A PAGEANT OF HISTORY

Uniform with this volume:

THE WONDERS OF SCIENCE

A PAGEANT OF
HISTORY

The Reigns of our Kings and Queens
Famous People and Events in our History

COLLINS
LONDON   GLASGOW

Opposite: H. M. QUEEN ELIZABETH II

CONTENTS

CONTENTS

CONTENTS

ACKNOWLEDGMENTS

The Publishers are indebted to the undernoted for permission to reproduce the photographs in this book.

AB Reportagebild, Stockholm: pp. 288. 290. *Lt. Cmdr. J. C Ackerman: p.* 203. *Thomas Agnew & Sons Ltd.: p.* 284. *The Autocar: p.* 13 *(bottom). Camera Press Ltd. pp.* 321, 323-8. *Carlisle City Museum: pp.* 59, 62-4. *Central Press Photos Ltd.: p.* 316. *J. Chettleburgh: p.* 93. *E.N.A.: pp.* 31-3, 305. *Fox: pp.* 35, 52, 88. *Harris's Picture Agency: pp.* 12 *(top),* 13 *(top left),* 18 *(bottom right),* 19 *(top),* 20 *(bottom),* 21 *(bottom). Hastings Museum: pp.* 86, 87, 90. *H.M. The Queen (by gracious permission): p.* 150. *Hulton's Picture Library: pp.* 9, 10 *(top),* 11 *(top),* 12 *(bottom),* 13 *(top),* 14 *(top right and bottom),* 15, 16, 17, 18 *(all except bottom right),* 19 *(bottom),* 20 *(top),* 21 *(top and centre),* 22 *(bottom),* 24 *(top),* 25, 26, 30, 38, 48, 49, 50, 57, 69, 70, 71, 77, 78, 79, 80, 81, 82, 84, 97, 100, 106, 107, 117, 118, 119 *(bottom),* 120, 121, 143, 165-7, 177, 178, 179, 185, 186, 189, 190, 192, 197, 209, 210, 211-17, 221, 222, 242-4, 267 *(bottom left),* 271, 274, 278-80, 282, 283, 286, 291, 294, 295, 297, 299, 301, 303 *(top),* 308, 309, 310 *(top left and bottom),* 312 *(top),* 313, 315 *(bottom),* 320, 330, 332-4. *Imperial War Museum: pp.* 275-7, 296, 298, 300, 302, 303 *(bottom),* 304, 335, 337-348. *Keystone: pp.* 22 *(top two),* 23, 24 *(bottom),* 89, 156 *(top),* 224, 226, 289, 312 *(bottom),* 317, 318. *The Provost & Fellows of King's College, Cambridge: col. plate facing p.* 96. *Leeds City Art Gallery: col. plate facing p.* 192. *Mansell: pp.* 53, 54. *Mondiale: pp.* 102, 103, 104, 126, 127. *National Coal Board: p.* 249 *(top). National Gallery: pp.* 66, 68, 136, 137, 139, 140. *National Portrait Gallery: pp.* 83, 92, 94, 116, 119 *(top),* 122, 124, 125, 130, 131, 132, 133, 134, 135, 146, 151, 152, 153, 155, 156 *(bottom),* 157, 158, 159-63, 168, 170-5, 182, 184, 207, 208. *Frank Newens: col. plate facing p.* 96. *Norval Ltd.: pp.* 292-3. *P.A.-Reuter: p.* 331. *The Parker Gallery: pp.* 265, 266, 267 *(top and bottom right),* 268-70, 272-3. *Paul Popper Ltd.: pp.* 27, 141, 249 *(bottom). W/Cmdr. Scrase-Dickins: p.* 11 *(bottom). Shakespeare Memorial Theatre: p.* 128. *The Times: frontis., and col. plate facing p.* 320, *also pp.* 310 *(top right),* 311, 314, 315 *(top),* 319. *Topical Press Agency Ltd.: p.* 307. *Weaver Smith Prints Ltd.: p.* 10 *(bottom). Josiah Wedgwood & Sons Ltd.: pp.* 193-6, 198-9. *Ministry of Works (Crown copyright): pp.* 58, 61. *Wright & Logan, Southsea : p.* 202.

ILLUSTRATIONS IN COLOUR

FROM VICTORIA
TO ELIZABETH

A Picture History of a
Century of Life in Britain

WITH the coming of Queen Victoria to the throne in 1837, a new era opened in Britain. The Crown acquired an honoured respect which had been sadly lacking for a very long time. The Queen's example of domestic happiness was an inspiration to all, and due to pioneering, inventiveness and hard work the country grew in prosperity.

On this and the following pages you will see some of the things which made up everyday life during the last hundred or so years. There are also pictures of "news" events which affected in some measure the life of everyone in the country. These photographs and illustrations will give you some idea of what people did, what they read or heard of and what

Queen Victoria in 1854. One of the first photographs for which she ever posed.

they achieved. The heritage which is ours is spread before you.

A dashing young cyclist photographed proudly holding his penny-farthing bicycle, a dangerous contraption, in about the year 1880.

A very "posed" family group in 1864. Father shows mother a book, whilst the eldest son rather unwisely looks down his gun-barrel.

Part of the lavish festival which attended the opening of the Suez Canal in 1869 by the Empress of the French. The Canal had a tremendous influence on trade with the East.

Traffic congestion on London Bridge even in 1886. Nose to cart, rather than bumper to bumper, but it was perhaps even more difficult to get the carts moving again.

Recruiting sergeants at Westminster in 1876 on the lookout for likely material.

IN CITY AND COUNTRY

A sight never to be seen nowadays—recruiting sergeants forgathered at a street corner in Westminster to discuss how the day was going before marching off to impress more would-be recruits with their smartness.

A short-service system of enlistment had been introduced a year or two previously which proved popular and provided the Army for the first time in its history with a trained Reserve.

The headgear of the two bystanders is typical of the time.

The leisured life of the wealthier people was made possible by the employment of plenty of staff. Although wages were low, if they rendered faithful service, they were regarded as part of the family and the employer looked after them in sickness and health with paternal solicitude. The "rural" clothes of the outdoor staff, seated on the horses in the picture below, show how untouched by sophistication a district within forty miles of London was at the turn of the century.

The indoor and outdoor staff at a Sussex country house in the late nineteenth century. They numbered thirty-four, and this was quite a small estate.

The well-to-do go racing at Sandown Park in the early 1900s. The elaborate hats and dresses were typical of this period and a straw "basher" was smart wear for the men.

A middle-class family goes for a picnic about the same date, but even on this less formal outing, the group is very carefully dressed for the occasion. Hats had to be worn and arms, necks and legs must be well covered, but they all enjoyed themselves.

Queen Victoria died in 1901 and the whole nation mourned her passing, for she had reigned longer than most people could remember. Everyone donned black, hats and clothes were dyed if nothing black was otherwise available, and for the funeral procession the route was lined with the public and soldiers. Many of the monarchs of Europe gathered in England for the funeral and amongst these mourners was the Kaiser, Wilhelm II, a grandson of the Queen, seen here on the left slightly behind King Edward VII. The scene is the arrival at Paddington Station in London of the cortège prior to entraining for Windsor.

A 20 h.p. T.T. Rolls Royce car of 1906. There was no protection from the weather and little comfort, but by this date the "horseless carriage" was here to stay.

Dr. William Gilbert Grace (1848–1915), the cricketer of legendary fame.

Mrs. Lambert Chambers, an early woman tennis champion, in play at Wimbledon in 1908.

Grace, the cricketer, played in first-class cricket for thirty-six years and set up many records not overtaken for many years. Cricket itself may not have changed much, but so far as tennis is concerned it was a very different game in 1908, as you can see. Aeroplanes, too, have changed since the pioneering days.

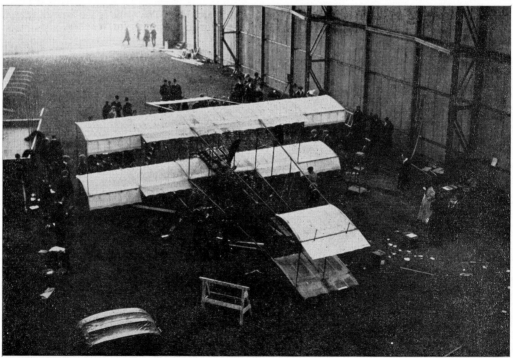

In 1910 Graham-White's Farman aeroplane, seen here, made the 183-mile flight from London to Manchester, finishing second to Louis Paulhan, who won the *Daily Mail* £10,000 prize.

Flower-sellers in the streets of London in 1911. In the background is a hard-wheeled, horse-drawn bus.

A travelling grandstand: a unique car brings a party to Epsom to watch the Derby in 1911. It roused considerable interest.

Pausing to buy flowers in the street, going to the Derby or spending a day at the seaside, these are simple pleasures, which we still enjoy to-day, though our clothes are different and some of the amenities change.

Britain before 1914 was a quiet leisurely place where everyday life followed a calm, even tenor, but this was to be disturbed most disastrously and completely by the outbreak of war in 1914. The whole world, indeed, was affected and nothing was ever quite the same again.

If you had gone to Scarborough in 1913, you could have had a horse-drawn bathing hut or a ride on a donkey, but you had to be fully and properly dressed.

War had been declared and a battalion of Territorial soldiers mustered one hot day early in August in the grounds of Somerset House, London, and awaited instructions.

Naval Reserve men left Cowes, Isle of Wight, by ferry to join their units for active service in August 1914 and waved farewell to their families.

Air raid warning cars toured the streets of London to warn pedestrians and others of raids. Even air raid warnings could be communicated in this comparatively leisurely fashion.

Down Whitehall in August 1914 went a recruiting car to rally men to the colours, passing on its way a newsboy with the latest war news.

At the outbreak of the war, the enthusiasm to join up and " finish the job " was there, but before there was time to set up proper recruiting centres, recruiting cars were put on the road to provide assistance for those who did not know what to do, or where to go and so help to swell the services with the greatest possible speed.

For the first time ever women worked as bus conductresses, releasing men for the forces.

To help food production the first land girls learned to drive a motor plough.

The Women's Ambulance Corps marched smartly by to do their bit.

And there were even women in the Fire Brigade, here seen saluting at dismissal.

The factories, too, were "manned" by women, some making lenses for gun-sights.

And when it was all over, the women cheered as loudly as the men.

This civil version of the Bristol bomber triplane was produced in 1919 and was "luxuriously" fitted for fourteen passengers. It was the first large airliner to be produced.

Women's new-found freedom caused some odd reactions as in this "smoking-suit" of 1922.

The magnificent "J" class yachts racing. These were the largest racing yachts ever built.

THE AGE OF WIRELESS AND TELEVISION

Broadcasting began officially in 1921, the first station being at Chelmsford and it was licensed by the Post Office. The next year the Marconi Company opened the London station (known as 2LO) and concerts were regularly transmitted. Later that year it amalgamated with other wireless concerns and became the British Broadcasting Company. Rex Palmer, carefully and formally dressed for the part, although it was only sound broadcasting, was one of the announcers. In those early days of broadcasting, however, jobs were often ill-defined and everyone on the staff had to be prepared to handle any situation which might arise, such as filling in unexpected gaps at a

Rex Palmer announcing a programme from the 2LO studio in London.

The original television apparatus used by Baird in 1925, now on exhibition in the Science Museum, London. His first demonstration of true television was on 27th January, 1926.

moment's notice in order to ensure continuity.

It may be surprising to some to realise how long ago television was invented. A public service, admittedly on a very limited scale, was inaugurated in 1929 and continued until the outbreak of war in 1939. Naturally the service was suspended during the war years, but at the end of hostilities the British Broadcasting Corporation began to get the service going again, and now there is a nation-wide coverage.

Baird, the Scottish inventor of television, worked hard to improve his invention despite bad health. After several years of tests, the B.B.C. decided to adopt another system—a sad blow to him.

Progress in scientific matters proceeded apace in the 1920s and 1930s. Radar experimental work began to produce results; atomic research, then very much in its infancy, was absorbing some of the best scientific minds in the country. Advances were being made in medicine and surgery.

But there was very considerable industrial unrest during the same period. Returning soldiers had not found the country to be one " fit for heroes to live in." Due to many and complex world conditions coal-pits and cotton mills had to close, unemployment rose and wages were reduced. A nation-wide strike took place.

The Times

No. 44263   London Wednesday, May 5, 1926.   Price 2d

WEATHER FORECAST. Wind N.E.; fair to dull; risk of rain.

THE GENERAL STRIKE.

A wide response was made yesterday throughout the country to the call of those Unions which had been ordered

N.Derbyshire and Monmouthshire.

Evening papers appeared at Bristol, Southampton, several Lancashire towns and Edinburgh, and typescript issues at Man-

The front page of *The Times* issued during the General Strike in May 1926 by volunteer printers, who were thus able to keep the public informed despite the strike.

Buses had to have their bonnets wired to prevent strikers getting at the engine.

THE GENERAL STRIKE

In 1926 a coalminers' strike developed into a General Strike of the leading trades unions, which lasted nine days. All public transport and services stopped, and it was due to the efforts of volunteer workers that newspapers, trains, buses, bakeries, dairies, etc., were kept going. Violence was feared and the military, particularly in the London area, were out. However, the situation remained calm and the public behaved with good-humoured tolerance, but all were very thankful when industrial peace was restored.

An astonishing sight in this country: armoured cars patrolling London streets during the General Strike. "Incidents" were few and after nine days the strike was called off.

AIRCRAFT

For a number of years after the First World War, there were many supporters of the lighter-than-air craft and many experimental airships were built. Hopes were pinned to Britain's R101, but when it caught fire, crashed and was burned out, killing all the passengers, all confidence in airships was not surprisingly destroyed too.

The airship R101 over St. Paul's in 1930.

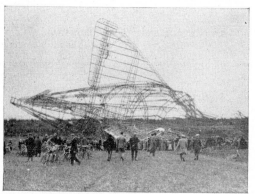

The burned-out wreckage of R101.

Miss Amy Johnson on her arrival at Croydon Aerodrome after flying in hops from Japan in September 1931. She had flown alone to Australia in 1930 in a small single-engined de Havilland Moth biplane. The 11,000-mile journey took her nearly three weeks.

Shortly after his election as Chancellor in 1933, Adolf Hitler's popularity was evident at this May Day rally. This was the man mainly responsible for the Second World War.

HITLER IN POWER

The effect that this one man had, not only on his own country, but on Britain, the Commonwealth and, indeed, on the world as a whole, was immense and on that account this picture has been included here.

Born an Austrian, Adolf Hitler worked as a house-painter in Germany before the First World War. During that war he served as a corporal and was wounded in 1916. After the war he was one of the founders of the National Socialist German Workers' Party, whose main plank was anti-Semitism. He led an unsuccessful rising in Munich in 1923 and, as a result of the part he had played in it, he was sentenced to five years' imprisonment. Released after a shorter period, he continued his work with the National Socialist Party (" Nazi ") and soon assumed its leadership.

In 1932 he became a naturalised German, having hitherto been an Austrian, and the same year unsuccessfully stood for the Presidency of the German Reich against Hindenburg (the former German Commander-in-Chief). The latter, realising the power and popularity of the Nazis made Hitler Chancellor in 1933.

At this date Hindenburg was already over eighty and with Hitler as Chancellor it was inevitable that when Hindenburg died in 1934 Hitler would assume full powers in Germany. This he did by abolishing the office of President and proclaiming himself *Führer* (i.e. Leader).

From 1934 until the outbreak of war Hitler concentrated on the complete militarisation of Germany. The Nazi organisation spread an almost crusading spirit with the aim and object of making Germany supreme in Europe. But Hitler's eyes rested not only on the immediate frontiers of his country, he dreamed of Ukrainian wheat and Romanian oil, and the tokens of the " disgrace " of Versailles, Gdynia and Danzig.

The outbreak of war grew closer. London's Green Park was dug up in 1938, when war first threatened, and air raid shelters were built. Piccadilly is in the background.

German troops were already seizing territory in March 1939. Here they are goose-stepping through Friedland (Czechoslovakia).

THE FATEFUL YEAR BEFORE THE WAR

For more than a year before the outbreak of war, Hitler had been threatening action in Europe. He claimed that Germany needed more living space and he claimed that there were areas on the fringes of Germany where Germans were living in other countries and they wished their areas to be re-absorbed into the German Fatherland (this they called "self-determination"). The "war of nerves" became so acute that in September 1938, it seemed as if war must break out. Trenches were dug in London's Green Park and the Prime Minister, the Rt. Hon. Neville Chamberlain flew to Germany to discuss the situation sympathetically with Hitler and so ensure peace. Although Chamberlain's intentions were of the best, he did not reckon with Hitler's fanaticism. Despite concessions, Hitler's "take-over" programme continued. The outcome was inevitable—Britain declared war on Germany on 3rd September, 1939.

How numbers of Londoners slept during the worst of the air raids in a tube station, the lines boarded over and double bunks set up.

After a rocket attack, a nurse is led through the wreckage to the injured by a young, but experienced, air raid worker.

Shortly after the outbreak of war, vast numbers of children were evacuated from cities thought to be liable to attack. Paddington station was one of the busiest centres.

Damage from a flying-bomb being cleared up. The damage was often more widespread than appeared superficially, for walls were cracked, windows blown in and main pipes severed.

Women of the Auxiliary Territorial Service helped to fight the enemy. The battery is in action and the predictor (in the background) directs the guns on to the target.

H.M. the Queen, wearing St. Edward's Crown and holding the Royal Sceptre and the Rod of Equity, waits to receive the homage of her peers after her Coronation.

VICTORIA AND ELIZABETH

In mid-nineteenth century a Queen was on the throne. Queen Victoria was remote from her people, making journeys only occasionally, so that a great many never saw her and few, indeed, heard her voice. She was at heart, however, an essentially simple person, and it was on that account that the common people understood and loved her.

During her long life, which spanned almost a century, change had been constant, yet by the fixed steadiness of purpose with which she handled affairs, she seemed to be the symbol of stability in the nation. Her method of dealing with all matters of State remained constant, thereby firmly establishing the position of the Crown in the Constitution of the country.

Now, more than a century later, we again have a Queen on the throne. Queen Elizabeth II has many of the attributes of her famous great-great-grandmother. In her case, however, the people, not only of Britain but of the Commonwealth, know her almost personally. She has travelled tirelessly, far and wide through the length and breadth of her lands; she has appeared on television; her speeches have been transmitted by radio and photographs of her activities appear regularly in the daily press. The love and affection which surround her are deeply felt and freely given, with none of the awe-struck element which was part of the feelings of the people of the Victorian age for their Queen.

When Queen Elizabeth mounted the throne in 1952, it was felt and hoped that the post-war struggle, military, economic and social, would be at an end and that a new Elizabethan age would dawn, matching the first Elizabethan age for glory of achievement. Whether or not that hope will be fulfilled lies in the hands of each one of us, for nothing is achieved without a struggle and hard work. What we make of this second half of the Twentieth Century lies in our own hands. Let us be worthy of that challenge.

ENGLAND BEFORE
THE NORMAN CONQUEST

(1) The Growth of England

TO-DAY we think of England as a part of the British Isles, and it is difficult to imagine a time when there was no division between England and Scotland or between England and Wales. Yet, there was a time, for the countries did not become separated until after the Romans had left and the Anglo-Saxon invaders landed.

In the fifth century, various Teutonic tribes struck at the heart of the Roman Empire, causing the Romans to leave Britain, never to return. Various others, from the part of Europe around Denmark and North Germany, turned their attention to the Roman province of Britain.

As we trace the arrival of these tribes, we can easily see how they settled eventually in kingdoms, which combined later to form England, or Angle-land.

The first to arrive were the Jutes. After having helped the people of Kent to beat off some of the savage tribes of the north, they decided that they would like to settle in Kent. After a few battles or skirmishes with the Britons, this became a Jutish settlement and later a kingdom. This was found to be a pleasant part of the country, but it was bounded on the west mainly by forest and barren land. To push past this, or to cross the Thames in the north, would be difficult and unnecessary, so these natural boundaries marked the borders of Kent.

Other Jutes settled in the Isle of Wight and in the coastal lands around Southampton Water, but, as they were overrun later by the Saxons, these settlements are of little importance.

To the west of Kent lay a piece of open country, which was hemmed in on the northern side, and this was occupied by groups of Saxons. This became the Kingdom of Sussex (South Saxons). About the same time, others had settled in the land north of the Thames Estuary, and this later became Essex (East Saxons).

THE NORTH FOLK AND THE SOUTH FOLK

Another group of people who invaded England were the Angles. They settled in two distinct places on the east coast, one of which, East Anglia, still bears their name to-day. This kingdom was bounded on the western side by the fen country, and this limited the spread in that direction. East Anglia consisted of the North Folk and the South Folk (Norfolk and Suffolk). Other Angles settled in Lincolnshire, but it was not until later that they were joined by others to form Mercia. The strongest were those who settled in the land north of the Humber and which became known as Northumbria.

It was a little later that other waves of Angles pushed in from the coast and occupied the middle of the country, which became Mercia, and other waves of Saxons landed to the west of the Isle of Wight and pushed west, north and east to occupy the remaining land in the south of England, which became the Kingdom of Wessex (West Saxons).

Thus, we find the formation of seven kingdoms, known as the Heptarchy, and named Northumbria, Mercia, Wessex, Sussex, Essex, East Anglia and Kent, the first three being much larger than the others. Though the boundary of Wessex ran along the course of the River Thames in the north, there were many of the Saxons who pushed farther north and settled in the southern part of Mercia.

Do not imagine, though, that all this happened quickly, nor that the kingdoms were formed immediately the people arrived. They did not mark off a piece of land and say, " This will be our kingdom." What happened was that each party of raiders settled in their own little township or village and, later, these combined either for their own protection or by being defeated in battle, until the kingdoms were eventually established.

Moreover, it must be remembered that the Britons had to be pushed out of the land

THE ANGLO-SAXON
INVASIONS

STRATHCLYDE

GALLOWAY

NORTHUMBRIA

NORTH
WALES

MERCIA

North Folk
EAST ANGLIA
South Folk

ESSEX

WEST WALES

WE S S EX

KENT

SUSSEX

Occupied by Britons

Angles

Saxons

Jutes

Boundaries of Kingdoms

before the new races could settle, and it was a long time before all the Britons were driven to the west. Just as was suggested earlier that the kingdoms had natural boundaries, so we find that the western boundaries of Northumbria, Mercia and Wessex were caused by the inability of the invaders to push the Britons any farther west.

WHEN KINGDOMS BECAME SHIRES

Some time after the seven kingdoms had been formed, they had the desire to spread. The kings, especially of the larger kingdoms, wished to become stronger; and it was not long before Mercia had absorbed the kingdoms of East Anglia and Essex, while Wessex gained the submission of Sussex and Kent. This meant that for about four hundred years there were three kingdoms that could be considered of any account. For a time the smaller kingdoms had retained their kings, who were vassals to the greater kings, but later ealdormen took their place and the kingdoms became little more than shires, the divisions into which each kingdom was cut to make the government of it the easier.

It was about this time that the re-Christianisation of England took place. Augustine found support for his ideas in the King of Kent, and made his headquarters at Canterbury, the capital of Kent. When Kent was overrun, and possibly even before, his work spread towards the north and the west.

When the daughter of the King of Kent married the King of Northumbria, she took a Christian priest with her, and he first took Christianity to the Northern Kingdom. The priest, Paulinus, became the first Archbishop of York; but when Northumbria was defeated by Mercia, Christianity was wiped out. Later, a monk from Iona re-established Christianity in Northumbria. Gradually it spread from the north and the south, until the whole country had accepted the Christian faith.

Each of the three Kingdoms had its turn as the most important, the first being Northumbria. In the seventh century it obtained the overlordship of the whole country, but, surrounded by hostile people, it was difficult to keep it. The Mercians, Britons and Picts all gave trouble, and Edwin, King of Northumbria, was defeated in 685. This marked the ascendancy of Mercia.

THE FIRST KING OF THE ENGLISH

For just over a hundred years, Mercia was the chief Kingdom in England and it remained strong until the death of Offa, in A.D. 794. It was not much later that King Egbert of Wessex became the chief King, and it was Wessex which retained the lead until the invasion of William I, with the exception of the period when the Danes were very strong, as you will see later.

King Egbert was a strong king and had been King of Wessex for twenty-six years before he became King of the English. Our Queen, Elizabeth II, is directly descended from

St. Paulinus became first Archbishop of York. Here, in a wooden church on Easter Day A.D. 627 he baptised King Edwin. York Minster to-day is on the very site of that church.

Egbert. When Egbert died, his son, Ethelwulf, succeeded him, and he was succeeded by his sons in turn—Etherbald, Ethelbert, Ethelred and Alfred, the last-named being one of our greatest kings.

However, there was a new danger to be faced, for, though the danger from the other kingdoms was gone, there was an even greater danger from the Danes, who had begun to make raids on the east and south coast. It was Alfred, who was mainly responsible for limiting the advance of the Danes.

ENGLAND BEFORE
THE NORMAN CONQUEST

(2) English and Danes

This reconstruction shows the type of ship in which the Vikings came to Britain.

A LITTLE before the time of Egbert, the people who lived on the coast and on the sides of the large rivers were greatly troubled by the " Dragon-ships " which attacked their villages. These were manned by some of the hardiest seamen of all time. In shallow open boats, propelled by oar or sail, they made voyages which make those of to-day seem just child's play.

In these fearsome-looking craft, with their gruesome figureheads, the Norsemen, or Vikings, had sought new lands in which to settle. They had landed in the Orkneys and Shetlands and they had travelled to Greenland. Some had even landed in America, long before Christopher Columbus was born. Others had settled in the part of France which we now know as Normandy. It was from their leader, Hrolf or Rolf, that William the Conqueror was descended.

The Norsemen who attacked England were mainly Danes and, at first, they had no intention of settling in Britain. Their ships would descend quickly and silently upon a village settlement, and the fierce warriors would carry off all they could find that was of value. Their main objective was usually the church, for they knew that this was where the English usually kept their best treasures. Men would be killed and women and children often

King Alfred the Great (A.D. 871–901) was a scholar, a fine ruler and a clever leader against the Danes.

carried off as slaves. Then, with their plunder, the Danes returned to winter in their own land.

In A.D. 851 these invasions took a new turn, when the independent Danish bands united and decided to winter in England. Their settlements were on the coast at first, as had been those of the Angles, Saxons and Jutes, but, like these people, they gradually pushed farther and farther west, defeating the inhabitants as they went.

ALFRED DEFIES THE DANES

Their main opposition was found in Alfred, King of Wessex, who is often referred to as Alfred the Great. He was the grandson of Egbert, and a member of a great family of leaders. He was only sixteen when he came to the throne, and, seven years later, in 878, his kingdom had collapsed. The English king went into hiding in the marshy land of Somerset, and the Danes thought themselves to be the masters of England. They had not reckoned on Alfred. He was not the type of man who sits around and does nothing, but spent all his energies in finding out how the English were placed and what the Danish plans were.

Then, at the opportune moment, he emerged from his hiding-place and well and truly defeated the Danes at Ethandune, in Wiltshire. The result of this battle was an agreement that the Danish leader, Guthrum, should become a Christian, and that his men should follow his example; also that the Danes should remain within the bounds of a part of the country to be known as the Danelaw. This was the part to the north-east of a line drawn between London and Chester.

The section to the south-west remained under the kingship of Alfred, who did not waste any time, but used this peaceful period as an opportunity to organise defence both by land and sea on a great scale. Moreover, he saw to the needs of his people, who greatly loved him.

Alfred's son, Edward, succeeded his father in A.D. 901, and he proved more than a match for the Danes. Many towns were conquered, and Edward called himself the King of all England.

During the period that followed there were several great English kings, who continued to struggle with the Danes. Athelstan, who succeeded Edward, was a great King, who improved the way of life of the people and who defeated not only the Danes, but the Scots and the Welsh, who were all compelled to accept him as overlord.

DUNSTAN, ARCHBISHOP OF CANTERBURY

His half-brother Edmund, who was only eighteen when he began to reign, showed himself to be a great leader and succeeded in getting the Scots to help him against the Danes. During his reign Dunstan, Abbot of Glastonbury, proved to be of great service to the Kingdom. Dunstan continued his work under Edred, after his brother Edmund had been murdered and, in this reign, a further step was made towards uniting the country.

Edred was succeeded by his nephew Edwig or Edwy, in whose reign Dunstan was sent out of the country; but Edwy was not popular, and his half-brother Edgar, who became King in 959, recalled Dunstan and made him Archbishop of Canterbury. He was a great king, and it is said that, on one occasion, his barge was rowed by eight kings of other parts of the country who were his vassals.

When he died, the power of the English began to decline. His son, Edward, reigned only four years before he was murdered on the instructions of his step-mother, who wished her son, Ethelred, to become King.

Ethelred, who ruled from 979 to 1016, was known as the Unready or Redeless, because he would not take the counsel of others. He did a very foolish thing in trying to buy off the Danes by paying them money, known as the Danegeld. Naturally, the Danes came back for more, and Ethelred, who was extremely angry, had many Danes murdered. One of these was the sister of the King of Denmark, Sweyn Forkbeard, and he determined to have his revenge. So strong was the Dane, that Ethelred was forced to flee to Normandy, the home of his second wife, Emma, who was a great-aunt of William the Conqueror.

Sweyn was never crowned, and, when he died in 1014, his son Canute made up his mind to become king. Ethelred returned but, before he could do much, he died. Canute married his widow, Emma, and, though Ethelred's son, Edmond Ironside put up a valiant struggle, he was compelled to give up his throne to Canute after only a few months.

CANUTE COMMANDS THE WAVES

Canute proved to be a great King, and he was respected by the English, to whom he showed his goodwill by sending all the Danes home that he could spare. In 1028 he conquered Norway, making himself ruler of three countries. It is said that his advisers flattered him by saying that he was so great that even the waves would obey him. To prove them wrong, he ordered his throne to be taken to the shore, where, after he had commanded them to stop, the waves washed over his feet,

thereby proving his advisers wrong. Whether this story is true or not is a matter of doubt, but it does show the respect which he commanded.

Canute was succeeded by his son Harold in 1035, but he died a few years later, and Canute's other son, Hardicanute (Harthacanute) became king. Within two years he died and the throne passed back to the English line of kings, to Edward, the son of Ethelred, who because of his piety became known as Edward the Confessor.

THE BUILDING OF WESTMINSTER ABBEY

Edward was not very good as a king and was quite unable to control the great earls, who were becoming more and more powerful. Eventually, Edward left the government of the country to the earls, and spent his energies in building Westminster Abbey.

The greatest of the earls was named Godwin and he had been related to Canute by marriage. In the time of the Danes, he held great authority, and he opposed Edward the Confessor, his son-in-law, because he was favouring his Norman friends too much. Godwin was forced to flee, and, while he was away, Edward, who was childless, promised the crown to William of Normandy.

Eventually, Godwin was allowed to return, but he died soon afterwards, and his son, Harold, became the leading earl in the country. When Edward died, Harold, Earl of Wessex, which was still the strongest kingdom of England, declared himself to be king.

Later, in the same year, William of Normandy invaded and Harold was defeated and killed in the Battle of Hastings. So ended the Anglo-Saxon period of English history, which had lasted for about six hundred years.

An artist's impression of the famous incident when Canute defied the waves.

WILLIAM I

The Story of William the Conqueror

THERE were two men who claimed the English crown when Edward the Confessor died. One of these was Earl Harold, and the other Duke William of Normandy. William claimed the crown on three different grounds, none of which was particularly good, but which, nevertheless, gave him a good excuse for invading. Firstly, he claimed the crown through a relation of his; secondly, he maintained that he had been promised the crown by Edward the Confessor; and thirdly, Harold himself had been captured while in Normandy, and had promised the crown to William to obtain his release. Whatever truth there may be in these claims, there is no doubt that William was prepared to stake all to get the crown.

But, who was he anyway? No doubt you will remember that the Vikings invaded Britain at the time when Alfred was King. This same race of people had also attacked France, and, because the French were unable to defeat them, their leader, Hrolf, was granted the district of Normandy and became the first Duke of Normandy. William, who was a descendant of Hrolf, was of a similar adventurous nature.

William had an ally in England. Tostig, the brother of Harold, had quarrelled with Harold, and was prepared to help William to secure the crown. To do so, he first invaded the south and east coasts, and joined up with the King of Norway on the Tyne. Then he marched south with an army, and Harold had to march north to fight and defeat him. William invaded while the army and navy were away, and when the weather conditions were right.

WILLIAM I. 1066-87.

THE BATTLE OF HASTINGS

William's men landed at Pevensey Bay and marched to Senlac Hill, near Hastings, where they awaited the arrival of the English. It was here that the important Battle of Hastings was to take place. Harold and his men fortified their position on the top of the hill, and looked as though they were to prove a match for the Normans, who were unable to break through the defences. Then William put into practice two plans which proved very effective. One was to get his bowmen to shoot their arrows into the air. Even William could not have hoped that the result of this would end in the death of Harold, who was struck in the eye and mortally wounded. The other plan was to get his armies to pretend to run away. The English gave chase, and, when they were in confusion, the Normans rounded on them, thus winning the battle. Later, William built on the site of the battle an abbey, which is still known to-day as Battle Abbey.

William then marched on London. There was no need to hurry, and he decided first to strike fear into the Londoners. Marching via Dover to Canterbury, he had to stay for a month in that old city owing to illness, but while he was there he received the surrender of Wessex. He marched south of London to Wallingford, where he received the acknowledgement of the Church, and then to Berkhamsted, where the people of the city of London received him.

Amidst great jubilation, he was crowned King of England, after being accepted by the Witan, on Christmas Day, 1066, in Westminster Abbey. So great were the cheers after the people had been asked in English and French whether they would accept him as king, that the Normans outside the Abbey, thinking it to be a rebellion, set fire to some of the outhouses. William became William I of England in an almost empty abbey.

THE FEUDAL SYSTEM

One of his first tasks was to organise the country to his liking. He had conquered the land, and he claimed that it was all his. There were, however, many people to whom he owed something. Some of his followers had given up lands in Normandy to come to England,

and he had to repay them. He did this by giving some large areas of land to tenants-in-chief. The land was then further divided between barons, knights and farmers, all of whom owed allegiance to the king and also to their immediate overlords. At any time, they could be called upon to give advice or military service. This system was known as the Feudal System.

There were, however, many English people who resented the Norman overlords, and they rebelled. Shortly after William had been crowned, he returned for a short while to Normandy, and the English, especially in the north, took the opportunity of rebelling. When the king returned, he quelled the rising and destroyed great expanses of land, burning down houses and crops and killing many people. As a precaution against a similar rising in the future, he built a number of castles to house the Norman soldiers. One of the most famous of these castles, built by the Conqueror, is the White Tower of the Tower of London.

Another small rising, which took many years to quell, was that of Hereward the Wake, who withstood the Normans in the Isle of Ely, hiding in the marshes, and causing quite a lot of trouble to the Normans.

William the Conqueror built a number of castles to house his Norman soldiers and to protect them against their enemies. One of these was the White Tower of the Tower of London.

PLANTING THE NEW FOREST

Yet another cause of discontent was the planting of the New Forest. William greatly enjoyed hunting and he ordered that all the houses in the area where the New Forest is to-day should be destroyed. Many people resented the fact that people should be made homeless, just because the king liked privacy while he was hunting the deer.

William was also able to achieve many good things in his reign. It is no easy task to subdue a conquered people or to get the country working efficiently, but William succeeded in doing both. His royal court, consisting of a number of the great barons, dealt with all matters of government, finance and justice; while the moots, which had been kept from Saxon times, were able to keep an eye on local matters. It says much for William's organisation, that he was able to compile the Domesday Book.

This book gave details of all the land in the country, and showed how much was open land, how much was forest, how many mills there were, and so on. Moreover, it told William just how much he could expect by way of money and military service from those who held the land.

William's reign ended rather abruptly after he had reigned for twenty-one years. While in France, his horse trod on some hot ashes and threw the king against the protruding part of the saddle. He died later, as a result of this injury.

William was a great king. He had a sense of purpose and allowed nothing to stand in his way. He may be regarded as cruel, and yet he felt that some of these actions were necessary to keep the country in order. One thing is certain. He set a standard for the Norman kings, which was going to be very difficult to live up to.

HARVARD AND YALE

MOST people could name the United States equivalents of Oxford and Cambridge Universities, though of course these universities cannot claim the ancient establishment of their British counterparts.

Harvard and Yale is the answer, but few know how they arose or anything about the men whose names are thus perpetuated.

John Harvard (1607-38) was of humble origin and he migrated as a Puritan minister to Charlestown, Mass., after taking his M.A. at Emmanuel College, Cambridge.

In 1636 the General Court of the colony voted £400 towards " a schoale or colledge " in memory of Cambridge, where some sixty or seventy of the leading men of the settlement had been educated. For similar reasons the township was to be called Cambridge.

Harvard left to this wilderness seminary half of his modest estate, some £780—and his library of some 260 books. Thus small are the acorns from which great oaks can grow.

The college took his name; the first building was erected in 1637, and seven years later the first graduating class was established.

You can see a memorial to Harvard in England, for St. Saviour's Church, Southwark, where he was baptised, has a Harvard Chapel. Southwark is often known as " The Borough," and St. Saviour's, once the priory of St. Mary Overy, is now the cathedral.

Elihu Yale, in contrast, was born in New Haven, Connecticut, in 1648, the site of the university which was eventually to bear his name. He came to England, entered the service of the great East India Company, and became Governor of Fort St. George, Madras.

He sent to the college of the colony, whose charter was granted in 1701, a cargo of gifts, including books, and East India goods that were sold for several hundreds of pounds.

This was in 1718, when it was finally decided to establish the college in New Haven, the birthplace of Elihu Yale. The benefactor, whose name lives on, died three years later.

To-day it is one of the richest universities in the United States, and almost any subject can be studied there. It has Schools of Law, Medicine, Divinity, Music, Nursing, Forestry, Science.

WILLIAM II
An Unpopular King

WHEN William I died, he left a good inheritance to whichever son was to succeed to the English throne. Of his sons, it had been agreed that Robert should become Duke of Normandy on the death of his father, and that William should become King of England.

William, who was known as Rufus, because of his flaming hair, hastened to England, where he was crowned king. He gained the support of many of the English, because he promised them relief from their taxation. Soon, however, it was found that William was not a man to keep his promise. In fact, he was probably one of the worst kings ever to sit on the English Throne.

Robert, now Duke of Normandy, had no interest in who was King of England; but William, on the other hand, was anxious to rule over Normandy as well. He seized several important places, but eventually came to an agreement with his brother.

About this time there was trouble in the East, where the Turks were molesting the Christians, who were on pilgrimages to the Holy Land. Soon it was decided by the Christian leaders of Europe, that there should be a crusade to the Holy Land, to attempt to break the power of the Turks. Robert of Normandy was anxious to go on this crusade, but he needed money. William was only too pleased to supply him with the money, in exchange for his being allowed to rule in Normandy for five years.

THE KING WHO WAS A BULLY

In the meantime, the king was becoming more and more disliked at home, for the barons found him to be a bully, who could not keep the promises he had made. Moreover, the people also found that they were being oppressed by the king and they resented it.

Rufus also managed to quarrel with the Church. William I, his father, had established the Archbishop Lanfranc at Canterbury, and he was still holding this office, when Rufus became king. When Lanfranc died, William

WILLIAM II. 1087-1100.

called another Bishop, Anselm, from France, to become Archbishop of Canterbury. Anselm was most unwilling to accept the office, but had to do so. He had heard of the way in which Rufus exploited people, and knew that there would be quarrels. Sure enough, there were. The king looked upon the lands and wealth of the Church with envy, and told the Archbishop that some of them should be his. Anselm, who was very popular with the people, fled to France, and yet another grudge against the king was found.

Like his father, the king was very fond of hunting, and spent many a day in the New Forest. It was here that he was to end his life. There were few regrets and probably many sighs of relief, when it was learned that the king had been struck in the chest by an arrow and slain.

HOW DID RUFUS MEET HIS DEATH?

The story of what actually happened will

never be known, but it is told that Sir Walter Tyrrel shot at a deer, but missed his mark, and the arrow, glancing off a tree, hit the king. This may or may not be true, since the king had so many enemies that anyone might have been responsible. Tyrrel, fearing for his life, fled to France, leaving the body of William where it lay. Later in the day, a peasant discovered the body, which was placed on a cart and taken to Winchester, where it was laid to rest in the cathedral. When, seven years later, the tower of the cathedral collapsed, it was said that it proved that the king was not fit to have had a Christian burial.

THE BUILDING OF WESTMINSTER HALL

Rufus did, however, do one thing in his reign which might be regarded as good, and which stands as a memorial to him. He was the king who was responsible for the building of Westminster Hall. Perhaps you have seen this to-day, for it is here that recent sovereigns have lain in state before their funerals. To-day, it is a part of the Houses of Parliament.

Also as a reminder of the king is a stone, which may be seen in the New Forest, and was erected on the spot where William was slain, part of the inscription on which reads as follows: " Here stood the oak-tree on which an arrow, shot by Sir Walter Tyrrel at a stag, glanced off, and struck King William the Second, surnamed Rufus, on the breast; of which stroke he instantly died, on 2nd August 1100."

Few people have been more disliked than William II and most people were thankful when he died.

Westminster Hall, the one magnificent reminder to-day of the reign of Rufus, the Red King—William II. Here Parliament has met, Kings have lain in state, and here Sir Winston Churchill was honoured in 1954 on his 80th birthday.

HENRY I

The King Who Helped Trade

WHEN William Rufus was slain, his brother, Robert, who should have succeeded to the throne, was still on the Crusade and unable to do anything about it. Their younger brother, Henry, immediately stepped in and took every possible step to get himself crowned King of England. The first step was to get hold of the Crown Jewels, which were in the keeping of a friend of Robert's, and this he did by force. Soon, he was on his way to London, where he was accepted by the people and crowned.

Right from the start it was obvious that here was a much greater man than Rufus. In fact, there was much in the life of Henry which reminded people of his father. Henry was a man who had done all he could to make himself wise. He had received a far better education than his father, and to have a king who knew how to read and write and to speak in three languages, was a decided advantage.

Moreover, Henry soon made himself very popular with the English people. He promised that he would relieve them of some of their taxation, and, unlike his brother, he kept his promise. Another thing which appealed very much to the English, was that Henry had married an English princess named Matilda, and he had been brought up to understand the English.

A PROMISE THAT WAS BROKEN

So we find that, when Robert came home from the Crusade, and was anxious to get the crown, which he believed was rightfully his, he did not have many supporters. The brothers met and agreed that Henry should have England. However, a few years later, Henry invaded Normandy and took Robert prisoner. With Robert safely away in a castle, Henry took Normandy for himself, so becoming ruler of the same lands as his father.

His reign was a good one and he is noted for a number of changes which he made. One of these which was to affect a large number

HENRY I. 1100-35.

of people was the reorganisation of justice. The old ideas of determining whether a person was guilty or not by the ordeals of fire and water, were being replaced by Justices, who were able to judge in the name of the Crown, and who gave a verdict on the evidence they heard. Henry has been known as the Lion of Justice, for he was a very just man.

His attitude to the Church was also very different from his brother's. One of his earliest actions was to recall Anselm from France, and, though the King and the Archbishop did not agree entirely, there was certainly not the trouble there had been in the reign of Rufus. Moreover, he invited a number of monks from Cisteaux, in France, to come and settle in England. These Cistercians, as we know them, built many monasteries and did much good work among the people. One thing for which they were noted was the rearing of sheep, and they were to do a great deal for the sheep-rearing industry.

THE FIRST TRADE GUILD

Here, again, is another thing for which Henry I is noted. He did much to encourage trade and industry, especially the woollen industry, and it was during his reign that the first Trade Guild was formed to protect the master craftsmen in their particular trade.

The favourite of Henry's children was a prince by the name of William. The King had fond hopes that William would succeed him, and he did everything in his power to secure the throne for the young prince and to ensure that he was brought up in the arts of kingship. Unfortunately, his hopes were not realised.

In 1120, Henry took Prince William, who was then eighteen, to Normandy, with the intention of getting the barons to swear allegiance to him. Having achieved his object and having secured the hand of a princess for William, the King was about to embark, when a sailor, whose family had been in the employment of William I, begged to be allowed to carry the King to England in his *White Ship*. Henry told him that he had already made arrangements for himself, but entrusted the young prince and his brother and sister to the charge of Fitz-Stephen.

THE KING WHO LOST HIS SMILE

Henry went on ahead and little dreamed of the disaster which was going to happen. Before sailing, there had been much drinking and merry-making on the *White Ship*, and the crew was determined to overtake the King. Unfortunately, it struck a rock and began to sink. A boat was quickly lowered, which would have enabled the prince to escape, but, hearing the cries of his sister Marie, he returned to rescue her. Panic-stricken, those on board all tried to jump into the small boat, and all, save a butcher, perished. He alone carried the news to court, where everyone feared to tell the King. At last, however, a page bore the sad news, and on hearing it Henry fainted and thereafter was never seen to smile again.

The remaining fifteen years of Henry's life were spent in trying to secure the throne for his daughter Matilda, and, by the time he died, he had received the promise from his nephew Stephen and from the barons that they would accept her as Queen. What in fact happened after his death was another matter.

On 1st December, 1135, the King died in France and his body was laid to rest in Reading Abbey, which the King himself had founded.

A WORD SQUARE

CLUES

1. Foremost.

2. Angry.

3. Runs swiftly.

4. Stalks.

5. Girl's name.

Complete this square so that it reads the same across as down.

Solution on page 91.

1	2	3	4	5
2				
3				
4				
5				

STEPHEN

A Reign of Terror

IF the barons had kept the promise which they had made to Henry I, they would have accepted his daughter Matilda as Queen when he died. The barons, however, did not like the idea of Matilda becoming Queen. For one thing, they were very doubtful whether a Queen reigning would be a good thing or not, and for another they disliked her husband, Geoffrey of Anjou. They had, however, made a promise to Henry, and a promise could not be broken.

There was another claimant to the English throne. Stephen, who was the son of Adela, and grandson of William the Conqueror, thought he should be King, and many of the barons agreed that he would be better than Matilda. So an excuse was sought to put Stephen on the throne instead of Matilda. An excuse was found. A man swore on oath that Henry had disinherited the princess, though it is doubtful whether he ever did, and Stephen was crowned.

So began a reign of terror. Throughout the country it soon became quite clear that the barons had no intention of doing as Stephen said, and, for that matter, Stephen seemed quite powerless to do anything about it. To secure the favour of the barons, he had allowed them to build castles, and the barons used them as bases from which to plunder.

MATILDA FIGHTS BACK

In the meantime, Matilda refused to sit back and see the crown taken from her. Right from the start, she began to organise an army to assist her. One of those who was to help her most was Robert, Earl of Gloucester, who gave up his lands in England, in 1137, and went to Normandy, from whence he defied the King.

Matilda also found support in her uncle, David, King of Scotland, who invaded England and massacred many men, women and children in the north of England. The people of the north rose for their own protection and the King of Scotland was driven back.

STEPHEN. 1135-54.

None of this helped Stephen, for, while he had to spend all his energy in defeating Matilda, the barons were able to do just as they pleased, many of them becoming stronger and stronger. Some were able to do well for themselves in other ways, too. It was no uncommon thing to find one supporting Stephen while he seemed to be winning, and changing sides with the tide of the battle.

HOW STEPHEN WAS CAPTURED

Once it seemed that Stephen's cause was lost, for, at the Battle of Lincoln, he was captured. It has been said that the King was weak-willed, but it must also be said that he was a man of valour. At Lincoln he fought " like a lion " with his sword until that broke, and then he continued fighting with a mace, with which he fought " with the fury of a wild boar," until he was struck on the head and captured.

At last, Matilda was in power. She had Stephen as a prisoner, and could do with him as she wished. However, she did not use her power to the best advantage, and soon she had lost much of the support that she might have had. Moreover, her friend and close adviser, the Earl of Gloucester, was captured by Stephen's men, and the Queen had to release Stephen in exchange for Gloucester.

Some time later, Stephen caught up with Matilda at Oxford, and she only escaped by slipping out of the city wearing a white robe which did not show up against the snow. In battle with Gloucester, soon afterwards, the King only just avoided capture for the second time.

Matilda sent to her husband in Normandy for support, and he sent their son, Prince Henry, with a formidable force of men.

A STATE OF ANARCHY

The armies of Henry and Stephen met at Wallingford and agreed to come to terms. Stephen's son, who guessed that this would cut him off from the throne, rebelled and caused some damage in Cambridgeshire, but he died suddenly, and Stephen was then quite ready to listen to Henry's claim on the throne.

It was agreed that, on the death of Stephen, Henry should become King of England. Stephen, who had already lost his lands in Normandy, was ready to accept such a plan, and Henry and Stephen, together, rode through the land.

Only a few months later, in October, 1154, Stephen died at Dover at the age of fifty, and was buried in the monastery at Faversham.

But what of the country? It was in a deplorable state. Nobles exploited the people. Anyone with property was seized by the barons, who devised all manner of tortures in their castles to get riches from these unfortunates. People went in fear of their lives, and it was commonly reported that " Christ and His Saints slept." Soon people came to realise that a state of anarchy is bad for everyone, and they welcomed a strong King, in Henry II, who was able to keep order.

A KNOTTY PROBLEM

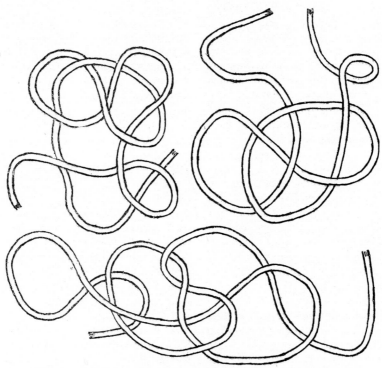

Which of these would form true knots? Solution on page 91.

HENRY II

The First Plantagenet

WHEN Stephen died, Henry of Anjou became King as Henry II of England, and so began a new line of kings. They were known as the Plantagenets, from the Latin words " Planta genista," being the Latin name for the broom, a sprig of which was the family's sign.

From the time that he became King, Henry showed the barons that he would tolerate no nonsense. He had the people behind him, for they had been subject to these great barons for far too long. One of the first things he did was to break down the power of the barons, and destroy many of the castles.

He realised, however, that he could not rely upon the old feudal idea of getting his knights and soldiers from the barons, for they could use them for their own advantage against him. Instead, he introduced the idea of an army. According to their social state, all men who were freemen had to arm themselves with the weapons prescribed by the King, so that in an emergency they could be called upon.

But what was this man like, who was able to keep the barons in order after so many years of lawlessness? Henry II is described as being of great strength and of a strong will. It was nothing, when he went on a journey, for him to out-pace his courtiers, who had the greatest difficulty to keep up with him and who tired long before he did. Nor was it strange for him to change his mind quickly and expect everyone else to fall in with his plans at a moment's notice. He was always active and always had his mind engaged on one plan or another. It is even said that when in church, if the priest were engaged at the altar, he would take out a script to read or would talk over some of his plans with his counsellors.

A DESCENDANT OF THE DEVIL?

His physique was such that he would have made a good wrestler, and he had a fiery countenance, but the feature that was most noticeable was the eyes. They were normally grey, but if he was enraged they were like balls of fire. Sometimes, when he was in a violent temper, he would throw himself on the floor and roll around. So furious did he get at times that there were many who said that there was no doubt but that the Devil himself must be one of the King's ancestors. It was this temper of his that was later to get him into serious trouble.

Great changes were made in justice and government, many of which were designed to increase the amount of money that came to the King. Fines were imposed upon sheriffs or jurors for failing to do their duty, while taxes were levied on those who had the money. Henry realised that, in those days, strength depended upon wealth, and he was determined to be strong.

THE FIRST ASSIZE COURTS

Justice was taken out of the hands of the moot altogether, and travelling judges, who sat at the various towns, did their work instead. Where they sat, they held an " Assize "—the beginning of our Assize Courts.

Henry passed more laws than did any of his predecessors, most of which were aimed at strengthening his position; but few people worried about this, as the barons were no longer to be feared. One man, however, stood out. He was Archbishop Becket of Canterbury. Until taking that post, he had been the chief adviser to the King, and the two had been inseparable friends, but when the King wanted all clergymen to be tried, for any offences they might have committed, in civil courts, not Church courts, Becket quarrelled with his King, because he refused to allow this. Henry banished him to France, though he allowed him to return again a few years later. When Henry heard of the welcome accorded to Becket on his return, he flew into a great rage and said : " What a parcel of fools have I in my Court, that not one of them will avenge me of this one upstart priest." Four knights then went to Canterbury and murdered the

Archbishop at the altar of his own cathedral.

Everyone was shocked and Henry not the least of them, for he had never meant such a thing to happen. To save himself in the eyes of the people he had to walk to Canterbury and submit to being flogged by each of the priests at Canterbury. What was even harder for Henry was that he was no longer in a position to make demands upon the Church and he had lost the battle with Becket. It may happily be said that Henry was on better terms with his next great adviser, Bishop Hugh of Lincoln.

A SAD ENDING

The lands over which Henry ruled were very extensive. Not only was he King of England, but his lands in France were many. From his parents he inherited large domains, and by his marriage to the wealthiest princess of his time he increased them considerably. By the end of his reign, he owned more land in France than the King of France did. Even so, he was always ready to conquer new fields, and gave permission for Strongbow, Earl of Pembroke, to go to the assistance of an Irish chief. As a result, he gave John, his son, the title of Lord of Ireland.

However, with large amounts of land such as he had, there were bound to be difficulties. For one thing, the barons were annoyed at having lost many of their rights. Moreover, Henry had lost much of his prestige over the matter of Thomas à Becket. Towards the end of his reign, even his sons revolted. Henry's wife had been kept imprisoned for many years, and she intrigued with her sons and the King

HENRY II. 1154-89.

of France. His eldest son, named after him, died after a revolt against his father, while Richard and John also took part with the rebels.

John had been his father's favourite and it is said that, when the King heard that he had been unfaithful, he turned his face to the wall and died with the words: " Now let all things have their way; I care no more for myself nor for the world."

THE OWL

When cats run home and light is come,
  And dew is cold upon the ground,
And the far-off stream is dumb,
  And the whirring sail goes round,
  And the whirring sail goes round:
    Alone and warming his five wits,
    The white owl in the belfry sits.

When merry milkmaids click the latch,
  And rarely smells the new-mown hay,
And the cock hath sung beneath the thatch
  Twice or thrice his roundelay,
  Twice or thrice his roundelay:
    Alone and warming his five wits,
    The white owl in the belfry sits.

Lord Tennyson

RICHARD I

Richard the Lion-heart

AS a King, Richard I was not of very great value to his people, but as a warrior there were few to beat him in the period in which he lived.

He succeeded Henry II at a time when there was trouble in the Holy Land and when all the important people of Europe were planning to overthrow the Saracens (Turks), who were in possession. For many years there had been struggles between the Turks and the Christians, and for about a hundred years the Christians had held Jerusalem; but the news reached Europe that a great Turkish leader, Saladin, had captured the city. Plans were made for the Third Crusade, the object of which was to recapture Jerusalem.

Three nations took part in this: Germany, led by the Emperor Frederick; France, led by King Philip; and England, led by King Richard.

Money was to play a very important part in financing the expedition, and Richard sold many of his possessions, including some of the Crown Jewels, and even said that he would sell London itself if he could get a high enough offer.

The German Army went first, travelling by land, because the Emperor feared to travel by sea. It is rather strange that he should lose his life before reaching the Holy Land, by falling into a river and drowning.

DISASTER AT SEA

Richard and Philip met in France, and decided that they would make the journey by sea. For the first time the English ships sailed into the Mediterranean, and they joined the French ships at Sicily.

Unfortunately, the English ships were scattered by a great storm, and Richard found himself seeking refuge with a few of his ships on the island of Rhodes. There he learned the news that two of his ships had been wrecked on the island of Cyprus and the crews had been thrown into prison. Determined to rescue them and to make an example of the ruler of the island, Richard sailed there and, after sailing round the island, he attacked and

RICHARD I. 1189-99.

made the ruler submit and surrender the men who had been imprisoned.

Wherever he went, Richard was renowned for his fighting, and when he arrived at Acre, on the coast of the Holy Land, he found that the French and the Germans, who had been there for about two years, had accomplished nothing. He gave new courage to the Crusaders, who went into battle and soon captured the town. Saladin fled to Jerusalem, and Richard was delighted, for he thought that at last he would have the opportunity of capturing the Holy City itself.

However, he was to be disappointed. Things had not gone too favourably for the Crusaders. Even the leaders had squabbled. The King of France, who had never liked Richard because he owned more land in France than the French King did, found illness the excuse to withdraw from the Crusade. Leopold of Austria, who had succeeded the Emperor

Frederick, disliked Richard intensely, especially as, on one occasion, Richard had torn down the Austrian flag and trampled on it.

RICHARD'S BRAVERY IN BATTLE

But Richard was not one to give in easily. His own strength and valour were sufficient to make his men rally round him and fight to the end. It is said that as he went into battle, wielding his famous battle-axe, the enemy broke before him, and that on one occasion he rescued some of his men almost single-handed. His name became a byword among the Moslems, who even told their children that, if they did not behave themselves, King Richard would get them.

Pressing on towards Jerusalem, Richard still hoped to be able to accomplish what he had come out to do, but day by day it seemed as though he were tackling an almost impossible task. Squabbles among the Crusaders, lack of good food, dreadful conditions in which to live and move, all told on the gallant little army, until, in sight of Jerusalem itself, Richard had to admit that he was unable to go on. Moreover, he had learned that his brother John in England, and the King of France, were endeavouring to take away his possessions, and, sad at heart, he made peace with Saladin for three years, three months, three days and three hours, intending after that time to attack the Holy Land again, but this was not to be so.

While on his way home again, he was unfortunate to be caught in another storm and driven off his course, which led to his being attacked by pirates, who forced him to continue his journey home by land. This meant danger, for he had to pass through the lands of his enemy, Leopold of Austria, and he knew that Leopold would be a difficult man to encounter.

DISGUISED AS A MERCHANT

Disguising himself as a merchant, on a pilgrimage from the Holy Land, he hoped to escape, but was given away by some of the fine articles which he carried, and fell into the hands of his enemy, who demanded a heavy ransom from Britain for his safe return. The story is told of his minstrel, Blondel, who travelled through Europe to find where the King was, and eventually discovered him through the singing of one of Richard's favourite songs, and the King, from his dungeon, responding.

The ransom money was duly raised, and Richard returned to England, where he showed his greatness by forgiving his brother John for his attempt to seize the crown.

However, his reign was to be brought to a sudden end only ten years after he had ascended the throne. While at war with the King of France, the mighty Richard was killed by a humble bowman in the French Army.

Richard was not a great King, but he was certainly a great warrior and one who undoubtedly earned for himself the title of the " Lion-Heart."

THE LAMB

Little lamb, who made thee?
Dost thou know who made thee,
Gave thee life, and bade thee feed
By the stream and o'er the mead;
Gave thee clothing of delight,
Softest clothing, woolly, bright;
Gave thee such a tender voice,
Making all the vales rejoice?
Little lamb, who made thee?
Dost thou know who made thee?

Little lamb, I'll tell thee;
Little lamb, I'll tell thee:
He is called by thy name,
For He calls Himself a Lamb,
He is meek and He is mild,
He became a little child.
I a child, and thou a lamb,
We are called by His name.
Little lamb, God bless thee!
Little lamb, God bless thee!

William Blake

JOHN

The King Who Signed Magna Carta

FROM the earliest records, there is little good that can be said of John, who became, undoubtedly, the worst king ever to sit upon the English throne.

The first real record that we have of him concerns his infidelity to his father, Henry II, which probably helped to hasten the death of that great king. The second thing that is said of him is that, while Richard I was away at the Crusades, John intrigued with the King of France to take the throne away from Richard. It says much for Richard that he was prepared to forgive this scoundrel when he eventually landed in England.

When Richard was killed in battle in France, he named as his successor to the English throne his nephew, Arthur, the son of Richard's elder brother, who had died; but John, who was completely selfish and greedy, had no intention of allowing Arthur to have the throne that he believed was his, though the claim of Arthur was stronger; and he proceeded to get himself accepted as King. This may have been all right in England, but on the Continent, and especially in Brittany, the people looked upon Arthur as the rightful king.

A BRUTAL MURDER

The result was a number of wars in France, which eventually meant that nearly all the land that had belonged to the English crown was lost. In the course of the fighting, young Arthur was captured; and, after being taken from one place to the other, he eventually disappeared. Many stories are told, and it is difficult to know which has the greatest foundation of truth, but one thing is certain, and that is that Arthur was killed, and most probably in a brutal fashion by the King or by his followers.

Shortly after this, Normandy was lost by John.

Next came trouble with the Pope. In 1205 Hubert, the Archbishop of Canterbury, died, and there followed a dispute as to who should succeed him. The monks appointed one man and, as soon as he heard of it, John appointed

JOHN. 1199-1216.

another. Thus, two candidates were on their way to Rome. To settle the matter, the Pope appointed yet another, by name Stephen Langton, who was later to have great authority in England.

A QUARREL WITH THE POPE

John refused to allow Langton to land, and sent an offensive letter to the Pope, who immediately put England under an interdict, which meant that no church services could be held; and excommunicated John, that is, cut him off from the Church.

Now, the King realised that he was in a difficult position, for he knew that the next step of the Pope would be to dethrone him.

To try to get support, it is said that he even approached the Moslem leader to see if he could get help from him. Whether this was the case or not, we do not know for sure, but, at any rate, he did not get the help. He next raised as much money as he could to equip an army.

He then made his way, plundering as he went, to Ireland, where he stole as much treasure as he could. Next he attacked Wales, and captured twenty-eight sons of chieftains as hostages, but, on hearing that the Welsh would not accept his rule, he hanged them all.

Eventually, he arrived at the conclusion that he could not continue opposing the Pope, who, by now, was ready to attack England, through the army of the King of France. He therefore accepted the Papal delegate, who was sent, and agreed to allow Langton to land and act as Archbishop of Canterbury.

It became obvious that Langton was going to take the side of the barons, for he could not possibly agree to working with John. By this time no one, barons, clergy or common people, had any time for John or for his ideas, and the barons determined to force the hand of the King.

SIGNING THE GREAT CHARTER

They endeavoured to get the King to call a council with the intention of forcing him to sign a Charter, but he was very elusive. Eventually, after capturing the city of London, they persuaded the King to meet them at Runnymede, on the Thames, near Windsor, on 15th June, 1215. On the appointed day, the King met the barons and all the assembled company of people, and was compelled to place his seal of approval on a Charter which was presented to him, and which has become known as Magna Carta—the Great Charter.

Having signed against his wishes, John was determined to break his promise, but he could only do so by getting the Pope to release him from his oath. This he proceeded to do, but the barons forestalled him. Rather than waste any more time arguing with John, they offered the crown to the French Prince, Louis, on the understanding that the French would drive John out.

Later, a French army, under the leadership of the prince himself, landed at Dover, where

John's seal on Magna Carta 1215.

it wasted too much time in trying to break the siege of that town. In the meantime, some of the barons were disillusioned by the length of time the French were taking. Moreover, as a conspiracy was uncovered, by which the French were likely to break their agreement with the barons, many deserted Prince Louis.

THE CROWN JEWELS ARE LOST

John, in the meantime, had been pillaging and plundering, setting fire to houses and massacring as he went. Arriving at the Wash, near King's Lynn, he decided to take a path which was dry at certain periods of the tide, but which became covered very quickly. Unfortunately for him, he had picked the wrong state of the tide, and though he got across safely, all his baggage, his jewels and many men were lost.

He went to a nearby abbey to spend the night, and there he became ill with the most violent pains in his stomach. The next day he died, and was later laid to rest in the cathedral at Worcester.

So ended a reign which was marked by murder and bloodshed, pillaging and plundering. John had remained faithful to no one, and it is doubtful if anyone mourned his death. The outstanding event of his reign was the signing of Magna Carta, but as is so often the case, a step in the progress of freedom only came about through great misery on the part of the people.

THE GREAT SEAL

Traditional Symbol of Royal Authority

THE history of the GREAT SEAL OF ENGLAND began nine hundred years ago when Edward the Confessor, in 1053, fixed the first hanging double Seal to a little writ which he sent to Leofwine, Bishop of Eadwine Earl, and his thanes in Staffordshire.

For hundreds of years every message and order from the King had to be sealed with his Great Seal, which has been called " the Key of the Kingdom," nothing of importance could be done without it. A new one is made for each King or Queen who comes to the throne, the old one being broken by the Monarch who at one time used to direct that the silver of which it was made should be given to some poor person. In more recent years, and at the present time, the old Seal becomes the property of the Lord Chancellor.

HOW THE SEAL IS USED

The Seal itself, which has always been round, is made of silver; this is the mould, or matrix. It is made in two halves, with projecting lugs; a disc of wax, softened in hot water, is placed on each half of the mould, with the lugs exactly matching. A press is used to make the impression of the Seal, any excess wax being scraped off with a knife, and then the wax seal is hardened in cold water. This wax impression is the Seal that is attached to certain documents by strings called " laces." In our time the Great Seal is not used so often, but is just as important as it has ever been. When the Queen gives her royal assent to the election of a bishop or an archbishop, when a writing called a Letters Patent gives the right to an invention or discovery, when power to sign and confirm treaties is given, and on many other occasions, her Great Seal is used.

The Great Seal of William the Conqueror.

To protect the wax impression of the Great Seal on documents it used to be carefully tied up in a bag usually made of wool or silk; there still exists a splendid white linen bag painted red outside and decorated with a silver and gold lion used for the Seal of Edward I. The bag was then put into a metal box, which in the past used to be made of solid silver, but to-day a japanned iron box is used without even the Royal Coat-of-Arms and the bag is omitted.

EXCEPTIONAL SEALS

Nowadays red or green wax is used, but in the twelfth century a white wax was used for the Great Seal. When coloured wax was needed it was painted light brown or red, or stained with verdigris to colour it green for certain special documents. Although it was the custom to make wax impressions, not metal ones, of the Great Seal of England, there have been occasions when gold has been used. This was done in 1213 by King John, two years before the signing of Magna Carta, when he had a gold Seal fixed to the document by which he gave his realms of England and Ireland to the Pope. A Great Seal of solid gold, different from any other, hangs from the document confirming the Treaty Henry VIII made with Francis I of France, but both these gold Seals are exceptions.

THE KEEPER OF THE SEAL

From earliest times the Great Seal has been in the keeping of the Lord Chancellor, who is appointed when it is handed to him, and who retires when he surrenders it, or " gives up the Key." In the Middle Ages the Chancellor was the King's Chaplain who also wrote the King's letters, and he was Keeper of the Seal, which was later called the Great Seal to distinguish it from other and smaller seals. He began in 1199 to keep on parchment rolls copies of all important letters he dispatched. When the Chancery lost its connection with the Royal Household, the records were moved to a place which thus became Chancery Lane, where to-day the Public Record Office stands, where some of the Great Seals can be seen.

In the Middle Ages sealing went on continuously every day except on the principal festivals, and it can be said that it was Bishop Salmon who made Sunday a holiday by forbidding sealing on that day.

GENTLEMEN SERVANTS IN ATTENDANCE

Gradually there grew up quite a large staff of Gentlemen Servants in attendance on the all-important Great Seal; these were ordered to be " dressed not in cote or jerken but decently in a gown as the clerks of long time used to be." Until 1832 the attendants were:

  The Clerk of the Hanaper (hamper holding documents for sealing).
  The Spigurnel (Sealer).
  The Chaffwax (who prepared the wax for the Seal).
  The Porter.
  The Purse-bearer.

The Clerk of the Hanaper took charge of the money paid for the use of the Great Seal. He had a special apartment in the Palace of Westminster, for himself and his parchment and wax, and his livery was also given to him. The Spigurnel, or Sealer, had to be on duty at all hours and must never take a holiday. He was paid £83 6s. 8d. in the time of Charles I, with a small payment for the towels he used to clean the oil and wax off the Seal, for his riding charges following the Seal round the country, and finally for four red cloth bags to protect the seal in its Purse. At one time he and the Chaffwax kept a servant called the Portjoie who kept the sumpter-horse, which was used to carry the books and parchment rolls. Changes made in 1832 left only the Purse-bearer, who was given an extra hundred pounds a year for doing the work of the others.

THE SPECIAL PURSE

The Great Seal itself, that is the silver mould, has always had a special purse in which it is kept. At first this cost 6s. 8d., but later the purses were made of better material with handwork for ornament. Every year a new one was provided, and when Roger Nelham, maker of the 1652 purse, sent in his bill for £28 16s. it included " embroidering the rich purse for the Greate Seale of England with best double refined gold and silver upon a rich velvet, ingraine with the arms of the Commonwealth of England at large." The old purse was always given to the Chancellor's wife, and one

The obverse and reverse of the Great Seal of Commonwealth, which was struck in 1651.
The interior of the House of Commons replaced the figure of the monarch.

Chancellor's wife collected so many purses she used them to make curtains. In the nineteenth century for a great many years the new purse was made by Elizabeth Berry, who earned her living—£70 a year—by doing so. After she died in 1882 it was agreed that the purse must be used till it was worn out, and the new one was to cost not more than £65. Sometimes the purse is carried in procession by the Lord Chancellor as a symbol of the Great Seal and when he reads the Lords' address to the Queen he holds in his left hand the purse in which the address has been carried.

EARLIER SEALS

In the British Museum and the Public Record Office there are Great Seals (some in wax impressions, some the actual silver mould) from the time of Edward the Confessor to George VI. The thin, tall King on this first Royal Seal looks like a trussed bird, arms raised from the elbows, knees nearly to his chin, as he sits on a low seat. Right up to the time of Queen Victoria that was the way each Monarch was pictured on the Seal (the obverse) and on the reverse side always on horseback.

Sometimes the Monarchs changed their Great Seals, or had more than one in use. Queen Elizabeth I wanted a second one, so she told the famous miniature painter Nicholas Hilliard to design it. The silver Seal, which measures $4\frac{1}{2}$ inches across, gives a fine picture of the Queen in royal robes, fur cloak, ruff and crown, seated on a curved throne curtained and cushioned. The reverse shows her upon a spirited horse with embroidered saddle-cloth riding over ground tufted with grass and little plants, with two flowering rose trees in the background.

CROMWELL AND CHARLES II

One of the finest Great Seals belonged to Oliver Cromwell's Commonwealth. It measures $5\frac{1}{2}$ inches across and is so beautifully engraved that every county's name can be read on its map of the British Isles, framed boldly by these words: "In the first yeare of Freedome by God's blessing restored in 1648." When, twelve years later, Charles II was restored, he ordered Thomas Simon, the man who made Cromwell's Seal to design the new one. The King sits on a curved shell-backed throne under a canopy bearing the Royal Arms. On the reverse the mounted King wears a cloak and cutlass, and he has a laurel wreath about his head. London Bridge and the Thames form the background. Charles had carried a plainer Seal, when, as a daring young King of twenty-three, he marched at the head of his Scottish soldiers to Worcester. After his defeat in battle he threw the Great Seal into the River Severn for fear that Cromwell's men would take it. It was never recovered.

JAMES II's SEAL

But when his brother James, a King in disguise, stole from Whitehall on that cold December night in 1688, he carried the Seal of England in his pocket to the horse-ferry at Westminster. There, attended only by Sir Edward Hales, he took a river-boat with one sculler. When close to Lambeth Bridge the King threw the Key of the Kingdom into the Thames, believing that without it the Government of the country he had deserted could not be carried on. The Seal was, however, netted by a fisherman at Vauxhall. As it was useless to him, and as it would have been high treason to use it, he took the Seal to the Lords of the Council, who gave it into the hands of William of Orange, who, with his wife, had just come to the throne. William used the Seal until 1689 when a new one bearing his own and Queen Mary's images was ready. The abdication of James II was dated legally from 11th December, 1688, the night on which he threw the Great Seal into the Thames.

STRANGE ADVENTURES

Other strange adventures have befallen the Key of the Kingdom. George IV's Lord Chancellor was careless enough to allow the Great Seal to be stolen from his house in Great Ormond Street. Perhaps he felt that it was safe in two bags, one silk and the other leather. Neither thief nor Seal was ever found. That burglar was luckier than the man who had broken into the house of an earlier Chancellor and was determined to steal the Seal of the Realm. All he got was the Gold Mace, as the Chancellor had taken the Great Seal to bed for safety, and had it under his pillow. The thief was caught and hanged.

At least one Great Seal has been buried and was in danger of remaining so. This happened in 1812 when fire broke out in the Lord

Chancellor's country house, burning so fiercely that he was anxious for the safety of his precious charge. Carrying the Seal into the garden, he hastily buried it. Next morning he had no idea which flower-bed held the Key of the Kingdom, so he turned out the entire household to join him in digging and delving until it was found, protected by one of Elizabeth Berry's handsome purses from any harm.

The Lord Chancellor no longer takes the Great Seal about when not in use. Queen Elizabeth II's Great Seal of England is kept safely in the House of Lords. The new Great Seal of Scotland is kept at the Record Office in Edinburgh, although the Secretary of State for Scotland is its official Keeper.

THE SEALS OF ELIZABETH II

For seventeen months Queen Elizabeth used the Great Seal of her father, George VI. Then she " broke " it, that is, lightly tapped it with a tiny hammer so as not to damage its engraving, and handed her new Great Seal to the Lord Chancellor, who is its Keeper. He also received the " broken " Seal of King George.

The Queen's Great Seal was designed by

The reverse side of the Great Seal. The Queen is shown throned and robed, holding the Sceptre and the Orb.

The obverse of the present Queen's Great Seal. Her Majesty is wearing the uniform of Colonel-in-Chief, Grenadier Guards.

Gilbert Ledward, R.A., and engraved at the Royal Mint. It has a diameter of six inches and weighs 135 ounces. On the obverse the Queen is shown mounted, in the uniform of Colonel-in-Chief, Grenadier Guards. The reverse shows her throned and robed, holding the sceptre and orb.

In July, 1954, Queen Elizabeth approved the new Great Seal of Scotland, which had also been designed by the same artist, and engraved at the Royal Mint. It is slightly different from the English Great Seal. The obverse shows the Queen, " Elizabeth II," crowned and throned in her robes of state, holding the sceptre and orb. She wears the collar of the Order of the Thistle, with its motto as the background to her head and shoulders. Her throne is flanked by two shields showing the Royal Arms of Scotland. The reverse, which has been unchanged since 1903, was designed by the Lyon King of Arms, and bears these Royal Arms in the Scottish form. The Seal is silver, half an inch thick, and six inches in diameter.

The Great Seals of the two Kingdoms are the traditional symbols of royal authority, and though used less frequently than formerly they are still of great importance to the realm.

JULIUS CÆSAR
A Great Figure in World History

TO MOST of us, Caius Julius Cæsar is merely a dim figure who suddenly brought anxiety into the latter part of our school days: but the man who wrote that famous sentence about all Gaul being divided into three parts was one of the greatest and most versatile figures in the history of the world.

He was born into the Roman aristocracy at a time when Rome was surging towards the peak of her power. He was educated at the famous school of rhetoric at Rhodes from which he emerged, a man of wide culture, brilliant, witty, and one of the finest orators in a city of great speech-makers. He had, too, his share of ambition and since politics offered the greatest prospects of a profitable career, it was, naturally, to politics that the young aristocrat turned. For almost eighteen years, he was engaged in various complicated intrigues during which time he was financed by his friend, the very wealthy millionaire, Crassus; and it is possible that all Cæsar's magnificent talents might easily have come to nothing had he not accepted the governorship of Western Spain. Here he had his first taste of military life which he took to as though he had never known anything else. When he returned to Rome, he had not only pacified his province but had added north-western Spain to the Roman dominions.

Caius Julius Cæsar, soldier and Emperor. The details of his clothes are here clearly seen.

CONSUL OF ROME

Back in Rome, Cæsar was unanimously elected a Consul of Rome by the Senate; and immediately the Senate had cause to regret the appointment, for Cæsar introduced a Bill to give free lands to soldiers who had fought in the wars abroad. Until then, such lands had been quietly taken over by wealthy speculators who exploited them to the full. The Senate tried, therefore, to block the new and revolutionary measure, but Cæsar outwitted them by proclaiming his Bill publicly to the citizens in the market place. Pompey, the great soldier and idol of Rome, added his support. The Senate recognised defeat and the Bill became law.

GOVERNOR OF ROMAN GAUL

In 59 B.C., Cæsar's term as Consul ended and he was appointed governor of Roman Gaul. It was a job that called for the highest degree of courage, character and ability. Gaul was a turbulent province that was constantly being overrun by various barbarian tribes. Cæsar accepted the challenge and reacted to it brilliantly. With consummate skill, he out-manœuvred and smashed threat after threat. He brought the Gauls into complete subjection. He drove the fierce Helvetii back into Switzerland. He crushed the overwhelming and very dangerous German tribes and conquered the forces of the Belgians. Twice he crossed the Channel and defeated the aggressive Britons. Soon Gaul was a peaceful Roman province that was to carry the imprint of Julius Cæsar for centuries to come.

The scene in the Senate House after Cæsar had been assassinated in 44 B.C., as depicted in a painting by a nineteenth-century French artist, Gérôme.

JEALOUSY AND ENMITY IN ROME

As was to be expected, the magnificent achievements of Cæsar gave rise to jealousy and enmity back in Rome. The great three-man association of Pompey, Crassus and Cæsar now existed no longer. Crassus had perished on an African battlefield and Pompey, who was now Consul, was bitterly jealous of his former comrade's new renown. The situation came to a head when Pompey swung his influence and his legions over to the side of the Senate. Cæsar was well aware of what was going on. He was returning to Rome with his seasoned, victorious troops when he heard the news. The Senate had trumped up charges against him. He was ordered to disband his legions immediately and to return to Rome to face trial. The crisis had arrived. The Senate was obviously determined to take over complete power in Rome and Pompey was the instrument whereby they hoped to achieve this design. Cæsar halted his forces in the valley of the Po while he made his decision. He was confident of the support of the Roman people. He was even more confident of the fidelity of his battle-hardened veteran legions. In January, 49 B.C., Cæsar ordered his forces across the Rubicon, a small stream that was the northern boundary of Rome. There could be no going back now.

THE BATTLE OF PHARSALUS

During the next year and a half, the position remained inconclusive but gradually it became clear that events were tending to favour Cæsar. The soldiers who were sent to check the invader promptly went over to his side. At the Battle of Pharsalus, on 9th August, 48 B.C., the issue was decided when Pompey the Great and Caius Julius Cæsar, the two greatest warriors of the day, clashed fiercely. Pompey was decisively beaten and fled to Egypt, hoping to resume the struggle from there. The young King Ptolemy, hoping to placate Cæsar, promptly had Pompey murdered: an action which failed signally to win approval, for very soon, Cæsar had deposed Ptolemy and had replaced him with Cleopatra, Ptolemy's sister. Egypt was thus added as a protectorate to the Roman domain. Meanwhile, in Spain and North Africa, the shattered forces of Pompey gathered for one final attempt. Cæsar met them at Thapsus, near Tunis, and routed them. The struggle was over.

THE STATESMAN

Cæsar returned to find a Triumph arranged

for him in Rome and the Senate grovelling at his feet. He accepted the title of Imperator and set about reforming the government. He broke the power of the Senate by extending its numbers to include people hitherto excluded. He encouraged religious toleration. He planned to extend Roman citizenship to all free men throughout the entire Empire. He carried out a far-reaching programme of colonisation. He spent large sums of money on public works, checked profiteering and took the business of appointing governors out of the hands of the senate. He called in an astronomer from Egypt and with his help reformed the calendar, making the year a regular 365 days with a leap year every four years. He wrote his famous War Commentaries. Then, in 44 B.C. the Senate made its final and successful effort. In the presence of the Senate, Julius Cæsar was assassinated by a group of conspirators who wounded each other in their wild attempts to strike down the Imperator. With 23 wounds in his body, Caius Julius Cæsar, who had earned immortality several times over, fell and died at the foot of the statue of Pompey the Great.

THE LAST BUCCANEER

Oh, England is a pleasant place for them that's rich and high,
But England is a cruel place for such poor folks as I;
And such a port for mariners I ne'er shall see again,
As the pleasant Isle of Avès, beside the Spanish Main.

There were forty craft in Avès that were both swift and stout,
All furnished well with small arms and cannons round about;
And a thousand men in Avès made laws so fair and free
To choose their valiant captains and obey them loyally.

Thence we sailed against the Spaniard with his hoards of plate and gold,
Which he wrung with cruel tortures from Indian folk of old;
Likewise the merchant captains, with hearts as hard as stone,
Who flog men and keel-haul them, and starve them to the bone.

Oh, the palms grew high in Avès, and fruits that shone like gold,
And the colibris and parrots they were gorgeous to behold;
And the negro maids to Avès from bondage fast did flee,
To welcome gallant sailors, a-sweeping in from sea.

Oh, sweet it was in Avès to hear the landward breeze,
A-swing with good tobacco in a net between the trees,
With a negro lass to fan you, while you listened to the roar
Of the breakers on the reef outside, that never touched the shore.

But Scripture saith, an ending to all fine things must be;
So the King's ships sailed on Avès, and quite put down were we.
All day we fought like bulldogs, but they burst the booms at night,
And I fled in a piragua, sore wounded, from the fight.

Nine days I floated starving, and a negro lass beside,
Till for all I tried to cheer her, the poor young thing she died;
But as I lay a-gasping, a Bristol sail came by,
And brought me home to England here, to beg until I die.

And now I'm old and going—I'm sure I can't tell where;
One comfort is, this world's so hard, I can't be worse off there;
If I might but be a sea-dove, I'd fly across the main,
To the pleasant Isle of Avès, to look at it once again.

Charles Kingsley

HANNIBAL

The Story of a Great Warrior

MANY, many years before Christ there was a great sea power in the Mediterranean. The Phoenicians were great traders and had even been as far as Britain. They established various trading stations along the coast of the Mediterranean, and one of the most important of these was Carthage. For years, the city was one of the most important in the world, and was very rich, but it found a rival in a new town, the town of Rome, which was on the other side of the sea on the coast of Italy.

The Carthaginians had long wanted to control the island of Sicily, and they were successful in getting this, but no sooner had they done so than they found the Romans also wanting the island.

The Romans eventually won Sicily in battle, and even went across the sea to Carthage itself. The result was that Carthage had to ask for peace and gave up all claims to Sicily.

Hannibal, the Great General.

One of the Carthaginian generals had been very successful in Spain and was driven to a bitter hatred of the Romans. Hamilcar was a soldier, and he determined that, from an early age, his two sons Hannibal and Hasdrubal should learn to hate the Romans. He persuaded them to swear that, as long as they lived, they would fight against Rome.

ELEPHANTS USED AS TANKS

Hannibal was extremely young when he first went to war. An expedition was sent from Carthage to attack Rome by way of Spain, and Hannibal was given a small part of the army to command. When the time was ripe, war was declared and Hannibal, now at the head of a great force of men, set out for Rome.

Hannibal was a really great leader and one who was respected by all his men, so much so that they were prepared to follow him even to death itself, as many of them did on that eventful journey to the city of Rome.

Hannibal's army was a strange assortment of men made up of all nationalities. There were the Carthaginian soldiers, who were well trained in the arts of war. There were various tribesmen from Spain and from Gaul and even from the north of Africa. What could such a strange assortment do against a trained Roman army? With a leader of Hannibal's calibre that question did not arise. He even equipped his army with tanks! Not the kind that you think of, for *they* did not come for many hundreds of years. Those that Hannibal had were elephants with defensive towers called castles upon their backs, from which weapons could be used more effectively against an army on the ground.

AN ARMY WHO CROSSED THE ALPS

This army took the Romans completely by surprise. They had expected to fight the Carthaginians in Spain, and had never realised that such an army could cross the mountains in the north of Italy. They had not, however, reckoned upon Hannibal. Travelling was difficult, as the army had to go through hostile tribes and through snow and ice; but they were successful, and had soon beaten three Roman armies and descended upon the city of Rome itself.

Here, things did not go too well for Hannibal. The Romans were wise and avoided engaging the Carthaginians in battle, as they knew that the enemy would weaken slowly if they could not get supplies from home. Hannibal was forced to retire to the south of Italy.

Had the supplies arrived from home, the end of the story might have been very different, but, unfortunately for Hannibal, the people of Carthage did not give him the support they might have done.

Hannibal crossing the Alps, from a seventeenth century engraving. The artist has shown the elephants used by this great Carthaginian General. These huge animals with their loads of soldiers, struck terror into the hearts of the Romans. As Hannibal could not get stores he had at last to retire.

Hasdrubal set out from Spain to go to his brother's assistance, and was successful in eluding the Romans there. His army of 50,000 would have made quite a difference. He was, however, engaged later in battle with the Romans and defeated. Hannibal, waiting for news, received it in a rather gruesome way. The Romans sent him the head of his brother as a sign of what they did to those who opposed them.

Soon after, the news also reached Hannibal that Scipio, the Roman general, had attacked Spain and conquered it, and was on his way to Carthage. Hannibal was recalled to defend his own city. The great successes of his early drive into Italy had been wasted by the short-sighted policy of the Carthaginians.

Back in his own city, Hannibal set to work to organise the defences of the city, but after many years of fighting the Carthaginian army was no match for the Romans and the city was forced to surrender. The Roman peace terms were harsh, but there was no alternative. Much of the glory of Carthage was gone.

THE END OF A GREAT WARRIOR

Having finished Carthage, as they thought, the Romans went off to Macedonia to defeat

that country, but they had not reckoned upon Hannibal. Though now an old man, he was still very active. The Romans, fearing lest he should cause any more trouble, demanded that the people of Carthage should give Hannibal up. To escape the indignity, Hannibal fled towards the east, where he found refuge in the court of a Syrian king by the name of Antiochus.

There, he became the chief military adviser to the Syrians, and again he declared war on the Romans. Once again the Romans were successful, and once again one of their demands was that Hannibal should be surrendered.

Once again, the valiant old man fled and escaped his enemies. This time, going via Crete, he took refuge in Bithynia, but he was again hounded out by the Romans and the king received a demand that Hannibal should be given up. To save the humiliation of submitting to his foes, the great warrior took poison and died in 183 B.C.

It seems a great shame that such a great warrior should end his life in such a way, but it was felt by Rome that as long as Hannibal lived they were in danger. Now, without him, they were secure. What a testimony to the strength of one man!

An artist's impression of Housesteads Fort on the Wall during the Roman occupation.

HADRIAN'S WALL

ONE of the noblest surving memorials to the Roman Empire of ancient times is to be found in the north of England. This is the Roman Wall, sometimes wrongly referred to as the Picts' Wall, but best known as Hadrian's Wall. It was Hadrian, a great Roman emperor, who, on a visit of inspection in A.D.122, commanded Aulus Platorius Nepos, Governor of Britain, to undertake its construction.

The Wall was designed partly as a frontier line (and a springboard for military operations when need arose), but mainly it was to be a fortification against the tribes farther north, on what is to-day the Scottish Border. The Roman engineers planned that it should run from Wallsend on Tyne, a few miles east of Newcastle, on the North Sea coast, across the " backbone " of England, the northern tip of the Pennines, to Bowness on Solway, on the coast a few miles west of Carlisle. Its total length was just over seventy-three English miles, or eighty Roman miles, the Roman mile measuring 1,620 instead of 1,760 yards.

Before examining in detail the Wall and the forts, mile-castles and turrets that were built along its whole length for special purposes, let us see what remains of it to-day, nearly two thousand years after it was planned and built.

WHAT THE WALL LOOKS LIKE TO-DAY

If you could look down on it from above, hovering over it in a helicopter, you would notice a line of solid, turf-topped stonework zigzagging east and west through, for the most part, very empty country, and dotted at regular intervals with rectangular earthworks. Beneath the outskirts and centre of towns like Newcastle and Carlisle it would vanish completely; here and there, where roads or rivers interrupted it, it would be less clearly defined, and sometimes obliterated altogether. But on the high ground in the central sections, particularly where it clings to the edge of the famous Whin Sill that rises to 1,230 feet above sea-level, it would stand out clearly.

It is best, though, to see it from close to. This is quite easy. You may walk alongside it, or even on top of it, for many miles at a stretch, exactly as the soldiers of the Roman garrisons did. It is wide enough most of the way for two to walk on it abreast, and the turf that now grows between the massive facing-stones is firm and springy to the feet.

Seen from ground level, the Wall is usually no more than about four or five feet high, and built fairly close to the edge of the northward-falling slopes. Sometimes, as at Crag Lough and Greenlee Lough and the Nine Nicks of Thirlwall, in the central section, these are so steep that they are almost precipices; sometimes there is just a berm, or terrace, and a deep ditch on the north side to give greater height to the Wall and make it a more formidable obstacle.

Originally, however, it was built to a uniform height of about fifteen feet, and in addition there was a shoulder-high rampart on the north side for the protection of the soldiers on patrol. Unfortunately, enormous quantities of the quarried stone used for the Wall have been removed for building purposes. If you are observant, you can easily spot these stones in walls and farm buildings near at hand. One

farmhouse, known as Sewingshields, is built entirely of pillaged stones, and in the wall of one outbuilding you can see a centurial stone with an inscription on it stating that that section of the Wall was built by the century of Gellius Philippus.

In addition to the Wall and the ditch on its north side, there was a road running east–west behind it for the rapid transport of men and supplies; between the Wall and this road there ran an enormous ditch known as the Vallum.

The Vallum lies about seventy yards to the south of the Wall, and was cut, like the Roman roads, in ruler-straight sections up to five miles in length. It was flat bottomed, about eight feet deep and twenty feet across, the material dug out of it forming a long " bolster " on each side, about fifty feet from the middle of the ditch. To-day the Vallum has been largely overgrown and filled in, but it is still possible to pick out long stretches of it, especially when the sun is low in the early morning or late afternoon and casts a faint shadow on the turf. As you travel along General Wade's fine Military Road between Newcastle and Carlisle, it is close alongside nearly all the way.

An inscribed centurial stone from the Wall of Cawfields. It reads c(o)ho(rtis) vic(enturia) lepidiana, i.e. " The Lepidianian century of the sixth cohort (built this)." The Wall was built in short sections of 50 ft. each and the unit responsible " signed " each section.

Experts have been digging and searching along the line of Hadrian's Wall for a hundred years and have discovered a very great deal about the design of this great fortification, the arrangements made for the welfare of its garrison and the provision made for their support in time of need. They know what efficient engineers the Romans were, and much about the methods they used to build such an enduring monument. They have found many of the quarries from which the hard, heavy gritstone was hewn.

HOW THE WALL WAS BUILT

The method of building the Wall, whether the broad section that runs west from Newcastle to the midway point, or the slightly narrower section that replaced the original turf wall between the River Irthing and the western terminus, was bold and skilful. Squared stones, about ten inches long by six inches high but tapering backwards for as much as twenty inches, were laid in courses on the north and south faces of the Wall, the largest at the base, the smaller ones above, and the space between the two faces was filled in with cemented rubble. The tapering ends of the facing-stones were bonded into this rubble so that when the moisture dried out the Wall was solid. It is still possible to see, both in the quarries and on some of the bigger stones, the marks left by the masons' chisels, and sometimes even their private " marks," which show after nearly two thousand years the pride these craftsmen took in their skill.

Where the Wall came to a river, as it does for instance at the crossing of the North Tyne near Chollerford, twenty-five miles west of Newcastle, it had, of course, to be replaced by a bridge. This was of heavy timbers on stone piers, and these, at low water, can still be seen, with their upstream cut-waters. If you examine the enormous stones used here as buttresses on the river bank, you will find that they have been skilfully jointed, their grooves filled with metal. Some of the metal is lead, and if you scratch it with the point of a knife it shines as bright to-day as it did when the Roman engineers laid the stones. If you look very carefully, too, you may find some of the lewis-holes, the wedge-shaped holes for the lewis, or wedge-key, by which a block could be lifted and lowered without being encircled

by ropes. The same method is used to-day for manipulating the huge stone blocks in constructing harbour walls and lighthouses.

And now for the line of the Wall itself, and the forts, mile-castles and turrets which are spaced along its length.

The forts are the most important, and the chief of these (there were a dozen or more) are at Rudchester (Roman Vindobala), Halton (Hunnum), Chesters (Cilurnum) on the North Tyne, Housesteads (Borcovicium) and Birdoswald (Camboganna). These are rectangular enclosures covering several acres, and a good example of one is at Housesteads, situated almost exactly midway along the Wall, in one of its highest sections. It covers five acres and was large enough to hold with comfort a garrison a thousand strong. As it has been carefully excavated, it is possible to-day to wander about it and examine its lay-out for oneself.

The north wall of the fort is the Wall itself, built on the crest of a steep slope, and there is a gateway in each of the four walls. Small signboards to-day point out the various sections of the fort. There is the *principia*, which was the headquarters building, or G.H.Q.; not far away is the Commandant's house, the *praetorium*; and just beyond are the *horrea*, the all-important granaries, long narrow buildings with floors raised on short stone pillars to protect the grain from damp and vermin. You can see the remains of the men's barracks and workshops, stables and storehouses. Each barrack block housed a *centuria* of a hundred men, together with its commanding centurion.

MARKS LEFT BY ROMAN CHARIOTS

All these sections are enclosed, as usual, within a five-foot-thick stone containing-wall, backed by a massive earth-and-turf bank. The four gateways are wide enough for the passage of the Roman chariots and the vehicles carrying the corn supplied by a levy on the district which the fort protected. Some most interesting details are to be seen at these gateways. For example, each has a stone sill over which the chariots were driven, and in passing in and out during the centuries of occupation, grooves have been worn in the sills on each side of the massive door-step. You can see the marks of the chariot and wagon wheels. and if you

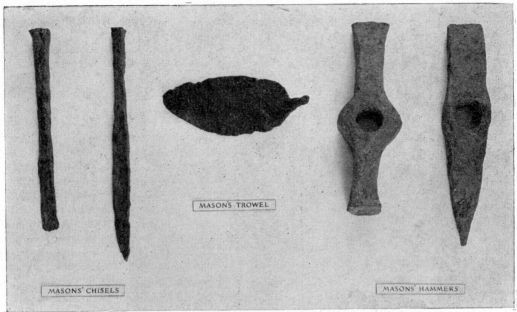

MASON'S TROWEL

MASONS' CHISELS

MASONS' HAMMERS

Some of the tools used by the masons who built Hadrian's Wall.

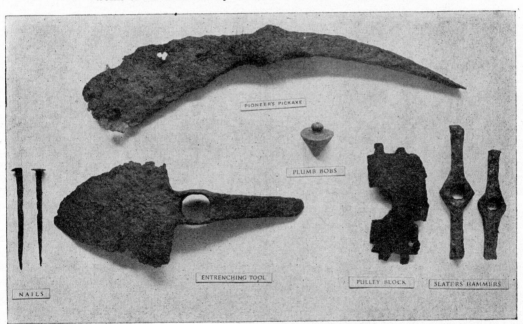

PIONEER'S PICKAXE

PLUMB BOBS

NAILS

ENTRENCHING TOOL

PULLEY BLOCK

SLATERS' HAMMERS

Found along the Wall, these tools, though worn by use and time, are modern in style.

measure them you will find that they are exactly four feet eight and a half inches apart. This happens to be the standard gauge of our railways.

The sockets in which the heavy door-pivots turned can also be seen at these gateways, and so skilfully have the great blocks of masonry been laid that often it is not possible to push a penknife blade down between block and block. The Romans, whatever they were building, whether roads or forts or aqueducts, saw to it that they were built to last.

The forts were carefully sited within reach of an ample water supply, and some of the springs used are still flowing to-day. There is evidence of an elaborate system of channelling and piping water from roofs to stone troughs. These were sometimes hewn out of massive blocks of stone, sometimes constructed of stone slabs skilfully fitted together, their joints packed with molten lead. Some of these troughs at Housesteads have scalloped edges where generations of Roman legionaries have sharpened their short, two-edged swords before battle.

Attached to the forts, but outside their containing-walls, was the *vicus*. This was a settlement of civilians, veteran soldiers on pension who had perhaps married and did not wish to return to the homes they had left when they were sent " abroad " to subdue the turbulent tribes in Rome's distant province, Britain, and all sorts of people who had attached themselves in one way or another to the garrison.

The *vicus* at Housesteads is tacked on to the south-east corner not far from the gateway by which the visitor usually enters (though it is perhaps more impressive to enter the fort by walking along the Wall itself till it joins the east or west corner and jumping down into it that way). It is a particularly interesting example, with relics of shops, inns, offices, chapels, bath-houses and other buildings. One of these is signposted Murder House, for here some years ago a skeleton was discovered buried beneath the floor, with a knife-point still wedged between its ribs.

THE SUN-GOD'S TEMPLE

Not far from the *vicus*, excavators laid bare a temple dedicated to the worship of the Persian Sun-God, Mithras. The Emperor Hadrian issued edicts to suppress this pagan religion, but there is evidence at several places along the Wall that his edicts were defied and temples were built for the secret practice of this banned religion.

Some of the discoveries made alongside the Wall have been made quite by chance. In a recent hot summer, when the swampy ground had dried out, a man walking across the turf stubbed his toe on a curiously shaped stone, bent down to examine it, and found himself looking at part of one of the most important of the Temples of Mithras, buried in the bog

The remains of the barracks for cavalry troops at the Fort of Cilurnum (now Chesters).

which was the Wall itself, and a second gateway for the entry of men and supplies, in the south wall. A roadway linked the two gates, and on each side of this roadway there were barracks capable of housing about twenty-five men. Thus the mile-castles were snug, self-contained garrisons of about fifty men each. From each mile-castle to the next, and so to the forts themselves, there was of course a protected way on top of the Wall, with the high parapet on the enemy side as extra security.

Though each mile-castle was less than an English mile from its neighbour, the Roman engineers also built yet smaller forts, known as turrets, two between each pair of mile-castles, so that actually there was a distance of only 540 yards between each strong-point and the next. These turrets were really small towers, about twenty feet square outside, with three-foot-thick walls, used for look-out and signalling purposes. It was possible to send messages very swiftly over long sections of the Wall by making use of these regularly-spaced points even the smallest of which would always have a platoon of men on duty.

From records found carved on centurial and

A local god inscribed: "To the god of the company, the company commanded by Bassius Crescens made this gift."

for hundreds of years. Now it has been excavated, the land drained and the temple's foundations cleared for everyone to see.

This temple is near Carrawburgh (Procolitia), the fort a few miles to the east of Housesteads. Close to the Carrawburgh fort some excavators in search of lead came across the upper lip of a well. When this had been excavated it was found to contain a hoard of nearly fourteen thousand coins of gold, silver and bronze. One can only guess why such a quantity of coins should have been thrown down the Carrawburgh well. Was it done in a sudden panic when superior forces overwhelmed the fort? Was it an accident? It remains one of the many puzzles still to be solved.

THE MILE-CASTLES

The mile-castles, as their name suggests, are castles, smaller than the great forts, established along the Wall at intervals of one Roman mile. Like the forts, the mile-castles were all built very much to a pattern. They were about fifty or sixty feet by sixty or seventy feet, rectangular, with a gateway in the north wall,

The tombstone of a Romano-British lady of the second century during the Roman occupation, shows the fashions of the time.

A horned head of an unknown deity by a native British sculptor, found near the Wall.

sufficiently docile. This simple but effective method involved the minimum of casualties among the legions themselves.

Little by little, the whole picture of life on Hadrian's Wall, and in the territory immediately behind it, is being built up. Excavators, scholars, decipherers of ancient monumental inscriptions, students of the Roman way of life, have pieced together the details they have found along the seventy and more miles of this tremendous Roman landmark. Wisely, the excavators have left the majority of their "finds" on the sites where they were uncarthed; so that visitors to-day can gain a fairly accurate impression of what life on the Wall was like eighteen hundred years ago. But some of the more precious and more easily weather-worn and damaged fragments have been removed to permanent safety.

other stones, it has been estimated that a total garrison of about twelve thousand men would be divided among the dozen or so main forts. In addition, a further four thousand men were needed to garrison the mile-castles, and supply relays of men for the intervening turrets. It is probable, therefore, that there was a secondary, mobile garrison working behind the line of the Wall for this purpose.

ROMAN STRATEGY

These units would of course combine in the skilfully planned military operations that took place from time to time against the skirmishing enemy from the difficult swamp ground that extended immediately to the north of the Wall. The Roman commanders were wise enough to see to it that their men did not penetrate too deeply into this ill-drained territory, where their heavy armour would put them at a disadvantage against the more freely moving enemy. The general strategy was to assemble the soldiers from certain forts and mile-castles under cover of the Wall, select two gateways in the Wall best suited to a sudden mass sortie by two forces at once, and then, with a strong pincer movement, roll the enemy back against the very Wall itself, through which they could be dragged if they were still alive, and be dealt with at leisure, or enrolled in the labour corps under Roman task-masters if they proved

HOW ROMAN SOLDIERS COOKED THEIR MEALS

In such museums as The Black Gate at Newcastle and Tullie House, Carlisle, in particular, and in the museums on the sites, such as the one at Housesteads, you may see the type of utensils in which the occupying soldiery cooked and ate their meals; the weapons with which they fought; the coins with which they were paid; the personal possessions which they cherished as reminders perhaps of the distant home so many of them were never again to see. There are ornaments and decorative work produced by artists among them who occupied their free time between forays in this more peaceful fashion. There are inscribed altar-stones, tombstones and memorial stones commemorating the deaths of comrades in battle and victories large and small over the tricky enemy against whom their Wall was the only safe barrier. There are curiosities such as small millstones made of Vesuvian rock for the grinding of their corn.

Well-nigh indestructible fragments such as these are continually coming to light in the vicinity of the forts and mile-castles; for there garrisons of men lived, played, fought, slept, during the whole period of the Roman occupation of this territory, which ended suddenly in A.D.383, two hundred and sixty years after the planning and first building of the Wall at the command of the great Emperor Hadrian, who gave it his own enduring name.

ST. PAUL: "And as he journeyed he came near Damascus: and suddenly there shined round about him a light from heaven: And he fell to the earth and heard a voice saying unto him, Saul, Saul, why persecutest thou me? . . . it is hard for thee to kick against the pricks."

ST. PAUL

The Greatest Christian Missionary

ST. PAUL was undoubtedly the greatest of all Christian missionaries. He carried the Gospel from Palestine across Asia Minor into Europe, founding flourishing churches and clearing up many serious confusions about the teachings of Jesus. The story of his wanderings is told in the Acts of the Apostles and, to some extent, in the famous letters he wrote to the churches he founded in Greece and Asia Minor. Impetuous and utterly fearless, he risked his life time and time again in long, adventurous journeys. Yet he began his career as a virulent persecutor of the Christians.

"Saul, who is also Paul, was a Hebrew of Hebrews," we read. The alternative names show that although he was brought up as a strict Jew, he was the son of a Roman citizen. To the Romans he would be known as Paulus, but among the Jewish community of Tarsus he would probably be called Saul.

There were many such communities along the Mediterranean, and they originated from the dispersion of the Jews after the Babylonian exile in 597 and 596 B.C. Paul, therefore, not only spoke Greek, but was familiar with a good deal of Greek literature and philosophy. His education was continued in Jerusalem, where he is said to have attended the school of the great Jewish teacher, Gamaliel.

THE CONVERSION

As a rigidly orthodox Jew of the Pharisee sect, Paul regarded the doctrines of the followers of Jesus of Nazareth as a blasphemous innovation that must be repressed. He joined in hunting down the Christians and was present at the martyrdom of Stephen. It was while he was actually travelling to Damascus on a mission of persecution that a tremendous event occurred which changed his whole life. He had a sudden vision of Jesus and heard a voice saying, "*Saul, Saul, why persecutest thou me?*"

This was the turning point in Paul's career. Unlike the original disciples, he had never seen Jesus, but now he was convinced that this encounter was as real as though he had come face to face with the risen Lord.

The meaning of it seemed plain: all the obligations of the Law which orthodox Jews followed so minutely were superseded by a new revelation. So, instead of entering Damascus as a persecutor, he went as a convert filled with a burning zeal to spread the new religion.

When he began to preach in the synagogues of Damascus the Jews were naturally incensed by this total change of front. There was a plot to kill him, but he made his escape by being lowered down the city walls at night in a basket. This was his first experience of the many hazards he would have to face. For the next thirty years Paul had to endure the bitter hostility of the orthodox Jews who regarded him as a renegade.

After leaving Damascus he spent several years in Arabia. He made his first visit to Jerusalem as a Christian about three years after his conversion. There he met the leaders of the original Church and formed a close friendship with Barnabas, who later joined him on some of his missions. In Jerusalem his preaching was mainly to his own Greek-speaking compatriots, and although the great central purpose of his life—to spread the Gospel far afield to the Gentiles—was forming in his mind, many years were to pass before he embarked upon this ambitious enterprise as fully as he wished.

A PROBLEM OF JEWISH LAW

Both he and Barnabas worked together in Antioch, where there was a mixed Church of Jews and Gentiles. Some of the Jewish Christians, especially in Jerusalem itself, were dubious about the extent to which Gentile converts should comply with regulations about circumcision and food.

This was an issue which might have split the primitive Church, but for the genius of Paul. It was bound to become more acute when churches sprang up composed of a majority of Gentiles. Was it necessary for them to obey the various prohibitions of the Old Testament in regard to unclean foods? Did they have to be circumcised?

P.H.

C

"St. Paul" by Niccolo di Pietro Gerini.

These questions led Paul to make a second visit to Jerusalem and he reached some agreement with the leaders of the Church. It was accepted that he and Barnabas should be entrusted with the momentous task of obtaining Gentile converts and forming new communities wherever the opportunities existed.

THE FIRST MISSIONARY TOUR

Paul then began the first of his three great missionary tours. We do not know the date of his birth, but it is probable that he set forth with Barnabas as his companion about A.D. 46–47. Barnabas was a native of Cyprus and they set sail for that island, following a procedure that became their rule. In most of the towns they visited there was a Jewish colony and Paul invariably preached his doctrine in the synagogue to start with.

Almost every time he met with bitter opposition. He was determined at least to give the Jews a chance to accept his message, and when they rejected it he became more than ever convinced of his own special vocation—to carry the Gospel into the very heart of the Roman Empire. " Lo, we turn to the Gentiles," he exclaimed when he was rebuffed.

There was a dramatic incident at Paphos when he clashed with a magician and the man was temporarily struck blind. Leaving Cyprus, he crossed to the mainland and at Lystra he cured a man whose legs were paralysed. This made such a deep impression on the populace that to Paul's horror he and Barnabas were venerated as gods. They would have been fêted and given divine honours if they had not indignantly protested that they were only men. The result was that later the mob turned upon them in a fury and they were driven out of the town.

The tour ended at Antioch, where trouble from another source awaited Paul. Those Christians who still failed to grasp that the Mosaic Law need not be followed by Gentile converts disapproved of Jews and Christians eating together in the mixed community at Antioch. So Paul returned to Jerusalem.

In the account given in the Acts of the Apostles we already see glimpses of Paul's dominating personality, selfless devotion to the task he had accepted, and physical as well as moral courage. His vision of Christianity as a world faith never wavered.

THE SECOND JOURNEY

On his second journey he was accompanied by Timothy, a young man for whom he felt a deep affection which lasted until the end of his life. Together they travelled across Asia Minor, putting fresh heart into the members of the newly founded churches, and Paul had another vision in which a Macedonian appealed to him, saying, " Come over into Macedonia and help us."

He crossed into Europe, to Philippi, where he soon found himself in trouble again. After listening to him a slave girl who told fortunes was unable to carry on her profession, and her owners protested to the magistrates. Paul and his companions were flogged and thrown into prison, but that night there was an earthquake and the terrified gaoler was converted. The magistrates ordered the prisoners to be released. Paul proudly retorted that he was a Roman citizen, and the city authorities were abject in their apologies.

At Thessalonica, the next town to be visited, it was the Jews who started a riot. Paul escaped to Athens, the centre of Greek learning and philosophy. The philosophers invited him to address the Areopagus, or Council of Public Morals and Welfare, and he made one of his most moving and inspired speeches.

He reminded the assembly that they had an altar in Athens to the Unknown God, and declared that it was He whose message of salvation was now being given to the world.

The Athenians were not very receptive, and he moved on to the great Greek port of Corinth, where he remained for some eighteen months in a Christian family who followed his own craft of tent-making. Yet again the synagogue Jews made mischief and he was brought before the Roman Proconsul, Gallio, on a charge of breaking the Jewish law. Gallio, however, decided that this was no affair of the Roman government.

THE THIRD JOURNEY

Paul's third tour took him to Asia Minor again. From Galatia he went to Ephesus, the centre of the worship of the goddess Diana. His preaching was so successful that the silversmiths who made idols complained that their trade was suffering. The populace were incensed and there can be no doubt that Paul's life was in constant danger during his stay in the city.

He returned to Corinth and began to consider an even more adventurous journey to the western Mediterranean, calling at Rome. First, however, he decided to pay another visit to Jerusalem, where he had heard of some dissension in the mother church. He had to change his route on discovering a plot to kill him, but even so the journey to Jerusalem was fraught with fateful consequences.

He was going into a hotbed of enemies and while entering the sanctuary of the temple he was recognised. He might have been lynched but for the intervention of Roman soldiers. The Jews took him before their own tribunal, the Sanhedrin, where he made such a bold defence that they were plunged into confusion. The Roman government would have dismissed the whole affair as a squabble between Jewish sects, but Paul made the tactical mistake of demanding that his case should be heard at Rome. As a Roman citizen he was entitled to appeal to Cæsar.

THE JOURNEY TO ROME

The last journey of Paul was therefore made as a prisoner. Such storms were encountered on the way that it seemed a miracle that he should survive. Starting from the Judaean port of Cæsarea, he was taken up the coast to Sidon, and then the ship followed a perilous, zigzagging course, hugging the coast, and at one point it seemed they would founder. Paul set a magnificent example of calm and courage. But when the ship finally ran aground off the coast of Melita (Malta) the soldiers would have killed him if they had not been prevented by the centurion. Three months later they embarked again, and after calling at Sicily Paul was landed safely in Italy.

He was technically a prisoner for several years although he managed to continue his preaching. The story of his last perilous voyage is told fully in the Acts, and then it ends abruptly.

Paul could scarcely have chosen a worse time to go to Rome. There were subversive movements seething throughout the Empire and the Jews in particular were an object of suspicion. The synagogue Jews, anxious to demonstrate their loyalty, were infuriated

"The Beheading of St. Paul," by Rubens. The artist has painted a poignant picture of the martyrdom of St. Paul, who died in the knowledge that his life's work had been completed.

with the Christians, whose predictions about the imminent end of the world disturbed the authorities. Moreover, a militant Jewish group called the Zealots, were instigating revolt against Rome. It was not easy for the Romans to distinguish between the Nazarenes and the Zealots.

HIS WORK AND DEATH IN ROME

While in Rome Paul continued to write letters to the various Christian communities, and these now form part of the New Testament. They supplement the story in the Acts of his trials and tribulations, but the end of it all is obscure.

It is certain that he suffered martyrdom during the persecution of Nero, and the date usually accepted is A.D. 64. It is generally believed that he was beheaded at a place three miles outside Rome on the Ostian Way.

He died in the knowledge that his life's work had been completed. He had laid the foundations of the Christian Church that sprang up from the blood of the martyrs and ultimately became the official religion of the Roman Empire.

THE BIBLE

The Sacred Writings of the Christian Church

THE teachings of Christianity are based on a collection of books, which was first named the Bible in catalogues of the ninth and tenth centuries. It is divided into two main parts, the Old Testament and the New Testament. The word "testament" really means covenant, or compact. The Old Testament is therefore regarded as the story of the compact between God and the Jews, who were "the chosen people." With the coming of Christ, there is a new covenant, and the message of Christianity is for both Jews and Gentiles.

The Jews were originally tribesmen, who settled in Palestine in very ancient times. There were already powerful Empires in existence—Babylon to the north and Egypt to the south. It seems clear that the author of the account of this migration was familiar with the civilisation of the Euphrates Valley.

HISTORY OF THE JEWS

The Old Testament is in part a history of the struggle between the Jews and the nations that surrounded them. For a time, they were enslaved by the Egyptians. Under the leadership of Moses, they escaped from Egypt and they believed that they owed their deliverance to divine intervention. All through their chronicles, the disasters that befell them are admitted to be a punishment for disobeying God.

The worst catastrophe was the invasion by Nebuchadnezzar in 597 B.C., when a large number of Jews were deported to Babylon. This period is called the Exile, and it marked the beginning of the dispersion of the Jews. The temple in Jerusalem built by Solomon was destroyed in 586 B.C., but in 583 B.C., Babylon was conquered by Cyrus and although a large number of Jews returned, some remained and formed a community that became a centre of learning.

THE SACRED WRITINGS

It was after this disaster that the Jewish priesthood re-edited the sacred writings. The first five books of the Bible, attributed to Moses

The opening chapter of St. Matthew from the Lindisfarne Gospel Book. Written about 680 in Latin by Eadfrith and illuminated 724-40 by Ethelwold, Bishop of Lindisfarne.

and known as the Torah (the Law), were firmly established as the supreme authority on religion and conduct. Although they took their present shape after the Exile, the originals of Genesis and Exodus go back hundreds of years. The most primitive parts of the Bible are thought to date from about 1200 B.C. From the eighth to the sixth century B.C., the major prophetic works were composed. After the Exile, we have the Prophets, Jeremiah, Ezekiel and part of Isaiah. Chronicles and Ezra were written in 250 B.C., Daniel 164 B.C., Ecclesiastes 160 B.C., and Esther 125 B.C. About 200 years elapsed between the writing of the last Book of the Old Testament and the first of the New.

TRANSLATIONS OF THE BIBLE

The Old Testament was, of course, written in Hebrew, although parts of such late books as Ezra and Daniel are in Aramaic, which had become the everyday language of Palestine by New Testament times. There were so many Jewish communities outside Palestine for

whom the language of the scriptures was unin
telligible that in the third and second centuries
B.C., they were translated into Greek. It was
through this Greek translation made in Alexandria that the early Christian Church received
the Jewish Bible.

At the end of the fourth century, however,
St. Jerome went to the Hebrew original and
translated it into Latin. He also provided a
Latin translation of the Greek New Testament.
and the two together became the Bible which
was accepted by the Western Church. It is
known as the Vulgate.

A LITERARY MOSAIC

Thus the Bible, as we know it to-day,
acquired its shape slowly. There must have
been a time for the ancient Jews, as well as the
Christians, when the various stories and moral
rules were passed on by word of mouth. Then
they began to be committed to writing; and
subsequently what was written down was
revised and added to.

A great deal of scholarship has been devoted
to the task of distinguishing the various parts
of what is in places a literary mosaic. It was
noticed that in the Old Testament, God is
sometimes called by the Hebrew name, Jahveh

One of the pages from Wycliffe's Bible translated into English from the Vulgate.

and sometimes by Elohim. It is thought that
this points to an important difference of
authorship and this is usually indicated by the
letters " J " and " E." The signs of priestly
editing and composition are indicated by the
letter "P." These devices throw a great deal
of light on how the Bible that we know was
written.

THE OLDEST MANUSCRIPTS

Naturally, we do not possess the original
rolls of papyrus on which the Old Testament
was written. The oldest manuscripts that are
more or less complete are in the British Museum
and the Vatican Library. They are not scrolls
but leaf-books and date from the fourth century.

The oldest Hebrew manuscript of any extent
does not go beyond the ninth century A.D.
There are, however, thousands of manuscripts
containing parts or the whole of the different
books. As printing was unknown, everything
had to be copied by hand. It was all too easy
for the copyist to make a mistake. For example, he might insert a marginal note which
another copyist took to be part of the original.

Again, early Hebrew was written without
vowel signs and this sometimes led to a faulty
rendering. Almost equally confusing were the
early Greek manuscripts in which the letters
of one word ran on to the next without a break.

Biblical scholars have sifted this mass of
material like detectives following a complicated clue. It is remarkable that in spite of all
the difficulties of correctly transmitting what

Facsimile of the beginning of St. John's
Gospel from the Latin Gospels, presented by
King Athelstane to the Church of Canterbury.

had been written down centuries before, no serious discrepancies have been discovered. We know more about the Bible to-day than ever before and we can now be confident of what was the original meaning.

CHAPTER AND VERSE

The present division into chapters was introduced into the Vulgate by Stephen Langton, the Archbishop of Canterbury who framed Magna Carta, but the system of numbered verses was not applied until the sixteenth century. This was a mere matter of convenience. What is important is the decision that had to be made about the list of books held to be inspired.

THE VULGATE AND THE APOCRYPHA

Roman Catholics used the Vulgate, and this includes some additional Old Testament writings to the Hebrew Bible that was finally accepted by the Jewish authorities. These extra books are called the Apocrypha (Greek for hidden). They were excluded by a council of Rabbis held at Jamnia in A.D. 90 to settle the long-standing dispute. At the Reformation the Apocrypha was also dropped by Protestant translators.

There is also a New Testament Apocrypha, but on this there is no difference of opinion between Catholics and Protestants; both reject it.

THE BOOKS OF THE NEW TESTAMENT

In the first years of the Christian Church the Gospels had yet to be written. What was afterwards turned into a permanent record was for some years an oral tradition. Not all scholars are agreed about the dates of the Books of the New Testament, or even about who wrote them. It is generally thought, however, that the earliest documents are some letters of St. Paul written about the middle of the first century.

The Gospel according to St. Mark is the first attempt that we possess to portray the life of Jesus. It may be that Mark had access to a document which has been lost. All knowledge of such a summary of the sayings of Jesus—usually referred to as " Q "—is a matter of inference.

Matthew and Luke probably wrote their versions about twenty years later. They seem to have acted independently of each other, but it is possible that they also used material from " Q."

The Fourth Gospel strikes a different note from the others. It is thought to be the last of the Gospels to be composed. An exciting discovery was made in the Egyptian desert of a tiny fragment of this Gospel, measuring $3\frac{1}{2}$ in. $\times 2\frac{1}{4}$ in., which strengthens the reason for believing that the traditional account of its authorship is correct.

Whether the Book of Revelations was written by the author of the Fourth Gospel has been contested, and it was a long time before the early Church admitted it to the Canon. For several centuries, there was no authoritative decision about the books that should form the New Testament. The bulk of the present contents was recognised by all Christian Churches, but there were certain differences of opinion about the remainder between the East and the West. The final form of the Canon, as the authoritative list is called, accords with the ruling of two Synods held in North Africa,

Fragments of ancient manuscripts have been discovered and, after being laboriously pieced together by an expert, have proved to be the earliest texts of parts of the Bible.

Bible production to-day is a highly skilled job. Here the craftsman " cases in " the Bibles.

at Hippo in A.D. 393 and Carthage in A.D. 397.

INFLUENCE OF THE REFORMATION

During and after the Reformation, the Bible was translated into the vernacular by Catholics as well as Protestants. There had been many partial translations into English by monks in the Middle Ages. John Wycliffe, with the help of a group of Oxford scholars, translated the Vulgate, and ten years after his death in 1384 his follower, John Purvey, revised his version.

William Tyndale turned back to the originals and translated the New Testament from the Greek, and part of the Old Testament from the Hebrew, between 1525–35. The Thomas Matthew Bible was the first to receive Royal licence. It was published in 1537.

THE AUTHORISED VERSION

In 1610, Roman Catholic exiles at Douai produced a version in English of the Vulgate, which is still used to-day. But the translation which is most familiar to people in this country is the Authorised Version of 1611. James I was responsible for this remarkable project in which at least forty-seven scholars took part. It incorporates a good deal of Tyndale's Bible

and yet in spite of being a composite work, it is a masterpiece of literature and has helped to mould the style of many of our best writers.

Its accuracy, however, did not satisfy all subsequent scholars and on the suggestion of the Convocation of Canterbury in 1870, work was begun on the Revised Version. Other translations have appeared in this century, but none can equal the Authorised Version in beauty and dignity.

THE WORK OF THE BIBLE SOCIETIES

No book in the world has been read by so many people or translated into so many languages as the Bible. In the early years of the nineteenth century, four great Bible societies came into existence in England, Scotland, the United States, and Holland. As the result of their activities, parts of the Bible have become available in more than nine hundred languages, and the entire Bible has been translated into one hundred and eighty-four languages. The total output of these Bible societies amounts to seventeen million volumes a year; and apart from this, eight million are distributed by other organisations.

HISTORY AND LITERATURE

In this article the Bible has been treated chiefly as a book. Parts of it undoubtedly rank with the world's finest literature. It is also of the highest value to historians. The raw material of its account of the Jewish people may be as old as 5000 B.C. and this

Applying the base to the edges of the pages of the Bible before putting on the gold leaf.

The Bible proof-reader ensures that no mistakes occur in the text. At the present time there are strict regulations governing the printing of Bibles in this country.

was given the literary form we know from about 800 B.C. The spade of the archæologist has recently uncovered a great deal of evidence about those remote times that confirms much of the Biblical story.

Compared with Babylon, Egypt, and Greece, the Jews did not contribute any important inventions or works of art or philosophical ideas. Their genius was expressed in the sphere of religion. So great was the gulf between their worship of one God and the debased and idolatrous cults that surrounded them that it is not surprising that they felt themselves to be unique.

THE REVELATION OF GOD'S PURPOSE

In no other religion do we find the idea of a continuous intrusion of God into history. It is not only in the writings that have come down to us, but also in the great turning points of Jewish history that both Jews and Christians see unmistakable signs of a divine purpose. Christianity is not intelligible unless it is viewed in the context of the history of the Jews and the prophecies contained in the Old Testament. Thus, although the Bible that we possess consists of a large number of separate books compiled over a period of more than a thousand years, it is in a very real sense *one* book. It begins with an account of the revelation of God's purpose and ends with its fulfilment in the appearance of the Messiah foreshadowed by the Jewish prophets. The stage on which this tremendous drama was enacted was Palestine.

HENRY III

A Foolish King who did Wise Things

HENRY III was only nine years of age when he succeeded his father, John, as King of England, in 1216. As a mere boy, he was in a most difficult position, for the country was split in two, some swearing allegiance to the new King, while others still thought the French prince, Louis, should take the throne. Up and down the country there were many hard feelings against John, and people naturally wondered whether it would be a case of " like father like son."

Being of such a tender age, it was necessary for someone to look after the matters which concerned the King; and the Earl of Pembroke, who was the Earl Marshal of England, was given this responsibility.

Ten days after the death of his father, Henry was crowned, not with the royal crown, for that had been lost in the Wash with the remainder of the Crown Jewels, but with a plain circlet of gold.

In the meantime, Louis refused to accept such a state of affairs, and determined to try to take the crown; but many of his English supporters had gone to the side of the new King. After a defeat of his army at Lincoln and of his fleet of ships off Dover, he gave up the struggle and returned to France.

But what of Henry? It was soon found that he was rather a weak King, who did some incredibly foolish things. On the other hand, he was a very cultured man who did some good things, which partly offset the foolish ones.

THE BUILDING OF WESTMINSTER ABBEY

One thing he did was to pull down the abbey which had been built by Edward the Confessor at Westminster and replace it with the building which still stands to-day as a masterpiece of architecture.

He was very fond of fine clothes, jewellery and banquets, which helped to give a full life at court, but in this he annoyed the English

HENRY III. 1216-72.

people. Many of the cultured people at Court were the foreign relations of the King, and, later, of his wife. They tended to think of themselves as being superior to the English, and the English resented their presence.

Another thing which angered the English people was that Henry was very good at giving lands and livings to foreigners. Often, when a church living fell vacant, the King allowed the Pope to appoint an Italian priest, who never came to England and could not even speak a word of English. It was only natural that the people should resent thousands of pounds being sent out of the country each year to someone they never saw, but who was supposed to be responsible for their spiritual welfare.

Henry was anxious to get as much money as he could for one reason or another. He imposed new taxes on the people, which they resented, especially as it seemed as though many of them were breaking the rules of Magna Carta. Though they were very annoyed they did little, until, in 1258, they were shocked into action by an incredible piece of folly.

The Pope had offered the crown of the island of Sicily to Edmund, the second son of Henry, provided that Henry supplied the army and financed the expedition. Henry approved the plan, and demanded one-third of the wealth of the country for this expedition. Moreover, the Pope demanded a tenth of the property of the Church, which was to be valued for this purpose.

The people had heard quite enough. For many years they had been discontented, but, if the King thought they would tolerate this idea, he was sadly mistaken.

THE MAD PARLIAMENT

A special Parliament was called at Oxford, which has been referred to since as the Mad Parliament. All the great nobles were there, determined to break the power of the King. By special orders, known as the " Provisions of Oxford," they took away from the King all his royal powers, which were placed in the hands of a council, known as the Council of Fifteen, or, more commonly, " The Fifteen." They took charge of the Royal Seal, without which no laws could be passed, and regulated the life of Henry as they thought fit. Henry was still King, but the barons held the power.

At this time, there were two groups of people in the country. One of these, known as the Bachelors, claimed that the knights and citizens should have some say in the government of the country. The other, the Royalists, began to think that some of the power of the King should be given back to him.

THE BEGINNING OF PARLIAMENT

Even the Fifteen split, and the King took the opportunity of seizing the Royal Seal. Then in 1263, the Royalists began to think of war. In the following year, the King was defeated at Lewes and put under the charge of the barons again. The important man in the land was now Simon de Montfort, the Earl of Leicester, who was the chief of the reformers. 1265 has become one of the most important dates in our history, for it was then that de Montfort called a Parliament, which, for the first time, included commoners as well as lords.

Later in the same year, Simon de Montfort was defeated and killed in battle at Evesham, for the reformers were not strong enough to withstand the Royalists. Once again, the King had regained his powers, and, with the reformers killed or disinherited, there was no one to oppose him. The country was again in a state of peace, and so it remained until his death in 1272. He was laid to rest in the new Westminster Abbey which he had been responsible for building.

He had done some foolish things, but they had led to the beginnings of a Parliament such as we have, and that was, indeed, a big step towards freedom.

THE ADMIRABLE CRICHTON

MANY people think that The Admirable Crichton was a character created by Sir James Barrie in his play of that name. In fact he was a real person, a boy prodigy, and his life story reads like a thriller.

He was born in 1560, probably in Dumfriesshire. His father was a Lord Advocate and his mother one of the noble Lindsay family.

James Crichton entered St. Andrew's University at the tender age of ten. At fifteen he graduated, being third on the list.

James went to France, and from the University of Paris issued a challenge to the world to hold discussions on any subject in any of twelve languages he named. He maintained a discussion for nine hours. He gave similar demonstrations of his amazing knowledge and memory in Rome. He was fêted in Venice, and when he retired to Padua, owing to ill-health, he improvised a poem in Latin for six hours. In it he extolled the virtues of the city.

But Crichton was not just an incredible scholar; he was also an athlete, a considerable musician and a man of much grace and charm.

The Duke of Padua made him tutor to his son, but jealousy caused the eventual assassination of this amazing personality. He was set upon in the streets by a masked gang, among whom Crichton recognised his pupil.

EDWARD I

A Brave Soldier and a Wise King

OUR first King Edward is a remarkably interesting figure. His character, like his body, was built on the grand scale. If his sinewy person towered head and shoulders over other men like a human Mount Everest, his personality was no less outstanding. He was a man's man: a mighty hunter and a doughty knight, and his long legs—which earned him the nickname of " Longshanks " —gave him the securest of seats in the saddle. He was, besides, royally masterful and utterly fearless and, in an age when a king's word was by no means always his bond, his motto was " Keep troth." In war, he became one of the most skilful captains of his age. In peace, his work is a landmark in our legal and constitutional history.

RE-ORGANISING THE LAW

He was gifted with a strong sense of justice and order. At the opening of his reign, in 1272, the old laws were in confusion. Edward clarified, improved and extended them. The administration of justice was harsh and chaotic. Edward reorganised the higher courts and put life into the popular assemblies of the hundred and the shire. It was his fixed policy to strengthen the Crown against the baronage and the Church; and, by the Statute of Mortmain, 1279, he checked the further accumulation of land in the " dead hand " of the clergy, who escaped many of the obligations due from feudal tenants.

But far more epoch-making than Edward's legal and judicial labours was his work in broadening the foundations of parliamentary government. In Simon de Montfort's famous parliament of 1265, that rebel baron had summoned not only clergy and barons, but representatives of the rising middle class as well. But Simon's revolutionary ideas of a parliament more truly representative of the nation might well have died with his defeat in battle. Edward, however, was in full sympathy with them. His just and progressive mind envisaged a realm ruled by a strong king with the affectionate support of his people. He would make the commoners his partners—though doubtless he meant sleeping partners. In 1295 he badly needed their support for his wars. Accordingly, in his parliament of that year he called together the barons, the higher and lower clergy, two knights from each shire and two representatives of every city and borough. It was in truth a " Model Parliament," one that freely recognised the people's right to a voice in their own government and served as a memorable precedent for future gatherings.

THE MAGNA CARTA IN PERIL

Yet a time soon came when the strong King found himself in conflict with his not so affectionate people. He was in desperate need of men and supplies for the war in Gascony— that last remnant of England's French possessions. Barons, clergy and people alike murmured at his enormous demands. Stung to rage by what he deemed their betrayal of the common cause, the King struck out blindly. He laid hands on the merchants' wool and hides, requisitioned provisions, levied crushing taxes, seized Church lands and summoned barons and knights and squires for service abroad. A universal cry went up that the Great Charter—Magna Carta—was in peril. The storm of national protest voiced itself in a demand for the formal confirmation of the cherished bulwark of English liberties. More than that, it called for a declaration that no such taxes or aids as had recently been exacted should thenceforth be taken without the common consent of the realm. Edward's sense of fair play had not been altogether extinguished by his wrath. He had already gone far towards satisfying the country's wishes. Now he put up his hands. He confirmed the Charter, with the addition of the clauses against taxation.

PARLIAMENT CONTROLS THE COUNTRY'S REVENUE

It was a notable surrender, though as things turned out the struggle was not yet over. The Charter was firmly buttressed. And, as in the course of time the principle of " no taxation without consent " became more fully established, it placed the keys of the public treasure

The Coronation Chair in Westminster Abbey, with the Stone of Destiny under the seat.

the North. Provoked by Llewelyn's repeated refusal, or neglect, to perform his customary homage, Edward overthrew him in two short wars and annexed his domain. Seventeen years later, in 1301, he created his heir, Edward, the first English Prince of Wales.

THE STONE OF DESTINY

Scotland, however, was to prove a harder nut to crack. Its people—made up principally of Pictish, Scots, British, Saxon and Norman stocks—were far from being welded into a single nation. A shadowy overlordship had long been claimed by the English Crown; but, when Edward tried to make it a reality, the people sprang to arms. In 1296, after a campaign of less than five months, Edward had overrun the country. Incidentally, he carried off from Scone the Stone of Destiny, on which the Scottish kings had formerly been crowned, and had it placed in Westminster Abbey, where it now rests under the Coronation Chair. But the heroic William Wallace raised the standard of revolt and the clans flocked to his side. While Edward was abroad in 1297, he annihilated an English army in the bloody battle of Stirling Bridge and Scotland stretched her limbs again in freedom.

Next year Edward set himself to avenge the disaster. Wallace was utterly overthrown at Falkirk and later taken and hanged. But meantime Scotland had produced another of her national heroes in Robert Bruce. In 1306 Bruce had himself crowned King and the country was once more aflame. Edward hurried north. But he was old and sick and next year death struck him down, leaving his work undone. Even the " Hammer of the Scots," as men called him, had proved unable to crack the iron-hard nut of Scottish independence.

chest in the hands of a national Parliament. So long as that assembly could keep hold of them it could, by withholding supplies, bring pressure to bear on the Crown in the conduct of public affairs. The people were no longer to be sleeping partners. These things are commonplace now; but they had to be battled for in the thirteenth century.

One of Edward's ideals was a united Great Britain and circumstances led him to attempt its achievement. Wales's turn came first. The native chieftain, Llewelyn ap Gruffydd, had been allowed to style himself Prince of Wales, though his actual principality was confined to

---

DO YOU KNOW?

How many hairs are in your head?

It would be difficult to tell exactly how many hairs are in your head; but it has been estimated that a brown-haired man has 109,000 hairs, and a fair-haired man 140,000 hairs in his head.

Dark brown hair is the most common in Britain, and each hair varies from the 250th to the 600th part of an inch in thickness.

It has been proved that a single hair will support a weight of about four ounces. Hundreds of years ago the Chinese and Japanese used to make rope from hair. One of these hair-ropes is in the British Museum. It is several thousand feet long and weighs about two tons.

EDWARD II

First Prince of Wales

THE story of Edward II's reign, beginning in 1307, is not a pleasant one. It is as full of blood and crime and cruelty as a thoroughly bad horror-comic. And it is a story without a hero. At twenty-three Edward was almost as fine a man physically as his father, Edward I; but his lack of moral fibre made him as great a menace to the community as an infant put in charge of a Rolls-Royce. Idle, vain, petty and cowardly, his boon companions were buffoons and ostlers. The duties of kingship wearied him—but he dearly loved a game of pitch and toss. He had not the spirit to continue his father's campaign against the Scots, and Robert Bruce, their King and champion, steadily strengthened his position.

" GOOD BROTHER PIERS "

Edward's weakness of character led him to a degrading dependence on a conceited and flashy young Gascon knight, Piers Gaveston. He loaded this odious favourite with honours and gave him the first place in his councils. The greed and insolence of " good brother Piers," as Edward fondly called him, and the errors of the unkingly King's feckless rule, stung the English nobility to violent action. Twice was Gaveston sent packing—only to return each time to his doting Edward—and the King was muzzled. He was compelled to accept a scheme for the complete fettering of the powers of government he had so wantonly abused. As for brother Piers, he sneaked back once too often. He was taken and foully murdered.

THE BATTLE OF BANNOCKBURN

Meantime, Bruce was making hay while the sun shone. In 1314, Stirling Castle, the last great Scottish stronghold remaining in English

Stirling Castle to-day still houses a garrison, though no longer for warlike purposes.

hands, stood in dire peril. Even Edward's feeble spirit was roused by the threat. He succeeded in mustering a mighty army and marched north. On Midsummer Day, the rival forces, the English by far superior in numbers, faced each other on the famous field of Bannockburn, some two miles south of Stirling. Famous, in truth, it was for the Scots, but infamous beyond measure for the English. Weary from forced marches and lack of sleep, ill-fed and ill-led, they had to face a body of men passionately determined to win their country's freedom or die on the spot and led by a masterly and inspiring captain. Their numbers were of no avail. They were checked, overborne, then completely routed. The inglorious Edward himself bolted from the fray and never stopped till he reached Dunbar, sixty miles off.

SCOTLAND GAINS INDEPENDENCE

Bannockburn clinched the question of Scotland's independence and crowned the movement towards the fusion of her assorted races into a single nation. The long and doubtful struggle begun by Edward I had drawn them together. Now the resounding victory over his son tightened the bonds as never before. The first Edward's attempt to unite the two realms under his own rule had returned like a boomerang on his country. For centuries to come Scotland was to stand, with hackles raised, the sworn foe of England, the friend of England's foes.

The shame of Bannockburn was followed by further evils, both at home and abroad. The English authority in Ireland was reduced to a shadow beyond "the Pale," the area around Dundalk, Dublin and Wicklow. Gascony was all but lost. The King took to himself two new favourites, the Despensers, father and son. Then he bit through his muzzle and bit the barons—hard. Meantime his afflicted people continued to groan under the extremes of misrule and oppression, to which fate unkindly added the horrors of famine and pestilence.

THE KING ABDICATES

At last a hope of relief came from an unexpected quarter. Edward and his favourites had humiliated and antagonised the young King's French wife Isabella, a lady of

This memorial to Robert Bruce stands at Stirling Castle not far from Bannockburn, where he defeated the English in battle.

uncomfortably strong character and violent passions. In 1326 the queen was in the Netherlands. With her were her thirteen-year-old son Edward and a band of English exiles which included her intimate associate Roger Mortimer, a baron of the Welsh marches. The party now crossed over to England with the avowed aim of evicting the detested Despensers. The country received the queen with open arms. Edward and the Despensers took to their heels and fled to the West with Isabella after them. Her followers captured the old Despenser and promptly hanged him. They hunted down his son and sent him the way of his sire. Edward, too, they took and held in captivity. But they did not stay their hands there. Next year, after Parliament had deposed him in favour of his son, they forced the King, in tears, to abdicate. And then—poor, shiftless wight—they murdered him.

An artist's impression of the Battle of Crecy, 1346. The Black Prince wields his axe in the thick of the battle. His banner as Prince of Wales is on the right.

EDWARD III
A Reign of Resounding Victories

EDWARD III was only fourteen when—in 1327—he came to the throne, and, for three years, the country was ruled by his mother Isabella and her greedy minion, Roger Mortimer, the Welsh Marcher-baron. And a poor show they made of it. In 1328 they concluded with the Scots what the disgusted English nation dubbed " the Shameful Peace." They bartered away England's claim to overlordship and recognised Bruce as Scotland's King. Two years later Edward decided that he was old enough to rule as well as reign. With a boldness that showed what stuff he was made of, he caused Mortimer to be seized, tried and hanged and sent his mother into retirement.

He was a fine-looking, splendidly-built youth and soon became immensely popular for his agreeable manners, good nature and amazing energy. He loved knightly chivalry, but above all things he thirsted after military glory. He sought it first in Scotland and presently found a pretext for side-stepping the Shameful Peace and reopening the war. He won some rousing triumphs and later called himself King of Scotland. But the Scots never did, and neither did he for long.

WAR WITH FRANCE

Meantime another field of glory was beckoning him. There were many causes of difference with France, the principal of which were England's claims on Gascony and commercial rivalry. Time, moreover, fomented the ill-feeling into ferocious hatred. The inevitable conflict was given a national character by Edward's preposterous claim to the Crown of France itself by right of descent through his French mother, Isabella. So, in 1337, began the stupendous folly of the Hundred Years War.

Apart from an annihilating victory (that even Nelson might have envied) over a powerful French fleet at Sluys in 1340, nothing noteworthy occurred till 1346— and then came Crécy. In that memorable contest, against odds approaching four to one, the English longbowmen and the new battle tactics won a spectacular triumph. They taught an astonished Europe the might of the English archer and the passing of the supremacy of the old heavy cavalry. Next year Edward took another mighty draught to slake his thirst for fame. He captured Calais and so opened a door into the Continent that English garrisons were to hold for 200 years. Then, in 1356, the lesson of Crécy was driven home. Edward's famous son, the Black Prince, won the hard-fought battle of Poitiers and captured the French King for good measure.

Longbowmen of the fourteenth century.

The peak of Edward's triumph was scaled in 1360. By the treaty of Calais, France ceded all the vast Duchy of Aquitaine in the southwest, which had been lost by John and Henry III, together with Calais and Ponthieu in the north. And then came the break-neck fall. The humiliating treaty could never be enforced against a proud nation. When Edward lay on his death-bed nothing of his dazzling conquests in the south remained save a strip of the Gascony coast. His one great lasting gain was Calais.

THE BLACK DEATH

In the full tide of the war another grim spectre had appeared to multiply the slaughter. In 1348 a fearful pestilence—the Black Death— swept across Europe and smote England. One person in every three was struck down. Life resolved itself into an hourly fear of death. Once a man discovered on his limbs the dreaded boils or dark blotches, he knew that his end was at hand. The dreadful scourge had other than physical consequences. For long there had been a rising discontent among the workers on the land. The plague brought it to a crisis. Labour became scarce, and labour, determined to improve its living conditions, put up its price. But times were already bad for the landholders and they resisted strenuously. The government met the situation by passing the Statute of Labourers in 1351, which sought to fix wages and living costs at the old rates. But the law proved ineffective and an obstinate class struggle ensued between the angry landholders and the repressed and sullen labourers. The next reign was to show its further development. The movement is worth pondering over. For the first time in our history the silent masses were taking the stage in a leading part.

TYRANNY OF THE CHURCH

The latter portion of Edward's reign was stormy. The once active King himself presently sank into helpless dotage and gave himself up to favourites and frivolities. The people complained of the mismanagement of the war, the taxes that reduced a man to the plight of Mother Hubbard, the corruption of the King's rascally friends and the labourers' wrongs. There was a long-standing grievance, too, against the Church. There had already been quarrels enough with the papacy over its interference in English affairs. Now, the country's anger was intensified by the worldliness and greed of the Popes and the conviction that they

Geoffrey Chaucer, author of *The Canterbury Tales*, had a very considerable influence on English literature.

that, beneath his attractive qualities, lay an over-reaching ambition, a lack of steady purpose in the government of his country and a selfish indulgence in the pursuit of war at whatever cost to his subjects. Yet his long reign was a fruitful age for England. It saw the final welding of alien Norman and native Saxon into a single English people, conscious of its nationality and proud of it. Parliament was establishing itself firmly as an assembly to be consulted in the general affairs of the nation, especially in connection with taxation. Another development, trivial enough to all appearances, had far-reaching effects. Parliament became definitely divided into " Lords " and " Commons." In this division the knights of the shire, who might have been expected to sit with the Lords, joined the representatives of the towns. Their presence gave weight and dignity to the Commons. And, by forming a link between the higher nobility and the people, it did much to preserve politics from those rigid class distinctions that proved fatal to the representative assemblies of other nations. Despite war and pestilence, the country made considerable advances towards prosperity through its expanding trade and commerce. Particularly was this seen in the export to Flanders of the wool of its teeming flocks and in the manufacture of cloth that was to bring such untold wealth to the country in the future. Notable, too, was the increasing ascendency of the once despised native tongue over the courtly French and the beginnings of our modern literature. In Edward's reign was born the first great outstanding figure of the movement, the soldier-courtier-ambassador-government official-Member of Parliament and supremely great poet, Geoffrey Chaucer.

were but the tools of England's enemy, France. It was insufferable to the independent islanders that the Popes should be allowed to appoint their foreign friends to rich English livings —which they never set eyes on—and to draw vast revenues from them. As for the English clergy, many of them were as depraved as their master. The lordly prelates revelled in pomp and luxury. The monasteries were ruined with riches. The country's demand for the correction of these and other abuses was vigorously voiced by John Wycliffe, a learned and earnest Yorkshire priest. But here again it was left to later times to complete the story.

" LORDS " AND " COMMONS "

When Edward died, in 1377, he had forfeited most of his early popularity. People realised

THE "ANTIENT SILVER ARROW" CONTEST

What is claimed to be the oldest sporting contest in Britain is the shooting for the " Antient Silver Arrow," held every August at Scorton, east of Richmond, Yorks. Nearly two hundred and fifty contests have been held, and records carefully kept, on this original ground.

Archers, who must be over 21, shoot at a 100-yard range, two arrows from each end.

The first to register a hit in the Inner Gold of the target wins the Arrow and becomes Captain for the ensuing year. There is an " Antient Horn Spoon " as a " booby prize," and on the same day a contest, open to archers born or resident in Yorkshire, for the Thirsk Bowmen's Insignia.

RICHARD II

A Foolish Tyrant

RICHARD II—son of the Black Prince, the eldest son of Edward III—is a mystery character. He was only ten when he mounted the throne in 1377 and only thirty-two when he toppled from it in 1399. He was a golden-haired, slightly-built youth who in many ways lacked manliness. His temper was so violent that he would hurl his hood or his boots out of the window. He was often foolishly arrogant and self-willed and sometimes outrageously rude. He loved fine clothes and pageants and was ruinously extravagant. Yet there were times when he showed remarkable spirit and the ability to rule wisely.

During his early years, while the country was governed by a Council, everything seemed to go wrong. The Scots were happily harrowing the north. The French, carrying the Hundred Years War into enemy country, were burning and raiding in the south. And the islanders themselves were at odds over the widespread troubles inherited from the previous reign.

Richard II. 1377-99.

THE WORKERS' GROWING DISCONTENT

The gravest of these was the unrest of the workers, particularly those on the land. It is strange to think that only five or six hundred years ago the English peasants, or " villeins," were still serfs. They were bound to labour on the landholders' home-farms at stated times and to render various other humiliating and burdensome dues. And they could not leave their villages: they were tied to the soil, like the cattle. None the less, an old practice of " commuting " the labour services for a money rent was spreading steadily, though it did not release the labourers from their other servile ties. Meantime, largely owing to the Black Death of 1348, labour had become scarce and dear and the landholders were at their wits' end. The labourers who had not commuted their field services worked grudgingly—if at all; and to hire free labour was both difficult and costly. Under these conditions the big feudal manors were breaking up. On the other hand, the peasant class was on the up grade. Wages being high and land cheap, many workers rented land on their own account and became yeomen farmers. It is not surprising, therefore, that they chafed under their feudal bonds and demanded to be set free. The Statutes of Labourers, passed in 1351 and later, had aimed at keeping wages at their former low level. But they had only inflamed the workers' sense of grievance and in 1381 the rumbling volcano of their discontent broke into violent eruption.

KING RICHARD AND THE REBELS

The Peasant Revolt, or Wat Tyler's Rebellion as it is also called after the most prominent —and insolent—of its leaders, gave fourteen-year-old Richard his finest hour. Bands of armed rebels from Kent and Essex surged on London (whose citizens also had their labour and other grievances) and spread fire and slaughter among their most hated oppressors. While the Council trembled with fear Richard boldly took the situation in hand. Riding out to face the angry mob, he demanded to know their grievances. " Free us for ever," came the answering shout, " us and our lands! " Richard granted their petition on the spot.

83

A monastery being burnt by Wat Tyler's mob.

reformer had begun by trouncing the clergy for their wealth and worldliness and the Pope for his interference in matters of Church government and discipline. Afterwards, he and his followers, the Lollards, went much further. They challenged some of the foremost spiritual teachings and practices of the Roman Church. Here, however, they were in advance of their time. Wycliffe, indeed, was a religious pioneer, one of the bold spirits who go forth and blaze a trail for others to follow. He began an organised campaign for purifying the Church and abolishing superstitious beliefs, many of which falsely exalted the authority of Popes and priests. The movement largely failed to have any immediate success, but it lingered on underground until finally its teachings were absorbed by the Reformation of the sixteenth century. Another great work of Wycliffe's was the part he took in giving the English people their first complete translation of the Latin Bible.

RICHARD TURNS TYRANT

While Richard was growing up, a gruelling game was being played for the control of the government. The principal players were the King himself and his youngest uncle, the Duke of Gloucester, together with his baronial confederates. Twice Richard got the ball into his hands and it was during the second period that he showed how wisely he could rule when he liked. But then came a remarkable change. Richard turned tyrant and openly gloried in his tyranny. He had the Duke of Gloucester and others of his former opponents executed, murdered or imprisoned. And then he rode rough-shod over the cherished rights of people and Parliament. But fortune soon sent a liberator. Richard's cousin, Henry of Lancaster (or Bolingbroke), was the son of John of Gaunt, the fourth son of Edward III. Richard had banished him and, in 1399, seized his estates. Henry thereupon suddenly returned from exile and raised the northern barons. Richard was made prisoner and induced to abdicate, and Parliament formally deposed him. Next year the imprisoned Richard died—which, of course, was very convenient for Henry. Did Henry murder him? Shakespeare gives one answer in his *King Richard II*. But no one knows the truth. Richard is a mystery in his death as in his life.

All labour services were to be commuted and villeinage abolished. But the insurrection was not yet over. Richard had to imperil his life in another parley with the more violent of the rebels. By sheer force of character and superb courage he pacified them and soon London was quiet again. And then came the great betrayal. The charters of liberation Richard had issued were revoked. The landholders in Parliament declared they were illegal without their consent and hotly refused to surrender their rights. The rebel leaders were everywhere hounded down and hanged or imprisoned. Villeinage continued as before. Yet it was already in decline and, as the changing times made it increasingly out of date, it gradually died a natural death.

But an interesting question remains. Was Richard sincere in that critical moment when he gave his promises to the rebels? Or was he just an unprincipled young scoundrel who tricked his simple-minded subjects into being quiet till he could crush them?

A RELIGIOUS REFORMATION

Another disturbing factor from the past was Wycliffe's religious crusade. The great

Here is Queen Elizabeth I's Charter to the Cinque Ports, confirming their privileges.

THE CINQUE PORTS

IF YOU fell asleep and could dream yourself backwards in time, right back to the days of Edward the Confessor, you would find yourself at the beginning of the Cinque Ports story. If you happened to live in Hastings, Romney, Hythe, Dover or Sandwich, you would actually be a citizen of one of those Ports, for those were the important harbours which for nearly a thousand years have been known as the Five Ports, or Cinque Ports. (Unless you are being very French you will pronounce them as "Sink" Ports.)

We can be sure that these towns were being made to work together in about 1155; this union of the Ports is known as the federation, though long before 1155 each harbour had its own separate importance. Even Edward the Confessor was interested in these Ports and their ships, realising how valuable they could be to England if they worked together, and William the Conqueror was probably the king who actually joined them into a federation.

Once the five were linked together they became not only useful but powerful. They grew more powerful still when Winchelsea and Rye were added to the original five, and these last two were called "Two Ancient Towns." As well as the "Ancient Towns" there were about thirty fishing villages included in the federation, and these villages were known as "limbs." They worked with the Ports, sharing their responsibilities and privileges.

The job of the people of the Ports was to provide fifty-seven ships with twenty men in each ship, to defend the south-east coast of England, for fourteen days a year. They did this without pay, but any defensive work they did over the fourteen "free" days was paid for by the king. The ships also acted as transport vessels for the king's armies, and when there wasn't any fighting or patrolling to be done, the Portsmen used their boats for fishing.

The Ports were at the peak of their usefulness during the thirteenth century. After this, owing to larger ships being needed, and also because of storms and cross-currents bringing in great sand-shoals, the harbours gradually

grew too shallow and tricky for bigger ships
to come and go. Although the Ports did
splendid work in many reigns, probably their
best was during that of King John. As you
know, he lost his crown in the Wash, but he
lost all the Norman dominions except Gascony,
as well, which was far worse. This meant that
instead of trading in peace and going happily
to and fro from England to France, the
English were faced with rather the same
situation as in the last war when the Germans
swept across France and occupied the whole
French shore: there was the English coast
wide open to attack.

King John had infuriated the Barons and
Portsmen because he refused to accept the
new Archbishop whom the Pope had appointed
to Canterbury, but in the face of great danger
from France, they forgot their quarrel with the
King, and mustered their boats and crews.
Sweeping out into the Channel, they attacked
the approaching enemy under much the same
circumstances, though by very different
methods, as in 1940, when the Spitfires from
Kent and Sussex, flown by the descendants of
these Portsmen, drove back the German
hordes from our skies. On this particular
occasion the Portsmen drove the French back
from the English coast and won a great victory
at Damme, now an inland village far from
the sea!

THE MEN WHO STARTED THE ROYAL NAVY

When you see the great ships of the Royal
Navy to-day, and their smartly uniformed
officers and men, it is surprising to realise
that it was the men from the Cinque Ports
(not forgetting the two Ancient Towns and
thirty villages), who really started the Navy—
in their queer long-shaped boats seventy to
eighty feet long, that is, only a little longer
than a cricket pitch. The early ships weighed
from twenty to thirty tons, and looked rather
like a slice of melon.

In the picture of the Cinque Ports Seal you
can get a rough idea of the shape of these
boats: the Cinque Ports ship has rammed
another vessel, cutting it in half, and a helmeted
soldier can be seen drowning. You can see the
Cinque Ports Standard in the bows, with its
half-lion, half-ship design. All the boats
were open; they had one mast and a square

This is the seal, now in Hastings Museum,
which was appended to the Charter.

sail. If there was no wind the men rowed,
and shields were slung along the side of the
ship to protect them. The steering was
managed, not with a rudder, but with one big
oar on the right of the boat, so our modern
word " starboard " comes from the fact that
this oar or " steerboard " was always on the
right of the ship. This was the type of vessel
which carried troops to one of the Crusades,
and the Ports provided thirty-three ships for
this. You can see a model of this type of
boat in the Victoria and Albert Museum,
Kensington.

A later type of ship, though still keeping its
sliced-melon shape, had peculiar-looking turrets built round a platform at each end of the
ship, just like those of a castle. From these
the archers could shoot down on to the deck
of enemy craft whilst remaining protected
themselves. Later ones still, in the fourteenth
century, had several " modern improvements."
The slice-of-melon shape changed. The hull
became more tubby, and though there were
still the raised parts at bows and stern, they
lost their castle-like protective screens; these
had been changed for a fence made of hurdles,
for shelter from the enemy. There was now a
huge hawse-hole for the anchor's cable, and
instead of steering oars, rudders were used.
This " improved " ship was the sort that was

sent from the Cinque Ports to the French Wars.

The method of fighting at sea in the Middle Ages was much the same as on land, the vessels carrying soldiers armed with bows and arrows. When they were close enough to the enemy, the armoured knights and squires on deck attacked each other over the sides, each trying to board and capture the other's ship.

It would need a very large book to tell you about all the battles the men and ships of the Ports took part in, but, as you can imagine, the Hundred Years' War, which began in 1338, kept them busy; though before this, in 1217 and on many other earlier occasions, there were battles off the Cinque Ports area of coast. Their ships fought at Bordeaux, Bouvines and Dover, to mention only a few places; and the men from the Ports were also involved in the Siege of Calais for which 710 ships gathered in Sandwich harbour. This was the only Port large enough to hold the fleet, though only 105 of these were actually Ports' ships, manned by Portsmen. In 1588 thirteen of them took part against the Spanish Armada, joining Seymour's squadron, and this was when they were long past the peak of their usefulness.

PRIVILEGES OF THE PORTSMEN

In return for supplying men and ships free for fourteen days in the year, Charters were given to the Ports. The Charters were a kind of licence, and these licences listed things the Cinque Port citizens might do that people in other parts of the country were not allowed to do. For instance, they paid no taxes or tolls anywhere they went in England or Normandy; they paid no Customs duties; Portsmen had the right of " den and strond " (dune and shore) at Yarmouth, for drying their fishing-nets. By Charter they also controlled the fish-sales and fishing rights, including those of Yarmouth, which even in those days had become a flourishing herring port—though not one of the important five. (You can picture how jealous the Yarmouth people must have been over this, because it brought much wealth to the men of the Ports, and none to themselves.) The Ports also had their own special flag and horn.

Each Port had its own Captain known as Baron, and under him they were allowed to govern themselves, much as a Borough Council to-day controls a town's affairs. The Baron was an important person allowed special honours at Court, such as attending as canopy-bearer to the king and queen at coronations, and being allowed to sit on their right at the banquet afterwards. There was only one man more important than a Baron, and he was the Warden of the Cinque Ports who lived at Dover Castle. If a Baron had a problem concerning his Port or the fishing villages also under him which he couldn't settle himself, he took it to the Warden. If the Warden couldn't solve it, then it was taken straight to the King himself, so you see the Warden was a very

Barons of the Cinque Ports are allowed special honours at Court. Here is an edging of the canopy which they carried while attending George IV at his coronation.

The official residence of the Warden of the Five Ports is Walmer Castle, near Deal. The Warden's standard flies from the Castle tower when he is in residence.

important man resembling a First Sea Lord of earlier days. The present official " residence " of the Warden is Walmer Castle, near Deal, and the Warden Sir Winston Churchill.

So respected by the rest of the country were the Five Ports that for centuries after they had ceased to be really useful, all other vessels were ordered to dip their topsails when passing one of the Ports or a Port ship. This was done as a mark of respect (just as a captain would salute an admiral), and in remembrance of the days when the Ports really had guarded England and the English Channel. In spite of the fact that the harbours had gradually grown impossible for ships of any size, and the town of Winchelsea had been entirely swept away, the Ports held on to their old privileges.

When Henry V came to the throne he decided that something must be done about extending England's sea forces. He saw that the Ports not only could not build big enough ships, but that they couldn't provide enough men to sail them, and so he chose Southampton as his chief naval base, but allowed the

Ports to keep their Charters. All the same, the Portsmen must have resented this blow to their pride. It certainly seems likely that Yarmouth men were tactlessly pleased about their decline—and showed it, and once a ship from Fowey, on passing Rye, refused to obey the rule of dipping its sail in respect. The men of Rye became so enraged at this insult that they leapt into their boats and chased after the cheeky Cornish vessel to show that they would not stand this treatment from an upstart " new port." However, they got such an unpleasant surprise when they reached the Cornish boat that they had to turn fast for home without stopping to worry about any sail-dipping!

This story is written by a Cornishman, but of course there may be another version written by a Sussex historian in which the Cornishmen were frightened out of their wits and were ready to come to the heel of the proud Portsmen! But in either case it does go to show that the Ports were being regarded as far less valuable to the rest of the world.

All the same, because of their long training and the fact that they knew more about the sea than any other group of men, the Portsmen were looked on for years as first-class sailors—even though their harbours were becoming useless. But even as far back as the Battle of Sluys, it seems that possibly Yarmouth men, jealous of the Portsmen's privileges, did not agree about this, for they so infuriated the men from the Ports that, at Sluys, instead of fighting the mutual enemy, the French, Portsmen attacked their own side. There, right in front of the King, they burned twenty of the Yarmouth ships and killed nearly all the crews. It was rather surprising that the English won this battle at all, after this shameful business.

Apart from this one disgraceful patch in the Ports' history, they seem to have a splendid record, and even after the Armada, Queen Elizabeth was so pleased with them that she gave them a special Charter saying that they were to keep their ancient privileges, and she sent her thanks for their help. The photograph at the beginning of the article shows a picture of the Queen at the head of this Charter. Yet the privileges she confirmed weren't quite the same as they were before the Battle of Sluys, for after the behaviour by the Portsmen there, although they did not have their rights taken from them, they were made to share them with the Yarmouth people. This particularly affected them over the Herring Fair.

THE FORTY DAYS HERRING FAIR

This Fair was held every autumn at Yarmouth—still famous for its herrings. The Fair was a huge business lasting for forty days; people came to it from all over England, from France, Holland, and countries even farther distant. There would be from seven to eight hundred visiting ships, and each ship had a toll of fourpence on it which had to be divided between the Cinque Portsmen and the Yarmouth people. Yarmouth people must have been delighted to be allowed a half share, and when as well their town became a Free Borough with a Mayor, they became very puffed up and dignified about it, quite naturally.

Yet, though the Portsmen must have been

Sir Winston Churchill, as Warden of the Cinque Ports, inspects the guard.

very annoying, they had certainly earned their privileges, because each Port had been burnt down by the raiding French more than once, except Dover with its nearly impregnable castle, and they had always had to be on the lookout for the enemy, and were in a much more dangerous position than Yarmouth. However, after their behaviour at Sluys, as well as having to share the fourpenny tolls on the visiting ships with Yarmouth, the Barons of the Ports and the magistrates of Yarmouth were to sit together in court, each judging their own people when they broke the law. This was bad enough, but of course it was the sharing of the toll which was worse.

As we know too well, you can't make four-pence go far to-day, but had you lived in the fourteenth century you would have been able to have bought a whole chicken for fourpence, and the best soles were only threepence a dozen, while oysters which to-day vary between six and twelve shillings a dozen were only two-pence a gallon—nearly given away! The ale you would have drunk with your oysters was only a penny a gallon, so you see the toll from one ship, let alone eight hundred, would

A Mayor of Hastings and Baron of the Cinque Ports during the reign of George IV— Edward Milward.

have given a large family a good square meal.

As the years passed, Yarmouth went up and up in importance, and the Cinque Ports went down, mattering less and less, until by the end of the seventeenth century they hardly counted for anything. Yarmouth finally broke away completely from the Cinque Ports about 200 years ago, and though now, as a modern port, only Dover really counts, something of their glory continues at Coronation times, just as it did in the time of Richard I's Coronation in 1189.

CARRYING THE CANOPY AT THE CORONATION

By Charter the Barons were allowed after the Coronation ceremony to keep the canopy that they carried over the King and over his Queen, who walked behind him. They were also allowed to keep the silver staves sup-porting the canopy, and the small silver bells which decorated the corners. In the picture on page 416 you can see a piece of the edging of the canopy (believed to be the only piece left in the world to-day), with its stars of the Orders of Knights of the Garter, Bath, Thistle and St. Patrick. This was carried at the Coronation of George IV.

In the picture on this page you can see the

These are the clothes worn by Edward Milward at the coronation of King George IV. They may be seen at Hastings Museum.

scarlet and gold clothes worn at that Coronation by the Mayor of Hastings, then Edward Milward, jun. If you look very carefully to the right just above Mr. Milward's waist, you can just see the wine-stain he made when, over-eager to drink his sovereign's health, he slopped the wine from his glass down his front. The original of this—wine stains and all—can be seen in Hastings Museum to-day, with the canopy edging.

In 1377 the Barons were allowed to carry a cloth of gold at the Coronation and to keep it afterwards, and the canopies were divided alternately between the Eastern and the Western Ports. The Kent Barons usually gave their share from the Coronation to Canterbury Cathedral, and the Sussex Barons to Chichester Cathedral. At Queen Elizabeth's Coronation in 1559 when Dover, Romney, Hastings and Winchelsea all claimed the canopy, it was sold for twenty pounds, and each Port had five pounds each. In 1727 the Sussex Barons pooled their share of Coronation " prizes " and had a silver punch bowl made which is used at Hastings Mayoral Banquets to this day.

There are still Barons of the Cinque Ports to-day, and a Warden, and though at Queen Elizabeth II's Coronation the Barons did not carry a canopy over her there were special seats reserved in Westminster Abbey for them and they wore historic costume, and of course a very special seat indeed was reserved for the present Warden of the Cinque Ports—Sir Winston Churchill.

NO!

No sun—no moon!
No morn—no noon—
   No dawn—no dusk—no proper time of day—
No sky—no earthly view—
No distance looking blue—
   No road—no street—no " t'other side of the way "—
No end to any Row—
No indications where the Crescents go—
No top to any steeple—
   No recognitions of familiar people—
No courtesies for showing 'em—
No knowing 'em!
   No travelling at all—no locomotion,
   No inkling of the way—no notion—
" No go "—by land or ocean—
No mail—no post—
No news from any foreign coast—
   No park—no ring—no afternoon gentility—
No company—no nobility—
   No warmth, no cheerfulness, no healthful ease,
   No comfortable feel in any member—
   No shade, no shine, no butterflies, no bees,
   No fruits, no flowers, no leaves, no birds,
     November!

Thomas Hood

ANSWERS TO PUZZLES

Page 40. 1. First; 2. Irate; 3. Races; 4. Stems; 5. Tessa.

Page 42. Only the top right-hand one forms a true knot.

HENRY IV

A Reign of Strife

WHEN, in 1399, Parliament deposed Richard II after his overthrow by Henry of Lancaster (Bolingbroke), Henry stood forward and claimed the crown. Yet he was not the immediate heir. The eight-year-old Edmund of March ranked before him. Henry was descended from John of Gaunt, Edward III's *fourth* son; but Edmund was descended from Lionel of Clarence, Edward's *third* son. The monarchy, indeed, was not strictly hereditary, but there was a very strong tradition in favour of the principle. Henry was the strong man on the spot, the popular liberator of his country from Richard's tyranny, and Parliament elected him with enthusiasm. The manner of Henry's accession had far-reaching consequences. The new king's best title to the throne did not rest on his pedigree, or on his conquest of Richard. It was based on his election by Parliament. This made Parliament's position strong and left Henry dependent on its favour. For, as Henry well knew, what one Parliament had done another might some day undo.

Henry IV. 1399-1413.

A TROUBLESOME REIGN

It was fortunate for him that he was a man who could act with caution and tact as well as with energy and determination, for his position was as generally insecure as that of a tight-rope walker. Risings and civil wars in quick succession lifted their heads against him like venomous serpents. Scotland and France were his ever active enemies. And in Wales the amazing rebel Owen Glendower, with his dash and spirit, his resourcefulness and tireless perseverance, was an incurable poison in his blood. For years Henry could do nothing with him. Glendower defied his barons. He defied his son, Henry of Monmouth, the Prince of Wales, whose title the rebel boldly assumed. He defied the King himself. The baffled English, out-fought and out-manœuvred, swore he was a magician in league with the devil. Till the day of his death, in 1415, though he had at last been reduced to the position of a fugitive outlaw, Glendower remained at large. It was mainly the Prince of Wales who wore him down. And it was in the Welsh campaigns that the young Henry learned much of the soldiering that later, when he had become Henry V, was to perform the miracle of Agincourt.

LOLLARD MARTYRS

While the King's energy was engaged in quelling risings, his tact was being employed in keeping Church and Parliament in good humour. Never before had Lords and Commons found a King so graciously eager to consult their wishes. Very wisely, they made the most of the opportunity. Through their control of the country's purse-strings, they did much to keep the obliging monarch at their feet. As for the Church, Henry won their approval by delivering the Lollards into their hands. Religious persecution was then unknown in England; but, in 1401, the first Lollard martyr was burned at the stake and a law was passed authorising the same monstrously inhuman punishment for all heretics. Thus did the blind and mistaken zeal that deemed it a sacred duty to destroy free-thinkers begin on its fiery course.

Henry must have been born under an unlucky star. In spite of all his efforts to please, he became increasingly unpopular. And, no sooner did his political troubles begin to dwindle and a prospect of peace and security come in sight than a new enemy took him by the throat. He was smitten with a horrible disease. His doctors said it was leprosy; but, whatever it was, his malady brought him, in 1413, to the grave. His snatch at the crown had gained him precious little joy in life.

The Marbles Championship in progress at Tinsley Green, Sussex.

THE MARBLES CHAMPIONSHIP

The quaintest sporting contest in Britain is the Marbles Championship, held every Good Friday outside the Greyhound Hotel, Tinsley Green, a few miles north-east of Crawley, and north of Three Bridges, Sussex.

The championship is said to have continued since the first Elizabethan days, when neither of two suitors for a village beauty could prove superiority in a sporting contest and eventually agreed to take a final decision in a marbles contest. (In fact, the familiar schooldays game dates back to Roman times.)

Teams of six compete on the circular rink, which is sanded. Forty-nine marbles are placed in the centre of the rink and the players shoot at them with " tolleys." The " tolleys," which must not exceed three-quarters of an inch in diameter, are rested on the first finger and " shot " or flicked with the thumb, much as a coin would be " tossed " horizontally.

The hand must not be moved, otherwise the player is penalised for " fudging."

The players endeavour to knock out of the ring as many marbles as possible without losing their own. The highest individual scorers compete for supremacy, and the winner, in a match in which only thirteen marbles are placed on the rink, challenges last year's Champion for the title. The Championship is locally organised and embodies much family tradition and skill. There are similar contests overseas, and United States troops, stationed in the area during the war, took the game back with them.

HENRY V

The Warrior King

Henry V. 1413-22.

HENRY V reigned less than ten years, but it was long enough to make him one of England's most splendid national heroes. When he succeeded his father, Henry IV, in 1413, at the age of twenty-five, serious-minded folks pursed up their lips, for there were hair-raising tales abroad of his wild youth. Doubtless the princely colt had kicked up his heels somewhat friskily; but the Prince Hal in the rollicking comedy scenes of Shakespeare's *King Henry IV* is mostly invented. In any case Henry's animal capers came to an abrupt end as soon as he was harnessed to the throne. He became a model king: courteous, earnest, just, wise and temperate. Henry was a fine athlete, a grand soldier and a leader whose comradely spirit and personal charm set men's hearts aglow with hero-worship. He was a strict churchman of almost monkish piety. His character was a blend of naked strength and simplicity and by no means free from fault. He could be narrow-minded and self-opinionated and he was often savage, or even spiteful, to any who presumed to cross him.

A BID FOR THE FRENCH THRONE

The stirring story of his reign might almost be summed up in one word—France. There were, of course, less noteworthy episodes. Henry continued the persecution of the Lollards because he abhorred their heresies and because, unhappily, the movement had become tainted with politics and sedition. Also, he had a jarring reminder that the crown his father had usurped for the House of Lancaster was a little wobbly on his head; for he was called upon to crush a plot for setting it on the true heir by descent, Edmund of March. But France was the main tune that England danced to. Henry early resolved to resume the Hundred Years War and to revive the preposterous claim of his great-grandfather, Edward III, to the French throne. He had complete faith in the righteousness of his cause, for he seems to have been a man who could sincerely convince himself of anything he wanted to believe. And he was shrewd enough to foresee that a successful war would strengthen his position at home.

THE BATTLE OF AGINCOURT

At this time France, under its mad king, Charles VI, was rent into two desperately warring factions: the Armagnacs and the Burgundians. To Henry it seemed a field ripe for his harvesting and, in the August of 1415, he crossed the Channel to gather in the crop. He secured a base in Harfleur, at the mouth of the Seine; but it took him till the end of September and by then his army was much reduced with sickness and the campaigning season was getting short. Henry, therefore, decided to ship his troops home. But not from Harfleur. He meant to march boldly across enemy country to Calais and embark thence. It was like a toreador trailing his cloak to bring on the bull. And, sure enough, on the eve of St. Crispin, the bull came on—a ferocious and powerful beast—at a place called Agincourt.

The French host was at least three times the size of the English; but its leaders, mostly Armagnacs, were divided and their suicidal battle tactics showed that they had not yet got by heart the painful lessons of Crécy and Poitiers. For, to begin with at all events, it was the same tale over again: their heavy cavalry could not withstand the murderous fire of the English longbowmen. Afterwards the battle was just a massacre. The French men-at-arms, dismounted but weighed down with their armour, got hopelessly bogged in the newly ploughed and rain-sodden field and the lightly equipped English, Henry in the thick of them, hewed them down by the thousand. Small wonder that, on Henry's return in triumph to England, the church steeples rocked with the pealing of the victory bells.

A SHAMEFUL TREATY

Nearly two years passed before Henry took to the warpath again. By January, 1419, Normandy was his. And then an astonishing stroke of luck befell him. Duke Philip of Burgundy's feud with the Armagnacs had reached such a pitch of blind fury that he was ready to promise the English invader anything in return for aid in crushing his rivals. So it came about that, in 1420, under his influence, the shameful treaty of Troyes was concluded. It was sealed by Charles and his queen, Isabella, who hated her son, the Dauphin, heir to the throne and leader of the Armagnacs; and it provided that Henry should be Regent of France till Charles's death and afterwards King, and that he should marry Charles's daughter Catherine.

Thus did Henry achieve the seemingly impossible and establish his claim to the crown of France. But the treaty was, in effect, only a compact with a French faction. Its execution depended largely on that faction's continued support. Meantime, most of the southern half of France and parts of the north were still in the Dauphin's hands. It would be too much to expect that England, in her delirious hour of rejoicing, should realise the folly and insecurity of it all. Men's ideas and standards of value were different then. So we may applaud Henry for a wonderful achievement while we wisely refrain from judging him and his people by the standards of our own day.

In 1421 Henry set forth on another campaign against the Dauphin. It was his last. He was worn out by his self-imposed labours. In the following summer an illness contracted whilst sharing the hardships of a winter siege laid him low and soon England was mourning the tragic death of her hero. Alas! that hero had left behind him an England sadly weakened in manhood and means and burdened with the evil legacy of an unrighteous, hopeless war.

THE NORFOLK GIANT

One of the best authenticated and normal giants of Britain was the Norfolk Giant, Robert Hales, who was born in 1813 at Somerton, near Great Yarmouth. He stood 7 ft. 8 in. and weighed 33 stones. He came from a remarkable family, for his father, a farmer, was 6 ft. 6 in. and his mother slightly over 6 ft.

Robert was one of nine children and the four sons averaged 6 ft. 5 in. and the five daughters no less than 6 ft. 3½ in. Robert's chest measurement was 62 inches.

At the age of 35, he decided to visit America and remained there for two years. When he returned to London he took over the Craven Arms, in Drury Lane. He was presented to Queen Victoria at Buckingham Palace.

Unlike many giants, Hales was cheerful and intelligent and quick and able in his movements. He died at Great Yarmouth in 1863, aged 50, and was buried at West Somerton where his epitaph records his great stature.

The Irish giant, Patrick Cotter, whose name was changed by showmen into O'Brien, was even larger than Hales, but by no means such a normal or healthy man. His memorial, which is perhaps more reliable than the showmen's handbills, says he was over 8 ft. 3 in. in height. He died at the age of 47, which is old for a person of such abnormal proportions.

HENRY VI

The Youngest Sovereign

IF Henry V had lived two months longer he would have been proclaimed King of France, for the insane Charles VI whom, under the terms of the Treaty of Troyes, he was to succeed, died in October 1422. As it was, his son, already Henry VI of England, was proclaimed instead. And he was only ten months old, the youngest sovereign who had ever toddled to the English throne. His Uncle John, Duke of Bedford, was made Regent of France and his Uncle Humphrey, Duke of Gloucester, became acting Protector of England under a Regency Council.

Duke John was a thoroughly sound man. From his headquarters in Paris he exerted himself to secure and extend Henry V's conquests. His chief concern was to maintain the alliance with Philip, Duke of Burgundy, whose support was as necessary to him now as it had been to the great Henry. The rightful French heir to the Crown, Charles VI's son, was duly acclaimed by his party as Charles VII. His power lay chiefly south of the River Loire and there seemed little likelihood of its ever being extended; for Charles was a poor, weak, misshapen youth with little spirit and no qualities of leadership.

JOAN OF ARC

The war fizzed and spluttered on with occasional bursts of flame, like a damp bonfire. Then, in 1429, it suddenly flared sky high at the siege of Orleans. Joan of Arc, with her heavenly voices and visions, appeared on the scene to save the city and France and to bring Charles to his crowning at Reims. The siege was raised, more astonishing successes followed and Charles was triumphantly crowned. Then came the Maid's capture—as sensational a prize as Hitler would have been in the Second World War—and her death at the stake in 1431. By her own fervent faith she had stemmed the tide of English conquest and rallied France to rise up and save itself. The English continued to battle on stubbornly, but four years later the staunch Duke of Bedford died and Philip of Burgundy went over to Charles. After that they were fighting

a losing battle. In 1436 Paris fell. By 1441 Henry V's northern conquests were reduced to Normandy and Maine. In 1444 Maine was practically given away as the price of a truce concluded at Tours. And in 1450 Normandy itself was lost. Then, three years afterwards, the last remnant of Guienne (Gascony) in the south, which the English had held for three hundred years, was torn from their grasp. Only Calais—Edward III's prize—remained. The Hundred Years War was over, leaving England with empty hands.

Empty and bloodstained hands they were. For a generation now England's leaders and England's fighting men had plunged recklessly into the carnage of war and learned the lawless life of the camp. The time was at hand when the horrors of civil strife, of which they had so blithely taken advantage in France, were to be let loose on their own homeland in the snarling dog-fight of the Wars of the Roses. The spirit of violence that infected the country was part of the legacy of Henry V's misguided lust for foreign conquest. But, to learn how the catastrophe came about, the course of events in England from the time of his death must now be followed.

THE STRUGGLE FOR POWER

For twenty years and more there is little worthy of record. The Lords of the Regency Council quarrelled like pigs round a food trough for power and profit and for a controlling influence over the growing King. One ever-recurring subject of their bickering was the question of seeking peace with France. The Council became sharply divided into a war party and a peace party. The truce of Tours was negotiated by the Earl of Suffolk, a prominent member of the peace party. In the hope that it would lead to the end of the war Henry, then twenty-two years old, was betrothed to Margaret of Anjou, a niece of the French Queen. But to secure this desirable though uncertain breathing space Suffolk, in secret, basely allowed himself to be persuaded by Charles into agreeing to the surrender of Maine.

Joan of Arc (1412-31) standing at the altar at the coronation of Charles VII of France. She is accompanied by her squire, chaplain and pages. Painting by Ingres.

A MARRIAGE OF OPPOSITES

The marriage duly took place and never was there a more startlingly contrasted pair. Henry was a most lovable youth, but he would have been better in a monastery than on a throne. He was extremely pious and soft-hearted and all too trustful and yielding. Margaret, a vivid and spirited maiden of fifteen, was a creature of entrancing loveliness and charm—with the vicious spirit of a wild-cat.

THE QUEEN'S INFLUENCE

The agreed surrender of Maine (which was trickily delayed for four years) was kept a guilty secret in England; but, when at length the cat was out of the bag, a howl of indignation went up. At this time the leader of the war party was Richard, Duke of York, Duke Humphrey of Gloucester, the former leader being dead. Richard's influence on affairs, and the people's respect for him, were strengthened by the fact that he had two possible claims to the throne. On his father's side he was descended from Edmund of York, Edward III's fifth son, and was Henry's heir, in the male line, if the latter died childless. On his mother's side he was descended from Lionel of Clarence, Edward's third son, and inherited the rights of Edmund of March (now dead) which Henry IV had usurped. The peace party was led by the King's ministers, Suffolk and the Earl of Somerset. They were hand in glove with the Queen and the three of them had the innocent Henry completely under their thumbs. Naturally, therefore, the King would not listen to any complaints against his trusted ministers. When, however, the fighting was resumed and Normandy lost, Henry could no longer shut his ears to the general outcry. He banished Suffolk overseas for safety; whereupon he was seized and beheaded in the Channel by some angry patriots. But he still could not bring himself to dismiss Somerset and the other friends of Suffolk. In 1450 the national discontent over the mismanagement of the war and the abuses of government reached flash point in " Jack Cade's Rebellion." The outbreak was one of many signs that the temperature of the country was dangerously feverish. The germs of civil war, indeed, were heating its blood; for the angry brawlings of the lords had spread from the Council to Parliament and to the country at large.

HEIR TO THE THRONE

When the war was just ending two dramatic events occurred at home. Poor Henry's most tragic weakness—one inherited from his mad grandfather, Charles VII of France—came to light. He became insane. Then, some months afterwards, Margaret gave birth to a son. The Duke of York was no longer Henry's heir, though his rights as a descendant of Lionel of Clarence still remained. The changed position brought the Yorkists into power. Somerset was clapped into the Tower and Duke Richard was appointed Protector. Throughout the emergency he acted with complete loyalty to the new Prince of Wales. But, at Christmas 1454, Henry recovered; the Duke's office came to an end; and Margaret gleefully released Somerset. The situation now became tense. Margaret's hatred of the Duke, as Somerset's avowed enemy, was deepened by her suspicions that he was reaching out for the sceptre. Soon their mutual enmity brought the first clash of arms and the suicidal Wars of the Roses—of the House of Lancaster against the House of York—were definitely on. What were they all about?

THE WARS OF THE ROSES

We can say, to begin with, that no higher principles were involved in the conflict than are to be found when two gunmen go stalking each other through a Wild West town or two dogs fight over a meaty bone. True, the war began as an attempt to liberate Henry from evil councillors who were misgoverning the country; but this praiseworthy object soon fell into the background. The lords lined up on one side or the other in accordance with their family connections or because they had a grudge to pay off. In time the crown was bound to become—like the dogs' bone—the ultimate aim. Again, as the struggle heated up and chieftains by the dozen were savagely slaughtered on the battlefield or mercilessly executed as prisoners, the war became a welter of ferocious blood feuds. The great nobles had become too powerful. They possessed enormous estates and commanded legions of armed retainers who wore their " livery " or distinctive badge. Family relationships, too, bound groups of nobles together in units of tremendous power. The Duke of York, his staunch ally and brother-in-law Richard Duke of Salisbury, and the latter's famous son Richard Earl of Warwick, were all linked in the mighty Neville group. The people had little say in the struggle and wisely stood aside —when they could.

From the beginning, the war was a violent see-saw. In the first battle of St. Albans, in 1455, Somerset was defeated and slain and the twenty-six-year-old Warwick showed himself a thrusting commander. An uneasy period of truce followed till 1459, when the Yorkists' end of the see-saw went down with a bump at Ludford.

Next year, however, saw them in possession of London; and, when Warwick won the battle of Northampton and captured the King, his party were right up in the air again. Then a marked change came over Duke Richard. Until now he had steadily declared that his only aim in taking to arms was to free the King. But now he brazenly claimed the crown. His supporters were aghast. By urgent persuasions they succeeded in getting the Duke to forgo his claim on being recognised by Henry as his heir.

Then came another and particularly violent bump of the see-saw. In the battle of Wakefield, Richard, his second son the Earl of Rutland and Salisbury were killed. The cause of the Yorkists and of Richard's eldest son, Edward, who inherited his dead father's claim to the throne, now rested solely on Warwick —Warwick " the King-maker," as he came to be known, and the hero of Bulwer Lytton's great book, *The Last of the Barons*. No cause could wish for a firmer support. The young earl held sway over vast estates and numberless retainers. He was a doughty fighter and a man of commanding will. His persuasive tongue and charming manner had won the affections of the people. Edward had been his pupil in war and was deeply under his influence.

EDWARD SEIZES THE THRONE

Early in 1461, however, Warwick suffered a reverse in the second battle of St. Albans and Margaret got her wild-cat claws on Henry again. But Edward, who was away in the west, winning triumphs on his own account, marched hot-foot to join Warwick and the pair re-entered London. And now a decisive step was taken. Reconciliation with Margaret and Henry had become impossible. Under Warwick's influence, Edward's claim to the crown was put forward to the people and accepted with a roar of approval. A few days later he was enthroned as King Edward IV, by right of descent from Lionel of Clarence. Thus did dog Edward wrest the bone from dog Henry's feeble jaws. He did not deem it necessary to be elected by Parliament—which only shows how the national assembly had declined. The snow-storm victory of Towton and the flight of Margaret and Henry to Scotland settled the crown comfortably on Edward's head.

The remainder of poor Henry's tragic story is best related under the reign of Edward IV.

SNOWDROPS

I heard the snowflakes whisper in the still dark night,
And when I peeped at bedtime, all the roofs were white.
Although the pussy willows their mittened buds unfold,
Although the hazel catkins are waving tails of gold,
Although the buds are bursting on the chestnuts by the gate,
And spring is in the countryside—the snow came late.

I saw it in the twilight, and I looked for it at dawn,
But all I found were thrushes on the smooth green lawn.
All the roofs were twinkling and sparkling in the sun,
And myriad buds were waking and opening one by one,
And all that could remind me of snowflakes on the beds
Were clusterings of snowdrops, with whitely drooping heads.

Ruth M. Arthur

After defeating the Welsh, Edward I gave them a Prince of Wales—his eldest son. Since then the eldest son of the Monarch is always created Prince of Wales on reaching a suitable age. This was the scene at Caernarvon Castle during the last "creation" in 1911.

LLEWELYN AP GRUFFYDD

IN THE north of Wales are many mountains, of which the highest is Snowdon, and in among the mountains, between Caernarvon and Portmadoc, is the little town of Beddgelert (" the grace of Gelert "). If ever you go there, you will find a small stone, in a small enclosure, and you will be told that this is the grave of Gelert. Who was he? Was he a great warrior? No. He was a dog.

If you ask more about him, you will be told that Gelert was a greyhound, given by King John to Llewelyn the Great, Prince of Wales. Loved by all, he was often left at home to look after the baby, when the Prince went out. The story tells how, one day, returning from a hunting expedition, Llewelyn was met by Gelert, who wagged his tail in greeting, but the dog was covered with blood. Quickly entering the house, Llewelyn found the baby's cot upturned and, thinking that Gelert had killed the baby, he thrust his sword through the dog, killing it instantly. Imagine

his grief, when, looking under the cot, he found the baby alive and well, by the side of the body of a wolf, which had tried to attack the child and which had been killed by Gelert.

The baby and his brother grew up, and became very strong. One brother was David and the other Gruffydd (Griffith), and it was the son of Gruffydd, named Llewelyn, after his grandfather, who was to fight against the English in a desperate attempt to free his native land.

THE WELSH PRINCE RAIDS THE ENGLISH

King Henry III of England had made Llewelyn ap Gruffydd (Llewelyn, the son of Griffith) Prince of Wales, but Llewelyn resented having to bow the knee to anyone. When Henry died, England was without a King, for the new one, Edward I, was out of the country fighting in the Crusade. Llewelyn took the opportunity to make raids upon the

100

English who lived on the borders of Wales. Moreover, he found great support in Simon de Montfort, who, together with a number of other barons, was tired of conditions in England and sought a change.

On his return, the King, who was a great fighter, defeated Simon and then made his way to Wales to put down the risings of this Welsh prince. Llewellyn was not very successful against the great and powerful English army, and he was compelled to fly to the mountains of Snowdonia and take refuge there. Here again, the weather was not on his side, and he and his men were compelled to come down again for food and shelter. Edward showed great generosity to Llewelyn and forgave him for the trouble he had caused, allowing him to keep his title of **Prince of Wales**.

A COUNTER-ATTACK ON WALES

Now Llewelyn was very fond of Simon de Montfort's daughter, and a marriage was arranged, but the ships that were carrying her from France were intercepted by the English and she was detained in London. Llewelyn was summoned to London, but, believing that it was a trap, and sending a message to this effect, he refused to go. Whether this was what Edward had hoped for, we are not sure, but it certainly gave the English King an excuse for attacking Wales.

This was to be no third-rate attack. Edward summoned all his strength and, with a great army, he departed for Wales. With the aid

Here is the emblem of the Prince of Wales, a crown and three feathers, with the motto *Ich dien*, meaning " I serve."

of a certain amount of bribery, certain of the Welsh chiefs and even Llewelyn's brother David, left the Prince of Wales and sided with the English King.

Llewelyn found himself at a definite disadvantage, and many a lesser man would have given up the struggle without much of a fight. Not so Llewelyn. He was ready to go on until his resources failed, and this, in fact, proved to be the cause of his downfall. Whether by accident or design, we are not sure, but Edward's ships and men were successful in cutting off Llewelyn's supplies just as winter descended. Once again, the Prince had to take to the mountains, which was anything but pleasant in wintry conditions, and there he remained as long as he could reasonably do so. Then he was forced to accept the conditions of surrender made by the King, which included giving up all his lands, with the exception of Anglesey.

Still Llewelyn was not beaten. In 1282 he made a last desperate attempt to regain what was his by right. He had also been reconciled with his brother David, and both brothers suddenly descended upon the English and caused great loss of life and equipment. The castle of Hawarden was captured, and those of Flint and Rhuddlan attacked, though unsuccessfully.

THE END OF THE RISING

Again an expedition was sent against Wales, and again Llewelyn stood by. With headquarters on the Isle of Anglesey, the Welsh waited for the English to land and then, when the tide had cut off their boats, drove them back to the sea and slew them. But it was a hopeless task. Llewelyn did his best, but there was an unending supply of English reinforcements compared with only a few of his own. Again he was forced to take to the mountains, and this was to be the last time, for there was a brief engagement, when some English soldiers came by accident upon a group of Welshmen. On the outskirts of this small battle was a solitary Welshman who was slain, and it was not until later that he was recognised as Llewelyn, the Prince of Wales.

Llewelyn was dead. Wales was lost. The King of England became the King of Wales too, and, but for Llewelyn, he might have done so very much earlier.

The famous painting which depicts the second meeting of Dante and Beatrice in Florence. Beatrice inspired him to write poetry and was for him the ideal of all that was good.

DANTE ALIGHIERI
The Great Renaissance Poet

IN THE year 1321, Guido Novello da Polenta, Lord of Ravenna, sent an embassy to the Doge of Venice to inquire into an incident which had resulted in the death of several Venetian sailors. The embassy was coldly received and when its members sought permission to return home by sea, this permission was abruptly refused. The journey was, therefore, made along the unhealthy, malarial coast and proved fatal to one of the ambassadors who died of fever shortly after returning to Ravenna. He was Dante Alighieri, aged fifty-six, a Florentine exile and the greatest literary figure of the Italian Renaissance.

THE BEATRICE LEGEND

Dante Alighieri was born in Florence in May, 1265. Little is known of his early years except for the famous episode of his meeting with Beatrice Portinari whom he saw when they were both nine years old and whom he never forgot for the rest of his life. He met her again when he was eighteen and it was following this second meeting that he wrote his first poem, a sonnet. In his great work, *The Divine Comedy*, it is Beatrice, too, who is the Spirit of Religion. The Beatrice legend has, perhaps, been unduly romanticised with the result that the real Dante Alighieri tends to become obscured. Far from the dreamy, love-sick youth he is so often pictured as being, Dante was very much a man of his time, practical, business-like, and prepared at all times to accept his responsibilities as a member of one of the great citizen states of Italy. For example, when war broke out in 1287 between Florence and Arezzo, Dante took part in the campaign and was present at the Battle of Campeldino, a great Florentine victory, in 1289. Within a year of his return from this battle, he learned of the death of

One of the illustrations from a fifteenth manuscript of Dante's Divine Comedy.

Beatrice and began to write his *Vita Nuova* which was probably completed four years later.

DANTE'S POLITICAL CAREER

In 1296, having reached the age at which the Florentine law allowed him the full rights of citizenship, Dante joined the Guild of Physicians and Apothecaries, one of the wealthiest and most influential guilds in Florence. His acceptance into this guild was perhaps due to the fact that, at that time, books, as a commodity, were handled by the apothecary. Furthermore, all practising artists were affiliated to the Physicians and Apothecaries and there is some evidence that Dante was interested in painting. The important thing, however, is that membership of the guild marked the beginning of the political career that was to lead Dante eventually to almost twenty years of exile. During the next few years, his name crops up regularly in Florentine records. In 1300, he is mentioned as being sent as an ambassador to San Gemignano. On his return, he was appointed as one of the six Priors of the Republic of Florence, this being the highest office in the state. In 1301, we hear of him voting against a motion to send a detachment of soldiers to serve with the Papal forces. Shortly afterwards he is a member of an embassy to Rome.

TWO WARRING FACTIONS

Meanwhile, trouble had broken out in Florence and the loyalties of the city were divided between two factions, the Blacks and the Whites. The Blacks were headed by the Donati family, ancient in lineage but reduced in circumstances; while the leaders of the Whites were wealthy upstarts called the Cerchi. Originally, the quarrel had been nothing more than a family feud, but soon it had become something bigger and more sinister, another phase in the struggle between the Guelphs and the Ghibellines that had devastated Italy for years. Florence became the scene of the kind of explosive street brawls that are depicted in the opening of Shakespeare's *Romeo and Juliet*; and Dante's attitude to the contestants seems to have been summed up in the dying Mercutio's remark—" A plague o' both the houses "— for it was during Dante's priorate that the authorities decided to exile the leaders of both factions. On All Saints' Day, 1301, Charles of Valois, the Pope's peacemaker to Florence, treacherously declared in favour of the Blacks who thereupon set about getting rid of their opponents. On 27th January, 1302, a decree of banishment was issued against Dante and two months later an even more severe sentence was promulgated, condemning him to be burned alive should he ever be caught. The charge of which Dante was supposed to have been guilty was fraud and corrupt practices whilst in office. No one, at any time, has ever been able to believe that there was the slightest foundation for this accusation, but the poet was doomed never to set foot in his native city again.

Another early illustration from the Divine Comedy, showing some of the horrors of hell.

TWENTY YEARS OF WANDERING

The next twenty years are mainly a chronicle of wandering as Dante moved from place to place, honoured and respected as a poet but unhappy and uprooted as a man. At first he dreamed of returning to Florence by forcible means but always he was doomed to disappointment. According to Boccaccio, he visited Paris and there is a vague report that he sojourned for a while in England and studied at the University of Oxford. Neither of these reports is substantiated. In his desperation to return home, Dante became involved more and more deeply with the enemies of Florence with the result that a pardon offered in 1311 to the Florentine exiles excepted him by name. At this time, Dante was pinning all his hopes on the Emperor Henry VII and wrote, in the Emperor's name, a thunderous and threatening letter to the Florentines. But the Emperor's death in 1313 blasted the poet's hopes and all chance of a reconciliation was finally shattered two years later, when the Ghibellines reconquered Florence and named Dante, with his sons, as rebels to be executed on sight. The dreary wanderings were resumed until finally Dante and his family settled in Ravenna somewhere about 1318. Here it was that he finally completed his wonderful poem *The Divine Comedy* on which he had been working for many years. Earlier, during his stay, he had finished and published the *Inferno*

and *Purgatorio*. Now the great work was complete. Then, in the summer of 1321, he set out on the embassy to Venice that was to lead to his death.

THE DIVINE COMEDY

There is no doubt that *The Divine Comedy* is one of the world's greatest poems. In it, Dante made use of a new verse form, the *terza rima*, a three-line stanza which takes the poem on at a great pace. The poem describes an imaginary journey through Hell, Purgatory and Heaven, and runs to some fourteen thousand lines. In its day, it was revolutionary, being written in the language of the common people with whom it was very popular. There is indeed a story of Dante beating a donkey-driver who was roaring out his verses loudly but inaccurately. In a way, this incident sums up Dante. He was a proud, vain, unhappy man. He knew he was a great poet and frequently acted as though he knew it. When he was dead, the Florentines, in the ensuing centuries, made great efforts to have his bones brought back to Florence but were foiled by Franciscan monks who hid them in a cavity where they remained until they were rediscovered in 1865. On 26th June, that year, the remains of Dante were re-interred with great ceremony in the original sarcophagus in Ravenna. Even in death, it seemed, the greatest poet in Italian history was still doomed to remain an exile.

EDWARD IV
A Period of Treachery and Intrigue

EDWARD IV's accession in 1461 marked the triumph of the Yorkists in the first period of the Wars of the Roses. The new King was a youth of barely nineteen years and a handsome, well-built one at that. He had shown that he could work hard and fight hard when necessary. He was henceforth to show that he much preferred to play—which, unfortunately, meant indulgence in the grossest of pleasures. So he settled down to enjoy life, leaving his older cousin, the Earl of Warwick, the "King-maker," to tidy up affairs in the north. This was entirely satisfactory to Warwick, who loved work and power. It was Warwick's strong arm that had hoisted Edward to the throne and he had every expectation that his controlling influence over affairs would continue. By 1466 the north had been more or less quieted, the poor, feeble-minded Lancastrian King Henry VI had been betrayed into Yorkists' hands; and his tempestuous Queen Margaret, with her young son, the Prince of Wales, had departed for France.

A SECRET MARRIAGE

Meantime Edward was discovering that it suited him better to stand on his own feet than to lean on cousin Warwick's broad shoulder. In 1464 differences arose between the pair. Warwick wanted the King to make an alliance with Louis XI of France and marry the latter's sister-in-law; and Edward deliberately allowed him to open negotiations. But he had no intention of leaguing himself with Louis and he could not very well marry his sister-in-law because, as he suddenly announced to a thunderstruck Council, he was already married. His bride was the Lady Elizabeth Grey. True, she was a widow with two grown children. True, too, that her father had been originally a mere country knight (Sir Richard Woodville), though he was now Lord Rivers, and that he was an old Lancastrian. Edward had fallen violently in love with the young widow and had married her in secret.

EDWARD IS TAUGHT A LESSON

Warwick, of course, was furious, but there were more slights and provocations in store for him. Edward began to marry his queen's relatives into the nobility and to build up a "Woodville" party to offset Warwick's powerful "Neville" party. In 1466 he opposed Warwick's plan for marrying his elder daughter Isabella to Edward's younger brother, George, Duke of Clarence. The King-maker was not the man to submit to being cold-shouldered; and, after biding his time for some years he decided, in 1469, to teach his ungrateful young cousin a sharp lesson. Clarence, a reckless and unruly youth, readily agreed to aid him. The Neville family rose in arms and the forbidden marriage was defiantly celebrated. Events moved with astonishing speed. Edward, taken by surprise, was captured. Warwick had no thought of dethroning his prisoner, but contented himself with showing his own power. Then, feeling doubtless that Edward would long remember the lesson he had received, he released him.

But Edward did not care for lessons of that sort and next year he turned the tables on Warwick and chased him and his new son-in-law clean out of the country. Seething with rage, Warwick, now in France, leagued himself with Queen Margaret. The Nevilles, with the remnants of the Lancastrian party, were to unite in a new rising and, to seal the bargain, Warwick's second daughter, Anne, was to wed Margaret's son, then a lad of seventeen. "False, fleeting, perjured Clarence," as Shakespeare aptly brands him, felt that he was being left out in the cold. So, true to character, he began to think of changing sides again.

TWO FAMOUS BATTLES

In September, 1470, Warwick and Clarence landed in England and proclaimed Henry as King. Edward, to his dismay, found his own forces dissolve in treachery. He fled to Holland. But he was back again in the following March. The faithless Clarence came over to his camp. Edward entered London and threw the unfortunate Henry back into the Tower. Two battles decided the final issue. At Barnet Warwick's power was laid in the dust and the King-maker himself slain. At Tewkesbury Margaret, newly-arrived from

This painting by Maclise, the Victorian artist, depicts William Caxton showing proofs from his printing press, the first set up in England, to his patron, Edward IV.

France, was routed and her son butchered, while a little later she herself was taken prisoner.

Henry was now the last of his line. He did not survive long and there can be small doubt that Edward had the unhappy, half-witted creature murdered. There was a dark streak of ruthless cruelty beneath his pleasing exterior.

Edward was now definitely standing on his own feet. For some years he toyed with the idea of reviving England's old claims to the

Queen Margaret of Anjou made prisoner of Edward IV after the Battle of Tewkesbury.

throne of France, then ruled by the crafty Louis XI. In 1475 he actually landed at Calais with an army. The expedition depended largely on the co-operation of his ally, Charles, Duke of Burgundy. But Charles failed him and Edward thereupon turned right about face and came to terms with Louis. He agreed to shelve his claims and take his army ingloriously home in return for a large immediate cash sum and a yearly pension. The sordid, though sensible, deal throws a revealing light on another side of his unamiable character.

DROWNED IN A BUTT OF WINE

Meantime he had been having trouble with Clarence. He bore with his brother's continuing insolence and his questionable intrigues for a long while; but in 1478, in a burst of wrath, he caused an overawed Parliament to attaint him of treason, whereupon he was sentenced to death. The exact manner of his well-deserved end has always been a mystery and it has given rise to the oddest of stories. The traitor was said to have been drowned in a butt of malmsey wine!

Edward's own death occurred in 1483 as the result of his persistent debauchery and self-indulgence. He is certainly not a desirable character; yet, with all his disgusting personal vices, he was not actually a bad king. His rich and splendid court was distinguished by a welcome revival of interest in the peaceful arts. Perhaps its best title to remembrance is that it gave its patronage to William Caxton when he set up the first printing press in England.

Neville, Earl of Warwick, "The King-maker."

EDWARD V

A Three Months' Reign

ON Edward IV's death in April 1483, a child once again inherited the throne. Edward had left two sons: the twelve-year-old lad who now became Edward V and Richard aged nine. For young Edward it was like being flung into a nest of vipers. A struggle for the post of Regent during Edward's minority began forthwith. The rival parties were the Woodvilles, headed by his mother, Queen Elizabeth, and the supporters of his uncle, Richard, Duke of Gloucester. Each party knew that the triumph of the one would mean the downfall of the other. It was Uncle Richard who struck first. Aided by the Duke of Buckingham, he seized the boy-King from the custody of the Queen's brother, Earl Rivers, and took the latter and his companions prisoner. Queen Elizabeth hastily gathered her younger son and her five daughters about her and fled for sanctuary to Westminster. And Uncle Richard got the regency.

TREACHERY !

Richard had earned an excellent record during his late brother's reign, but he now began to behave in a highly suspicious manner. He packed London with armed retainers. He heaped extraordinary favours on Buckingham. At a peaceful meeting of the Privy Council he suddenly summoned in an armed band and arrested Lord Hastings and other staunch friends of the late King. Having decapitated Hastings, he betook himself to Westminster. By fearful threats and artful persuasions he induced Queen Elizabeth to surrender her son Richard and sent him to join his brother in the Tower.

Proceeding step by step, the crafty schemer invented a remarkable fairy-tale. He told the people that Edward IV had not been legally married, so that his children were not lawful, and that he, good Uncle Richard, was the true heir to the throne.

Finally, by packing the streets with his and Buckingham's men-at-arms, he compelled a terrified Parliament to offer him the crown, which, on 26th June, he graciously accepted.

Some weeks passed by, and then a deed was done that sent a shudder of horror through the land. The innocent and helpless princes were brutally murdered. The story told later was that they had been smothered in their beds by a pair of heartless ruffians and their bodies buried at the foot of a staircase in the White Tower. There is no outright proof that the usurper was responsible for the monstrous crime. To-day many people hold him guiltless, but the general opinion of historians is strongly against them.

A VISION OF CHILDREN

I dream'd I saw a little brook
  Run rippling down the Strand;
With cherry-trees and apple-trees
  Abloom on either hand:
The sparrows gather'd from the squares,
  Upon the branches green;
The pigeons flock'd from Palace-yard,
  Afresh their wings to preen;
And children down St. Martin's Lane,
  And out of Westminster,
Came trooping many a thousand strong,
  With a bewilder'd air.

They hugged each other round the neck,
  And titter'd for delight,
To see the yellow daffodils,
  And see the daisies white;
They rolled upon the grassy slopes,
  And drank the water clear,
While buses the Embankment took,
  Ashamed to pass anear;
And sandwich-men stood still aghast,
  And costermongers smiled;
And a policeman on his beat
  Pass'd weeping like a child.

Thomas Ashe

THE BIBLE

The Old Testament Story

THE Old Testament provides a well documented history of the Jews down to about 300 B.C. It also contains some of the finest religious poetry ever written and some remarkable but obscure books foretelling the future. These various writings were composed at different times and with different objects; yet the total effect is a single, coherent story.

THE CREATION OF THE WORLD

It begins with the creation of the world by God. Man was formed in the image of God, but man sinned and evil and suffering were the inevitable consequences. The message of this profound allegory runs like a thread through the whole of the Old Testament. The history of the Jews is shown as an illustration of the disasters that result from disobedience. In their case the penalties were all the more severe because they had been shown special favour.

THE WORSHIP OF ONE GOD

They were surrounded by great empires, such as Babylon and Egypt, at a much higher material level. The Jews produced no magnificent buildings or works of art like other ancient nations, but they did possess an immeasurably superior religion. It shone out from the darkness of superstition and idolatry, with its insistence on the worship of one, unseen God, and its high moral code. Unfortunately, time and again, many of the Jews were seduced by the cults of their neighbours—the worship of Baal, Dagon, and Astarte, with its debasing accompaniments.

Solitary religious teachers, known as the Prophets, arose at different periods and denounced such apostasy. They predicted the downfall of the entire Jewish nation, and what they said came true. They also predicted the appearance of a Messiah who would bring deliverance from these tribulations. For the most part the Jews believed that this meant a leader would be sent by God to restore their lost kingdom and overthrow their oppressors. This was a mistaken interpretation and the story of the Old Testament was continued in the New in a way that was unexpected.

THE STORY OF ABRAHAM

The earliest part of the Old Testament story deals with a semi-legendary past. Abraham came to Palestine, we read, from Chaldea. He brought cattle, sheep and camels and settled down in the new country. God promised that his descendants would multiply because of Abraham's intense religious faith. Abraham had believed that God wished him to slay his son, Isaac, but he was prevented from doing so. His complete trust in God, even to the point of being willing to obey such a drastic command, was rewarded by a compact or covenant, promising future greatness.

The Jews certainly multiplied. The period of Abraham, Isaac and Jacob (from whom the twelve tribes of Israel claimed descent) was a time when pastoral nomads entered Palestine from more barren regions. But they did not achieve national unity until much later. No precise date can be assigned to the first immigration, though Abraham may have been a contemporary of the famous Babylonian King Hammurabi, a little before 2000 B.C. Nor is there any record in Egyptian history to date the time when the Jews were in " Egyptian bondage."

MOSES AND THE EXODUS

The Egyptians had many slaves, usually captured in war, working for them. Some of these were of Hebrew origin. They rebelled against their masters under the leadership of Moses. The struggle between Moses and the reigning Pharaoh is vividly told in the biblical narrative. Plague and pestilence swept over Egypt and Moses held this to be the judgment of God. Finally Pharaoh relented, but no sooner had the liberated Jews begun to leave than he tried to bring them back. They managed to cross the Red Sea, and in this also they saw the hand of God. For the waters engulfed their pursuers but they reached the safety of the Sinai peninsula. They were free, but they

The " stele," or code of laws, of Hammurabi, a great ruler in Babylon. The seated figure at the top is a portrait of the king himself.

had to endure considerable hardship in the desert, and some of them even looked back wistfully on the days when they at least had enough to eat.

" THE CHOSEN PEOPLE "

The march from Egypt is known as the Exodus. It marks the beginning of the history of the Jews as a nation. During their wanderings in the desert they received a direct revelation from God. It assured them of divine protection provided they were loyal to their religion. Moses inscribed the Ten Commandments on tablets of stone and laid the foundations of a set of religious observances which gave the various tribes a new sense of unity. Thereafter they were convinced that they had been singled out among all other nations in the world. They were " the chosen people " and they had the right to conquer the fertile country beyond the desert and make it their home. This part of Palestine was called Canaan. To the Jews it was " the Promised Land." They somewhat exaggerated when they described it as " a land flowing with milk and honey." Most of it was already occupied by an agricultural people akin to the Jews in language, but with a more advanced culture. Farther north the Phœnicians were well established as prosperous traders and they sent their ships as far as the coast of France and Spain. The Philistines, on the southern coast, were a warlike, non-Semitic race, who gave Palestine its name.

INVASION AND CONQUEST OF CANAAN

It was a desperate undertaking for ill-equipped nomadic tribes to invade these settled and well-developed regions, but they undertook it in the spirit of a crusade. The account of the early conquest can be read in the books of Samuel and Kings. The struggle was bitter and ruthless. Moses died before the entry into Canaan was made, but his main task was accomplished. He had formulated a set of laws and the tenets of the Hebrew religion.

The next stage was military conquest and this was carried through by such leaders as Joshua and David. The stories of this heroic age of the Jews read like a saga. They went into battle carrying a wooden ark, which was the symbol of the covenant made between God and the Jews in Sinai. Their enemies similarly carried idols of their own gods; and sometimes the ark and sometimes the idols were captured in the fighting. Joshua subdued the great Canaanite stronghold of Jericho in such a novel way that the Jews regarded it as a miracle. We are told that the Israelites marched round the city, shouting and blowing trumpets instead of attacking, and the walls collapsed. Archæologists have dug up the site of the original city of Jericho, and there can be no doubt that something very unusual happened to its walls.

Another hero of this period, whose exploits against the Philistines won him great renown, was Samson. He was a man of giant strength, but finally he was captured and his eyes put out. But he maintained a defiant resistance to the end. Blind but still strong, he pulled down the supporting pillars of a temple and perished with his trapped captors.

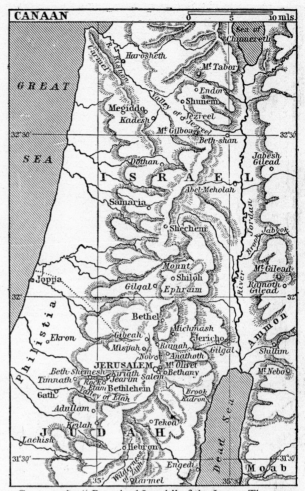

Canaan, the " Promised Land " of the Jews. The map shows the later division of the country into two parts.

THE FIRST KING

Unlike the surrounding peoples, the Israelites had no king. They were ruled by a number of chosen leaders called Judges. In time they became dissatisfied with this system and prevailed upon one of the most revered of the Judges, Samuel, to institute a monarchy. Somewhat reluctantly, he acceded to their wishes and made Saul, a warrior of the tribe of Benjamin, the first king of Israel. Saul reigned from 1030 to 1010 B.C., and he was succeeded by David, the author of many of the Psalms. David consolidated the new kingdom. He captured the hill fortress of Jerusalem and made it his capital. During his reign, Israel became a military power to be reckoned with in Palestine itself, and when he was succeeded by his son, Solomon, the Jews seemed to enter an era of peace and prosperity. They had enjoyed

nothing like this before and it is no wonder that subsequent chroniclers wrote so glowingly of Solomon's fabulous riches and deep wisdom. He preferred diplomacy to war and entered into a number of profitable trade agreements with other states. He built the great temple in Jerusalem which was made the centre of Jewish worship. To the Jews, Jerusalem was what Mecca became to the Mohammedans.

DIVISION AND DANGER

Solomon died in 933 B.C., but unfortunately the golden promise of his reign was not fulfilled. The Jews began to quarrel amongst themselves and the unity which David had forged was broken. The nation was split into

This is a model of the magnificent structure of Solomon's Temple in Jerusalem, built according

to the measurements given in the Bible. Its great size can be appreciated. (*See I Kings* 6)

two unequal parts under separate kings. Israel in the north made Samaria its capital, and Judah in the south retained Jerusalem. The Jews had so weakened themselves by this division that they might have fallen a prey to the other petty states with whom they had formerly been so long at war, but for the fact that the whole of Palestine was threatened by a new and predatory power. The Assyrians were on the move, plundering and burning cities and laying waste every land they entered.

THE JEWISH PROPHETS

Dark warnings were uttered by the Jewish Prophets. They declared that the Jews would have only themselves to blame for the evils to come. Instead of cherishing the pure worship of Jehovah and keeping faithfully to the laws of Moses, they had imitated the idolatrous rites of their neighbours and bowed the knee to Baal.

All the prophetic writings point back to the old days when life was stern and simple. In their new prosperity, the Jews had become luxury-loving, and so we find the prophets taking up the cause of the poor and oppressed. Thus Isaiah scathingly denounced the rich for " grinding the faces of the poor." The increasingly elaborate ceremonial of the temple is also condemned. What matters in the sight of God is the inner man and not the outward pomp. " To what purpose is the multitude of your sacrifices unto me? saith the Lord. I am full of burnt offerings of rams and the fat of fed beasts; and I delight not in the blood of bullocks, or of lambs, or of he goats. . . . Your hands are full of blood. Wash you, make you clean, put away the evil of your doings from before mine eyes; cease to do evil; learn to do well; seek judgment, relieve the oppressed, judge the fatherless, plead for the widow. . . ."

The prophets were feared and respected by all. Elijah denounced Ahab to his face. Ahab was king of the northern kingdom and had

Here is an Assyrian horseman hunting. So perfect is this carving that it gives a photographic impression of the hunter. The Assyrians absorbed Judah in their empire.

gone over to the worship of Baal. Elijah challenged the priests of Baal assembled on Mount Carmel to ask their god to bring down fire from heaven to consume a sacrifice on their altar. The story of their defeat makes a dramatic interlude in the plain historical record in the Book of Kings.

PALESTINE AND JUDAH INVADED

Elijah was a terrifying personality, dedicated to the task of turning the Jews from their degenerate ways. Their history entered a new phase when Israel was invaded by the Assyrians in 722 B.C. Thereafter Palestine was at the mercy of the great warring empires that dominated the Middle East.

The Assyrians moved on Judah next and in 701 Sennacherib besieged Jerusalem. The King of Judah was Hezekiah, and on the advice of the prophet Isaiah, he refused to surrender. The Assyrian army was stricken down by some epidemic and so many of them died that the siege had to be raised. Nevertheless, Judah was politically a part of the Assyrian empire and remained so until the rise of a new combination, the Medes and Chaldeans. The Assyrians then passed from history and Palestine came under the sway of the Chaldeans.

THE EXILE

The prophetic writings of Habakkuk and Jeremiah belong to this period. They are heavy with a sense of doom, but the sufferings of the Jews are seen as a judgment on their failure to observe their religion. Jehoiakim, the King of Judah, led a revolt against the Chaldeans in 597, but the only result was that Jerusalem was besieged and a large number of Jews taken into slavery. A second rebellion followed and in 586 Jerusalem was destroyed and practically all the inhabitants were deported to Babylon. This tragic landmark in Jewish history is known as the Exile.

THE TEMPLE REBUILT

The prophecies of Ezekiel are related to these world shattering events. Ezekiel foretold the return of the Jews from Babylon and the building of a new temple in which God would be worshipped with a purified ritual. In 539 B.C., Babylon fell to Persia and the Jews were released from captivity.

During their sojourn in Babylon, they had reorganised themselves as a religious community since they could no longer do so on a national basis. Cyrus, the Persian king, showed them considerable clemency, but there was no question of their regaining full independence. They were able to rebuild the temple in Jerusalem; and in the centuries that followed, they set about the task of codifying their laws and closing their ranks by preventing intermarriage with non-Jews.

It was a time of great literary activity and a good deal of the Old Testament as we now know it was composed or revised. But the breach between the northern and southern kingdoms was not healed. Until New Testament times it was still disputed whether the temple at Jerusalem had a superior claim to the temple on Mount Gerizim in which the Samaritans worshipped.

THE DISPERSAL OF THE JEWS

As empire succeeded empire, the Jews exchanged the rule of Persia for that of the Seleucids and finally they became part of the Roman Empire. They continued to dream of a Messiah who would liberate them and restore the glories of David and Solomon. They missed the significance of Isaiah's portrait of their saviour: " He was despised and rejected of men; a man of sorrows and acquainted with grief."

It was not until the Christian era that Jerusalem was finally destroyed (A.D. 70) and the Jews dispersed. Their story is a tragedy of lost opportunities and a triumph of endurance. This tiny nation which began its career like wandering Bedouin tribesmen has indirectly influenced the course of human history more than any other people.

RICHARD III

Last of the Plantagenets

Richard III. 1483-5.

RICHARD III's bloodstained climb to the throne in June 1483 and the murder of the princes in the Tower, are described in the account of Edward V's brief reign. Richard's own people had little doubt of his guilt and the dark deed ruined his cause forever. Thenceforth he went about like a haunted man, his furtive eyes dark with suspicion, his hand ever on his dagger. By the autumn his former confederate the Duke of Buckingham was leading a rebellion which aimed at deposing the detested ogre and ending the feud between the houses of York and Lancaster by uniting their present heirs in marriage and seating them on the throne. The Yorkist heir was Princess Elizabeth, the murdered Edward V's eldest sister. The Lancastrian heir was Henry Tudor, Earl of Richmond, a descendant of John Beaufort, Earl of Somerset, one of John of Gaunt's illegitimate children, whose line had hitherto been barred from the succession.

MISFORTUNE AND DEATH

The insurrection was scotched by Richard's skill, but the victory was his last piece of good fortune. His son Edward died suddenly in 1484. Eleven months later, his wife, too, passed away. In the same year a new rising was staged under Henry Tudor. The opposing forces met on the Field of Bosworth on 22nd August. Richard's army was twice the size of Henry's, but treachery was busy in his camp and his men had little heart to fight for such a captain. Richard's lean face was haggard with bodeful fears. Yet, when the crisis of the battle came and he saw that the day was lost, he died, battle-axe in hand, like a stout-hearted soldier. For a great fighter he was in very truth and no " Crookback," as later writers said. His only deformity was a withered arm that made one shoulder slightly lower than the other. Richard's last hour was his finest. When he fell his battered crown was discovered in a hawthorn bush and placed in triumph on Henry's victorious brows.

The Wars of the Roses had practically ended; and the last decisive battle, and the throne, had been won by a descendant of the House of Lancaster.

THE PIGEONS ROUND ST. PAUL'S

The pigeons round about St. Paul's
　Are happy all the year;
Amidst the rush and roar of things
　They seem to have no fear.
They boldly walk about the street,
And all amongst the horses' feet

They bob their heads and pick and preen,
　And congregate together;
And always they look neat and clean,
　However bad the weather.
No angry blasts, nor rain, nor squalls,
　Disturb the pigeons round St. Paul's.

Catherine A. Morin

An artist's impression of the scene at the Battle of Bosworth, 1485. Richard III in the foreground attacks Henry of Richmond, who later became Henry VII.

HENRY VII

First of the Tudor Monarchs

AFTER the Battle of Bosworth in 1485, the Lancastrian Henry of Richmond began the Tudor line of monarchs as Henry VII under promising circumstances. Thirty years of the carnage and anarchy of the Wars of the Roses had left the people yearning for peace and settled government. Henry was just the ruler to give them both. He was a young man of twenty-eight years, cold, reserved and calculating, yet possessed of outstanding courage. Having secured Parliament's confirmation of his right to the throne, he married the Princess Elizabeth, heiress of the House of York. Thus the rival factions of Lancaster and York at last more or less buried the hatchet. The power of the great baronial houses had been broken by the wars and numbers of the old nobility had passed away. Henry applied himself to tame the survivors. Their strength had always rested largely on the numerous retainers who wore their badge, or " livery."

Henry took strong measures to abolish these private armies and punish their misdeeds. In particular, he set up a tribunal, which became famous as the Court of Star Chamber, and armed it with drastic powers to bring over-mighty lords to book.

Meanwhile there were still some considerable flickers from the smouldering embers of the late wars. One of them was the Lambert Simnel plot. Lambert was a bright and promising boy whom some disgruntled Yorkists trained to impersonate Edward of Warwick (the son of Richard III's murdered brother Clarence), then a prisoner in the Tower.

Lambert got as far as being crowned in Ireland as Edward VI; but in 1487 Henry scotched the affair. When the hopeful Lambert fell into his hands he shrewdly brought him into public contempt by making him a turnspit in his royal kitchens.

117

Christopher Columbus, who discovered
America in 1492.

A VERY DARING MASQUERADE

Then, about 1491, began a most astonishing
adventure that would fill a book with its wild
exploits. Perkin Warbeck, a lad favoured
with good looks and an air of breeding, set
himself up as Richard of York, the younger of
the two princes smothered in the Tower. Such
were the grace and dignity of his bearing that
he hoaxed quite a number of foreign princes
and was presently used by the Yorkists as a
useful tool. When, after a whole string of
exciting adventures, Henry got hold of him,
he once again showed that he could be merci-
ful. But, in 1499, his slippery prisoner plotted
with young Warwick to escape from the Tower
and the King had had enough: he called in
the executioner.

Henry was unwillingly drawn into another
war with France. Charles VIII was trying to
swallow the half-independent Duchy of Brittany. His success would have meant a threat
to Calais and the command of the Channel,
and Henry intervened to check the French
King's growing power. But Brittany presently
gave in and Henry could do little alone.
Accordingly, in 1492, he made the best of
things by extracting a fat pension, or tribute,
from Charles and sailed away home. Doubtless he was fully satisfied, for he was a great
money-getter, shrewdly realising that money
was power.

HISTORIC ALLIANCES

In his dealings with other countries he was
more successful. He strengthened England's
dubious authority in Ireland by the Poynings
Law, which gave the Crown control of the
Irish Parliament, and by the daring step of
making the chief disturber of the peace, the
Earl of Kildare, Lord Deputy. He married
his eldest son, Arthur, to Catherine of Aragon,
the youngest daughter of Ferdinand and
Isabella of Spain, and, when Arthur died,
passed her on to the latter's brother, Henry.
He secured a spell of peace with Scotland by
wedding his daughter Margaret to King James
IV, thus uniting the Thistle with the Rose.
Future history held great events in store as the
result of these alliances.

When Henry died, in 1509, he had done
fine work in restoring peace and a settled
government to his realm. True, it was achieved
at the price of making himself almost an autocrat; for his wise rule kept Parliament purring
with satisfaction and made it his willing agent
and tool. But the country was content. He
had got what it yearned for.

THE DEATH OF FEUDALISM

What adds a special interest to the period
covered by Henry's reign is that it is in some
respects a dividing line in European history
between the Middle Ages and modern times.
Actually, the line is as artificial as the Equator;
but it has its uses provided we do not apply it
strictly. Certainly from this period men's
outlook on the world underwent fundamental
changes.

Feudalism was dying. Men were beginning to think for themselves instead of
accepting the traditional authority of priests
and scholars. Education was spreading. The
invention of printing was diffusing knowledge
and new ideas. A new thirst had arisen for
scientific facts and spiritual truth, and it was
stimulated and sustained by the re-discovery of
the treasures of classical Greek and Roman
literature. The hoary dogmas of the Church
were scrutinised anew and the Reformation
was on the way. The spirit of nationalism
grew apace and, following the example of
England, strong national monarchies arose in
France and Spain. The physical globe itself
was altering. Columbus, bucketing across the
dreaded " Sea of Darkness," blundered on
nothing less than a New World. There can be
no comparable voyage till we make a space
flight to the Moon.

HENRY VIII

A Man of Versatile Powers

"**H**ENRY the Self-Willed" would be a fitting title for Henry VIII, who succeeded his father, the seventh Henry, in 1509, when he was just on eighteen. He was a most remarkable character and he crowded his reign with remarkable performances. A handsome prince and every inch a king, he was gay, shrewd, deep and utterly selfish. His people held him in pride and admiration and much of his popularity lived on despite his deeds of blood and the despotism of his rule. Indeed, his masterful spirit, robust manliness and bluff independence made him a truly representative Englishman. As for his despotism, the country preferred it to the anarchy of the Wars of the Roses.

The high-mettled young King staged two early campaigns in France and won some

Henry VIII. 1509-47.

notable successes. Then, in 1513, James IV of Scotland, who was in league with France, stepped over the Border. But he never stepped back again. The Earl of Surrey slaughtered both him and his army on the fatal field of Flodden.

WOLSEY'S CLEVER DIPLOMACY

During these early years, the remarkable King discovered a remarkable minister. Thomas Wolsey had started life as a butcher's son. He lived to become Lord Chancellor of England and a Cardinal of Rome; and, as Henry's right-hand man, he rose to such a pinnacle of power as would have made an ordinary man dizzy. The political situation abroad gave his subtle brain good exercise. From 1519 two youthful monarchs, Francis I and Charles V, were competing for supremacy like two heavyweights boxing for the championship of Europe. Francis, was King of France. Charles was ruler of half Europe: Germany, Austria, Spain, the Netherlands and parts of Italy. The victory of either party would be a grave menace to light-weight England and Wolsey busily manœuvred to preserve the balance of power by succouring first one side and then the other as occasion suggested. His crafty

Thomas Wolsey, Cardinal, Archbisop of York.

119

Catherine of Aragon, first wife of Henry VIII.

PAPAL DISPENSATION REFUSED

It was not until about 1527 that the flames began to get a hold on England and then it was a purely personal concern of the King's that gave them a real start. Henry badly wanted an heir, for all his children by Catherine of Aragon, except Mary, had died in infancy. Catherine had been his dead brother Arthur's widow, and, as the Scriptures forbade such a union, a dispensation had been obtained from the then Pope. Henry was now troubled about the legality of his marriage and leaning to the conviction that the deaths of his children were a divine judgment on him. He had a most obedient conscience. Then he fell in love with a dashing young maid of honour named Anne Boleyn and his mind was made up. He told Wolsey to get the Pope to dissolve his marriage. But Catherine was the aunt of Charles V; and the Pope was in Charles's pocket; and Wolsey failed in his mission.

diplomacy raised his country's prestige to its highest pitch; but it failed in the end. By 1529, after Francis had been knocked out of the ring, Charles was definitely on top. Moreover, two years earlier, he had sacked Rome and the Pope was entirely under his control —a circumstance which happened to be extremely inconvenient to Henry at that particular time.

MARTIN LUTHER, PROTESTANT REFORMER

The Reformation had broken out in Germany, where Luther, from 1517 onwards, was striking right, left and centre at the abuses of the Roman Catholic Church. The movement spread over northern Europe like a forest fire. It was fanned by the new spirit of inquiry that was in the air, by the revived study of the Bible in the light of a better knowledge of the Greek, Latin and Hebrew texts, and by the utter spiritual and moral depravity of the Pope and his court of red-hatted Cardinals. The Bible was declared to be the sole guide to the truths of religion, and many of the fundamental doctrines and practices of the Church were denounced as without authority. In particular the reformers denied the spiritual supremacy of the Pope and the central dogma of transubstantiation on which much of the priestly power depended.

HENRY FLOUTS THE POPE'S AUTHORITY

That was the end of the great Cardinal. In 1529, Henry, without a thought for his long and arduous service, dismissed him from Court and toppled him down from his lofty pinnacle in ruin and disgrace. Shortly afterwards the fallen minister died heart-broken.

The King now favoured two new ministers: Thomas Cromwell, a gritty upstart, and Thomas Cranmer, whom he made Archbishop

Martin Luther, German religious reformer.

of Canterbury. In 1533 he set Cranmer to judge the question of his marriage in an English court and the court obligingly pronounced it illegal. Meanwhile Henry, not to waste time, had already wedded his Anne in secret, and later she bore him the Princess Elizabeth. The Pope promptly denounced the marriage, but self-willed Henry cared little for that. He had started on a particular course and meant to pursue it to the end. Next year he caused Parliament to pass a whole series of Acts of the most momentous consequence. The clergy were brought completely under his control. He was acknowledged as Supreme Head of the Church of England. And it was made high treason to deny his title and authority. Thus did the King boldly and resolutely retaliate on the Pope by repudiating his supremacy in England and clothing himself with his ecclesiastical powers.

A change so profound as to affect the eternal salvation of every individual in the land could not, of course, have been effected through a personal quarrel of the King's. It needed the people's co-operation. And the most active part of the people was sufficiently on their popular King's side to give him his head. They had nourished grievances against the papacy for centuries and the same influences that inspired Luther's movement were at work among them. As yet the country was little affected by the extremer opinions of the continental reformers; but it was ready for some change at least and the question of the King's marriage provided the occasion.

" THE SIX ARTICLES "

Quite unconcerned by the fact that the Pope had now excommunicated and deposed him, Henry proceeded on his self-willed way. He set his minion Cromwell to dissolve the monasteries, and their vast estates were seized and sold to laymen. In 1539 he set up an English Bible in every church for the people to read. Then, having made himself master in his own house and reformed or abolished a number of outworn popish practices, he called a halt. Henry, like the majority of his people, was still a Catholic, though not a Roman Catholic. He clung steadfastly to the principal doctrines of the Catholic Church. To check the more advanced Protestants who would have made a clean sweep of everything not supported by the Bible, he made Parliament pass the Act of " the Six Articles." This imposed the penalty of death, or lesser punishments, on any who denied the truth of transubstantiation and other fundamental Catholic doctrines. What the autocratic King believed his people too must believe, or . . .

THE PILGRIMAGE OF GRACE

Beside these memorable events the other happenings of the reign seem of minor importance. Anne Boleyn was heartlessly executed and Henry took to himself one wife after another: Jane Seymour, who bore him the heir, Edward, he was so anxious for; Anne of Cleves; Catherine Howard, who suffered the same cruel fate as Anne Boleyn; and Catherine Parr. In 1536–37 there was a dangerous insurrection in the north—the Pilgrimage of Grace—where Catholic feeling and political discontent were strong. It was brutally crushed, partly through Henry's treacherous dealings, and followed by mass executions. War with Scotland flared out again in 1542 and the week-old Mary, " Queen of Scots," began her tumultuous career.

Henry died in 1547, a diseased and bloated hulk. He left England half-way between Catholicism and Protestantism. He left it, too, as an autocrat who had reduced Parliament almost completely to his will. Truly he may be styled " Henry the Self-Willed."

Thomas Cromwell, Earl of Essex.

EDWARD VI

A Brief but Important Reign

HENRY VIII had won such a mastery over Parliament that it had empowered him to name his successor by will. He had appointed Edward, his son by Jane Seymour, and Edward, accordingly, at the age of nine, duly assumed the crown in 1547. He was an intelligent and serious-minded boy with an appearance of great charm. The government was conducted by a Regency Council under the presidency of his uncle Edward Seymour. Uncle Seymour dug himself well into power from the beginning; he had himself made Protector and Duke of Somerset. Then he set out on a mission in the North. Henry VIII had made a treaty with the pro-English party in Scotland for marrying Edward to Mary, Queen of Scots, then a seven-month-old baby. It was a statesmanlike plan, for it would have united the two quarrelsome neighbours. But, unfortunately, the treaty had been torn up by the Scots in their incurable hatred of England. In September, 1547, Somerset tried to revive it—with an army at his back. It was a sad miscalculation. Though he simply pulverised the Scots in the Battle of Pinkie Cleugh, the defeat only united those who favoured and those who opposed the marriage in a common loathing of the victors. The royal infant was bundled off to France for safety and betrothed to the French King's son, Francis.

Edward VI. 1547–53.

SOMERSET AND THE REFORMATION

In religious affairs Somerset belonged to the Protestant party. The late king, by throwing off the yoke of Rome, had left England moored half-way between Catholicism and Protestantism. Somerset, by reforming the doctrines and practices of the Church, slipped the moorings and sailed on. He found a valuable ally in Cranmer, the Archbishop of Canterbury. In 1547 Henry VIII's Act of "The Six Articles," forbidding the denial of transubstantiation and other basic Catholic doctrines, was repealed. In 1549 the First Book of Common Prayer, the earliest form of The Anglican Prayer Book, was issued. In 1552 (after Somerset's death) it was followed by a Second Prayer Book which carried the principles of the Reformation much farther. In 1553 Forty-two Articles of Religion, establishing the like principles, were published.

The Protestant movement was gaining strength in the country, but there was one new feature that deeply wounded the feelings of the mass of the nation. With the aim of removing the reminders of popish superstition, the churches were brutally and irreverently stripped of many of their sacred images and pictures, their richly carved woodwork and glowing stained glass. The services, too, were shorn of much of their former impressive ceremony and colourful ritual.

ENCLOSURE OF THE LAND

These over-hasty measures provoked extreme unrest, which was increased by long-standing grievances of another kind. For centuries land-holders had been steadily enclosing their farms and driving off the peasants from their intervening holdings. Often they enclosed the uncultivated "waste" of the different manors on which the peasants supported their little stock of beasts. Sheep-breeding, too, was becoming more profitable than corn-growing, because it required less labour. Thus the harassed peasants tended to lose both land and employment. Stringent laws were passed to check the growing evil, but with little success.

THE SCHEMING DUKE OF NORTHUMBERLAND

Somerset's mismanagement of affairs presently cost him his position and, in 1552, his head. By that time his rival, the Duke of Northumberland, had come to the fore. The Duke's main idea in life was self-advancement. He had no religion worth speaking of, but, as the Protestants were dominant at Court, he decided to be Protestant too. As time went on he had reason to be concerned about his prospects. The King was very weakly and Northumberland began to reflect on what would happen should his master die. Under Henry VIII's will, his daughter Mary, by Catherine of Aragon, would succeed to the throne. Now Mary was a staunch Roman Catholic and it seemed likely that, under her rule, the Reformation in England (and, what was of far more consequence to the worthy Duke, his self-advancement) would be undone. The prospect was one, indeed, that troubled all Protestants, including the young king himself. The anxious Duke conceived a daring plan for securing his power. Having, in May, 1553, married his son Guildford to the Lady Jane Grey (a granddaughter of another Mary, Henry VIII's sister), he persuaded Edward to grant the Crown to Lady Jane after his death. Of course it was a preposterous plan, but the unscrupulous Duke forced it on the government. A fortnight later Edward's brief life and briefer reign came to an end and the Duke put his outrageous scheme into action. How it fared is related in the account of Queen Mary's reign.

WRITERS WHO NEED A MICROSCOPE

Even in these days of typewriters and dictating machines, the majority of professional writers prefer to write by hand, and an astonishing study their manuscripts present.

Charlotte Brontë wrote a microscopic script. She might well have written with a needle, so scratchy are the characters, and most of the round letters are little more than blots.

Captain Marryat author of *Midshipman Easy*, wrote a script so fine and small that when the compositor ceased work he had to stick a pin in the page to mark where he left off. Charles Dickens often wrote a very minute hand, and added to the difficulties of reading by using blue ink on blue paper. At other times he would write a quite large open hand which looked almost like a schoolboy's.

Arnold Bennett, the solicitor's son, who set most of his famous books in the Potteries, wrote a beautiful hand, like a graceful script, and set out the page with all the precision and balance of an illuminated manuscript.

H. G. Wells, whose father was a professional cricketer, wrote a small rather feminine hand, and used to put a fancy scroll under his signature, such as great-grandmamma would do in the days of button boots.

Thackeray was marvellously neat, but his scripts could only be read with comfort through a magnifying-glass. Rafael Sabatini, an Italian by birth, though he described magnificent sea dramas in glowing colours, put them on paper in a handwriting so small that the printers often used a lens to decipher it. Balzac, one of the greatest novelists of all, used to defeat the printers, who would work on his scripts only for short periods, for reading his writing was like solving a puzzle.

But bad writing is not confined to novelists. It is told that once Sir Henry Irving, the great actor, dismissed one of the cast in a letter of a few lines. So unreadable was the writing that the actor in question used the letter as authority for free entry to the theatre for years after. Even the great Napoleon was an offender. It is recorded that some of his letters to Josephine from Germany were first thought to be rough sketch maps of the war front.

When you are great you may perhaps write as if a fly had staggered with inky feet across the paper, but writing, even of the great, is intended to be read. It is common courtesy that it should be read easily and unmistakably.

Mary I. 1553–8.

MARY I

An Embittered and Unwise Queen

IMMEDIATELY on Edward VI's death in July, 1553, the unscrupulous Duke of Northumberland made his carefully planned bid for power. He proclaimed his artless sixteen-year-old daughter-in-law, the Lady Jane Grey, Queen. Then he made a pounce on Mary, the rightful queen under her father Henry VIII's will. But Mary escaped his clutches and, when the thwarted Duke pursued her supporters, his forces dwindled away and the whole country rose. Protestants and Catholics alike shouted for the true Queen and Northumberland saw that the game was up. It ended, in fact, with his execution and the imprisonment of the nine-days' Queen and many members of the Duke's family.

RESTORING ENGLAND TO " THE TRUE FAITH "

On the all-important question of the national religion, the greater part of the people were still Catholics at heart, though not papists.

Probably they hoped that Mary, though herself a fanatical supporter of the Pope, would be content to restore the conditions of her father's time. But they little knew the emotions rankling in her heart. For the last twenty of her thirty-seven years she had lived in loneliness, neglect and suspicion. Her mother, Catherine of Aragon, had been heartlessly divorced. She herself had been declared illegimate. She had become morose and bitter; her religious creed was a consuming flame within her; and her one purpose now was to perform the sacred duty of restoring England to the true faith and purging the land of heretics.

She wasted no time. Within a few ,months the Latin Mass was heard again; Protestant bishops were replaced by Catholics; Edward's laws establishing the reformed faith were swept away; the ancient rites and ceremonies of the Church were revived. Protestants, in fear of their lives, fled in hundreds to the Continent.

MARRIAGE WITH PHILIP OF SPAIN

Meantime Mary was considering another vital question—that of her marriage. Her heart was fondly set on the haughty, sour-faced Philip of Spain, son of the Emperor Charles V, and as bigoted a Catholic as herself. Brushing aside all opposition, she arranged a treaty early in 1554. Her English subjects viewed the prospect with dismay. The marriage might set a line of papist children on the throne. And the country would almost certainly be dragged at the heels of Philip into another war with France; for the old contest between Spain and Charles V for supremacy in Europe still continued. Almost immediatley an insurrection flared up; but everything went wrong and it was quickly extinguished. Mary, whilst executing scores of the rebels, committed the unpardonable crime of beheading her imprisoned rival the innocent Lady Jane Grey.

PROTESTANT MARTYRS

Presently sour-faced Philip came over and the detested marriage was duly solemnised. He was followed by another unwelcome visitor, the Pope's legate, and an equally detested ceremony took place. England was formally received back into the bosom of the Roman Catholic Church. Then came a most sinister move. The atrocious laws for the burning of

124

heretics which had been repealed by Edward were re-enacted. Mary was collecting the faggots. Early in 1555 the systematic persecution began and from then onwards till the end of her days the long procession of Protestant martyrs trod their way to the stake. In all, nearly three hundred men and women died for their faith. Of that noble army three have earned imperishable fame. We can still hear in imagination the voice of the grand old Bishop Latimer calling out his ringing message of cheer to Bishop Ridley. And we can picture the dramatic scene when Archbishop Cranmer went to his agonising death. In an agitated conflict of mind he had signed a recantation of his principles. Now, nobly triumphing over his weakness, he thrust the offending hand straight into the flames and watched it blacken and burn.

Mary, in her fanatical zeal, had thought to stamp out heresy through terror. But the spectacle of her persistent and pitiless inhumanity and of the unshakable constancy of her victims only inspired the heart-stricken onlookers with a fiercer hatred of Rome and an increased sympathy for the reformed doctrines. " Bloody Mary " never understood the English people.

THE LOSS OF CALAIS

In 1557, to please her adored Philip, Mary declared war on France. From that act a shameful disaster followed. In 1558 Calais, England's proud possession for over two hundred years, was lost. Well might the Queen exclaim, " When I die Calais will be found written on my heart " ! Her time arrived only

Philip II of Spain, who married Mary.

ten months later. She died tormented with disease, neglected by her absent and cold-hearted husband and hated by her people.

I HAD A DOVE

I had a dove and the sweet dove died;
    And I have thought it died of grieving:
O, what could it grieve for? Its feet were tied,
    With a silken thread of my own hand's weaving;
    Sweet little red feet! why should you die—
Why should you leave me, sweet bird! Why?
You lived alone in the forest-tree,
Why, pretty thing! would you not live with me?
I kissed you oft and gave you white peas;
Why not live sweetly, as in the green trees?
                    John Keats

SHAKESPEARE THE BARD OF AVON

ALMOST in the centre of England stands the old town of Stratford on Avon. It is a beautiful old-world town which has thousands of visitors every year. They come from the four corners of the world to visit the birthplace of the most famous poet of all time, William Shakespeare. Stratford on Avon is always considered Shakespeare's town, although his great work was done in London, but there is no doubt that much of his inspiration came from the wonderful country near his home.

If you visit Stratford you will find many reminders of Shakespeare and his times. There is the house where he was born, the Grammar School which he attended, and the old farm-house in a neighbouring village where his wife lived. He was born on 23rd April, 1564, to parents who, whilst not very rich, were in comfortable circumstances. His father dealt in meat, skins and similar products, and when he was old enough William was sent to Stratford Grammar School. His schoolmaster, Master Roche, believed that to spare the rod was to spoil the child, and we can be sure school was not a very pleasant place. Lessons commenced at six o'clock in the morning, and with half an hour's interval for breakfast they continued until half-past eleven. Afternoon school started at one o'clock, and continued until half-past five, with only one half-hour's interval. At lunch William would wait on his parents at table, and when they had finished he would start. He would always address his father as " sir."

WHY DID SHAKESPEARE LEAVE STRATFORD ?

At thirteen years of age Shakespeare had to leave the grammar school, as his father's business had declined and he had become a poor man. Nobody really knows what Shakespeare did in the next five years. We do know, however, that when he was eighteen he married Anne Hathaway, a lady eight years his senior. We believe the marriage was not very successful, and when Shakespeare was twenty-one we hear of him going up to London. Some writers say that he left Stratford in a hurry as he had got into trouble poaching deer on the estate of Sir Thomas Lucy, at Charlecote, three miles

William Shakespeare (1564-1616) who is undoubtedly the greatest of our dramatic poets.

out of Stratford. It may have been so, but it was a common practice of bright young men in those days to go up to London to seek their fortunes.

Of his first eight years in London, nothing is known. Many people think he must have travelled abroad, so great is the knowledge of foreign customs and characters shown in his plays. Whatever he did, he must have mixed with " all sorts and conditions of men," and that is a fine education for an alert mind. We can be sure he had visited both the London theatres, the Curtain in Moor Fields and the Theatre in Shoreditch. Both theatres were outside London in those days, and gentlemen rode on their horses to either of them. Some people say that Shakespeare held the gentlemen's horses at one time. We do know for certain, however, that he soon obtained work in the theatre.

Later he became an actor, and afterwards was employed altering plays and making them suitable for stage production. Of course, there were no actresses in those days, women's parts being taken by boys. That is one reason

This old print shows the Globe Theatre, Southwark, about the year 1612. It was here that so many of Shakespeare's plays were first performed and met with popular acclaim.

hy several of the women in Shakespeare's ays act as men for part of the play (*e.g.* Rosa- nd, Portia). It is not a long step from dapting plays to writing plays, and when he as twenty-seven Shakespeare wrote his first ay, *Love's Labour's Lost*.

FAVOURITE AT COURT

During the next twenty years Shakespeare rote thirty-six plays. He became very rich nd popular, having many friends among the oblemen at the court. Queen Elizabeth was ery fond of his poetry which he read to her, nd of his plays which he had acted at court. ame and popularity did not spoil Shakespeare, he man. He was anxious to retire to his native own, and in 1597 he bought New Place, then large house in Stratford.

In the year 1610 Shakespeare settled for ood in Stratford. His mother was dead but is father was still living. His eldest daughter ad married a local doctor, and his other aughter Judith lived with her mother. In ebruary 1616 he attended Judith's wedding at tratford, and a few days later he entertained

some of his old London friends, among them Ben Jonson, a great writer. As soon as they departed people noticed that Shakespeare looked ill. On 23rd April, 1616, he passed away, leaving behind him his incomparable bequest to us.

The fact that we know so little of Shakespeare's private life has given rise to much speculation and much guesswork as to how he lived. Apart from parish registers, and a few references to him in the works of others, there is not a large amount of data available, but in his plays and poems we find many utterances from which learned men have gleaned many facts.

HOW DID SHAKESPEARE LEARN ABOUT FOREIGN LANDS?

The fact that the mean and spiteful Justice Shallow in *The Merry Wives of Windsor* is said to be a pen-portrait of Sir Thomas Lucy has led people to believe that the story of his deer poaching on Sir Thomas Lucy's estate is true. Other critics think that, because his references to foreign countries are so accurate, he must

The Shakespeare Memorial Theatre stands beside the River Avon at Stratford. The annual season of plays attracts large numbers of visitors both from home and overseas.

SCENES FROM SHAKESPEARE'S *RICHARD III*

The Court of Edward IV. The King's brothers, Richard (later Richard III) and George, Duke of Clarence, his young sons, the Princes in the Tower, and his Queen are in attendance.

On the instructions of their uncle, now Richard III, the little Princes in the Tower, Edward V and his brother Richard, are murdered by hired assassins, as they lie sleeping.

Colour photographs by courtesy of London Films International Ltd.

have been a much travelled man, and could not possibly be the man we think him to be. These people forget that the Elizabethan Age was one of travel and adventure, and that London was full of men who were much travelled.

The theatre for which Shakespeare wrote was a very different affair from the theatre of to-day. It was a crude structure with the stage in the middle and the pit open to the skies. In the pit apprentices and poorer workmen stood and jostled each other, while the people who could afford it sat in covered galleries round the outside. At the side of the stage, young gallants sat drinking and smoking. Ladies seldom went to the theatre, and if they did, they wore masks. It was not considered proper for ladies to visit such a place. There was no scenery, but a few properties such as a barrel for an inn, a sail for a ship, a few branches for a wood, would represent the scene. The audience no doubt had much more imagination in those days.

WHEN GENIUSES MET IN A TAVERN

Shakespeare was fortunate to live at a time when there were many famous poets and writers. It is said that he was friendly with Christopher Marlowe, who was a poet and dramatist of no mean order. There is no doubt that Marlowe's works had considerable influence on Shakespeare. Then there was " Rare Ben Jonson," Dekker, Middleton, Massinger and Webster, and Greene. What a fine company of geniuses these must have made as they gathered together at the Mermaid Tavern, in Bread Street, in the City. The advent of the plague during 1593-4 interrupted his play-writing, as the theatres were closed, and so he turned to poetry. He wrote two very long poems, *Venus and Adonis* and *The Rape of Lucrece*, dedicating them to the Earl of Southampton, who made him a present of £1,000, which was a large sum in those days and worth at least three times its present value.

Between the years 1600-6 Shakespeare wrote his most famous tragedies, *Hamlet, Othello, Macbeth*, and *King Lear*. He also wrote *The Merry Wives of Windsor* to please Queen Elizabeth, who, we are told, wanted him to write a play showing the huge, bucolic Falstaff in love. No writer ever portrayed such a large number of characters, all so different and yet so living. His characters are no ciphers, but real flesh and blood people with whom we laugh or are sad according to the occasion. To create such subjects consistently is the work of a genius such as the world cannot hope to see in every generation.

SONNET

CXVI

Let me not to the marriage of true minds
Admit impediments. Love is not love
Which alters when it alteration finds,
Or bends with the remover to remove:
O no; it is an ever-fixèd mark,
That looks on tempests, and is never shaken;
It is the star to every wandering bark,
Whose worth's unknown, although his height be taken.
Love's not Time's fool, though rosy lips and cheeks
Within his bending sickle's compass come;
Love alters not with his brief hours and weeks,
But bears it out even to the edge of doom.
    If this be error, and upon me prov'd
    I never writ, nor no man ever lov'd.

William Shakespeare

ELIZABETH I

A Glorious Reign

Elizabeth I. 1558—1603.

IT WAS with a deep sigh of relief that, in 1558, England learned that " Bloody Mary " was dead and her half-sister Elizabeth seated on the throne. But what a thorny path lay before the new Queen! Her realm was poor, ill-armed and simmering with religious discord. Her title to the throne was threatened. And two rival continental giants, France and Spain, with the Pope spurring them on, were trying to gain control of her country for their own ends.

But Henry VIII's proud and talented daughter soon showed herself equal to the occasion. She was a comely young woman of twenty-five, quick of intellect and fond of gay pleasures. But she was also shrewd and wily— and not above telling diplomatic lies. She had her own method of *getting* her own way. She would run fearful political risks, and her womanish whims and caprices often made her friends despair and her enemies gnash their teeth.

REVIVAL OF PROTESTANT LAWS

Elizabeth early tackled the vexed question of the warring creeds. She was not deeply religious and, whatever her own views may have been, she hated extremists of any kind. Her immediate need was to close the gulfs that were dividing and weakening the nation. So she devised a plan to open up a middle way and make it broad and accommodating enough for all except papists and advanced reformers to walk in. The plan was carried out by Acts of Parliament passed in 1559 and by other measures. The Protestant cause was continually waxing stronger and, recognising this, the Queen reversed Mary's backward step into Roman Catholicism and revived Edward VI's Protestant laws with some judicious modifications as a sop to moderate Catholics. Everyone was required to attend Church services and otherwise conform to the religious laws under pain of fines or more severe penalties. The Queen's wisdom was well rewarded. As time went on the bulk of the nation settled down to the new system and the independent Anglican Church, much as it exists to-day, was established.

THE RISE OF THE PURITANS

None the less, there were exceptions. The staunchest of the Catholics still clung to their popish creed. And the advanced reformers, influenced by their continental associates, felt strongly that the Reformation had not gone far enough. They sought to reduce the power of the lordly bishops. They condemned priestly vestments, church ornaments and music, the sign of the Cross in baptism and other ritual usages. All such rags of popish superstition, they declared, should be swept away and the Church restored to its ancient purity and simplicity: hence their name of " Puritans." Most Puritans were followers of Calvin, the great French reformer; and they believed in the grim doctrine of " predestination ": that every individual's salvation or damnation was preordained by God. For a while the Puritans as a whole remained in the Anglican Church; but soon certain extremists entirely rejected it and claimed that every church congregation

Mary, Queen of Scots, the beautiful but ill-fated Queen, who was beheaded.

in Europe. France, too, was Catholic, but strongly infected with the Protestantism of the Huguenot sect. The Pope was sternly bent on riveting the Catholic fetters on Elizabeth's kingdom again and Philip was his foremost champion. Thus religion and power-politics were inseparably joined together.

It was Philip who made the first forward move. Early in 1559 he sent Elizabeth a proposal of marriage. But the wary young queen found it rather too much like the spider's invitation to the fly and politely declined to be snared. Then France began to close in. She already had a firm footing in Scotland. French troops were stationed there and the two countries were in league. The Catholic Mary Stuart, Queen of Scots, had recently become Queen of France by marriage. And she claimed the English Crown, either immediately or as successor to Elizabeth, as a descendent of Henry VII's daughter Margaret.

RELATIONS WITH SCOTLAND

There was trouble going on in Scotland; there mostly had been during the two hundred years of Stuart " rule." But recently another disturbing factor had added to the turmoil. The Reformation had come and the people, with many of the powerful lords, had ardently adopted its more advanced teachings. A blazing patriotism combined with this religious zeal to fill the reforming party with a fierce hatred of the alien and papist French. In 1559 Elizabeth had grave fears that the French giant was about to force his way into her citadel by the postern gate of Scotland. So she took one of her inspired risks. She faced him boldly and, in 1560, with the help of the Scottish reformers, drove him out neck and crop.

should be a separate and independent unit, governed by self-chosen pastors and elders.

Elizabeth detested the Puritans for they disturbed her religious settlement. And opposition in religious affairs was apt to lead to opposition in political affairs—in Parliament for instance. So she sternly repressed the whole movement—for a time. There could be no question of tolerating different forms of religious belief. It would have been foreign to the spirit of the age. To most sincere believers heresy was a sin that ought to be suppressed. Moreover, religion and patriotism had became inseparable. There must be one national Church and every loyal citizen must conform to it or pay the penalty.

EUROPEAN POWER-POLITICS

Meanwhile, from the opening of the reign, the two continental giants, Spain and France, were cautiously circling round the island citadel of their hoped-for prey. The Emperor Charles V had abdicated; Spain and France were competing for dominance in Europe; and each coveted control of the little island kingdom as an almost decisive make-weight in the contest. Spain was now in the ascendant. Its rabidly Catholic king, Philip II, ruled also the Netherlands, parts of Italy and the vast regions of the New World, and his soldiers were the finest

MARY, QUEEN OF SCOTS

In the same year Mary, through her husband's death, lost the French throne. She was a passionate, vivacious and untameable creature. In 1565 she made a love-match with the contemptible Lord Darnley, whom she quickly learned to despise. An heir, James, was born and, next year, her husband was found strangled. Mary thereupon married the murderer, the ruffianly Earl of Bothwell. But the Scottish nobles, convinced that she had been a party to the crime, imprisoned her and forced her to abdicate. In 1568, however, she broke loose and, galloping across the Border, threw herself desperately into her rival Elizabeth's citadel.

She remained in the English Queen's custody for nineteen years. They were years of tremendous consequence in the battle of the giants and of Elizabeth's astute manœuvres in playing off one against the other. France was hamstrung by internal religious wars. The Protestants in the Netherlands revolted against Spain. The Pope excommunicated and deposed Elizabeth. In England there was a Catholic rising, followed by sinister Jesuit plots. And, in between, the most diabolical conspiracies were hatched by Elizabeth's enemies for " removing " the heretic queen, crowning Mary and restoring the Roman creed. Then came the Babington plot for Elizabeth's assassination. Mary's complicity was proved and, in 1587, she paid the penalty with her head.

SPAIN ROUSED TO ACTION

The hour had already struck for Philip, England's foremost foe in the existing weakness of France, to seek a show-down. Religious duty, political ambition and countless provocations received at the island Queen's hands, all urged him irresistibly forward. From the beginning Elizabeth had played cat-and-mouse with him. She was brazenly supporting his rebellious Dutch subjects. Her privateers were wantonly boarding his merchant ships in the Channel. And her sea-captains, with insufferable audacity, were challenging his monopoly in the New World. He began to build his Armada.

THE SEAMEN-EXPLORERS

England was ready for the death-grapple. She knew what were the stakes: freedom of country and creed waged against a foreign despotism and the Catholic fetters riveted on again by the tortures of the Spanish Inquisition. Her people, save for the most bigoted Catholics, were united in passionate loyalty to an adored Queen. A violent attack of " growing pains," sending them voyaging into unknown seas, had made them hardy and confident mariners. Hawkins, Raleigh and Drake had sailed boldly to the Spanish Main and beyond to trade or to flout and pillage the hidalgos, their ports and treasure ships. Frobisher and Davis had gone

Francis Bacon, lawyer, writer, favourite of the Queen and Lord Chancellor.

seeking a north-west passage to the East. Gilbert claimed Newfoundland. Raleigh— though unsuccessfully—attempted a colony in " Virginia."

THE ARMADA DEFEATED

So the Armada sailed out of Corunna in July, 1588. And the English fleet, with its new type of fast, handy and well-gunned ships, drummed it up the Channel, shot it to pieces off Gravelines and left the elements to do the rest. The stupendous victory, followed up by further successes and good fortune, saved England from her dire peril and made her the leading sea power of the time.

A REVIEW OF THE REIGN

The reign of Good Queen Bess, the last of the Tudors, which ended in 1603, saw England raised in power and prestige. She had preserved her independence and established her national Church. Trade and commerce grew

Sir Francis Drake, circumnavigator of the world, who vanquished the Spanish Armada.

by leaps and bounds as her ships ploughed the remotest seas, from the Russian north to the Far East and the American west. Another, but less creditable, performance was the conquest of Ireland. The whole country was brought into subjection. But the work was done by ferocious measures that laid great areas of the island waste and sowed the seeds of grievous evils.

In the field of literature the nation seemed to break into flower. Its joyous energy, stimulated by the new learning and the quickened outlook on life men call the Renaissance, or Re-birth, found expression in imperishable works of the intellect and the imagination. Spenser, Hooker, Francis Bacon, Marlowe, Ben Jonson and the matchless Shakespeare are but the brightest of the many jewels that shed their lustre over and beyond the reign.

A WORD IN YOUR EAR

If you asked a crowd of people which was the loveliest musical instrument, you would probably receive half a dozen different replies. Many might vote for the great range of the piano or the organ, others might prefer the solo qualities of the violin. The more thoughtful would ponder upon the claims of the human voice. It has a peculiar claim, because it is the only musical instrument that every normal person possesses.

Perhaps because it is universal, people give little thought to it. They acknowledge the greatness of a famous singer, or the art of an actor or actress who can make words sing; but they do not think of their own voices, in the same way as you probably seldom think about yours.

It is very odd that everywhere one is given advice about care and treatment of every part from the topmost curl to the toe-nail; advice about dress and colour, deportment, health. Yet the most charming man, or the most beautifully dressed woman, can ruin the effect if the voice is unpleasant or badly produced. And there are very, very few voices that cannot be attractive, if the best is made of them.

There are many young people who take great pains not to walk in a slovenly fashion, not to dress carelessly; yet when it comes to talking—and in the course of a year thousands of people hear your voice—they are slovenly indeed, lazy-lipped and wretchedly untidy.

Listen to the poets—and remember their words:

" I thank you for your voices—thank you— your most sweet voices." And of Cordelia, the daughter of King Lear: " Her voice was ever soft, gentle, and low: an excellent thing in woman."

Byron writes:

" *The devil hath not, in all his quiver's choice,*
An arrow for the heart like a sweet voice."

Nothing is more revealing of personality and temperament than the voice; there is no surer barometer of mood.

" *All thy smiles and all thy tears*
In thy sweet voice awaken."

James Russell Lowell was right when he wrote that. What does *your* voice betray? It ought to reveal the best in you; it can be a delight. It will not be unless you give it thought.

James I. 1603–25.

JAMES I

A Stuart becomes
King of England

O NE OF the few notable things that James I did was to found the Stuart line of English sovereigns. He was already James VI of Scotland, and he succeeded Elizabeth I in 1603, as the son of Mary Queen of Scots, a descendant of Henry VII. He was hardly the sort of man to give the new dynasty a good send-off. He could not, of course, be blamed for his grotesque figure and slobbering tongue, nor perhaps for his cowardice and indolence and arrogance. But he need not have been, as he so often was, as bookish and long-winded as a pompous dominie lecturing his class.

Two fortunate changes in England's position in Europe distinguish the reign. Scotland (still ruled as a separate kingdom) became more of an ally than a foe. And Spain, beginning to show evidences of decline, ceased to be the national bogy. The period was also one in which an extremely mixed collection of seeds was sown in the garden of England, to germinate in growths as stupendous as the one we used to read about in *Jack and the Beanstalk*.

THE COLONIAL EMPIRE

One of these high-powered seeds sprouted so lustily that its towering growth now overshadows the world. In 1607 a colony—the real beginning of England's colonial empire was successfully planted in Virginia. It was the first of a group that, later, was to expand into the United States of America. A little later the Bermuda Islands were settled.

THE PILGRIM FATHERS

The religious question led to the sowing of a second seed of the same character. James strongly supported the Anglican Church and the order of bishops. Like Elizabeth, he regarded the Puritans' opposition as the sign of a dangerously independent attitude that might presently extend itself to political concerns—as, in fact, it did. The persecution under which disobedient Puritans suffered drove a small sect of Independents—those who rejected the Anglican Church and wished to establish their own self-governing churches—to emigrate to Holland. In 1620 a number of this devoted band, with others from England (the Pilgrim Fathers), courageously crossed the Atlantic in the famous *Mayflower* and founded the Puritan settlement of New Plymouth.

THE GUNPOWDER PLOT

James was compelled, against his will, to deal severely with Catholics. One result was the Gunpowder Plot of 1605 which we celebrate with such explosive enthusiasm on 5th November. Guy Fawkes and other crack-pots tried to blow up the House of Lords, plus the King, plus the Prince of Wales, plus the Lords and Commons, with a couple of tons of gunpowder.

JAMES AND PARLIAMENT

James was a well-meaning and, in some ways, a wise ruler, but he completely failed to understand his new subjects. His overbearing attitude towards Parliament well illustrates this. During the storm and stress of Tudor times Parliament had allowed itself to be dominated by its popular and tactful sovereigns. Towards the end of Elizabeth's reign, however, the Commons had been getting restive and they now made it plain to the first of the Stuarts that they meant to assert their ancient hard-won constitutional rights again—with perhaps a few new ones. The race that had achieved so much under Elizabeth's rule felt itself fit for a larger share in its own government. The Puritans were strongly represented in the Commons, which was composed largely of middle-class country gentlemen, or squires, wealthy merchants and lawyers.

THE DIVINE RIGHT OF KINGS

The King was entirely out of sympathy with this mood. His notions of his own rights, indeed, were flatly opposed to it. He believed in the theory that kings ruled by divine right, that they could make and unmake laws at their pleasure and that opposition to their will was not only seditious but sinful. The preposterous claim was admitted by many perfectly sane people, including the Anglican bishops, who supported the king partly because he supported them. But they most emphatically did *not* include the members of the House of Commons. Apart from this James also had his own ideas about the extent of his prerogative. It was generally agreed that the sovereign enjoyed the sole right of dealing with certain special subjects, such as foreign affairs and other matters of state. But James stretched his powers far beyond these limits. Moreover, he gave the Commons a rap over the knuckles with his schoolmaster's ferule by forbidding them even to debate such subjects. The King was either too wise or too lazy to press his theories over-hard, but it was plain that this particular seed of his sowing was likely to produce a fatally poisonous weed. As it was, the Commons stubbornly insisted on their rights of free speech and of prosecuting any offending royal minister, besides denouncing arbitrary taxation.

ATTEMPTED FRIENDSHIP WITH SPAIN

James's friendly feeling for England's arch-enemy, Spain, was another of his offences. He

Elizabeth, daughter of James I, and grandmother of George I, married the Elector Palatine of the Rhine, who later became King of Bohemia.

made peace with the reigning Catholic king, Philip III. He tried to marry his son Charles to a Spanish princess. To please Philip he had England's admired Elizabethan hero, Sir Walter Raleigh, shamefully executed on an old charge of treason. At the end of his reign he was completely dominated by his favourite, " Steenie," the Duke of Buckingham. This court pet was an attractive individual, not without ability, but swollen with a vast conceit. He ardently supported the proposed Spanish marriage and, when it failed, a fit of pique drove him to favour an alliance with France. In 1624, the year before his father died, Prince Charles was betrothed to the French King's Catholic sister, Henrietta Maria.

A seed of particular interest to us to-day was sown when James married his daughter Elizabeth, the lovely " Queen of Hearts," to Frederick, the Protestant Elector Palatine of the Rhine. It is from that ancient union that our present line of sovereigns descends.

" The Nativity " by Piero della Francesca (1420-92), a symbolic painting of great beauty.

THE BIBLE

The Story of the New Testament

WE do not know precisely when the founder of the Christian religion was born, but it was during the reign of Herod, who died in 4 B.C. Palestine was then part of the vast Roman Empire, a fact which many of the Jews bitterly resented. They dreamed of the day when a leader would appear and restore the brief glories they enjoyed long ago when David was king.

There were various prophecies in the scriptures which spoke of a Messiah to be sent by God to deliver them. They expected a warrior prince who would organise a revolt and establish an earthly kingdom. But when the Messiah came they did not recognise Him. He was of humble birth and declared that His kingdom was not of this world.

Moreover, the message of salvation He

136

brought was not only purely spiritual, but was offered to Jews and Gentiles alike. This was not what the orthodox Jews wanted and they denounced the Messiah as an impostor and a blasphemer. They handed Him over to the Roman governor who somewhat reluctantly yielded to their demand that he should be crucified.

THE LIFE OF JESUS

The only written record of the life and teachings of Jesus Christ is found in the collection of books known as the New Testament. It also contains an account of how His followers spread His teachings far beyond the confines of Palestine to Rome itself. Just as the Old Testament predicted the coming of the Messiah, so the New Testament contains prophecies of His return and the end of the world. These are found in the last Book which is called the Revelations or the Apocalypse, but they are veiled in allegory.

For what is known of the life of Jesus, we must turn to the four Gospels—the word literally means Good News—written by some of the disciples, or later followers. Mark's Gospel is probably the first of the documents that have come down to us. Luke and Matthew made use of Mark's version, but they added interesting new material. Luke was not a Jew, and he addressed himself mainly to non-Jewish Christians; Matthew, on the other hand, wrote primarily for converted Jews, like himself.

The story that emerges from their writings is simple and profoundly moving. Matthew tells us that a carpenter called Joseph lived in Nazareth, and one night he had a dream in which an angel told him that his wife, Mary, would give miraculous birth to a child, whom he must call Jesus. According to Luke, Mary also had a vision that she would give birth to a child which had no human father and would be known as the Son of God.

THE BIRTH AND FLIGHT INTO EGYPT

Before Jesus was born the Roman authorities issued a decree for everyone to be taxed, each person going to his own city to register. Joseph and Mary, belonging to the House of David accordingly left Nazareth and went to Bethlehem where she gave birth to a son. There was no room for them in the local inn

" The Infant St. John with the Lamb " by Murillo (1618-82). On the banner are the words " Behold the Lamb of God " in Latin.

and they had to shelter in a stable. The child was laid in a manger.

In Luke's Gospel we read that neighbouring shepherds saw a vision of angels singing "Glory to God in the Highest, and on earth peace, goodwill towards men." Matthew, however, has an account of astrologers from the East who came to Jerusalem because they believed that a child had been born destined to be king of the Jews. Fearing that this might mean an insurrectionary movement, Herod caused a search to be made for the child. Joseph and Mary decided to take refuge across the Egyptian border until the danger had passed.

They remained in Egypt until the death of Herod, and this was a wise precaution because a number of babies born in Bethlehem and the neighbourhood were put to death.

JOHN THE BAPTIST

Meanwhile, another prophet was proclaiming that a tremendous event had taken place.

John the Baptist, as he was known, had attracted a considerable following by his preaching. He lived in the desert and baptized those who repented of their sins in the River Jordan. He continually repeated that he was only the forerunner of one who would be stronger and holier than he, and who would baptize with the Spirit and not merely with water.

No one knew to whom these mysterious words referred until Jesus Himself was greeted by John when He asked to be baptized. At first John refused, protesting that he was unworthy but finally he acceded, and we are told that on this solemn occasion a voice from heaven was heard saying, " This is my beloved Son, in whom I am well pleased."

There is a dearth of information about the years which Jesus spent with Mary and Joseph. It is presumed that He learned the trade of a carpenter, but His precocity made a startling impression. When He was taken to Jerusalem on a visit He amazed the learned Rabbis by His knowledge of the Scriptures. It has been calculated, however, that the accounts of the life of Jesus given in the Gospels only cover about fifty days. The short period about which we possess records is packed with dramatic incidents. It begins with the baptism at the hands of John when Jesus was about thirty years of age, and ends as a ministry with the crucifixion in A.D. 29 or 30.

THE FORTY-DAY FAST

One difficulty in understanding the momentous happenings described in the Gospels is that they cannot be judged by ordinary standards. To Christians, at least, Christ is both human and divine. Because they believe in His divinity the miracles He worked become intelligible. But there were times when the human side of His personality strongly showed itself.

It did so after His baptism, when He retired into a barren region and fasted for forty days. He fully realised then that He was the Messiah, whom the prophets had foretold. His temptations in the wilderness suggest that an appeal was made to His human side to make use of superhuman powers in order to demonstrate that He was indeed the Son of God. But He did not yield to this temptation and already foresaw the bitter ordeal through which He must finally pass.

JESUS SPREADS HIS MESSAGE

When He began to preach, John the Baptist had been thrown into prison, later to be beheaded. Jesus made Capernaum, a town on the coast, the centre from which He spread his message throughout Galilee. Large crowds flocked to hear Him, bringing their sick because of His reputation as a healer. He spoke to them in a language that the most illiterate peasant and fisherman could understand, making use of parables or stories, to illustrate His points.

But He did not wish to appear as a mere wonder worker—that was one of the temptations He had overcome after His long fast. He was more concerned with men's souls than with their bodies, although the sight of suffering never failed to move Him to compassion.

His fame reached beyond Galilee and Jordan. People flocked to hear this itinerant preacher about whom such remarkable rumours had spread. They found Him travelling with twelve of His most trusted followers and He would halt by the wayside or by the shores of a lake or on a hill to address the crowds. He not only cured many who were sick, but He seemed able to read their inmost thoughts.

What manner of man was this? The leaders of the Jewish Church were disturbed by His popularity. It seemed to them He was teaching doctrines that were novel and dangerous. They kept scrupulously to the letter of the Mosaic law, but He flouted it by healing the sick, for example, on the Sabbath.

His claim to be greater than the Prophets and to know the will of God better than the Scribes and Pharisees seemed blasphemous presumption. Worse still, He denounced them as hypocrites; and when shortly before His arrest He found that the temple in Jerusalem was used by some for conducting business He drove out the desecrators with a whip.

It is obvious that even His disciples were perplexed at first. Then Peter, a fisherman from Galilee, discovered the answer: " Thou art the Messiah! " he exclaimed. Jesus, at this point, warned them to keep it secret for the present.

The time was not yet ripe to announce publicly what He knew lay ahead, but He told His disciples that soon He would be arrested and crucified. They were incredulous.

The story now moves swiftly to the terrible climax. Jesus could have saved Himself by not

" Christ driving the Traders from the Temple," by El Greco (1541-1614).

going to Jerusalem for the Feast of the Passover, but He knew that His destiny must be fulfilled. They made the journey, with many other pilgrims, for this great annual event, and all disguise was at last thrown off. Jesus entered Jerusalem riding upon an ass, thus fulfilling the prophecy of Zechariah.

Enthusiastic crowds waving palms cheered Him—the same crowds who were soon to demand His death. The temple priests were thoroughly alarmed. This was a direct challenge to their authority. They moved cautiously, however, because this rebel and heretic—as He appeared in their eyes— evidently had a popular following.

JESUS IS BETRAYED

Judas Iscariot, one of the disciples, offered to lead them to Jesus so that He could be taken quietly and for this he was paid thirty pieces of silver. Judas sat down with the disciples at what has come to be known as the Last Supper, and Jesus said that one of them would betray Him, but He mentioned no names. After they had partaken of bread and wine, He withdrew to the garden in Gethsemane, and, although He shrank from the painful death that awaited Him, He submitted to what He had realised from the beginning was the inscrutable purpose of God.

Soldiers burst into the garden while it was still dark and Judas drew their attention to Jesus by an agreed sign—he kissed the Master he had been bribed to betray. Subsequently, overcome with remorse, he hanged himself. When Peter was asked if he was a follower of Jesus he denied it and afterwards wept bitterly because of his momentary cowardice.

THE TRIAL AND CRUCIFIXION

The disciples were dismayed at what they now thought was sheer disaster. For in spite

"Christ after the Flagellation contemplated by the Christian Soul," by Velazquez (1599-1660).

of what Jesus had told them it was hard to believe that if He were the Messiah He could end up like a criminal on the gallows. The priestly tribunal (the Sanhedrin) to which He was brought had no power to pass the death sentence, and they had to frame a charge against Roman laws.

Jesus faced his accusers calmly and when they asked Him if He was the Messiah, He quietly admitted it. To the Jews this was blasphemy; but to the Romans the whole affair was still no more than a sectarian squabble. In order to interest the Romans, the priests had to make it appear that Jesus was the ringleader of a seditious movement. They did so by charging him with having claimed to be " King of the Jews."

When He came face to face with the Roman Procurator, Pilate was impressed by His dignity and plainly baffled by His silence. Pilate appealed to the mob, offering to release either Jesus or Barrabas, a notorious bandit, also under arrest. They demanded that Barrabas should be freed and Jesus crucified.

The perplexed governor ceremoniously washed his hands to indicate that he took no responsibility for sentencing a good man to death. He dismissed the matter from his mind and Jesus was led away to be scourged, according to custom.

His jeering tormentors followed Him through the streets when He carried the cross to which He was to be nailed and left to die. A mock crown of thorns was placed on His head and an inscription " King of the Jews " placed on the cross. He was crucified between two thieves.

THE RESURRECTION

This seemed to be indeed the end, for how could the promised Messiah, the Son of God, suffer such a shameful death? But it was only the beginning of a chain of momentous happenings that changed the course of history.

The traditional site of the garden of Gethsemane on the outskirts of Jerusalem.

Three days after Jesus was crucified, His disciples were astonished to hear that the tomb in which His body was laid was empty. Then they *saw* Him walking towards them.

He was not only seen by the apostles but, according to Paul's version, by five hundred others. Had He been taken down from the Cross whilst still alive? Was it a mass hallucination? Those who witnessed this greatest miracle of all had no doubts. The sacrifice on the Cross was then seen as a prelude to the Resurrection, and this became the central Christian doctrine.

The original band of followers were aflame to spread an account of the wonders they had been privileged to see. They met together on the Day of Pentecost and underwent a profound spiritual illumination. They described this as " the descent of the Holy Spirit " and it is commemorated now at Whitsun.

Understanding of the tremendous happenings in which they were involved came to the disciples in gradual stages. When they were companions of Jesus on His wanderings some of His sayings mystified them, and it was not until His death that at last they understood everything.

THE FIRST MARTYR

Some of the Jewish converts had supposed that the Jews were to be the main channel of communication. They did not grasp that baptism had superseded circumcision, and a new church would take the place of the synagogue.

They preached at first to the Jews, and the orthodox priests regarded them as heretics who must be suppressed. The Nazarenes, as they were at first called, were hunted down, flogged and imprisoned. The first martyr was Stephen who was stoned for blasphemy—the same charge that had been brought against his Master.

Saul of Tarsus, a Greek-speaking Jew and a Roman citizen took a leading part in this persecution. But one day, on the road to Damascus, he had a vision which totally changed his life. He was converted to Christianity.

He then threw all his amazing energy into the task of spreading the new religion. His long, perilous journeys by land and sea, his sufferings and escapes from prison are described in the *Acts of the Apostles*. He founded churches in Asia Minor, Greece and Rome, where, like Peter, he finally met a martyr's death.

From the very beginning the Christians aroused the hostility both of Jews and the ordinarily more tolerant pagans. They would not compromise. Yet the more they were persecuted, the more they multiplied.

HOW THE TESTAMENT WAS WRITTEN

In the early days, of course, they did not possess any writings to which they could appeal as an authority. Those who had walked and talked with Jesus remembered some of the things He had said and made a record out of the oral tradition. The meaning of His sayings —and of His life—was interpreted in letters written by Paul and others to the various scattered communities. That is how the New Testament, which is the source-book of Christianity, came gradually into existence, the earliest part about ten years before the destruction of Jerusalem by the Romans in A.D. 70 and some after that catastrophe.

VASCO DA GAMA
A Famous Portuguese Navigator

THE fifteenth century was the Age of Discovery, an age when the men of Europe suddenly seemed to realise simultaneously that the world was not bounded by the limits of a man's eyesight; and in the swift, almost explosive, expansion that followed, no nation was more venturesome or progressive than the Portuguese. Prince Henry the Navigator, the son of the King of Portugal, with his enthusiasm for maritime discovery, raised Portugal from pettiness to a place among the great powers. The rulers who came after him were less mystical perhaps but no less practical. King John II, who came to the throne in 1481, was a great patron of exploration and discovery; and among those who sailed to the East with his blessing was Vasco da Gama.

THE EXPEDITION TO THE EAST

Vasco da Gama was born, somewhere about 1460 at Sines, his father being governor of the province of Alemtejo. While still a young man, he distinguished himself as both soldier and sailor but it was not until he was thirty-seven years of age that opportunity catapulted him into history. In 1497, he was entrusted with the command of an expedition that was to extend Portuguese sovereignty over the lands of the East. The expedition consisted of no more than four ships, one of which was a small store vessel. Two of them, the *São Raphael* and the *São Gabriel* were of 120 tons burthen. The third, the *Berrio*, was a mere 50 tons. The two large ships, if the term " large " is permissible, were specially constructed for the expedition and incorporated several suggestions from the very experienced explorer, Bartholomeu Diaz. They were larger and sturdier than previous ships had been because Diaz had learned, from bitter experience, the phenomenal power of the storms round the Cape of Good Hope. The *São Gabriel* was da Gama's flagship while the *São Raphael* was commanded by his brother Paul. The total personnel of all the ships was one hundred and seventy. On Saturday morning, 8th July, 1497, the tiny fleet set sail amid great ceremony and the farewells of the king and court. Nineteen days later, the four ships arrived at the Cape Verde Islands. From there, they continued the voyage, at first along the African coast, then later, to avoid storms, on two successive courses that brought them, at one point, to about two hundred leagues from the American coast. Heading south-east, the fleet fought its way back, in the teeth of contrary winds and, on 7th November, dropped anchor in a sheltered mooring which they christened St. Helena Bay. Between 27th July and 7th November they had sailed four thousand, five hundred miles without a landfall.

DIFFICULTIES ENCOUNTERED

Nine days after the arrival in St. Helena Bay, the fleet was on its way again, having in the meantime become embroiled in a skirmish with the Hottentots during which Vasco da Gama narrowly escaped death from a spear. On 22nd November, the store ship, no longer seaworthy, was broken up, its cargo and crew being shared out among the remaining vessels. On Christmas Day there was another christening ceremony and the name of Natal was added to the world's maps. The next halt was at the mouth of the Zambezi. Here the ships were careened and the crews relaxed and recovered from a new disease, that was soon to be familiar as the deficiency disease, scurvy. It was not until the last week in February 1498 that the voyage was resumed; and by the beginning of March, Vasco da Gama and his crews were staring, rather superciliously, at the Arab vessels in the harbour of Mozambique. These vessels seemed, to Portuguese eyes, to be designed rather to sink than to float; but the cargoes they carried were something far more impressive, the Arab ships being loaded down to the water-line with gold, silver, rich spices and the most exquisite silks. It was, however, sufficiently clear that the infidel Europeans were scarcely welcome in Mozambique; so the three ships set off northwards until they reached Mombasa where, if anything, they were even more unpopular. They continued on to Malindi where the ruler was much more amenable. He

Vasco da Gama, who discovered the sea route
to India and later became its Viceroy.

being equally careful, at the same time, to spread a report that his small fleet was merely the forerunner of another fleet twelve times as great in size. Despite this, however, he was kidnapped one day and, but for the presence of mind of his brother, would probably have been murdered. Paul checkmated the attempt by seizing half a dozen of Calicut's leading citizens and holding them as hostages for the safe return of the fleet's commander. The following day, the Portuguese decided wisely to abandon Calicut. They went on to Cannanore and from there to Cochin. Early in August, they began the long voyage home.

THE RETURN JOURNEY

The return journey across the Arabian Sea was a nightmare of calm seas and capricious, unworkable winds. Scurvy broke out among the crews, killing the sailors off like flies. At Malindi, the *São Raphael* was left to its fate because the disease had reduced the ship's complement to such an extent that there were not enough sailors left to work her. Those who survived were barely able to stand. After Malindi, which they.left in January, 1499, their troubles continued. Sickness spread throughout the two ships and the weather was foul. The months dragged on and on until they began to despair of ever seeing their homeland again. Still they persevered, fighting the sea and the wind and the disease that made their hands and feet swell and caused their gums to grow over their teeth. And on 5th September, 1499, they sailed up the Tagus. They were home. They were received as heroes and conquerors, as indeed they were. Honours and rewards were showered upon them. The King of Portugal immediately added to his titles, the new sonority of " Lord of the Conquest, Navigation and Commerce of Ethiopia, Arabia, Persia, and India " and sent out, almost at once, another fleet of thirteen ships whose mission it was to justify, with sword and powder, the new title he had used in a letter to the Pope.

received them courteously, entertained them sumptuously for almost a fortnight and, when they left, provided them with a pilot who guaranteed to navigate the fleet to India.

DA GAMA REACHES INDIA

On 24th April the fleet once more put to sea and for over three weeks sailed steadily towards the north-east. 18th May saw them altering course to sail due east and in another four days they had reached the Malabar coast and were anchored at Calicut, the place that immortalised itself by giving its name to the cloth calico. The situation here was difficult and there was no relaxation for the weary men who had left Lisbon almost a year previously. The Arabs, who controlled the industries of Calicut, had no wish to lose their monopoly and stirred up the natives against the newcomers. Vasco da Gama behaved diplomatically, being careful to avoid all friction and

A PUNITIVE EXPEDITION

In 1500 Vasco da Gama entreated the King to allow him to lead a punitive expedition against Calicut. He had a long memory and the recollection of his almost fatal kidnapping during the earlier voyage apparently still rankled. He repaid his score in full, reducing Calicut to a bloodstained heap of ashes. He returned from this second and less praiseworthy voyage in 1503 and was honoured by the title of Count of Vidigueira. A new office, that of the Admiralty of India, was created especially for him and the revenue from this office made him one of the wealthiest noblemen in the country. For the next twenty years or so, he was content to live quietly on his vast estates.

But the sea was not yet finished with him. In 1524 he was offered the post of Viceroy in the East and accepted it eagerly. He sailed off, a man of sixty-four, to take up his duties. He was not to be long in office. The onerous duties of his new dignity combined with the Indian climate to limit his term of office to a mere two months. At the end of that short period, he fell sick of fever and on Christmas Eve 1524, Vasco da Gama died.

TWO PROBLEMS

A TIME PROBLEM How many minutes is it to three o'clock if twenty minutes ago it was three times as many minutes past one?

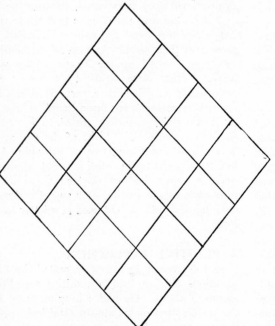

ALL DIAMONDS How many diamonds are there altogether?

For solutions see page 147.

SIR WALTER RALEIGH

A Famous Elizabethan

IF ONE figure had to be taken to typify the first Elizabethan era in all its turbulence, restlessness, and imaginative brilliance, then that figure would surely be Sir Walter Raleigh, politician, poet, sailor, soldier, explorer and writer of history, a man whose versatility makes him almost unchallenged as the spirit of his age.

He was born, probably in the year 1552, at Hayes Barton in Devon. He arrived into a large family, his father having married three times, the third time to a widow who already had three children of her own. Altogether, there were nine children in the family. One of these went to Eton; the rest grew up and were educated at Hayes Barton. When they were not being schooled, they roamed the countryside and no doubt spent many pleasant and profitable hours at the nearby ports of Exmouth and Budleigh Salterton. At the age of fifteen, in pursuit of more formal teaching, Walter was sent to Oriel College, Oxford, where he remained until the beginning of 1569, when he joined a band of volunteers who went to France to help the Huguenots. Four years later, he was back in London, a tough, hardened, sunburned man who was both soldier and sailor. The new plan was that he should study law, but this dry-as-dust subject did not fire his imagination and was soon abandoned in favour of the fascinating business of exploration. In 1578, Raleigh's half-brother, Humphrey Gilbert was given the royal permission for an attempt to discover a north-west passage to the Indies and Raleigh joined him in the enterprise. The expedition was a failure but Raleigh's appetite had been whetted. It was an appetite he was never to lose.

A GALLANT KNIGHT

In 1580, Raleigh obtained, through influence, the command of a hundred men in the suppression of the Desmond Rebellion in Ireland. Here, he rapidly distinguished himself and in 1581, as a mark of favour, he was sent to London with dispatches for the Queen. From this moment, he was a made man. The tall, handsome, witty Raleigh was immediately established as the court favourite. Honours were showered on him. He was rewarded with huge tracts of the confiscated Desmond lands in Ireland. He was granted patents for selling cloth and licensing the sale of wine. Another appointment gave him control of the mining industry in Devon and Cornwall. In 1584 he was knighted. Later he was presented with the manor of Sherborne. He was not, however, content with the life of a parasitic court favourite and in 1583, he again joined with his half-brother in an attempt to establish an English colony in the New World. For this he built a four-masted ship, the *Ark Raleigh*, which later became the *Ark Royal* and, as flagship of Lord Howard of Effingham against the Armada, began a famous naval tradition. It was Raleigh's intention to command the new ship but the Queen refused to sanction this and the expedition sailed without him. The five ships reached Newfoundland and, for eleven days, England had a colony there. Then the settlers demanded to be taken away from the land of cold and fogs. On the homeward voyage, all but one of the ships foundered. Humphrey Gilbert was among those drowned. Raleigh promptly had the dead man's patent transferred to himself and, along with several friends, he formed a Fellowship for the Discovery of the North-West Passage. In 1584, the first Fellowship expedition set out and founded the colony of Virginia, returning the following year with a number of settlers. Again the venture failed and the survivors were brought back to England by Francis Drake. Two further ventures failed, and it is interesting—and tantalising—to speculate on what might have happened had Queen Elizabeth allowed Raleigh to lead his ventures in person.

RALEIGH INCURS THE QUEEN'S DISPLEASURE

Raleigh was in Ireland when news of the Spanish Armada reached him and he hurried home to take up his duties as Vice-Admiral of Devon and Cornwall. There is no certain record of his activities about this time but the following year he was very prominent in an

Sir Walter Raleigh with his son, painted in
1602 by an unknown artist.

Dorado. Early in 1595, he set out with a fleet
of five ships and having overcome the Spanish
at Trinidad, he embarked with a hundred men
towards what he hoped was the final goal of
his ambition. The story of his four-hundred-
mile journey up the Orinoco may be read in
The Discoverie of Guiana which Raleigh wrote
and published on his return to England. Apart
from this fine book, the expedition was mainly
abortive. In 1596 and the year following, we
hear of Raleigh engaged in various pin-pricking
raids against Spain.

ON TRIAL FOR CONSPIRACY

In 1603, Queen Elizabeth died and James VI
of Scotland came to the throne. Raleigh
appears to have been somewhat laggard in
declaring his loyalty to the new monarch,
whereupon James dismissed him from the
Court and stripped him of both honours and
lands. It is possible, although no satisfactory
evidence was ever produced, that Raleigh,
infuriated by this unjust and peremptory action
on the part of James, joined one of the
numerous conspiracies that were afoot against
the new and unpopular monarch. In any case,
he was arrested and tried on a charge of conspiring against the King's life. While awaiting
trial, he tried to commit suicide; but when he
was finally brought to trial, his conduct, in face
of the hectoring Attorney-General was calm,
brave and entirely admirable. " When the trial
began," an enemy said, " I would have gone
a thousand miles to see Raleigh hang; before
the trial closed I would have gone a thousand
miles to save his life." The thousand-mile walk
would have been futile. The trial was a sheer
fabrication and an obedient jury convicted
Raleigh of treason. He was, accordingly,
sentenced to death. Public outcry, however,
persuaded the always cautious James to com-
mute the sentence to life imprisonment.

IN THE TOWER

For the next thirteen years, therefore,
Raleigh was left in the Tower of London.
Characteristically, he made the most of his
time. There were the chemical experiments by
which he thought to discover the elixir of life
or the magic stone of the philosophers. There
were the beautiful poems he wrote which stand
comparison with anything else in the Elizabethan anthology. There was the prose *History*

action against the Spaniards off Gravelines.
He took part, too, in an attempt, which failed,
to set a king, hostile to Spain, on the Portuguese
throne. By this time, his star, as favourite,
had set, at least temporarily. The new favourite
was the Earl of Essex, and Raleigh was severely
reprimanded for challenging him to a duel. A
tactical retreat seemed to be in order and
Raleigh retired to his estates in Ireland. By
1590 he was again in London and reinstated
in favour. Two years later, he was in prison
for having dared to marry Elizabeth Throg-
morton, a lady-in-waiting. He languished in
the Tower for several months and only obtained
his release by making over to the Queen most
of the proceeds brought back by his fleet of
privateers which had had a most successful
encounter with Spanish treasure-galleons.

THE SEARCH FOR EL DORADO

Now, at last, Raleigh was free to attempt
something that had long been in his mind—
the discovery of the fabled city of gold, El

of the World which he was writing for Prince Henry, the ill-fated heir to the throne who died in 1611 and who, with his mother, was one of Raleigh's great admirers and champions. There were, too, the letters to the King himself in which Raleigh pleaded to be allowed to renew his search for El Dorado.

A MAN OF COURAGE AND ENTERPRISE

At last, in 1617, James agreed and sent Raleigh, now 65, to find a fabulous mine in Guiana of which he had heard and which had aroused his cupidity. Before he left, Raleigh was forced to promise not to come into conflict with the Spaniards, a promise which he broke largely because, it almost seems, attacking Spaniards had become as automatic as drawing breath. The Spanish Ambassador demanded his execution as a pirate when he returned home, having failed in his object and leaving his son dead on a foreign shore. James hurried to placate the Spaniard and Raleigh was executed under his former sentence which had never been revoked. On the scaffold, he asked to see the axe and commended the sharpness of its edge. " This is a sharp medicine, but it is a sure cure for all diseases." Thus, bravely, died Sir Walter Raleigh, a man who never succeeded in founding a colony but succeeded in establishing the colonising spirit, the man who introduced tobacco to this country, the man who had enough talents for several ordinary men, one of the greatest figures in one of the greatest eras of English history.

A THANKSGIVING TO GOD, FOR HIS HOUSE

Lord, Thou hast given me a cell
    Wherein to dwell;
A little house, whose humble roof
    Is weatherproof;
Under the spars of which I lie
    Both soft and dry;
Where Thou, my chamber for to ward,
    Has set a guard
Of harmless thoughts, to watch and keep
    Me, while I sleep.
Low is my porch, as is my fate,
    Both void of state;
And yet the threshold of my door
    Is worn by th' poor,
Who thither come and freely get
    Good words, or meat:
Like as my parlour, so my hall
    And kitchen's small:
A little buttery, and therein
    A little bin,
Which keeps my little loaf of bread
    Unchipped, unflead:
Some brittle sticks of thorn or briar
    Make me a fire,
Close by whose living coal I sit,
    And glow like it.
Lord, I confess too, when I dine,

    The pulse is Thine,
And all those other bits, that be
    There placed by Thee;
The worts, the purslane, and the mess
    Of water-cress,
Which of Thy kindness Thou hast sent;
    And my content
Makes those, and my beloved beet,
    To be more sweet.
'Tis Thou that crown'st my glittering hearth
    With guiltless mirth,
And giv'st me wassail bowls to drink,
    Spiced to the brink.
Lord, 'tis Thy plenty-dropping hand
    That soils my land,
And giv'st me, for my bushel sown,
    Twice ten for one:
Thou mak'st my teeming hen to lay
    Her egg each day;
All these, and better Thou dost send
    Me, to this end,
That I should render, for my part,
    A thankful heart;
Which, fired with incense, I resign,
    As wholly thine;
But the acceptance, that must be,
    My Christ by Thee.

Robert Herrick

Solutions to problems on page 144: A TIME PROBLEM: Twenty-five minutes to three. ALL DIAMONDS: There are 30 diamonds.

CERVANTES—
AUTHOR OF *DON QUIXOTE*

YOU may have heard some one described as "quixotic," and although you may know that it means extravagantly romantic or chivalrous, like Don Quixote, the principal character in the novel of that name by Cervantes, you may not know very much about this book or its author.

Miguel de Cervantes Saavedra was born in 1547 at Alcalá de Henares, north-east of Madrid, the second son of an apothecary-surgeon. Like many of the world's most famous men of the past, little is known of his early life, but it appears that he enlisted in the regular army in 1570 and was wounded at the Battle of Lepanto in 1571 (when Don John of Austria, son of the Emperor Charles V defeated the Turks). Although permanently maimed in his left hand as a result of his wounds, he continued in the army until 1575. On his way home to Spain, when he carried letters of recommendation addressed to King Philip II and also to the Duke of Sessa, viceroy of Sicily, the ship in which he was travelling was captured by Barbary corsairs, and he and his brother were taken as prisoners to Algiers. In view of the letters which he carried, Cervantes was thought to be a man of importance and in a position to pay a high ransom.

The following year he attempted unsuccessfully to escape and he was thereafter treated with additional severity. In 1577 his parents sent, with two priests of the Order of Mercy, a sum of 300 crowns as ransom money. The price on Cervantes's head, however, was too high and the money was devoted to releasing his brother.

A further attempt, equally unsuccessful, to escape, resulted in his being threatened with death, but in view of his heroic bearing the viceroy of Algiers, Hassan Pasha, remitted the sentence and bought Cervantes from his owner for 500 crowns. Yet again Cervantes attempted to escape with equally ill-fated results, but meantime his family had gathered more ransom money, and this only arrived just as Hassan Pasha's household and slaves were to be embarked for Constantinople, as his term of office was drawing to a close. On this occasion the ransom money was again insufficient, but the balance was made up by the Christian traders of Algiers. At last Cervantes was able to return home to Spain.

TRYING TO EARN A LIVING

From about 1582–7 he wrote a great many plays, but only two of these have survived, neither showing any very great merit. He also wrote a novel called the *Galatea*, which had a small success, but it was written in the artificial pastoral vein and did not allow Cervantes's rich and glowing realism any play. Play-writing was not a lucrative occupation at the time in Spain and Cervantes realised that he must find some other means of earning money. His father had died and family responsibilities were heavy, especially as his wife, whom he married in 1585, had not brought a substantial dowry, for it only consisted of five vines, an orchard, some household furniture, four beehives, forty-five hens and chickens, one cock and a crucible.

He went to Seville to seek employment in connection with the provisioning of the Invincible Armada, and he helped to gather wheat for this purpose. After the defeat of the Armada, he was retained as commissary to the galleys. There was, however, no prospect of advancement in this work and Cervantes accordingly applied for one of several posts then vacant in the Spanish American colonies. In this he was unsuccessful and he found himself in dire financial straits, because his official accounts were so badly kept that he was accused of swindling public funds. He even served several terms of imprisonment.

"DON QUIXOTE" PUBLISHED

From the time of the publication of the *Galatea* in 1585, his literary production was limited to occasional poems. But he had apparently started writing his masterpiece during one of his terms of imprisonment, and in 1604 *Don Quixote* was published.

This novel was intended by Cervantes to ridicule the romances of chivalry (absurdly artificial accounts of knights-errant and their ideal ladies for whose honour they fought) and in this he was entirely successful, but somehow the story grew and developed into a brilliant panorama of Spanish society as it existed in the sixteenth century: knights and nobles, poets and priests, farmers and inn-keepers, muleteers and convicts, barbers and traders, ladies of all sorts and conditions—they are all here with life-like vividness.

What appealed to readers in Cervantes's day was the variety of incident and the humour, which so frequently bordered on farce, together with the jibes at well-known contemporaries. But *Don Quixote* has more to it than that. It has timeless qualities in its understanding of human nature, in its penetrating criticism of life and in its touching pathos.

The story, in simple terms, recounts how Don Quixote imagines, after reading too many romances of chivalry, that he is a knight-errant and that his old nag Rocinante is a noble steed. A simple peasant called Sancho Panza, mounted on his donkey, acts as his squire and accompanies him when he sets out on his travels. Sancho is full of common sense and although he understands little of his master's idealism, he is very fond of him

The Knight thinks he has captured a helmet.

and helps him when he gets into difficulties.

The second part of *Don Quixote* was published in 1615, and although the characters of the knight and his squire remain basically the same, there is more dignity in the knight, more sense and manners in the squire than in the first part. The construction of the plot is better, too, and there are fewer digressions.

Between the publication of the first and second parts of *Don Quixote*, Cervantes produced in 1613 his *Novelas Exemplares*, short stories, perfect of their type, which alone would entitle Cervantes to rank with the greatest masters of Spanish prose. He also published a burlesque poem and a collection of short plays, though neither was of the highest merit.

Cervantes died in 1616 without having reaped much financial gain from his master-piece. The first part of Don Quixote had been translated into English in 1612 and into French in 1614, and since that date it has been translated into more languages and sold in more countries than any book other than the Bible. He was, without doubt, one of the greatest writers of all time. Changes in literary taste have not diminished the popularity of *Don Quixote* of which it is said: "children turn its leaves, young people read it, grown men understand it, old folk praise it."

Don Quixote, thinking that some windmills are giants, attacks them unsuccessfully.

An unusual painting by Anthony Van Dyck of Charles I (1625–49).

CHARLES I

An Attempt to Reign as an Absolute King

JAMES I's inflated claims concerning the divine right of kings and the royal prerogative had sown the seeds of discord amongst his people. Would the seeds germinate? It depended on his son, Charles I. There was high promise in the young king. He was virtuous, pious and cultured, and his subjects hailed his accession in 1625 with joyful hopes.

Those hopes were quickly overshadowed. Charles, it appeared, had learned all too well his father's autocratic doctrines. The seeds of discord soon put forth their shoots. When the Commons attacked the Duke of Buckingham (the favourite of both James and Charles) for his misdeeds, the King haughtily bade them

mind their own business. The Commons retorted by impeaching the offender and withholding money supplies. Charles's dealings with religious affairs were another grievance. In fact, he was devoted to the Anglican Church; but, under the influence of his Roman Catholic Queen, Henrietta Maria, he was being lenient to the papists. And he was favouring " High Churchmen," those who were introducing elaborate ceremonial and ornaments into the services.

THE PETITION OF RIGHT

Charles's reply to the Commons was to raise money by forced loans and unauthorised

Henrietta Maria, sister of Louis XII of France, married Charles I in 1625.

affairs. He was wholly sincere and well-intentioned but severe and narrow-minded. He corrected many abuses that were defiling the Church and its ministry. As leader of the High Church party he established the elaborate ritual that aroused the horror of all good Puritans. In his hatred of the severe code of those earnest men he persecuted them mercilessly in the tyrannous Star Chamber and Court of High Commission. Wentworth, afterwards Earl of Strafford, was the King's strong man in civil and military affairs. He despised Parliament and Puritans equally. Thousands of Puritans sought political and religious freedom by crossing the Atlantic, where they built up the colony of Massachusetts and other New England settlements.

A rank crop of discontent was now growing vigorously and poisoning the whole kingdom. In 1637 its first-fruits appeared in open resistance, a notable instance of which was John Hampden's sturdy refusal to pay ship-money. But it was from Scotland that the self-willed King received an outright slap in the face. Charles and Laud tried to establish there the use of a Prayer Book after the pattern of the English liturgy. Now the Scots were fiery Presbyterians and they hated the " popery " of Prayer Books as an unbroken colt hates the bridle. The angry nation rose almost to a man and swore a solemn Covenant to preserve their threatened Church. Charles, foolishly obstinate, sent an army against them. But it had no stomach for fight and in 1641 the King was driven to yield.

customs dues and to cast into prison those who refused to pay. Parliament spoke up. In its Petition of Right of 1628 it denounced all such practices. Next year it declared that whosoever should propose changes in religion was an enemy of the kingdom. Charles had accepted the Petition of Right; but, as he was to prove on many an occasion, his word could not be trusted. He now resolved to do without Parliament, and did so for the record period of eleven years. The money he needed for carrying on the government was raised by various unpopular means, including a " ship-money " tax to pay for new ships.

LAUD AND STRAFFORD

Amongst the party that supported him none were more devoted than Laud and Wentworth. Laud, who became Archbishop of Canterbury, was the King's right-hand man in church

THE LONG PARLIAMENT

Meanwhile his empty pockets had at last forced him to summon Parliament. The assembly of 1640—the historic Long Parliament—met in the mood of a lion roaring after its prey. No more eleven-year gaps for them! Henceforth Parliament must be summoned every three years. Under the lead of the great parliamentarian Pym, they swept away the hated Star Chamber and Court of High Commission. Ship-money and fines were declared illegal. Strafford and Laud were imprisoned and, in due course, executed. Then, unfortunately, the Commons started roaring at each other over their Grand Remonstrance of 1641. The majority of the Puritans clamoured for sweeping reductions in the power of the untrustworthy King and his allies the bishops. But those who still deeply reverenced the monarchy and the Church thought this was going too far. The members were lining up in opposite camps—King and Church against Parliament and Puritanism. Taking advantage of the cleavage, Charles committed one of his greatest follies. He suddenly descended on the House with an armed retinue to seize Pym, Hampden and three other prominent leaders. But the birds had flown. His high-handed breach of the privileges of the House brought the struggle to a crisis. Agreement between King and Parliament was plainly impossible. Each side prepared for war.

RISE OF OLIVER CROMWELL

In the first Civil War of Cavalier and Roundhead, which opened in 1642, there were several occasions when it looked as if the King would win. But two major circumstances ruined him. One was the spirit and military genius of Oliver Cromwell, a plain country squire and stern Puritan, in whom a solemn sense of religious duty burned like a steady flame. His successes at Marston Moor in 1644 and Naseby in 1645 stamped him as the foremost cavalry leader of his day. The other circumstance was the intervention of the Scots. Pym bought their aid by promising extreme reforms in the Anglican Church, including the exclusion of bishops as in the Presbyterian system.

The First Civil War ended in 1646 after Charles, in despair, had thrown himself into the hands of the Scots. Next year his countrymen, unable to bring him to terms, handed him over to the English Parliament. Meantime the Presbyterians who now dominated the assembly had started to force their system of worship on the country. They never succeeded. The country was against it and so was the Army, with the mighty Cromwell as its champion. The soldiers were largely Independents who favoured toleration for all creeds except Romanism.

THE END OF THE WAR

The wily Charles once again made the most of his enemies' disagreements. His well-intentioned double-dealing won back the Scots to his side (with a promise to establish Presbyterianism in England for three years and

Oliver Cromwell, the Roundhead general who defeated the Royalists, and signed the death warrant of Charles I.

suppress all other creeds) and plunged the country into the Second Civil War of 1648. But Cromwell crushed the Scottish army near Preston and the new outbreak was soon over. And now his blood was up. The Army was weary of Charles's trickery. It was enraged with Parliament for carrying on negotiations with him. And the Army knew that the Presbyterian majority was unfriendly to it because that majority feared the Army's power and detested its religious and political principles. Straightway the Army marched on London and violently purged Parliament of its hostile members. The " Rump " of a few score individuals—mostly Independents—who were suffered to remain then proceeded to the mockery of bringing the King to trial. On the 30th January, 1649, to the horror of all Europe and the vast majority of Englishmen, the condemned King, steadfast as he had ever been in heart to the principles of Church and Monarchy as he conceived them, was executed as a tyrant and public enemy.

Charles II, 1660–85. His restoration to the throne, in 1660, was greeted with acclamation by the people, who were glad to be released from Puritan rule.

CHARLES II

The Interregnum and the Restoration

HAVING executed Charles I in 1649, the Rump Parliament set up a Commonwealth and abolished the House of Lords. The Rump was wholly dominated by Independents and controlled by the Army. It was no more a representative Parliament than a piston-rod is a railway engine. England lay under the dictatorship of the sword. Meantime the dead King's elder son was proclaimed in Scotland as Charles II and Ireland was in revolt. Cromwell struck down both. Ireland was crushed by a savage terrorism that ever after made the ruthless victor's name a byword. The Scots were defeated at Dunbar in 1650 and afterwards brought under the English yoke. Prince Charles was soundly beaten by the invincible Cromwell at Worcester in 1651 and, after countless hair-raising adventures, fled to France.

CROMWELL IN CONTROL

The problems of government and religion now demanded attention. Between them the English had taken the household clock to

153

pieces. Now Cromwell had to reassemble the parts and get it to go again. He was not an autocrat. He firmly believed in Parliament. But, Parliament or no, he was determined to carry out his plans for the reformation of England and the creation of a godly State. First there should be, within limits, toleration for all creeds except popery. True, the Anglican Church, to which the greater part of the country was still loyal, had already been hit hard. Its bishops and its Common Prayer Book had been abolished. But at least no man was any longer compelled by law to attend services offensive to his beliefs. Secondly, the reform in morals which the Puritans had already begun must be sternly enforced. The vices of drinking and swearing, the popish Christmas festivities and pagan May Day revels, the profaning of the Sabbath and such-like vanities and frivolities must be rooted out.

DICTATORIAL VIEWS

But Cromwell knew that the bulk of the people were against him and his military rule. He dared not, therefore, summon a free Parliament. Finding the miserable Rump Parliament unsatisfactory, he bundled the members out of doors in 1653. From then on, until his death in 1658, the Lord Protector, as he became, tried one government experiment after another to carry out his purposes. But all failed because of the fundamental conflict of views that divided him from the mass of the nation over his aims and methods—his reliance on the support of the Army, his severe treatment of Anglicans, his advanced ideas on religious toleration, his harsh and joyless " moral " laws. So his work crumbled away and collapsed like a badly-built house.

FOREIGN POLICY

But the same cannot be said of his work abroad. Cromwell was a true Englishman and his rule restored his country's prestige to Elizabethan heights. He was ready to fight anyone anywhere. England, Scotland and Ireland were not enough. He fought the Spaniards. He fought the Dutch (they had just won their long struggle with Spain for independence). Holland's offences were various. The Dutchmen had helped Charles's cause. They were England's foremost rival in commerce. They refused to dip their flag to

English ships in the Channel as an acknowl- edgment of the islanders' sovereignty over the Narrow Seas. And so on. In the First Dutch war of 1652–4 Blake brought them to their knees. Spain, of course, was always fair game and, in 1655, Jamaica was filched from her. The destruction, later, of two treasure fleets beggared her and left England supreme at sea.

KING CHARLES BROUGHT BACK

Cromwell's son Richard, who succeeded his father, was a harmless political nonentity. Quarrelling broke out in the Army and its power broke. General Monck, who com- manded the English forces in Scotland, voiced the wishes of almost the entire nation when, in 1660, he negotiated for the restoration of the monarchy. When Charles entered London the roads were strewn with flowers, the bells rang peals of joy and the fountains ran with wine. It was as though a shadow had passed from the land.

The cynical Charles was vastly amused by these raptures. But, in the sunshine of his gay presence, everyone hoped that the Merry Monarch would speedily restore the " Merrie England " of old. In truth he restored it to excess. His own tastes were all for ease and pleasure. His character was scandalously lax and unprincipled, his habits shamelessly immoral. His personal vices were speedily copied by the Court and society. Cromwell had kept them overlong in school. Now that they were out at play again they ran wild.

THE CAVALIER PARLIAMENT

Next year saw the assembling of the " Cavalier " Parliament, elected in the first flush of royalist enthusiasm and filled with the ardent champions of King and Church. Charles had promised religious toleration, subject to Parliament's sanction. The majority of the Cavalier Parliament, however, during this and the succeeding years, were eager only for a reckoning with their old Puritan oppres- sors. The Act of Uniformity required all ministers to accept the Revised Common Prayer Book, the Thirty-nine Articles and the order of bishops. The great majority con- formed. Those who refused were expelled from their livings. These stalwarts are the fathers of our modern Nonconformist sects. By the Corporation Act no one was allowed to serve

Sir Christopher Wren (1632–1723), architect of St. Paul's and other famous buildings.

on the town corporations and councils without receiving Holy Communion according to the Anglican rites. Rigid Puritans were thus excluded from local government. The Conventicle Act forbade all religious meetings of Nonconformists. This was hardly the religious toleration the Puritans had been led to expect and they rightly felt that they had been betrayed.

TROUBLES ABROAD AND AT HOME

Very soon the country had other troubles to bear. The Second Dutch War of 1665–7, arising out of the old commercial rivalry, brought England little credit. None the less the Dutch colony of New Netherland in North America was captured and later became the English colonies of New York, New Jersey and Delaware. In 1665 came the Great Plague that made London a city of the dead. And in the following year the afflicted capital was two-thirds destroyed by the Great Fire.

CHARLES'S AIMS

Shortly after these unhappy events Charles began to show his true colours. Beneath his indolent exterior he nursed two aims; to rule unshackled by Parliament, and to secure toleration for the Catholic creed to which—so far as he had any religion at all—he himself was secretly attached. His chosen ally was Louis XIV of France, a young king with dazzling ideas of power and glory in his head. Louis was bent on the utmost expansion of the power and dominion of France and the crushing of Protestantism. The Treaty of Dover, which he and Charles secretly concluded in 1670, is almost unbelievable in its cynical disregard for popular English feeling. The precious pair of royal conspirators were to divide Protestant Holland between them. Charles was to declare himself a Catholic. And Louis was to pay him a pension (to make him independent of parliamentary supplies) and, if necessary, send over troops to put down opposition.

In execution of this despicable plot Charles duly began the Third Dutch war of 1672–4. He likewise issued—solely by virtue of his royal prerogative—a Declaration of Indulgence suspending the penal laws passed by Parliament against Catholics, and (to cloak his primary aim) those against Puritan Nonconformists as well. But he had woefully mistaken the temper of his people. The Nonconformists scorned to accept toleration at such a price. A cry of indignation burst from the country and a wrathful Parliament demanded the withdrawal of the offending Indulgence. Here, then, were the makings of another struggle with a Stuart king. Was Charles II to go the way of Charles I?

PARLIAMENT ACTS

Not so. If the second Charles had one steady purpose in his life it was this: he would never do anything that might " send him on his travels again." He now realised that he had gone too far. He withdrew the Declaration. Whereupon Parliament clinched their triumph by passing the Test Act of 1673 which excluded from offices of State all who refused to receive the Anglican Holy Communion. In this way they ejected from office certain of Charles's ministers and his brother James, Duke of York, who were known to be Catholics.

TITUS OATES AND THE POPISH PLOT

But Charles had not given up hope of gaining his ends. The leader of the opposition against his supporters in Parliament was the Earl of

Shaftesbury. The Earl guessed something of the King's designs. When the scoundrelly Titus Oates came forward in 1678 with his infamous story of a widespread popish plot to murder Charles and crown James with the help of French troops, he made the most of it. The very mention of a popish plot made Englishmen as nervous and agitated as an old lady crossing Piccadilly Circus in the rush hour. The country became panic-stricken. Shaftesbury and his friends brought forward a plan for excluding the Catholic James from the royal succession and substituting one of Charles's illegitimate sons, the dashing and popular but brainless young Duke of Monmouth.

It was during the excitement of these events that the two great opposing parties in Parliament first became organised under the nicknames of " Whigs " for those who supported the exclusion of James and " Tories " for those who opposed it.

In the end Charles managed to defeat his opponents; and, as the clamour died down, he quietly went on with his plans. He was not too proud to pocket the cash Louis paid him to further his own schemes. For some years he was able to do without Parliament. And, in the meantime, he was scheming to control the

The Monument, built by Wren to commemorate the Great Fire of London in 1666.

next elections. But in 1685 those subtle scheme suffered a mortal blow. Charles died.

EXPANSION OF OVERSEAS POSSESSIONS

During this and the previous reign England' overseas possessions gained many addition beyond those already mentioned. In Charles I' time the American colony of Maryland wa founded and Barbados colonised. Unde Charles II the Carolinas and Pennsylvani were colonised and the settlement of th Bahamas established. In India, the East Indi Company, formed in 1600, had opened severa factories, or trading stations, by the end o the same reign.

The outstanding literary figure of the da was John Milton, the Puritan poet, who in hi *Paradise Lost*, wrote one of the grandest epic of all time.

Samuel Pepys, the diarist (1632–1703).

JAMES II

The End of Absolute Monarchy

RULING a kingdom is rather like sitting for an examination: you earn good marks and bad. James II, in 1685, began with what was considered in England a very bad mark indeed: he was an avowed Roman Catholic. Yet he was given a fair chance. The Tories were dominant in Parliament and they were cordially inclined towards him. Tories and Whigs alike, of course, supported constitutional government by King and Parliament. But, in any contest for power between the two institutions, the Tories would generally side with the King, while the Whigs would defend the rights of Parliament. In religion, the Tories stood stoutly for the Anglican church; the Whigs stood as staunchly for toleration for Nonconformists; and both held Roman Catholicism in horror.

SEDGEMOOR AND ITS CONSEQUENCES

James was not long in revealing an ugly side to his character. His brother Charles II's legitimate son, the hare-brained young Duke of Monmouth, got the idea that all England would support him in a Protestant rising. So he rose. And very soon afterwards he fell. His rabble of brave but untrained West-country yokels and miners were routed at Sedgemoor in July, 1685, after their valiant leader had decamped. Later, James's soldiers found him hiding in a ditch and hauled him out. His next journey was to the block. But it was James's pitiless treatment of the rebel's ignorant followers that shocked the country. In the merciless " Bloody Assize " of his minion, the atrocious Chief Justice Jeffreys, over a thousand of these deluded rustics were condemned to death or slavery in the West Indian plantations. It was another bad mark for James.

DECLARATION OF INDULGENCE

This success encouraged the King to proceed with the dearest wish of his heart—the restoration of Catholicism. He selected papists for his councillors. He created a Court of High Commission, similar to the tyrannous organ

James II. 1685–8.

of religious persecution which had been abolished by the Long Parliament. He openly encouraged Roman Catholic rites and institutions. He vastly increased the existing small standing army to strengthen his power, and officered it extensively with Catholics. In 1687 he repeated Charles's disastrous experiment of issuing a Declaration of Indulgence suspending the penal laws against Catholics and Nonconformists. But, while Charles had had the good sense to yield when he encountered the iron core of popular resistance, James obstinately persisted in his folly.

IMPRISONMENT OF THE BISHOPS

The succeeding year was a fateful one for England. In May, James issued a further Indulgence and ordered it to be read in the churches. It was *not* read, save in a very few. Sancroft, Archbishop of Canterbury, and six other conscientious bishops mildly petitioned the King to withdraw the order. James, in a fury, hauled them before the judges for sedition. It was a test of strength. The whole nation hung tensely on the court's decision. For once Anglicans and Nonconformists were united in common opposition to a papist autocrat. When the judges acquitted the heroic

157

The Duke of Monmouth, who headed an unsuccessful rebellion against James II.

bishops, London blazed with triumphal bonfires.

THE BIRTH OF AN HEIR

One circumstance which had consoled the country during James's tyranny was that he had no heir to carry on his policy and was unlikely to have one. In that event his successor would be his elder daughter, Mary, who, some years before, had become the wife of that champion of Protestants, William, Prince of Orange, the head of the Dutch republic. Imagine, then, the general consternation when, in 1688, the birth of an heir was announced!

Mary's succession was forestalled and England might well shudder at the prospect of a line of Catholic monarchs. Half the country refused to believe the announcement. They suspected a trick, and soon the tale went round that somebody else's new-born baby had been smuggled into the Queen's bedchamber in a bed-warming-pan.

INVITATION TO WILLIAM OF ORANGE

The event, however, was genuine enough and the immediate result of it was to speed up certain secret negotiations which had been in progress for some time. A group of leading men, representing both Tory and Whig opinion, invited Prince William to come over and restore the liberties of England and the Protestant religion. It is true that England and Holland had recently fought three wars against each other; but they were brought together now by a number of common interests. Not the least of these was the need to combine against the towering ambitions of Louis XIV which had made France a growing menace to all Europe. William eagerly accepted the invitation. In November he landed at Torbay with an army that included English and Scottish regiments. James marched west to encounter him, but, to his dismay, his forces fell away piecemeal, as leaders and men deserted to the popular side. His eyes were opened at last. He saw that his only hope lay in flight. William was anxious to get him off the premises, for he had no thought of using extreme measures against him. So he left a loophole for escape. And, on the 23rd December, 1688, James took his chance and scurried away to France.

He had failed woefully in his exam.

THE WIND

What way does the Wind come? What way does he go?
He rides over the water, and over the snow,
Through wood, and through vale; and, o'er rocky height
Which the goat cannot climb, takes his sounding flight.
He tosses about in every bare tree,
As, if you look up, you plainly may see;
But how he will come, and whither he goes,
There's never a scholar in England knows.
Dorothy Wordsworth

MARY QUEEN OF SCOTS

A Favourite of Misfortune

I AM certain that, at some time or other, you must have come across the name of Mary Queen of Scots. So much has been written about this ill-fated monarch; books, plays and poems, and even a film, all of which would probably astonish her. She would, perhaps, be most pleased about the poems, for she wrote poetry herself.

Mary Queen of Scots was born at Linlithgow Palace, on 6th December, 1542, and at that same moment her father, King James V, lay dying not twenty miles away. So, you see, Mary was practically born a queen and was, as a matter of fact, only one year old when her coronation ceremony took place. Henry VIII saw an opportunity of gaining control of Scotland by arranging a betrothal between his son, Edward, and the infant Queen. Mary's mother, a Frenchwoman, refused and an English army was sent to Scotland to kidnap the child, more or less. Mary was hidden away in Stirling Castle and, later, was smuggled off to the Priory of Inchmahome, on an island on the Lake of Menteith. Here she remained for a very short time, for, in the meantime, the King of France had decided that the Queen of Scotland would be a fitting bride for his son, Francis, when they both grew up. And so, in August, 1548, Mary was taken on board a French galley at Dumbarton and sailed away from her native land.

LIFE AT THE FRENCH COURT

The next ten years in France were, perhaps, the only really happy years of Mary's life. The French Court, at that time, was the most glittering place in Europe. In this atmosphere, Mary grew up into a beautiful and accomplished girl. " She is so perfect and accomplished in all things, honourable and virtuous," wrote the Cardinal of Lorraine, " that the like of her is not to be seen in this realm." She sang beautifully and could accompany herself on the lute. She wrote excellent verses. Her embroideries were things of sheer beauty. She was a fearless horsewoman who loved

Mary Stuart aged 16, by an unknown artist.

hunting, a skilled archer, and she excelled at the ancient game of pall-mall.

In April, 1558, Mary was married in Paris to the Dauphin, the heir to the French throne. One year later, King Henry II, the Dauphin's father, was accidentally slain in a tournament by a Scottish knight and Mary became Queen of France and Scotland at the age of seventeen. It seemed that Mary was, indeed, one of fortune's favourites and then, on 6th December, 1560, her world collapsed around her when her husband, who had always been sickly, died, leaving her a widow at eighteen. It soon became obvious that there was no longer any place for her in France, but she was still Queen of Scotland and so she decided to return to her native land. In August, 1561, she set sail from Calais and, after sailing for five days, landed in Leith.

THE RETURN TO SCOTLAND

It was hardly a pleasant homecoming. To begin with, it was a dreadful day of rain and mist and, as no one was expecting her, there was no assembly to meet her. Also, one of the French ships that had been escorting her had been captured by an English vessel, and as this ship had carried all Mary's splendid thoroughbred horses, her retinue

159

found themselves stranded. So Mary and her companions had to make their way to the gloomy palace of Holyrood, riding on borrowed, broken-down horses. In a way, Mary's arrival in Scotland had something ominous about it. And after the gaiety of France, Scotland, poor, wretched and war-battered, was a sad disappointment.

It would have been very difficult to find two more different countries. In France, the royal word had been law, but here in Scotland there appeared to be no law at all. The country was ruled by the turbulent barons who fought the English and who warred among themselves, and who would have fought anyone as long as they thought that it was to their own advantage. They were, as Mary soon discovered, both treacherous and disloyal. Then there was Master John Knox, a terrifying, bearded figure, the leader of the Reformers who wished to destroy the Old Church of which Mary herself was a faithful member. In this, Knox was supported by the Scottish Lords, not so much because they believed in Knox's ideas but rather because the Old Church was very rich and, if it were destroyed, there would be plenty to plunder. In France, Knox would quickly have lost his head had he

Mary leaves France, the only place she was ever truly happy, never to return.

presumed to talk to his Queen as he did at Holyrood: but here, in Scotland, things were otherwise. You can easily sympathise with Mary, therefore, in her attempt to build for herself a tiny corner of France in Scotland. In Holyrood she had her own little circle, made up of poets and courtiers who had accompanied her from France: and, of course, there were also the four Maries, her maids of honour, who had grown up with her: Mary Beton, Mary Livingstone, Mary Seton and Mary Fleming. In time, there was added to the circle an Italian called David Rizzio, who sang beautifully and who became Mary's private secretary.

MARRIAGE TO DARNLEY

In 1565, Mary married again. Her bride-groom, this time, was Henry Stuart, Lord Darnley, a tall, handsome young man but rather weak and stupid. For a while, things went smoothly until Darnley became dis-satisfied. He wanted to be king rather than merely the Queen's husband, but Mary would not agree to this, with the result that Darnley began to plot secretly against her. The cunning Scots Lords saw their opportunity here and encouraged the foolish Darnley. They whispered to him that Rizzio was the real ruler of Scotland, that he drew up and signed all the decrees and that it was monstrous that a base-born Italian should have such power while Darnley himself, a prince of the blood, should be allowed no say at all in the government of his country. The weak Darnley believed it all, and one March evening in 1566 he led a group of conspirators, by way of a secret staircase, into the Queen's apartments in Holyrood. The conspirators were led by Patrick, Lord Ruthven, a ghastly figure who was, popularly, supposed to be a sorcerer. He had risen from a sick-bed to lead the traitors and now they dragged the hapless Italian from the Queen's presence and mur-dered him. Mary managed to escape and rode off to the castle of Dunbar.

BOTHWELL

Mary never forgave Darnley for the assassina-tion of Rizzio and, naturally, she never trusted him again. In fact, sometimes it seemed as though there was not, in the whole country, anyone she could trust. There was, however,

With the help of a young page, Willie Douglas, Mary Queen of Scots escaped from Loch Leven Castle and joined her friends shortly before the disastrous Battle of Langside.

Henry Stuart, Lord Darnley, Consort of Mary and father of the future James I of the United Kingdom, with his brother.

one man on whom she came, gradually, to rely more and more. His name was James Hepburn, Earl of Bothwell, a strong, ruthless warrior whose loyalty to the crown had already been proved. Bothwell now stood between her and the schemes of her nobles.

In February, 1567, a mysterious event happened. Darnley was lying ill at a place called Kirk o' Field in Edinburgh. Suddenly, at two o'clock in the morning, the house was blown up and Darnley and his servant were killed. Everyone was convinced that Bothwell had murdered Darnley but by this time Bothwell was too powerful for anyone to dare to accuse him; and the reason for the crime seemed clear when, three months later, Mary

married Bothwell. The result was a rebellion and once more Mary sought sanctuary in Dunbar Castle. From here, she and Bothwell sallied out to meet the army of the Scottish nobles. The two forces met at Carberry Hill, where, after a great deal of parleying, the Queen's forces refused to advance to the attack. Mary sent a message, requesting a further discussion, and one of the Scottish Lords rode up to offer her terms. The Queen must return with the Lords to Edinburgh—alone. They did not care where Bothwell went as long as he did not go with the Queen. There was nothing for it but to accept, and so Bothwell rode off, never to see the Queen again.

IMPRISONED IN SCOTLAND

Once more Mary was a prisoner, and this time there seemed little prospect of escape. The Lords had decided to shut her up in Loch Leven Castle until such occasion as she would agree to give up the throne. She did so. Her half-brother, the Earl of Moray, was made Regent to govern in her place, and preparations were made to keep her imprisoned in Loch Leven Castle for the rest of her life. Once more, though, the Lords reckoned without Mary's courage and resource. Assisted by a young man, George Douglas, she made one attempt to escape which failed. Douglas was banished from the castle and a stricter vigilance was imposed on the Queen. Despite this, however, she finally did escape through the devotion and quick-wittedness of a sixteen-year-old page, Willie Douglas. When the guards came into supper, the gates of the castle were locked and the keys were laid on the table beside the Laird, who later took them with him to bed and slept with them under his pillow. One spring evening in 1568, Willie Douglas dropped a napkin over the keys and later picked them up quietly. When the castle was quiet, Mary, dressed as one of her tire-women, made her way downstairs, accompanied by Willie Douglas. They opened all the doors and when they had won their way outside, locked them all again. They stepped into a boat and Willie began to row towards the faraway shore. To make sure that there was no pursuit, he dragged the other boats behind him and when they were well out in the loch, he threw the keys of the castle overboard. They reached

The conspirators enter Queen Mary's apartments to seize and kill the Italian Rizzio.

the shore, where George Douglas and Lord Seton awaited in the darkness with a small force of horsemen. By the end of that week, Mary found herself in command of an army totalling six thousand men.

On 13th May, at Langside, near Glasgow, Mary fought her last battle against the Scottish Lords, led in person by her half-brother. In forty-five minutes, Mary's army was in flight and she herself was spurring her horse madly away from the battlefield. She rode desperately, hardly knowing where, drinking sour milk and eating only oatmeal, spending, as she later wrote, " three nights with the owls." On 16th May, she sailed across the Solway Firth in a fishing-boat and landed at Workington in Cumberland. She never saw Scotland again.

EXILE IN ENGLAND

The presence of Mary Queen of Scots in England was a very thorny problem for Queen Elizabeth. They had, in the past, exchanged letters which were very friendly and perhaps these letters had been quite sincere at the time. But circumstances were different now that the Scottish Queen had turned up in person; for there were people in England, especially those who still clung to the old Pre-Reformation faith, who thought that Mary had a better claim to the English throne than Elizabeth: and, indeed, Mary herself, at her wedding to Francis II of France, had made just this claim. You will appreciate, then, that the Queen of England was in a very difficult position and one about which she did not appear able to make up her mind.

There were, however, other people who already had their minds made up, and these people suggested that the fugitive Queen should be kept in what they described as " honourable custody." So, for nineteen years, Mary wandered from castle to castle, Bolton Castle, Chatsworth, Sheffield, Tiltbury,

Mary Queen of Scots dressed as she appeared at her execution.

plot were smuggled into Mary by way of a small beer barrel and her replies were smuggled out in the same way. Every letter was scrutinised by Walsingham's agents and soon he was in possession of one in which Mary agreed that the assassination of Elizabeth should proceed. This was what Walsingham had been waiting for and now he swooped. Anthony Babington and his friends were arrested and executed; and, after a great deal of hesitation, Elizabeth agreed that Mary, too, should be put on trial for treason.

TRIAL AND EXECUTION

On 14th October, in the hall of Fotheringay Castle, the trial opened. Mary defended herself skilfully and courageously but to no avail, for her English judges had already made up their minds as to the outcome of the proceedings. On the 25th of the month, the commissioners gathered at Westminster and considered their verdict. With one exception, they declared Mary to be guilty and decreed for her the punishment of death.

In the early morning of 8th February, 1587, Mary Queen of Scots dressed herself, for the last time, in her state robes, black velvet stamped with gold. Over her wig she hung a long white veil. Her shoes were of white Spanish leather, her petticoat of crimson velvet. She walked firmly into the hall where the dreadful preparations had already been made. She showed no sign of fear, even when the black-clad executioners came to kneel before her and crave pardon, as was the custom, for carrying out their duty. "I forgive you with all my heart," Mary told them, "for I hope this death shall give an end to my troubles." After that, it was soon over, and Mary Queen of Scots had died like a queen.

In the end, however, Mary did triumph over Elizabeth for when the English Queen died in 1603, she was succeeded by James, the son of Mary and the ill-fated Darnley; and in another way, Mary can be said to have triumphed still further. Elizabeth is remembered as a symbol of a great era but Mary is remembered as she was, a beautiful, tragic woman, an eternal mystery whose solution has been sought by a great many writers of all nationalities and will, in the future, be investigated by many more.

Wakefield and Fotheringay, while, all the time, Elizabeth tried to decide what to do with her embarrassing guest; and, make no mistake about it, the guest was embarrassing, for Mary was continually engaged in plotting with sympathisers in England and abroad, and wherever she happened to be, there was sure also to be a crowd of spies and agents and go-betweens, plotting, plotting, plotting. But clever as they were, the English statesmen were still cleverer and, as often as not, they knew what was afoot before Mary knew herself. That was why, when the Duke of Norfolk planned a revolt in favour of the Scottish Queen, he was quickly arrested, tried and executed. In no way deterred, Mary went on with her schemes, and then Sir Francis Walsingham, one of Elizabeth's ablest ministers, decided to produce to his Queen definite evidence of what Mary of Scotland was planning. He knew that a young man, Anthony Babington, was an adherent of the Queen of Scots and often carried letters for her to and from the Continent. Walsingham managed to insinuate his own spies into the councils of the conspirators and secretly encouraged the conspiracy until its aim was nothing less than the assassination of Queen Elizabeth and the establishment of Mary in her place. Some of the letters about this

SOME FAMOUS DWARFS

THE antics of dwarfs have always fascinated mankind. Few royal courts of bygone days have been without them, and it used to be fashionable for persons of rank to be attended by one or more of these quaint little creatures.

So great, indeed, was the demand for dwarfs in ancient Rome that, in order to increase supplies, many were artificially bred. It is said that this was achieved by compressing children into boxes so that their growth was stunted. The majority of these manufactured freaks came from Syria and Egypt, and rich Romans delighted in decking them out in sparkling jewels so that they might show them off to their friends.

This desire on the part of powerful personages to amuse themselves at the expense of the undersized has persisted from the reign of the Pharaohs to quite recent times when the Bey of Tunis kept a troupe of dwarfs for his own entertainment.

One of the earliest accounts of a dwarf in Britain occurs in an old ballad which begins: " In Arthur's Court Tom Thumb did live." But we have to wait until the reign of Mary Tudor before the first authentic specimen can be chronicled. He was John Jarvis, just two feet high, and he carried out the duties of court page.

Edward VI was supposed to have had a favourite dwarf, called Xit, who is mentioned in Harrison Ainsworth's book, *The Tower of London*. He was the boon companion of the giants Og, Gog and Magog, and all four of them stood guard before the gateway of the Tower.

One of the most delightful of these tiny court attendants was Jeffrey Hudson, who was born at Oakham in 1619, and lived to the age of 63. He was the son of normal parents but, although perfectly proportioned, he measured no more than eighteen inches when he was nine years old. His father was a butcher in the service of the Duke of Buckingham.

THE DWARF WHO WAS BAKED IN A PIE

One day the Duchess happened to catch sight of this lovely little creature and immediately took him into her household. Shortly afterwards she and her husband had the honour of entertaining King Charles I and his Queen, Henrietta Maria, to dinner. In the hope of amusing the royal couple the Duchess ordered Hudson to be placed in a pie and set upon the table. No sooner was this done than the pastry lifted up like a lid and out stepped the manikin. Her Majesty was so fascinated by his engaging ways that the Duchess felt obliged to make her a present of the tiny page.

Hudson remained in the service of the royal family for a great many years. The Queen doted upon him and perhaps the finest compliment she paid him was when she dispatched him to France on an important errand. Unfortunately the ship in which the dwarf and his companion were returning was seized by Flemish pirates and Hudson was taken into captivity. When at last he escaped the fortunes of his royal mistress were at a very low ebb.

Soon the Civil War broke out and this tiny gallant donned Cavalier uniform and became a Captain of Horse. It is hard to imagine that he could have been a very great thorn in the Roundhead side, but he evidently spared himself no effort, for he earned the nickname of " Strenuous Jeffrey " for his deeds of derring do, the daring actions which the valiant little fellow performed. But the title he must have treasured most was conferred upon him by King Charles when he dubbed his miniature follower Sir Jeffrey Hudson.

A DUEL WITH A TURKEY-COCK

When the Queen was forced to flee to Paris, Sir Jeffrey accompanied her into exile, and it was here that he fought his two famous duels. The first was with a turkey-cock and the second with a Mr. Crofts.

His human opponent treated the whole affair as a good joke, and arrived at the scene of action armed only with a squirt. Hudson, on the other hand, was in deadly earnest. Seated on a horse, that brought him up to Croft's level, he fired a pistol and shot his opponent dead.

After that Paris was too hot to hold him, and he took ship for England. But, in mid-Channel, he was again captured by pirates and

children, five of whom were of normal proportions.

A PORTRAIT PAINTED ON CHICKEN SKIN

Gibson, who was born in Cumberland in 1615, was a gifted artist, and had been discovered by a lady living in Mortlake. She made him her page, and then arranged for him to receive lessons in art from Francis Clain, the manager of the tapestry works in that town. Later the dwarf passed into the service of the Queen. A large head of Her Majesty, which Gibson painted upon chicken skin, is still among the treasures of Windsor Castle.

Another of this little artist's paintings, depicting the parable of the lost sheep, so impressed Charles I that he asked his Keeper of the Royal Pictures to take special care of it. The unfortunate man put it into so safe a place that he was unable to lay hands upon it when the King wanted it. Thinking it was lost he committed suicide and, a few days afterwards, the missing picture was found.

Gibson's marriage to Anne Shepherd must have been a charming event. The King himself gave away the diminutive bride, and the poet, William Waller, wrote some verses in celebration of the occasion. A portrait of the midget couple, standing hand in hand, was painted at the time of the ceremony by the famous court artist, Lely.

Gibson was held in high regard as a painter of miniatures and, in the reign of James II, he was appointed drawing-master to the young Princesses, Mary and Anne. He was 74 when he died, in 1690, and he was buried in St. Paul's, Covent Garden. His wife outlived him by nineteen years, dying at the age of 89. She was buried in the same grave as her husband.

The last dwarf to figure in the English court was a German, named Coppernin. Contemporary accounts describe him as "a lively little imp" who helped to cheer the days of the Princess Augusta of Wales, mother of George III.

HOW A "BABY" SMUGGLED DISPATCHES

In other European countries dwarfs have also been popular. One of the most famous

Sir Jeffrey Hudson, who was presented to Charles I and his Queen in a cold pie.

sold into slavery. This time the shock of his sufferings was so heavy that it caused him to shoot up to a height of three feet nine inches.

Even after his return to his own country Hudson's troubles were not over. The truculence, which is so often part of a dwarf's nature, persuaded him into taking part in some Popish plot, and he was arrested and imprisoned in the Gate House, Westminster. Shortly after his release he died.

We know exactly what this doughty manikin looked like, for there is a portrait of him at Hampton Court. His little blue satin waistcoat, slashed and ornamented with pink and white silk, and his one-piece breeches and stockings, made from the same material, are in the Ashmolean Museum, Oxford.

Henrietta Maria delighted in dwarfs. As well as Sir Jeffrey Hudson she sought diversion in the company of Richard Gibson and his wife, Anne Shepherd. These two little people measured between them only seven feet two inches, and yet they eventually had nine

was Richebourg, whose height never rose above 23 inches. He served the Orleans family, and played an important part in the French Revolution. Disguised as a baby, he was carried in and out of Paris by his " nurse," with vital dispatches hidden under his swaddling clothes, thereby cheating the guillotine of many a victim. He died in Paris, aged ninety, as recently as 1858.

If it were necessary to prove that dwarfs are much more high-spirited than giants, we might turn to an account handed down from the seventeenth century about a certain Empress of Austria who decided to assemble together all the dwarfs and giants in the Germanic Empire and exhibit them in Vienna. The people responsible for carrying out this queenly whim were anxious lest the giants should bully the dwarfs. But, instead, the undersized were so rude to the oversized that these huge creatures were reduced to tears and obliged to beg for protection against their tiny tormentors.

" GENERAL TOM THUMB "

The term midget is thought to have had its origin in the entertainment world and, for the majority, this word serves to remind them of the most celebrated midget of them all,

The young Queen Victoria was captivated by Tom Thumb's impersonation of Napoleon.

" General Tom Thumb." So much has been written about this diminutive creature that he has almost become a legend.

His real name was Charles Stratton, and he was born, of British stock, in 1837, at Bridgeport, Conn., U.S.A. Curiously enough his weight at birth was above that of an average baby, for he turned the scale at nine pounds, two ounces. But when he was six months old, and had attained the height of two feet one inch and weighed fifteen pounds, he suddenly stopped growing. Prosperity in later life not only fattened him but increased his height to well over three feet.

The great American showman, Barnum, discovered Tom Thumb one day while visiting Bridgeport. He was immediately impressed by the commercial possibilities of this minute child and, finding the parents only too willing to make money out of their unusual son, he took little Charles away so that he might be put on show for the rest of his life.

He was taught to dance, sing, recite and strut about the stage in the guise of certain notable persons. Owing to his intelligence, sense of showmanship and graceful movements this

One of the most famous dwarfs, "General Tom Thumb," in highland dress.

Charles Stratton ("General Tom Thumb")
and his tiny wife Lavinia.

Before long Tom Thumb was summoned to Buckingham Palace where his elfin appearance quickly captured the heart of the youthful Queen Victoria. He also enacted his well-known impersonation of Napoleon before the Duke of Wellington, who declared it to be "Boney" to the life.

On his second visit to England Tom Thumb acted the part of Hop-o'-My-Thumb in the Lyceum pantomime while, during the day, he entertained gaping crowds in a London hall. The tragic outcome of his popularity, on this occasion, is revealed by the artist, Haydon, in his diary. It appears that while thousands flocked to see the remarkable dwarf only a paltry handful stepped into an adjacent room where Haydon's masterpiece, "The Banishment of Aristides" was on view. Such humiliation was too much for one of Haydon's temperament to bear and, shortly afterwards, he committed suicide.

Altogether the little "General" came to England three times and, on each occasion, the Queen expressed a wish to see him. At one such audience he introduced Her Majesty to the now familiar song, "Yankee Doodle." On his last appearance here, in 1863, Tom Thumb brought along his midget wife, Lavinia Warren. Sad to relate their only child died shortly after birth while the tiny parents were on tour.

There have been other show midgets in this country as attractive as "General Tom Thumb," but he was the first to capture public imagination and, as such, his name is likely to be remembered for many years to come.

Meanwhile a perfectly proportioned midget is worth far more than his weight in gold to the showman of to-day. For modern audiences are just as fascinated by these intriguing little people as were the kings and queens of old.

little creature proved an instantaneous success.

After raking in plenty of dollars in his own country, Barnum decided to try the "General" out in England. So, in January 1844 they crossed the Atlantic accompanied by the seven-year-old midget's parents as well as his tutor. No sooner had the party landed on these shores than the English took Tom Thumb to their hearts and his appearance everywhere was greeted by enthusiastic crowds.

TOM THUMB'S CARRIAGE

The London carriage-makers presented the "General" with a smart little barouche, twenty inches high and eleven inches wide, in which he could drive in state. It was painted a bright blue and red, with the dwarf's coat-of-arms emblazoned upon the door.

A WONDERFUL BIBLE

One of the most remarkable Bibles in the world was written, entirely by hand, in an exquisite script, by a Presbyterian named Russell, who lived in Montreal. He completed it in 1924, after 22 years of spare time work. There are nearly 2,000 pages and there is not a single error or omission. The title pages are most beautifully illuminated and the Book, which weighs about 18 lb., is bound in leather.

William III (1688–1702) and Mary II (1688–94).

WILLIAM III AND MARY II

Limitation of the Monarch's Power

THE reign of William and Mary set the seal on the " Glorious Revolution " of 1688. With the flight of James II the nation had shaken off a would-be Catholic autocrat. The time had now come to fill the vacant throne and to establish once and for all the constitutional rights and principles for which the nation had so long battled with the Stuarts. Here are some of the things Parliament did during the reign. It declared that it was illegal to use the royal prerogative for suspending laws, or to levy loans and taxes or raise a standing army without parliamentary sanction. Parliament was to be called frequently. The Crown was settled on William and Mary (from the 13th February, 1689); then, if there were no children, on Mary's sister Anne, all Catholics being excluded; and, finally, on the next Protestant heir, the Electress Sophia of Hanover, a child of James I's daughter Elizabeth, the lovely " Queen of Hearts." Further than this, liberty of worship was granted to practically everyone except Catholics and Unitarians (those who denied the doctrine of the Trinity); although the Nonconformists were still barred from holding official positions.

PARLIAMENT'S ASCENDANCY

By these and other provisions Parliament finally won its great victory. The control of the nation's purse (more especially by the House of Commons) led to an increasing share in the general control of public affairs and resulted in the calling of regular annual Parliaments. And there could be no more talk of the Sovereign's claim to rule by divine right, for now the Crown was held under a parliamentary grant.

THE KING'S UNPOPULARITY

The new King's position was not a happy one. He never loved the English and they never loved their " Dutch William." The leading men around him were a sorry crowd: quarrelsome, spiteful, self-seeking and faithless. Queen Mary, with her bright smiles and warm heart, helped greatly to smooth his path; but, when she died in 1694 and William was left to rule alone, he became even more unpopular than before. Unfortunately he was not a man to command affection. He was surly and unsociable and his wretched health often made him peevish. Moreover, he was only interested in English affairs for a particular purpose—to save Holland, his homeland, from the grasping ambition and cruel Catholic bigotry of Louis XIV, King of France.

THE STRUGGLE WITH LOUIS XIV

The mighty Louis's dream of extending his boundaries to the Rhine was a nightmare to Europe and its Protestant communities. It threatened the seizure of a number of petty German states and of the Spanish Netherlands —now limited to the region of modern Belgium. This was an obvious menace to Holland, situated next door, and William had been steadfastly struggling against it for nearly twenty years. His undersized and fragile frame housed an unconquerable spirit, a soldier's heart and a statesman's head. The little David had already administered a check to the great Goliath, France, and was busying himself now with bringing Spain and the Emperor, Leopold of Austria, into a league against France. It was in the hope of enlisting England in what was the common cause of Europe that he had come over and accepted the Crown. The hope was duly realised. England joined the league in September, 1689.

RESTORING PEACE AT HOME

But William had to wait awhile before he could come to grips with his principal enemy. Resistance to his throne at home had first to be suppressed. In England it arose from a number of true-blue Tories and ministers, Anglican, or Church of England, but these made no active opposition. In Scotland however, there was a rising in the Highlands and it was some time before the new King was generally accepted. Charles II's restoration had brought with it Scotland's restoration as a separate kingdom and now religious peace was furthered by making Presbyterianism the established creed. In Ireland William had to fight hard. The vast majority of the population was Catholic and anti-English, and, when in March, 1689, James, with the help of Louis,

landed, he controlled most of the island. However he controlled precious little of it by the time William had finished with him at the battle of the Boyne in July, 1690. He bolted back to France and never showed his face again on this side of the English Channel. Bitter fighting continued throughout the next year. Later, the Irish Parliament, from which papists were excluded, reduced the Catholics almost to the condition of outlaws.

PEACE THEN WAR AGAIN

William was now able to turn to the war in the Netherlands. For several years a ding-dong series of campaigns was fought till both sides grew war-weary. In 1697, peace was signed in the Treaty of Ryswick. The exhausted Goliath was forced to disgorge most of his later gains and to acknowledge William as rightful King of England.

But four years later a far greater war began. King Charles II of Spain had died in 1700 bequeathing his empire (Spain, the Spanish Netherlands, Milan and Naples, Sicily and Sardinia and boundless territories in the New World) to Duke Philip of Anjou, Louis's second grandson. The acceptance of these vast dominions as an addition to the existing possessions of the Bourbon House of France would completely upset the balance of power in Europe and threaten another war. Actually, the danger had long been foreseen and Louis had agreed to a treaty for the peaceful partition of the Spanish empire between his heir, the Dauphin, and the Emperor Leopold's second son, the Archduke Charles. Now, however, he threw over the Partition Treaty and greedily accepted the rich legacy for his grandson. This, and his further actions, made war unavoidable. And, when, on James II's death in 1701, he proclaimed the latter's bed-warming-pan son as James III, England's entry became assured.

THE GRAND ALLIANCE

It was in this explosive state of affairs, when the cannon were already growling on the Continent, that William, in March, 1702, died. But, six months before his passing, he had crowned his life's work by binding together England, Holland and the Emperor in the Grand Alliance that, with its later adherents, was to cross swords with the Grand Monarch in the titanic War of the Spanish Succession.

ANNE

The Last of the Stuarts

QUEEN ANNE had not many queenly qualities beyond her sense of dignity. She was just a plain, homely, affectionate and obstinate woman.

At her accession in 1702 the man of the hour was John Churchill, present Earl and future Duke of Marlborough. He stood high in the Queen's good graces through the boundless influence exercised over her by his Countess Sarah—a lady whose character combined the force of a whirlwind with the fury of a volcano. The War of the Spanish Succession had opened at the end of William III's reign and the Churchills' favour at court supported the Earl in his eagerness to prosecute England's part in the contest as commander of the English and Dutch armies.

THE WAR OF THE SPANISH SUCCESSION

In 1702 Marlborough commenced operations in the Netherlands. And in the succeeding years one dazzling victory after another took Europe's breath away. In 1704 a combined army of the French and their Bavarian allies was threatening Vienna. Suddenly, to their consternation, Marlborough (who was supposed to be far away in the Netherlands) appeared on the scene. He had made an astounding forced march of some three hundred miles across Germany. Now he completely broke the enemy forces in the battle of Blenheim. Austria—and with it Germany—was saved. The shock to the current belief in French invincibility was shattering. In 1706 he overwhelmed another Franco-Bavarian host at Ramillies and sent their disordered remnants flying. In 1708 he scattered the French at Oudenarde and led the way to the mastery of the Netherlands. And in the following year he gave them another trouncing at Malplaquet. Such were the mighty hammer-strokes of the greatest general England had ever produced.

While Marlborough was thus writing his name across the map of Europe the war was raging on the other fronts. The French were driven out of Italy; but they were more successful in Spain. The allied navies, too,

Anne. 1702–14.

were not idle and in 1707 England picked up Gibraltar—the key of the Mediterranean—and the island of Minorca.

MARLBOROUGH OUT OF FAVOUR

But in 1710 troubles began to thicken round "Corporal John," as his adoring soldiers called the great Duke. They did not come in the field—he never lost a battle or failed in a siege—but from enemies at home. Party politics were a hard-hitting affair in those days. The country was weary of the war, which it was the policy of Marlborough and the Whigs to continue. Louis had twice made offers of peace and the Tories, eager to displace the Whigs from office, declared that they should have been accepted. The Duke had lost favour with Anne, who had rebelled against the whirlwind-volcano Duchess. The Whigs added to their growing unpopularity by laying themselves open to the charge of a Nonconformist attack on the Church.

The upshot was that, in 1710, the Tories

returned to power. They opened peace negotiations with Louis. They accused Marlborough of corruptly accepting gifts and bribes. The Duke was able to answer the charges, but they gave a sufficient pretext for dismissing him from all his offices. His conduct had been no worse than that of other men of the times. The pity is it had not been better. We like our heroes to be beyond reproach.

VALUABLE GAINS

The Tories afterwards came to terms with Louis. By the Treaties of Utrecht and Rastadt of 1713–14 the victorious allies got some good pickings. Charles, the new emperor, received most of the Spanish Netherlands and possessions in Italy. Holland was given the garrisoning of the " barrier fortresses " lying along the French north-eastern frontier. Gibraltar and Minorca were ceded to England, together with Newfoundland (which had been disputed with the French), Nova Scotia and territories around Hudson Bay. England also received valuable trading rights, and the Protestant succession was recognised. Louis's grandson Philip kept Spain and its New World possessions, but the crowns of France and Spain were never to be united. Thus England's main object in the war was substantially achieved and the threatened French domination of Europe was checked. She had, moreover, increased her trade and colonies and made herself a controlling power in the Mediterranean.

UNION WITH SCOTLAND

While the war was still tearing Europe apart, England and Scotland were being drawn together. By the Treaty of Union of 1707 they became linked in the Kingdom of Great Britain under one King and one combined Parliament, Scotland retaining her own laws and Presbyterian creed. Thus the two quarrelsome neighbours at last sheathed the sword, shook hands and went into partnership.

A HANOVERIAN SUCCEEDS

After peace was secured abroad a storm-cloud gathered over England. Anne's health was failing. Under the Act of Succession passed in William's reign the House of Hanover was to inherit the throne. Now there were a great many Tories, faithful to their belief in

The Duke of Marlborough, one of the most famous soldiers in our history.

the divine right of hereditary succession, who still hankered after the Stuarts. They were called " Jacobites," the Latin form of James being *Jacobus*. James II's son—the Old Pretender—was, however, a Catholic, which made him quite unacceptable to the greater part of these malcontents. But there were a number of extremists who had no such scruples. They knew that, if the Hanoverians (whom the Whigs supported whole-heartedly) wore the crown, they, as Jacobites, would lose their power. So they were quite prepared to plot for bringing over the Pretender. Anne's sudden death, in 1714, however, scotched whatever designs their leader, the impetuous Viscount Bolingbroke, may have formed before they were sufficiently advanced. Whereupon George, the son of the recently deceased Sophia, Electress of Hanover, was peacefully proclaimed King.

George I. 1714–27.

GEORGE I

The German King who knew no English

IN 1714 George I, Elector of Hanover, dawdled to the throne of Great Britain and Ireland. He did not trouble to come over from his beloved homeland till seven weeks after the death of Queen Anne. When he did arrive he aroused little enthusiasm for the new Hanoverian dynasty. He was a reserved, plodding, awkward German, as dull in personality as in looks. He knew not a word of English. He did not understand English politics. And he did not want to. The Whig party, as outright upholders of the new monarchy, now came into power. The Tories were left out in the cold as suspected Jacobites. The thirteen-year reign was as dull as George's expression, though it had a few sparkles. The temper of the English people had changed in the eighteenth century. The strife and agitation of the seventeenth century were over. The fight for Parliament and Church was won. A period of calm replaced a period of passion. The fires that had blazed so fiercely in the struggle for high ideals and noble causes died down. They were replaced by the feebler glow of practical pursuits. Worldly welfare and national stability became the general aim. With this mood came an increased toleration—and likewise lukewarmness—in religion. It was as though England had become middle-aged.

POPE AND WALPOLE

Two outstanding figures illustrate the character of the times: Alexander Pope with his witty, polished and artificial style of verse; and Sir Robert Walpole, the coarse, good-humoured, unsentimental country squire who headed the Government for twenty-one years from 1721. Walpole's long and mainly peaceful "rule," coupled with his financial genius, gave the country a healthful breathing space between wars; but his cynical outlook, his lack of ideals and his corrupt parliamentary methods lowered the moral standard of public life.

PARLIAMENT GAINS CONTROL

One of the interesting things to note in this reign is the way relations between Parliament, the King and his council of ministers developed. In earlier times the administration of public

Sir Robert Walpole, later Earl of Orford.

172

Alexander Pope, the famous poet.

affairs had been directed by the King with the advice of his Privy Council. When this body proved too large for practical purposes a smaller council, the germ of our modern cabinet, was selected from it. The members were chosen, or dismissed, by the King, whose servants they were; and they might be men drawn from different political parties. But these conditions had for some time been undergoing a change. The smaller council was becoming more like the cabinet of to-day, in which the members are the servants of Parliament, chosen by the leader of the party in power (the Prime Minister) from his own followers. It was far from having reached this stage under George I, but the King's disposition speeded up its progress. His lack of interest in English affairs, and his hankering after frequent holiday jaunts to Hanover, made him only too pleased to resign the burden of government to his ministers. So Parliament gained through the indifference of the King.

THE COMPOSITION OF PARLIAMENT

Parliament itself was a vastly different gathering from that of to-day. It stood for government by the property-owning classes. The masses of the people had no votes. The great aristocratic families—possessors of vast landed estates—formed the bulk of the governing class. They dominated the House of Lords and powerfully influenced the Commons. The House of Commons, composed of upper and middle class members, was very unequally representative, even of those particular ranks of society. And the elections to it were scandalously corrupt. There were many constituencies, containing only a few voters, which returned as many members as the whole of Yorkshire or Devonshire. Peers and other local magnates controlled numerous " pocket " boroughs and " rotten " boroughs, either by nominating the candidate to be elected or by selling the seat to the highest bidder. For many members, Parliament was the road to an easy living. These unscrupulous placemen sold their support to the Crown, or the ministry, for pensions or offices of profit. It is a sordid picture, but there are some purer colours in it. The House of Commons, despite its faults, could, on great occasions, display a robustly independent and truly national spirit. And it could boast a distinguished succession of gifted statesmen and powerful orators devoted to the public service.

THE JACOBITE REBELLION

One of the notable sparkles of the reign was an alarming Jacobite rising in 1715. Outbreaks were planned in both England and Scotland. The former made only a feeble flicker, but up in the Highlands there was quite a considerable flash. It was not till a set battle had been fought that the insurrection fizzled out in 1716.

THE SOUTH SEA BUBBLE

The next excitement was the South Sea Bubble. The South Sea Company was a prosperous trading venture. In 1719 it offered to take over the National Debt in return for certain commercial privileges. The Company's plan was to persuade the individual government creditors to transfer their rights to the Company in exchange for some of its shares. A bargain was struck and the Company's prospects looked so golden that there was a wild public rush to buy shares. The market price of the £100 shares leaped to £1,000. Fortunes were made in a day. The bubble was swelling. Presently it came to be realised that the golden prospects were not so golden after all. The tide turned. Panic set in. There followed a rush to sell, with few to buy. Fortunes were *lost* in a day. The bubble had burst. A public demand for vengeance on the Company and the Government blazed up. There had been bribery in high places. Before the blaze died down the Government had been all but consumed.

George II. 1727–60.

GEORGE II

A Period of Expansion

GEORGE II, who inherited the throne in 1727, was a fussy little man, but shrewd and straightforward and stout-hearted. In 1745 he had something to fuss over. Bonnie Prince Charlie, the dashing and glamorous Young Pretender, and son of the Old Pretender, landed in Scotland and raised a Jacobite insurrection. He seized Edinburgh. He made the English run like rabbits at Prestonpans. He crossed the Border. Though few English Jacobites rallied to his standard, the gallant prince marched blithely on and actually reached Derby. London shivered with fear. But his prudent captains, seeing his army melting away, persuaded him to turn back to Scotland.

And there, at Culloden, in 1746, his cause was laid in the dust, never to rise again.

THE WAR OF THE AUSTRIAN SUCCESSION

In foreign affairs, trade and dominion had become Britain's main concern. The conflict with Spain in 1739 arose out of the aggravating persistence of English merchants in the forbidden ports of South America. It was the first real break in the long peace of Walpole's rule, which ended in 1742. In 1740 the far bigger War of the Austrian Succession began. The Emperor Charles VI had persuaded most of the European powers to concur in the descent of his immense dominions to his young daughter, Maria Theresa. But, on his death, their greed for possible spoils made all their promises worthless. The Elector of Bavaria stepped forward with *his* claims and France and Spain supported him. Meantime there came a lightning stroke from King Frederick II of Prussia. The unscrupulous royal thief seized Silesia, a part of the Austrian inheritance. Britain entered the arena on Maria's side and at Dettingen in 1743 our little King George fussed like a hen and fought like a lion. When the war ended in 1748 Maria Theresa secured most of her rights, except Silesia.

OVERSEAS RIVALRY WITH FRANCE

For Britain and France the peace was scarcely a truce. In the competition for worldwide trade and dominion they were natural rivals. During the war they had been energetically jumping each other's claims in America and India. Now, they continued to face each other, ready to carry on the fight.

The English colonies in North America (Georgia had been added in 1732) stretched in a line along the Atlantic coast. Behind them to the south lay French Louisiana. In the north was French Canada. The French had conceived a grandiose design. They would connect their two great possessions with a chain of forts behind the English settlements. They would pin their enemies down. Then they would drive them into the sea. Meantime, after the " peace " of 1748, the rivals continued to batter each other vigorously.

INCREASE OF POWER IN INDIA

In India the vast Mogul empire was falling

174

Prince Charles Edward Stuart, son of the Old Pretender and grandson of James II, who raised a rebellion in favour of his father's claim to the throne in 1745. The venture ended in complete defeat.

to pieces and its provincial nawabs and rajahs were setting up as independent rulers. The principal English settlements were Bombay, Calcutta and Madras. The headquarters of the French East India Company were at Pondicherry. The struggle between the rivals took two forms: direct fighting, and manœuvres for winning the favour of the dusky local rulers. This is where that determined young man, Robert Clive, comes in. At the age of nineteen he had arrived in India as a clerk to the English company. Presently he abandoned his desk for the field of action. In 1751-2 his

astonishing dash and courage won and held Arcot, the capital of the Carnatic, against odds of twenty to one and restored the pro-British nawab to power.

THE SEVEN YEARS WAR

1756 brought the Seven Years' War. Maria Theresa hungered for the recovery of Silesia. Most of Europe joined in the general scramble, this time with Britain on the side of Prussia, and France supporting Austria. As usual, Britain started badly. Then William Pitt took charge of affairs. Pitt was a strategist on the grand scale. His eye took in the four corners of the world of combat. His energy was terrific, his self-confidence boundless, his enthusiasm and burning oratory irresistible. He gave new vigour to the operations in Europe; but his eyes were fixed on the lands beyond the oceans. 1759 set England's bells ringing till they were like to crack. Guadeloupe, in the West Indies, was taken. The battle of Minden brought imperishable glory to Britain's redcoats. The French navy was crippled in the battles of Lagos and Quiberon Bay. Quebec, the key to Canada, fell to the dauntless determination of the dying hero Wolfe. In 1760 Montreal went the way of Quebec and the French dreams of an empire in America were ended.

Meantime, in 1757, Clive in India had scored the sensational victory of Plassy—a matter of three thousand men against a mere fifty thousand. By 1760 he had established English supremacy in Bengal, while other captains were winkling the French out of the regions farther down the coast.

It was in the same year, with the Seven Years War still blazing, that King George died. He left Britain with her head held high and the foundations of her empire immeasurably broadened.

THE METHODIST MOVEMENT

A work of a higher character was the organisation of the Methodist movement by John Wesley and his colleagues from 1739 onwards. The Church had lost its former vigour and left the masses of the people without spiritual uplift. The passionate zeal and earnestness of Wesley's life-long crusade made the teachings of the Christian faith once more a living inspiration in daily life.

CLIVE OF INDIA

Soldier and Statesman

ON 29th September, 1725, there was born at Styche, near Market Drayton, a son and heir to Richard Clive, man of law and petty squire. The newcomer was christened Robert and in his early years at least was not regarded particularly highly by his choleric parent. Certainly, he was a wild boy who delighted in fighting and in such wild pranks as climbing the church steeple at Market Drayton and sitting astride a gargoyle with his legs dangling. There is a story, too, of how he laid his body across a street gutter to deflect the water into the shop of a tradesman who had annoyed him. In the circumstances, it is hardly surprising that the general attitude to young Clive could be summed up in the report of one headmaster that he was the most unlucky boy they had ever had. Only one, Dr. Eaton, differed from this finding and foresaw the greatness that was to come.

IN THE EAST INDIA COMPANY

In 1743, when he was eighteen, Clive was appointed as a writer in the service of the East India Company and was posted off to Madras. To begin with, he was far from happy. He was poor and friendless and his sensitive pride made him keenly aware of this. He reached such a state of depression that in 1744 he tried to commit suicide. The gun, however, failed to go off and Clive decided, thereupon, that he was spared for a greater future.

The conditions for that future were slowly coming into being. With the collapse of the Mogul Empire, India had split up into a number of warring states which were too busy fighting each other to be aware of dangers from the outside. Dupleix, the French governor of Pondicherry and a cunning, subtle man, realised this long before anyone else and began to carve out an empire for himself and France. In 1746, the French captured Madras with ridiculous and shameful ease and young Clive was made prisoner. He escaped dressed in native attire and in 1747 he asked for and was granted a commission as an ensign in the Company's forces. He showed his quality at the siege of Pondicherry; but in 1748, the Treaty of Aix-la-Chapelle gave Madras back to the British and Clive returned reluctantly to his ledgers.

SUCCESS IN SOUTH INDIA

The peace between France and Britain, however, was only real on paper. Both sides began a kind of underground struggle for control of South India by supporting rival claimants to its various thrones. In 1751, the British-sponsored rival for the Carnatic was penned up in Trichinopoly. Clive, now a captain, put forward the suggestion of creating a diversion by an attack on Arcot, the capital of the Carnatic. The suggestion was approved and Clive was placed in command of the expedition. He marched off with a force that consisted of two hundred Europeans and three hundred sepoys. Their artillery consisted of three light field pieces. Eight officers commanded the sepoys and of these eight, only two had ever smelled gunpowder. In less than a week, Clive had created, out of this unpromising material, a disciplined and formidable force that marched across the Carnatic plains through a fierce thunderstorm to take the fort of Arcot without firing a shot.

The plan was completely successful, four thousand men being detached from the force that was attacking Trichinopoly to deal with the sudden threat at Arcot. Clive and his small force, however, beat off all attacks. The attackers withdrew and Trichinopoly was then relieved. The name of Clive was suddenly famous and when he married and returned, a wealthy man, to England in 1753, he was received with great honour. His ambitions now tended towards a career in politics but they failed to be realised and, disappointed, Clive began to think of India once more. He applied again to the East India Company and was welcomed back with open arms. In 1756, he returned to India as lieutenant-governor of Fort St. David in Madras.

"THE BLACK HOLE OF CALCUTTA"

His arrival was perfectly timed. For, twenty-four hours after he disembarked,

Robert Clive, Governor of Bengal. A great soldier, statesman and administrator.

Suraja Dowlah, ruler of Bengal, captured Calcutta and herded one hundred and forty-six British prisoners into the notorious "Black Hole of Calcutta," a low oven-like room from which only twenty-three survivors staggered the following morning. When news of this outrage arrived at Madras, the Governor immediately sent Clive to recapture the city and punish the tyrant. By the end of the year, Clive had retaken the city and had also captured the French settlement of Chandernagore. Suraja Dowlah, however, was still in power but Clive saw clearly that there would be neither stability nor peace in Bengal until Suraja Dowlah was deposed. He decided, therefore, to replace the weak, capricious tyrant with Mir Jafar,

Fort George, on the Coromandel coast, the property of the East India Company.

a man of his own choosing, and with this in view, a great deal of secret and not always very creditable intrigue was set afoot. This led up to the Battle of Plassey on 12th June, 1757. Suraja Dowlah brought into the field thirty-five thousand infantry, fifteen thousand cavalry plus fifty-three heavy guns and a small detachment of French soldiers. Against this force, Clive opposed eleven hundred Europeans, two thousand one hundred sepoys and ten light field guns. Despite their overwhelming superiority in numbers, Suraja Dowlah's forces were routed and Clive retired the victor with the loss of only seventy men. The tyrant fled and was very soon murdered. The French power in Bengal was broken. Mir Jafar was enthroned and the career of Clive was at its zenith.

GOVERNOR OF BENGAL

When he came back again to England in 1760, he was created a Knight of the Bath and an Irish baron. He was also elected to Parliament; and when reports reached England of corruption and mismanagement in Bengal, Clive was reappointed governor and during the period 1765 to 1767 he completely reorganised the province, removing abuses, improving the administration and putting the armed forces on a sound basis. This, naturally, made him many enemies and when ill-health forced him to return home after two years, he found that his enemies had been at work there too.

CLIVE CHARGED WITH CORRUPTION

A committee was set up to investigate the charges made against Clive, particularly the charge of bribery. The House of Commons inquiry lasted for two years and ended in a complete vindication of Clive. Yet, in another way, his enemies had achieved their purpose. The proud, sensitive Clive, broken by ill-health and smarting under the stigma of unfair criticism, became subject to fits of depression. On 22nd November, 1774, for the second time in his life he put a pistol to his head; and this time the pistol did not misfire. But his work did not die with him; and long after he was dead, posterity awarded him a title that he would have been proud to have acknowledged —Clive of India.

Captain James Cook, who planted Britain's flag in Australia and New Zealand.

CAPTAIN JAMES COOK

JAMES COOK was born in 1728, one of the nine children of a poor farm labourer who lived in the village of Staithes, near Whitby on the Yorkshire coast. This was hardly an auspicious start for a man who later became one of the greatest navigators of all time. Thanks to his father's employer and a friendly old lady, young Cook managed to get an education; but he had a more ambitious use for it than a career in the grocer's shop where

he was employed as an apprentice. So one day he walked out of the little shop and joined a ship that was sailing to London.

SURVEYOR AND EXPLORER

In London, he joined another ship whose destination was Canada. Here, James Cook saw action and took part in the capture of Quebec by General Wolfe. Here, too, his natural navigational genius first displayed

179

itself and soon James Cook was well known as a surveyor with a particular talent for charting tides and currents. It is hardly surprising, therefore, that when an expedition was sent out to Tahiti to observe an eclipse of the sun, James Cook was one of those chosen to go. Apart from its astronomical duties the expedition was empowered to conduct geographical research and this led to the discovery of the mainland of Australia and the annexation of a new colony for the British Crown. The party also explored New Zealand. Cook's career almost came to an abrupt end in these uncharted seas when his ship struck a rock, some distance from the coast. The rock pierced the ship's bottom and broke off, leaving a plug of solid rock wedged in the gaping hole. On his return to England, in the year 1770, James Cook received promotion and became a commander.

THE HEALTH OF THE CREW

Two years later, he was off again, this time towards the South Pole, where he hoped to discover a few facts about the great ice mass of the Antarctic Ocean. The Antarctic regions were explored, Easter Island, the Marquesas

Cook's renowned ship *Resolution* (467 tons).

and the Friendly Islands were visited and charted. Even more important were Cook's experiments, on this voyage, to promote the health of his crew. Dirt and disease killed more sailors than the sea ever did and James Cook was one of the first responsible people to tackle this problem. He demanded so high a standard of cleanliness on board his ships that someone once said that on Cook's ships it was always Sunday. He saw that his crews were always amply supplied with fresh water. He experimented with various foods in an effort to prevent scurvy, the dreaded skin disease caused by malnutrition. He had a kind of dried soup made from meat and bones and resembling in appearance very hard glue. A century and a half later, in 1938, this stuff was found to be still fresh. The Antarctic voyage proved to be one of the healthiest on record, and Cook was honoured by the Royal Society for his work on hygiene.

THE LAST VOYAGE

His third and last voyage was an attempt to discover the North-West Passage. His ships were driven by a storm to take shelter at Hawaii. A dispute arose concerning a stolen boat. A man was killed, the natives rose in anger and the men in Cook's boat opened fire. As Cook turned to give the order to cease fire, a native sprang at him and stabbed him in the back. Screaming natives then pounced on the defenceless man and hacked him to pieces within sight of his own boats. Thus, on 14th February, 1779, the gentlest of explorers met the most gruesome of deaths.

CONQUER THROUGH FRIENDSHIP

James Cook was unlike many great men, he had no harsh or brutal traits in his character. He did not hate anyone as Drake had hated the Spaniards. He did not plunder as the Sea Dogs of earlier centuries had done; he maintained that the best way to conquer was through friendship. Killing, to him, was abhorrent. It is interesting to note that, when Britain and France were at war, the French captains were instructed that there was one Englishman who was not to be touched—Captain James Cook. This was indeed a great tribute from an enemy power to James Cook, the brilliant explorer and navigator, who always remained simple and unassuming.

GEORGE III
A Long and Troubled Reign

THE long reign—from 1760 to 1820—of George III, grandson of George II, was packed with tremendous events. The new King was a sincere, brave and well-meaning young man, but not over-bright, and very narrow and obstinate in his views. Unlike the earlier Georges, he " gloried in the name of Briton." He opened his innings with the fixed idea of doing most of the scoring himself, instead of leaving it to the cabinet, as his predecessors had done. So he appointed his own chief ministers and organised, largely by bribery, a party in the House of Commons on whose support he could depend. Among these " King's friends," as they were labelled, the Tories were predominant, for the Tory party had now become reconciled to the Hanoverian succession.

THE END OF THE SEVEN YEARS WAR

The Seven Years War was yielding further successes, including the capture of Pondicherry, the last of the French strongholds in India. The struggle ended in 1763 and, under the peace treaty, France ceded Canada, her claims on the country east of the Mississippi, several West Indian islands and the African settlement of Senegal, while Spain handed over Florida. France, however, received back her settlements in India, on condition that she should not fortify them.

THE LOSS OF THE AMERICAN COLONIES

Shortly after pocketing these marvellous prizes, something in the nature of a gale warning came from across the Atlantic. The war had left Britain loaded with debt. Much of this had been incurred in securing the American colonies from French designs, and the mother-country thought they ought to bear a small part of the burden she was now carrying. Accordingly, in 1765 and 1767, several duties were imposed, mainly on tea and other imports into the colonies. They aroused hot resentment and active opposition, being condemned as an infringement of the colonists' rights of self-government. By 1770 the situation had become critical. Pitt, who had been made Earl of Chatham, had finally retired from office; and King George, with his new tame minister, Lord North, was bent on scoring a boundary. To pacify the colonists, all the duties were repealed except that on tea; but the obstinate George insisted on retaining this so as to assert Britain's right of taxation. His attitude was neither unfair nor illegal and it was strongly supported in Parliament and the country. None the less, to persist in it in the face of the strong colonial feeling aroused, was crass stupidity. The colonists stood out mainly for the time-honoured English principle of " no taxation without representation." And, quite apart from this, they declared that they were no longer children subject to their mother's arbitrary authority.

The result of the long and unhappy dispute was calamitous. Arguments were followed by deeds, deeds led to bloodshed, and so in 1775 the bitter War of American Independence commenced. On the 4th July, 1776, the colonies which had revolted issued their Declaration of Independence, and the history of the United States began. During the next four years France and Spain flung themselves eagerly into the fight against their old enemy and Holland was added to the circle of Britain's foes. The sorry tale came to an end in 1783, when Britain was driven to acknowledge defeat and let her children go. It was like the loss of a limb. And there were further losses: Minorca and Florida to Spain; Senegal and other possessions to France.

AUSTRALIA COLONISED

Perhaps it was some consolation for this gloomy failure, to reflect that we were soon to begin to help ourselves to a new continent. Captain Cook had explored the east coast of Australia in 1770 and eighteen years later the penal settlement of Botany Bay was founded.

BRITISH INFLUENCE IN INDIA

But things were certainly looking more cheerful in India. Acts of Parliament which were passed in 1773 and 1784 made the East

George III. 1760–1820.

approaching the powder-barrel of national discontent. And, when the explosion came, it rocked Europe. Within four years the Revolution, in a frenzy of destruction and reconstruction, had turned France upside down and drenched it with blood. Monarchy, aristocracy and Church alike were overthrown. A free republic was proclaimed. The King was mercilessly guillotined. The reign of " liberty, equality and fraternity " had begun its stormy career.

EFFECT ON EUROPE

The wild excesses of the upheaval, and the revolutionaries' encouragement to other nations to rise against their rulers, created sharp alarm throughout Europe—and with good reason. In 1792 Austrian and Prussian troops invaded France. In the following year, with the exultant French patriots overrunning the Austrian Netherlands and threatening Holland, Britain was inevitably drawn into the fray.

The Earl of Chatham had died in 1778 and his son, William Pitt the younger, was now chief minister. He was lacking in many of his father's great qualities, but his unshakable resolution and self-confidence were to prove Britain's main driving force in the perilous years ahead till he died in harness in 1806.

THE NAPOLEONIC WAR

Soon France was beset with a coalition of enemies in arms. But the flaming ardour of her citizen-soldiers hurled them back. By 1797 Britain faced her alone. Worse still, Spain and Holland were now leagued with victorious France; and France had produced the all-conquering military genius of Napoleon Bonaparte. But, if we could not fight the Corsican ogre on land, we could fight his power at sea, as Jervis and Duncan and Nelson showed in the terrific victories of Cape St. Vincent and Camperdown in 1797, the Nile in 1798 and Copenhagen in 1801.

In 1803, when the war was renewed after a brief truce, it had ceased to be merely one against republican France. It had grown into a struggle against Napoleon's attempted domination of Europe. His plans for invading Britain were foiled by her navy and nicely disposed of in 1805 by Nelson's smashing victory off Trafalgar—won, alas! at the cost of the victor's priceless life. By 1807 Napoleon,

India Company's rule subject to Crown control. The succession of able Governors-General sent out, beginning with Warren Hastings, extended the sphere of British influence, British justice and settled government step by step. By the end of the reign it embraced almost the entire sub-continent.

THE FRENCH REVOLUTION

In Europe the peace of 1783 was shattered, six years later, by the convulsions of the French Revolution. France had suffered the insufferable too long—a despotic monarchy, an oppressive government, a privileged and selfish aristocracy and higher clergy, a despised peasantry burdened with outworn feudal services and a load of taxation from which the nobility and the Church were exempt. Ideas of an enlightened popular government, and of the natural rights of man, had long been filtering in from free England, and, later, from the newly-free United States of America. They acted like a long, slowly smouldering fuse

now Emperor of France, had reached such a height of power that most of western Europe lay prostrate at his feet. But soon events that were to mark the beginning of his decline began to shape themselves. Arthur Wellesley (some day to be better known as the Duke of Wellington) drove his marshals' armies from Portugal and Spain in the Peninsular War of 1808–1814. Meantime Napoleon had overreached himself in an invasion of Russia and a disastrous retreat from Moscow in 1812. Next year he suffered defeat at Leipzig by a new coalition of enemies. His final ruin came in 1815 with the epoch-making triumph of the Duke of Wellington, clinched by the timely co-operation of the Prussian Blücher, on the field of Waterloo. Europe breathed again.

The Bourbon kings were restored in France. Belgium (the former Austrian Netherlands) and Holland were united as an independent state. Britain retained various conquests she had made, including Malta and Mauritius from the French and the Cape of Good Hope from the Dutch.

BRITAIN'S OTHER TROUBLES

A year earlier a harassing little additional war had closed down. The proudly independent

United States of America had resisted Britain's claim to stop neutral ships trading with France or her allies, and war had followed in 1812. So Britain and her former colonies once more fell to slogging each other, till peace—but not, unfortunately, goodwill—was restored two years later.

Yet another untimely hornet-sting had come from Ireland. The lot of the down-trodden Catholics had been greatly improved by the abolition of some of the harsh penal laws passed against them after William III's conquest. And the Irish Parliament had been made independent of the British legislature. But the demand for further concessions, and even for complete independence of Britain, led to a rebellion in 1798. It was quickly stifled, but it had an important sequel. By the Act of Union of 1800 Ireland was united with Great Britain, the Dublin Parliament closed its doors and henceforth Irish members sat in the Parliament at Westminster.

THE INDUSTRIAL REVOLUTION

George III's reign saw the development of the Industrial Revolution which completely transformed the daily life of the people and

In 1773 colonists at Boston protested against the Stamp Act by dressing up as Red Indians and throwing chests of tea overboard at Boston. This became known as the Boston Tea-party.

James Watt, the inventor and engineer, who realised the mechanical capabilities of steam and developed the steam engine.

changed Britain from a mainly agricultural to a mainly industrial country.

During the eighteenth century agriculture itself was revolutionised. New methods of cultivation and the growing of root and other crops vastly increased the yield. Scientific breeding and improved feeding doubled the weight of cattle and sheep. Millions of acres of open land were enclosed. Large farms, progressively managed, took the place of small backward holdings. But now the machine age had come. Mechanical inventions in the textile industry had begun in the previous reign. They now followed each other in a steady succession. Then the Scotsman, James Watt, brought out his improved steam engine, which began the age of steam power for machinery, and George Stephenson built his first locomotive. Discoveries were made for smelting iron with coal and coke instead of with charcoal. New canals and better roads facilitated inland transport of goods of all kinds. The national wealth rose by leaps and bounds.

DISCONTENT IN THE COUNTRY

But there was another side to the picture. The growing wealth was unequally shared. The war, and the slump that followed it, dislocated trade and industry in the midst of these fundamental changes. The altered agricultural conditions dislodged large numbers of small farmers and peasants from their holdings. The population to be supported was increasing fast. In large areas of the country, as in the rapidly growing towns, to which many countrymen were drifting, the evils of unemployment, low wages and dear food appeared. Factory hours, and working and living conditions, were becoming positively inhuman. In many districts the workers were reduced to the gripping extremes of want and squalor and hopeless misery.

The outcome was a deep and sullen discontent. Riots and other disturbances became frequent. Parliament, ignorant of the true conditions of affairs, was unsympathetic. Accordingly, a long-standing demand for its " radical," or root, reform was pressed forward with increased emphasis. The House of Commons, it was asserted, should be made more fully representative of the people, the mass of whom were voteless. But the government feared that these agitations were inflamed with the lawless spirit of the French Revolution—of which, indeed, there were signs —and rigidly repressed them. The era of reform had not yet come, but it was on the way.

PROLIFIC LITERATURE

Only a brief mention can be made of the prolific literature of the times. The reign is filled with illustrious names, of which the most familiar to us all are the English poets, Wordsworth, Coleridge, Shelley, Keats and Byron, the Irish Oliver Goldsmith, and the Scottish national bard Burns and " the wizard of the North," Sir Walter Scott.

Poor King George's active career came to an unhappy end. Following on previous attacks, he became quite insane and from 1811 his son, the future George IV, acted as Regent.

RAFFLES OF SINGAPORE

A Practical Visionary

O N THE 6th July, 1781, a boy was born on board the merchant ship *Ann*, off Morant Point in Jamaica. His father, Benjamin Raffles, was the master of the vessel, trading without much success between London and Jamaica; and in due course the boy was christened Thomas Stamford Raffles, a name that was to become famous throughout the tropics.

A CLERK IN THE EAST INDIA COMPANY

It would almost appear that young Raffles had no childhood at all. There is a brief mention of him at a boarding school in Hammersmith; but details of his life until his fourteenth year are very sketchy and add up to very little more than that he was interested in botany and had a passion for animals. The picture becomes clearer in 1795 when he was appointed to an extra-clerkship with the East India Company: and it is a picture worthy of Dickens. Young Raffles's earnings, small as they were, represented an important contribution to a family in such straitened circumstances that the burning of a candle in a room was an extravagance; and for five years, the boy worked with an almost incredible eagerness and application, by day at his desk in the Leadenhall Street office, in the early dawn and late into the night at his private studies. Fortunately, this devotion did not go unnoticed and by 1800 Raffles was earning £100 a year and ruining his health in the process. Five years of grinding work ensued until, in 1805, there came his moment of destiny. The East India Company had recently taken over the Island of Penang along with a strip of territory on the Malayan mainland. It was now decided to constitute this as a Presidency with a Governor and Council and Raffles was made Assistant Secretary to the new body at a salary of £1,500. The days of debt and drudgery were over. The family's future was assured. Raffles could marry and did.

APPOINTMENT TO PENANG

It was typical of Raffles that he spent the long months of the voyage east learning to

Sir Thomas Stamford Raffles (1781-1826), founder of Singapore.

speak and write the Malay language, an achievement that to a great extent shaped his career; for very few men have understood the Malays as Raffles did. His studies did not cease, moreover, when the ship docked. In fact the pattern of his new life showed little difference from the pattern of the grim days in Leadenhall Street. The surroundings were rather more exotic but that was all. There was the same overwhelming amount of work that made him, with each day that passed, more and more indispensable to the Governor. There were, too, the dedicated private studies in the hours before dawn and in the evenings after work. In 1807, he was promoted to be Secretary. He was appointed the official Malay Translator. He was the pivot of the whole organisation and he could not even take time off to recover from illness. " We shall not be able to make up any dispatches for the Court without your assistance," the Governor wrote, begging him to cut short his convalescence. The strain was superhuman and in 1808, Raffles collapsed under it. He was ordered to spend a few months in Malacca where the

185

climate was kindlier. He arrived at a crisis in the history of Malacca and, although he did not know it, at a crisis in his own. The Directors of India House had decreed that Penang was to be the only settlement. Malacca as a trading post was to be abandoned and destroyed. The fort was to be demolished and the native population was to be lured and persuaded to Penang.

A PROTEST ABOUT MALACCA

Raffles was aghast at the stupidity of this policy and immediately sat down to draft a report that was also a protest. He pointed out that Malacca was a more suitable trading centre than Penang; that other European powers would not be slow to take it over in the event of its being abandoned by the British; that should it be occupied, there would be a threat, not only to Penang but to the whole China trade. The report, miraculously, went forward and, even more miraculously, was acted upon. The evacuation of Malacca was cancelled. Raffles was pompously commended by his superiors. More important, the report brought his name to the notice of Lord Minto, the Governor-General in Calcutta. Raffles returned to Penang where for the next two years he found himself increasingly discontented. It seemed to him that through short-sightedness and excessive caution, Britain was losing a wonderful opportunity of establishing a great eastern empire. He dreamed of complete British control of Malaya and the extension of sovereignty to Java, Borneo and Celebes; and in 1810 he made a bold decision. Having been granted leave, he set off on a dangerous voyage across the Bay of Bengal to find out how receptive the Governor-General might be to his ideas.

PLANS TO ATTACK JAVA

Lord Minto was extremely receptive. He had long had Java in mind as a link in the chain of defence against Napoleon's threatened encirclement of India. Raffles was eagerly welcomed and when he returned to Penang, he was wearing a new title, that of " Agent to the Governor-General with the Malay States." His immediate task was to prepare the way for the expedition that was, in due course, to attack French-held Java. Raffles threw all his incredible energy into the task and his reports

were masterpieces of keen, accurate detail. Soon Lord Minto had organised the expedition and was ready to move, and on the 29th July, 1811, Lord Minto and Raffles, his agent and secretary, saw the coastline of Java loom up from the deck of H.M.S. *Modeste*. The landing of the British force was hardly opposed since the Franco-Dutch forces had decided to withdraw inland to the strong fortification of Cornelis. This was stormed on 26th August and by 18th September, all resistance was over and the French general had capitulated. Java was now a British possession and its new lieutenant-governor was the ex-clerk, Thomas Stamford Raffles. It was not to prove a long appointment. His far-sighted reforms and brilliant administration were not popular at home because, to begin with, they cost money. Lord Minto died and his successor was hostile. The Company was beginning to rue its bargain as far as Java was concerned and when the Peace of Vienna was signed, Britain handed back to Holland all her former East Indian possessions including Java. Raffles was curtly relieved of his duties and left Java in March 1816. Behind him he left, too, his wife and all his children who had died during his term of office. A severe illness followed and when he recovered he took leave and returned to

Gilbert Elliot, Earl of Minto.

England. His ship called in at St. Helena where the exiled Napoleon showed a great deal more interest in Java than had been evinced by his British conquerors; and by July, Raffles was back in England.

A NEW APPOINTMENT

He was home only for a crowded year during which he wrote a two-volume History of Java, was knighted, and married again. An inquiry was held into his Javanese administration and, his character having been cleared, he was created Lieutenant-Governor of Benkulen, on the west coast of Sumatra, and in November 1817 he was back east again. He found his new domain broken-down and neglected and with characteristic energy set about re-establishing it. He travelled widely getting to know the place and the people and the rulers. He saw that the Dutch, who were also established in Sumatra, were likely to crowd the British out. He came into conflict with them at Palembang and published, on his own initiative, a biting protest. The furious Dutch protested to the British Government. Raffles was severely censured and for a while his dismissal seemed certain. It was almost as though the Directors of the East India Company were going out of their way to destroy themselves by handing over complete control of the East Indies to the Dutch; and there is no doubt that, but for Raffles's tenacity and vision, this is precisely what would have happened.

SINGAPORE ESTABLISHED

Once again, however, a perilous voyage across the Bay of Bengal saved the situation; and Raffles was instructed by the new Governor-General to establish a British Post in a situation that would be commercially advantageous and, at the same time, outside the Dutch sphere of influence. Raffles went off, happy with this commission and established the post at Singapore on 29th January, 1819. The Dutch were furious and abusive. There were threats of violence. But the Governor-General stood by Raffles in the face of attacks from both London and Holland. The value of Singapore suddenly became obvious. The Dutch climbed down. Raffles was satisfied. He had finally defeated them.

He returned to Benkulen and he quietly resumed his duties. He knew that Singapore had justified his life and his work. For the next year he was, perhaps, happier than he had ever been. Benkulen flourished under his guidance. He indulged in his hobby of botany. Two young tigers and a bear roamed about the house and played with the Raffles children. An orang-utan strolled about, dressed, rather oddly, in white linen. A cat played with a parrot. Then suddenly, within three weeks, all the children were dead with the exception of the youngest who was saved by being sent off immediately to England. Raffles and his wife were seriously ill. Heart-broken, he wrote home, asking that a successor be sent out. In 1822 he paid a final visit to Singapore; and spent nine months there, leaving it for the last time on 4th June, 1823. Months passed before he could get a ship home and it was not until August 1824 that he landed finally in Plymouth, lean, yellow and ill, with 173 cases containing books, stuffed animals, birds, and coral, paintings and musical instruments.

IN ENGLAND

He threw himself busily into public life and found himself the lion of the hour. He made maps of Sumatra and Singapore and had them engraved. He founded the Zoological Society for which the Government gifted a site in the new Regent's Park. He bought a farm and settled down to live quietly at Mill Hill. Then suddenly, his conduct in the east was brought in question again and another inquiry was opened. The Government exonerated Raffles but the India Company presented him with a bill for £22,000 which he had allegedly expended during his period of service with them. This blow was followed by the news of the failure of a Calcutta firm and the loss of a further £16,000. Raffles began a correspondence with the Company but before anything was settled, he was found dead, one morning, on the eve of his forty-fifth birthday. Apoplexy, the doctors said. After his death, the Company generously accepted £10,000 from his widow in settlement of its claims. It took later generations to appreciate the full extent of his achievement and to implement the dream he dreamed when he founded what has since become one of the greatest and most important ports in the world.

THE DUKE OF WELLINGTON

A Brilliant Soldier

IT IS a nice coincidence that Arthur Wellesley (one day to be Duke of Wellington) and Napoleon Bonaparte, who were fated to meet each other forty-six years later in the shock of Waterloo, should have been born in the same year of 1769.

Arthur's parents came of an old Anglo-Irish line and his birth took place in Dublin. The family belonged to the aristocratic governing class, Arthur's father being Earl of Mornington and his mother a viscount's daughter. The child developed into an unpromising and rather sickly youth, and his handsome and brilliantly gifted elder brother, Richard, once tolerantly dubbed him " the biggest ass in Europe." When he had idled long enough at Eton and in Brussels, his mother sent her "awkward son" to a sort of French military, or " finishing," academy at Angers. Then, in his eighteenth year, he donned the soldier's red coat with an ensign's commission.

EARLY MILITARY CAREER

Even so he performed little, if any, regimental duty during the next six years. Instead, he served as A.D.C. to the Lord Lieutenant of Ireland and entered the Irish Parliament. In those days, however, army promotion often went by favour; and family influence, plus generous brother Richard's purse, made him a lieutenant-colonel at twenty-four. Still, he did some serious reading and began to give that marked attention to the practical details of his profession that was to be such a notable feature of his career.

Private and public events combined to quicken his interest in the service. In 1789 the French Revolution had blazed up and subsequently set Europe afire. Britain was drawn into the conflict and the young colonel had his first, and extremely unpleasant, experience of fighting the French in 1794–95. His brigade covered the retreat of the Duke of York, King George III's second son, in the Netherlands.

The whirlpool of the war in Europe washed to the shores of the East. The territory then controlled by Britain in India embraced only Bengal, the Northern Circars and various areas in the south including Madras, together with Bombay on the west. But even there her position was threatened. The French hopes of empire had, indeed, been rudely dashed by Clive and his successors; but French agents were busily engaged in inciting the discontented native princes to rise and training their troops for the total overthrow of British power.

WITH HIS REGIMENT TO INDIA

At this juncture Arthur's regiment was ordered to India, where it disembarked in 1797, and his brilliant brother Richard went out as Governor-General. Arthur, now a full colonel, was a neat and slightly built young man of nearly twenty-eight. One can think only of predatory birds when describing his features, for he had an eagle eye and an immense hawk nose. Self-confidence had always been his strong point: now his ambitions had grown. His studies had already gone far to make him a human encyclopædia of the technical details of the soldier's calling, besides educating him in the general principles of war and the special problems of India. The new Governor-General, who had once dubbed his brother a superlative ass, was quick to recognise, and to depend upon, his sound judgment in both political and military affairs.

ACTION AGAINST NATIVE RULERS

Tippoo Sahib, the wily " Tiger of Mysore," was conspiring with the French; and, to stop his capers, war was declared against him in 1799. During the ensuing campaign Colonel Wellesley's growing military reputation suffered a slight check in the attack on Seringapatam. He was unsuccessful in a subsidiary night operation entrusted to him by the general in command. None the less, when the city was taken, his brother appointed him Governor. The manner in which he discharged the duties of that responsible office was a revelation of his accomplished generalship in the field and of his understanding, tact and good faith in dealing with the natives.

Four years later, when he had become a major-general, he won fresh laurels in a war

The Duke of Wellington (1769–1852), who served his country long and faithfully as a soldier and, later, a politician.

against certain of the central Maratha States. In the battle of Assaye his cool and calculated daring shattered a strongly placed army four times his own strength. Two months afterwards he took another scalp at Argaum and later stormed the " impregnable " fortress of Gawilghur. The Maratha chieftains sued for peace.

By 1805 there remained little prospect of serious fighting and Wellesley sailed for home. He was Sir Arthur now. Eight years of arduous service in the East had grounded him in war and statecraft. His once weakly frame had waxed tough and wiry. He had matured into a serious-minded man of thirty-six, tirelessly engrossed in his duties. The Governor-General's Indian career ended at the same time. The period had been gloriously fruitful. Britain's modest eastern mansion had been enlarged into a vast palace, thoroughly disinfected of the germs of French intrigue. Britain had, indeed, established herself as the dominant power in the great sub-continent.

And to the winning of this achievement Sir Arthur had made a conspicuous contribution.

THE BEGINNING OF THE PENINSULAR WAR

In 1807 Napoleon, who had become Emperor of France, had brought well-nigh all western Europe under his heel. Britain alone continued to defy him. Napoleon had thoughts of seizing the neutral Danish Fleet for use against the incurably stubborn islanders. But Britain forestalled him and pounced on it herself. A combined expedition to Copenhagen carried out the judicious little act of brigandage, and Wellesley was engaged in the land fighting and in arranging the terms of the Danes' surrender. This, however, was small fry and in 1808 he got his real chance. Promoted to the rank of lieutenant-general, he was given the command of an expedition to Portugal. Napoleon had already annexed the kingdom of our oldest ally and also seated his brother Joseph on the throne of Spain. Sir Arthur's mission was to aid the two nations in their struggle to throw off the alien yoke.

Within three weeks of his landing he broke the army of Marshal Junot at Vimeiro. But, unhappily, army jealousy at home had already caused him to be superseded and he returned to England in disgust. The campaign ended lamentably with the embarkation of the British Army at Corunna, after the death of its then commander, the heroic Sir John Moore, in January, 1809.

Lisbon and Cadiz, however, remained in British hands and in April Wellesley was sent out to try again. It was a weighty task and the difficulties that were thenceforth continually to beset him quickly revealed themselves.

SPANISH AND PORTUGUESE ALLIES

His Spanish and Portuguese allies were as exasperating as a hair-shirt. The Portuguese troops, indeed, behaved excellently once they had been stiffened by British training. And the Spanish irregular combatants, or guerrillas, performed priceless service; for the furious war they everywhere waged against the hated French pinned down large numbers of the enemy troops. But the regular Spanish generals and officials were fantastically unreliable and incompetent.

Wellesley's own British army—apart from

An artist's impression of Wellington encouraging one of the squares at the Battle of Waterloo.
For eight long hours the British troops had to withstand the repeated assaults of the French.
When Wellington's troops finally advanced, it was against an exhausted foe.

the Spanish and Portuguese troops who shared in its battles—was woefully small compared with the French. Yet there was one factor, over and above the Spanish guerrilla operations, that helped to correct the balance of numbers. Spain was a poor and mountainous country and could not feed large armies for long at a time in any one district. They had to break up and seek their dinner elsewhere. Wellesley's supplies came largely from overseas. (Their efficient distribution was one of the major problems he had to tackle.) But the French were accustomed to " live on the country." Accordingly, they could only concentrate their superior numbers against Wellesley for limited periods and particular efforts.

With such allies and such forces the harassed British commander was called upon to face Napoleon's celebrated veteran marshals and some of the finest troops in Europe.

THE CAMPAIGN

He faced them with his customary assurance. First he drove Marshal Soult over the hills and far away out of Portugal. Then he made a bold dash into Spain towards Madrid. At Talavera

he won a hard-fought and costly triumph over Marshal Victor and King Joseph. He was rewarded with a peerage and became Lord Wellington. But it was a barren victory. The food supply failed and Soult was threatening his communications with his base in Portugal. There was nothing for it but to retreat. Napoleon, arrogantly confident of ending the whole business by driving the British into the sea, poured reinforcements into Spain. Next year, 1810, Wellington was pressed back on Lisbon by the great Marshal Masséna. Then, to the stupefaction of that redoubtable general and the astonished delight of the retreating British, Wellington cheerfully led his men behind the impregnable system of defences, the famous Lines of Torres Vedras, which he had secretly constructed for such an emergency.

Next spring, 1811, he had the satisfaction of hustling the disgruntled Masséna's starving and bedraggled army out of Portugal. Wellington, clearly, was not to be driven into the sea. But would he ever be strong enough to advance and sweep the French legions from Spain? He decided, at all events, to prepare the way. He would besiege the great fortresses of Ciudad

Rodrigo and Badajoz: their possession would close the gates of Portugal against the enemy and open the roads into Spain for himself. The operations brought his army two more hard-won successes—Fuentes de Oñoro and Albuera; but it was not till 1812 that the grim sentinel fortresses were triumphantly stormed. The victor was honoured with an earldom.

SUCCESS AND FAILURE

And now Napoleon's own soaring designs began to play into Wellington's hands. The Emperor had withdrawn a number of his best troops from the Peninsula to join the Grand Army in the invasion of Russia. Wellington marched once more into Spain. At Salamanca he continued his game of ninepins with Napoleon's generals by scoring a brilliant triumph over Marshal Marmont. In August he was in Madrid, and England jubilantly created him a marquis. Then once again the prize of victory was snatched from his grasp. His prolonged siege of Burgos, on the vital line of communications of all the French armies in Spain, failed. Profiting by the delay, the French concentrated from all quarters in overwhelming force and Wellington had to scramble back towards the safety of Portugal as best he could.

VICTORY

But he was not disheartened—he never was. During 1812 he had taken two key strongholds and, by drawing the French northwards, freed southern Spain. And the position in 1813 was heartening. Napoleon's Grand Army had practically perished amid the snows of Russia. The French forces in Spain had been further weakened, while Wellington's were reinforced and in high fettle. In May he began his third advance; and this time, like King Bruce's spider, he did not fail. By skilful manœuvring he forced the enemy to abandon Madrid and Burgos. In June his crushing defeat of King Joseph at Vitoria forced the miserable remnants of that hapless monarch's army across the Pyrenees. By the end of October the frontier fortresses of San Sebastian and Pamplona had fallen and Wellington's troops had crossed the frontier and set foot in France. Meanwhile, in the battle of Leipzig, the armies of a new coalition, embracing Britain, Prussia, Russia, Austria and Sweden, had taught Napoleon the bitter taste of total defeat. When Wellington

fought his last battle at Toulouse in April, 1814, the Emperor had already abdicated.

WELLINGTON'S GENIUS

Wellington had won his campaigns by clear military insight, able strategy and masterly tactics, by careful planning and organisation, by calm determination and cool self-confidence. His merciless discipline and watchful care, and the respect and confidence he won from his men—he never gained their love—had moulded his troops into an army with which he could " do anything, or go anywhere." Finally, his operations had fostered, and made effective, the disjointed guerrilla resistance of the Spanish people. This is a point we need to remember when valuing Wellington's achievement. For the guerrilla fighters in turn performed a major part in the winning of the final triumph.

The Peninsular War was one of the mighty punches that helped to knock out Napoleon. It was a continual drain on his strength: he himself inelegantly called it " a running sore." And the spectacle of a nation in arms for freedom's sake served as an inspiring and infectious example to the other oppressed peoples of Europe.

Britain could hardly do less than make her illustrious son a duke.

THE BATTLE OF WATERLOO

In 1815 Wellington represented Britain at the Congress of Vienna which assembled to resettle the chaotic affairs of Europe. Then, in March, came the thunder-clap. Napoleon, who had been exiled to the island of Elba, had escaped. By 20th March he was in Paris, having conjured up a new and deliriously enthusiastic army on the way. While the Allies were gathering their armies to overwhelm him, Napoleon struck at the most threatening of them—a British, German and Dutch-Belgian force under Wellington, and Blücher's Prussians.

On Sunday, 18th June, Wellington and Napoleon faced each other for the first time near the little Belgian town of Waterloo. Blücher was pressing forward to join his ally. For eight long hours Wellington's troops indomitably hurled back the repeated assaults of the massed French infantry columns and the charging cavalry. Then came their turn: the Duke gave the order to advance on the

UP AND DOWN
POLITICAL SEE-SAW

A contemporary cartoon showing (*left to right*) Lord Grey, William IV and the Duke of Wellington. Wellington, out of office, is advising against the Reform Bill, Grey, the Prime Minister, perilously perched has popular " support," whilst the poor King is in a dilemma.

exhausted foe. Blücher's timely appearance aided and clinched the historic victory. The French retreat became a rout. Napoleon's lurid star had set; and Wellington, in the crowning triumph of his military career, had finally delivered Europe.

WELLINGTON AS A POLITICIAN

Till 1818 the victor commanded the allied army of occupation in France. Then, returning to England, he held, from time to time, various offices in the government, including the premiership. He did not, however, excel in party politics. He strove to serve the best interests of his country as he conceived them. But his ideas were those of a member of the privileged governing class, a rigid Tory and a convinced Protestant; while the country itself was in a ferment over more democratic and progressive movements of reform. Wellington opposed " Catholic Emancipation " in Ireland, which would have admitted Roman Catholics to Parliament and various public offices. He opposed the Reform Bill of 1832, which sought to give the middle classes the vote. Yet on both these questions he had the good sense, in the end, to bow to the storm of public opinion.

There was a marked strain of aloofness and reserve in the duke's character and he made few friends. He was considered hard and unfeeling (did they not call him " the Iron Duke "?), and his manner was very commonly curt and gruff and autocratic. He was in fact a man of plain common sense and no nonsense, and he detested gush and heroics. His temperament and politics brought him much dislike and unpopularity. But he could not long remain in general disfavour. The country gratefully recognised his sincerity, honesty, courage and ingrained sense of public duty. The wise and moderating statesmanship of his later career made him something of a public oracle. The splendour of his military deeds could never be forgotten. When he died, in 1852, all England mourned the loss of a great soldier, a true gentleman and a national hero.

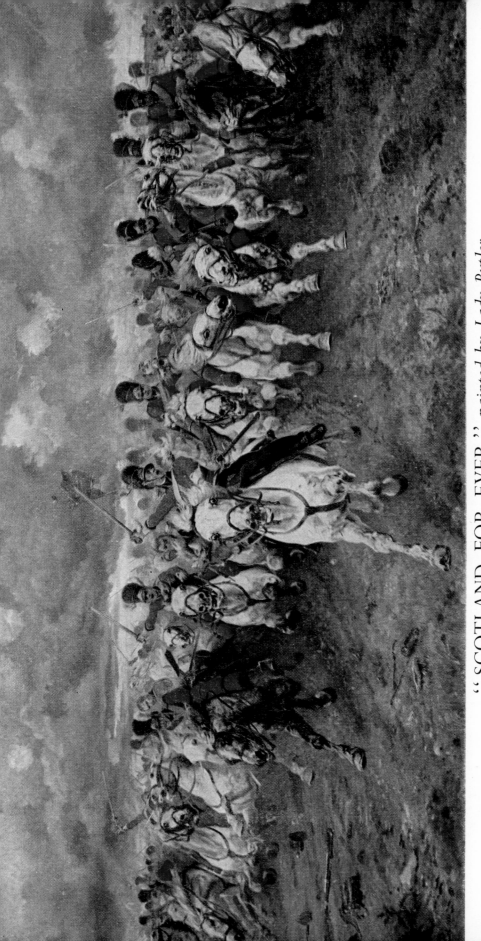

"SCOTLAND FOR EVER" *painted by Lady Butler*

The Charge of the Scots Greys during the Battle of Waterloo, 1815, has been magnificently portrayed in this famous picture. The dashing gallantry of the men, their determination and courage can be plainly seen. With an already brilliant record, the regiment covered itself in further glory on this occasion, putting a French column to flight and capturing the eagle, or standard, of the 45th French Line Regiment. Mounted on splendid grey horses, this regiment of excellent horsemen presented an awe-inspiring sight to the enemy, and even drew grudging admiration from Napoleon.

A trolley load of biscuit ware is here seen being pushed into the oven for firing. When clay pieces are hard and chalk white they are described as biscuit ware.

POTTERY AND CHINA

CERAMICS is the name given to the manufacture of all articles of baked clay, whether for use or ornament. But there are many kinds of clay, and it is mixed with various other ingredients to make it hard. The hardest of all is called china, or porcelain, because the recipe was first discovered by the Chinese some twelve hundred years ago. Stoneware is less hard, earthenware comparatively soft and porous.

If you buy a cup and saucer to-day it is likely to be of hard, white earthenware or of bone china, so called because the clay has been mixed with the ashes of ox bones. True porcelain is less common in England and America, but it is preferred on the Continent and in the Far East.

THE POTTER'S PROBLEMS

To understand what these distinctions mean, we must consider the problem that confronts the potter when he wishes to make something out of clay, say a bowl. First he must find the right sort of clay. Not all kinds are suitable; and only one kind, china clay (or kaolin) will do for porcelain. Clay is plastic and can be kneaded like dough; when baked it becomes hard and retains its shape. But if the oven is very hot it will be spoiled unless it is mixed with some other substance.

As a result of early experiments it was found that powdered flint and even powdered glass helped the clay to stand up to a high temperature. Kaolin mixed with petuntse (a silicate of potassium and aluminium) can be safely subjected to at least 1,350° C. The result is porcelain. Another body-material, not quite so hard, which can stand up to about 1,150° C. is stoneware. Temperatures even lower than 700° C. suffice for soft earthenware.

These classifications are useful, but they are not absolutely rigid. There are intermediate

Throwing is the most ancient method of making pottery. Here the thrower is at work at his wheel, the method unchanged.

kiln. The heat causes them to fuse and so provide a glassy surface.

UNDERGLAZE AND OVERGLAZE

Sometimes designs are painted on the pot before the glaze is applied; colours of this sort are called underglaze. When the painting is done after the glazing the colours are called overglaze, or enamel. The principal overglaze colours are oxides of copper, iron and manganese. The same metal produces quite different colours if the temperature is varied. Iron can be made to yield yellow, black and bright red; copper gives a range of blues and greens, and in the presence of carbon monoxide a glorious red called Chinese *flambé*.

Most of these metallic glazes will only fuse at a high temperature. They cannot, therefore, be applied to earthenware. So the early potters—outside China—had a very limited palette. They relied on form and design rather than on subtle combinations of colour.

THE HISTORY OF POTTERY

The history of pottery stretches back to the dim beginnings of civilisation. Neolithic man made pots of soft earthenware decorated with

grades. There are, for example, ' soft ' and ' hard ' porcelains. These terms refer to the temperature of the kiln during firing, as the baking process is called. ' Hard ' or ' true ' porcelain requires the highest temperature and in the firing it is really transformed into a natural glass.

GLAZING

There is nothing very glassy in the appearance of earthenware. Yet earthenware can be given a glass-like finish by coating it, or giving it an external 'glaze,' as with tiles in a modern fireplace. The progress of pottery through the ages is bound up with the continual discovery of new methods of glazing.

The original purpose of glazing earthenware was to prevent it from being porous. But it was found that different glazes produced different colours and so the search went on for more beautiful effects. All glazes are mineral dyes and they are ground to powder and the particles are suspended in a liquid in which the pot is immersed. The particles adhere to the clay, which is then placed in the

The casting mould, comprising two or more parts, is removed, leaving the finished article in a soft clay state.

simple lines. In ancient Egypt and Babylonia the need for glazing porous earthenware was appreciated and a high standard of workmanship was reached. For sheer elegance the pottery uncovered in the buried cities of Crete is unsurpassed in the ancient world. This civilisation came to an end about 1000 B.C. and the next important development took place on the mainland of Greece, reaching its zenith in fifth century Athens.

You can see in the British Museum many examples of Greek vases, bowls, drinking vessels and oil jars. Some of the finest are in a black and red ware. They are decorated with scenes from daily life, war, mythology and religion, drawn with a fidelity that was something new. The main focus of Greek art in pottery as well as sculpture was on the human figure. The materials then available were used to perfection; only variety of colour was lacking.

This limitation persisted throughout classical times. With the decline of the Roman Empire

The handler applies the cup handles with just a touch of clay mixed with water.

The plate-jolleyer makes the plates on a machine called a jolley, which has a rotating head and a lever to which is attached a profile to give the correct shaping.

The famous " Portland " Vase, copied by Josiah Wedgwood in 1790 from the original Vase in the British Museum, and pronounced to be " a correct and faithful imitation."

the potter's art suffered an eclipse, but it was revived under the remarkable Arab civilisation that flourished in Baghdad, Alexandria and Córdoba between the ninth and eleventh centuries A.D. The Arabs improved the technique of glazing, but for religious reasons they did not use animal or human forms in their decorations. Not so the Persians, however, whose glazed tiles and bowls and plates are covered with miniature figures. The Persians introduced a cobalt glaze that the Chinese called Mohammedan blue. They used it for a popular blue and white ware.

ADVANCE OF POTTERY IN EUROPE

Before turning to China, however, let us glance quickly at Europe. No great progress was made in the Middle Ages, but pottery advanced, especially in Italy, during the Renaissance. As soon as Chinese porcelain began to be imported attempts were made to imitate it. In Venice, a centre of the glass industry, this took the form of a white, opaque glass to which tin oxide had been added. It was not genuine porcelain.

In Italy there was a thriving industry in glazed earthenware painted in enamel colours. This is known as Majolica; but in France it was called Faience, and in Holland it received the name of the location of the potteries at Delft. The Dutch excelled in making plates and tiles in blue, with landscapes or scenes from the Bible.

Stoneware jugs were made in Germany and the vogue led to the development of English stoneware, culminating in the famous Wedgwood ' china.' Wedgwood made very little porcelain, which in any case remained a mystery to European potters until the eighteenth century.

CHINESE PORCELAIN

The first recorded reference to porcelain comes from an Arab merchant who visited China in A.D. 851. He wrote: "the Chinese have a fine clay of which they make drinking vessels as fine as glass; one can see the liquid contained therein though they be made of clay."

Marco Polo, the famous Venetian traveller, went to the court of the Mongol Emperor, Kublai Khan, in 1275, and he used the word *porcellana* to describe some of the wares he saw being made. Their exquisite glaze reminded

Eighteenth century rustic candlesticks, " Summer and Winter," in sage-green jaspar.

A beautiful porcelain vase with lid made at the famous Sèvres factory in France in 1757.
Sèvres was renowned for the exquisite work of such vases as this. They were, of course,
designed for a small luxury market.

him of the shells of the genus *porcellana*, but the name he coined did not become current in Europe for several centuries. When the first examples reached the West, the European potters were mystified by this strange new substance—so hard that it could be cut like a gem. When struck it gave a resonant note. It was translucent when held up to the light.

Chinese porcelain is dated according to the dynasty of the reigning house. Some porcelain was undoubtedly made in the Tang dynasty (618–906), but we have many more specimens of the Sung dynasty which followed. Compared with later work they are somewhat austere. The Sung potter often achieved a superb effect with a simple bowl in one or two colours. On one such bowl, for example, we find the inscription " For the Imperial fondling of Chien Lung." This means there was an appeal to touch as well as sight; even a blind man could feel the beauty of the texture by gliding his finger-tips over the surface.

CELADON

A type of grey-green ware called Celadon reached perfection in the Sung dynasty. The name is thought to be derived from Saladin, the twelfth century Sultan, who imported it from China. It was much sought after by Islamic collectors and a few pieces found their way to Europe. Celadons were thought to have the magical property of changing colour or even cracking in the presence of poison—a highly desirable property in oriental courts.

" BLANC-DE-CHINE "

In the Ming dynasty (1368–1644) there was a striking change in fashion. Instead of relying mainly on form and colour for their effects, the Ming potters delighted in intricate designs, sometimes of flowers and fruit, fish and dragons, sometimes of landscapes. Small cream-coloured statuettes in a porcelain called *blanc-de-chine*, are also typical of the period.

They are usually gods, goddesses and sages with real hair inserted through tiny holes.

There was constant competition between master-potters to discover new glazes and colours, and to combine them to produce novel effects. Thus one sort of glaze had the mottled appearance of chicken skin; another left a pebbled surface due to a myriad tiny bubbles.

SACRIFICIAL RED

The rival kilns closely guarded their secrets and the experiments were sometimes drastic. There is a story of one potter who so despaired of attaining a certain copper red that he threw himself into the furnace. The pots were fired with exactly the colour he had sought, and because he had paid for it with his life this glaze was named *chih hung* or sacrificial red. It should be remembered that unless a potter carried out the often impossible orders of the Emperor he was liable to be executed.

CENTRES OF MANUFACTURE

The most famous of the many centres of

A traditional Wedgwood pattern, still very popular, which decorated tableware used by Napoleon when he was exiled to the island of St. Helena.

The first ornamental ware to be developed by Wedgwood was " black basalt " and this was used for the Egyptian-style inkstand made in 1780.

manufacture from the Ming period onwards was at Ching-te-Cheng, near Nanking, the old Imperial capital before Peking. A European missionary, who visited it in the early eighteenth century, found that there were a million inhabitants in the city. It contained at least three thousand kilns and their products went all over the world.

Korea and Japan had learned from China, but the secret of true porcelain was not discovered in the West until just after 1700 when a German alchemist, Friedrich Böttger, turned his attention from trying to make gold to a more rewarding task. A factory was started at Meissen and this was the beginning of Dresden china.

Like the Chinese, the Germans also tried to keep the process secret; but a runaway workman took it to Vienna and further leakages resulted in factories being started in France. Dresden and Sèvres china are world-famous names. Dresden is renowned for its exquisitely modelled figures—shepherds and shepherdesses, gallants and ladies, Turks, harlequins, birds and animals. The most distinctive feature of Sèvres porcelain was the production of elaborate vases. It was mainly designed for a small, luxury market.

ENGLISH POTTERIES

From the mid-eighteenth century there was a considerable demand for figures of various kinds and the English potteries joined in the competition. William Cookworthy of Plymouth was the first to make porcelain in England. Factories were started at Chelsea (1743–85), Bow (1744–76), Derby (1745), Worcester (1748) and by the end of the eighteenth century a number of factories were making porcelain in Staffordshire. The Worcestershire Royal Porcelain Company has continued from the earliest years without a break and celebrated its bicentenary in 1951.

Josiah Wedgwood, perhaps the greatest name in English pottery, is most widely known for his coloured jasper stoneware with figures in relief illustrating classical themes. He also introduced a black basalt ware with designs in red enamel. But his most significant contribution was to start pottery as an industry that could reach an ever bigger market.

MODERN POTTERIES

To-day, machinery has made mass-production possible. Instead of the traditional wheel, worked by foot, the industrial potteries use electric power. Gas- and electrically-heated ovens replace the coal-heated kilns. The lathe is used for polishing. Modern potteries must not only cater for ornaments and tableware, but such necessities as baths, drain-pipes and insulating materials. Times are not easy for the craftsman-artist, and some fear that the art of ceramics will become one of the glories of the past and that the masterpieces in our museums will never be repeated.

HORATIO NELSON
The Terror of the Seas

Portrait of Lord Nelson, by Abbot, in the National Portrait Gallery.

THE people of the little village of Burnham Thorpe, in Norfolk, are very proud of their church and of the association with their village of one of our greatest seamen, for it was here that Horatio Nelson was born. His father was the rector, and Horatio was one of a large family.

He was never very strong and, when an uncle decided to give one of the boys a start in life as a seaman, he was amazed to think that Horatio should be the one who wanted to go. Life was not too good at sea in those days, and his uncle was doubtful whether Horatio could stand up to the hardships. He soon proved that he was able to stand up to as much as most men could.

He was only twelve when he first went to sea, and within a very short time he was on his way to the Arctic. Here he had an early escapade, one of many that he was to have

An artist's impression of the Battle of Trafalgar, where Nelson won a great victory. This picture gives some idea of the carnage wrought by massed batteries at close quarters.

The famous artist Turner painted this picture of the death of Nelson in the *Victory*.

during his lifetime. Truanting from his ship, he was seen, when the fog cleared, fighting with a polar bear. Needless to say, he found himself in further trouble when he returned aboard.

Nelson soon decided to go out for promotion, and by the time he was twenty he had reached the rank of captain and had been to many parts of the world. Moreover, he had won the respect of his men by his inspiration and leadership. Clearly he was heading for great things.

His great chance came when he was thirty-five and the power of Napoleon had begun to threaten Europe. Nelson was given command of the *Agamemnon*, a 64-gun ship, which was to be his for some time.

HOW NELSON LOST HIS EYE AND HIS ARM

One of his first engagements was in Corsica, in the Mediterranean. The garrison was taken by surprise by the British party, which landed and made a daring raid, led by Nelson himself. It was during the attack on Corsica, that Nelson lost the sight of his eye, through gravel being scattered by a cannon ball.

Then came his first great battle. Off Cape St. Vincent, with a fleet of fifteen British ships, he attacked a Spanish fleet which was almost twice the size of his own, and defeated it. At one time, the *Agamemnon* was attacked by five Spaniards, but Nelson was successful in capturing two of them.

Several months later, Nelson was sent to Santa Cruz, in the Canary Islands; but the Spaniards were aware that he was coming and had prepared. In spite of the defences, which were particularly strong, Nelson insisted on landing. His bravery amazed everyone, for he led a very determined attack, and it was on this occasion that he lost his arm.

The next engagement was to make Nelson famous. Napoleon was determined to conquer the East, and Egypt seemed to be his main objective. A fleet was dispatched under

The *Victory*, as she is to-day, well kept and preserved, at Portsmouth, so that all may see the kind of ship that, with brave sailors aboard, gave Britain command of the seas. She is flying the famous Trafalgar signal.

The Jack Tars of Nelson's Day were dressed like this.

Sectional drawing of H.M.S. *Victory*. A. Poop Deck. B. Capt. Hardy's Cabin. C. Upper Gun Deck. D. Middle Gun Deck. E. Lower Gun Deck. F. Orlop Deck. G. Hold. A.1. Quarterdeck, 2. Waist, 3. Forecastle, 4. Binnacle, 5. Four Boom Boats, 6. Belfry, 7. Galley Funnel, 8. Carronades. B.1. 12-pounder guns, 2. Steering Wheel. C.1.

Nelson, to attack the French. At last he found the French anchored off the Nile. Dividing his force in two, the French were engaged on both sides at once, and ten ships out of thirteen were captured. Great honours were showered upon him by a joyous nation after the Battle of the Nile, and Nelson became Lord Nelson.

Further fame came to him as a result of the Battle of Copenhagen. Denmark was not on very friendly terms with Britain, and a fleet was sent to attack the Danes. Lord Nelson was the Vice-Admiral and second-in-command. The Danish fleet proved stronger and gave more trouble than had been expected, and the order was given to break off the engagement. It was then that Nelson did one of those things which were to make him famous. Putting his telescope to his blind eye, he said, "I see no signal," and continued the battle, which ended in defeat for the Danes. On his return he received a hero's welcome.

Napoleon now decided to attack Britain, and prepared great fleets of ships to carry his men across the Channel. He was wise enough to realise, however, that unless he had the mastery of the seas, such an invasion would never be successful. He also realised that, as long as Nelson sailed the seas, it was very doubtful if *he* would be master. Nevertheless, he was determined to get his ships out into one large fleet if possible, but many were trapped in French and Spanish ports by the British.

Some, however, were successful in escaping from Toulon and they were joined in the West Indies by other ships that managed to escape. Nelson gave chase, but missed them at sea, and he had to chase them back across the Atlantic, where he found they had reached Cadiz.

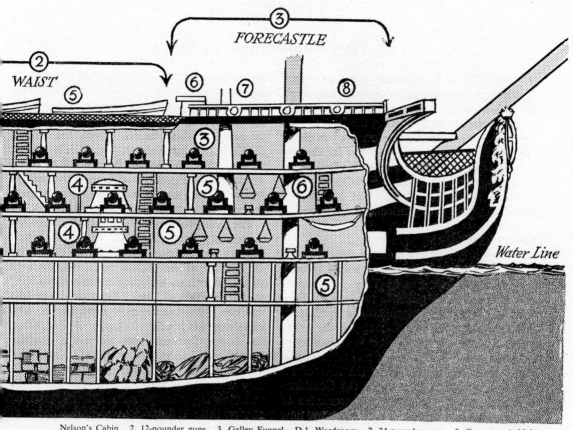

FORECASTLE

WAIST

Water Line

Nelson's Cabin, 2. 12-pounder guns, 3. Galley Funnel. D.1. Wardroom, 2. 24-pounder guns, 3. Capstan, 4. Main Capstan, 5. Galley, 6. Crew's Quarters. E.1. Gunroom, 2. 32-pounder guns, 3. Capstan, 4. Main Capstan, 5. Crew's Quarters. F.1. Dispensary, 2. Cockpit, 3. Main Hatch to Hold, 4. Grand Magazine, 5. Canvas Locker.

THE BATTLE OF TRAFALGAR

On October 21st, 1805, the British fleet was off Cape Trafalgar when the combined French and Spanish fleet hove in sight. It was slightly larger than the British one, which had been divided into two squadrons, with Nelson leading one in the *Victory* and Collingwood the other in the *Royal Sovereign*.

Having spent some time in prayer, and in preparation, Nelson donned his full uniform, complete with decorations, and went on deck. Though it was suggested that he should not wear the decorations for fear that he might be a good target, he insisted on doing so. The famous signal was hoisted, " England expects that every man will do his duty," and the battle commenced.

The British did well, and victory was in sight, when a marksman on one of the enemy ships fired a shot at Nelson, which lodged in his spine. In the arms of the captain, Hardy, he died below deck where he had been carried, his last words being, " Thank God, I have done my duty."

That was the end of Napoleon's chances of invading England, for, at the Battle of Trafalgar, the French fleet was well and truly beaten. Britain was overjoyed at the removal of the threat from Napoleon, but it was marred by the death of the one who had made it possible.

Nelson was laid to rest in St. Paul's Cathedral, where a monument was also erected; Nelson's Column was erected in Trafalgar Square, so-named after the battle; the *Victory* lies as a constant reminder in Portsmouth Dockyard; Trafalgar Day is observed every year; and Nelson holds a great place in the esteem of most people. These remain a fitting tribute to a national hero.

GEORGE IV

" The First Gentleman in Europe "

GEORGE IV had already acted as Prince Regent for nine years when he succeeded his poor mad father, George III, in 1820. The less said about the new King the better. But the least that *can* be said is a lot. He was clever and not without wit and taste, but for the rest he was a faithless and completely selfish man, an undutiful son, a ruinous spendthrift and a dissolute dandy and rake. Yet his toadies called him " the first gentleman in Europe."

SOCIAL REFORM

The country was still agitated over the vital question of parliamentary and social reform, and a freshly constituted Tory government now adopted a new attitude towards it. They tried to show that a sympathetic Parliament was fully competent to correct popular grievances without reforming its own constitution. Amongst the " Safety first " measures passed in the previous reign, under the fear of revolutionary disturbances, were the Combination Acts which had forbidden workmen to combine in trade unions. These Acts were now repealed. Steps were also taken to promote freer trade and reduce the cost of living.

Under the savage criminal laws an offender could be hanged for stealing five shillings or a sheep. Indeed there were more than two hundred crimes punishable by death. In 1823 Sir Robert Peel, the Home Secretary, reduced the number by a hundred. (It was the same Sir *Robert* who gave us our " Bobbies " by establishing the London Police Force in 1829).

FOREIGN AFFAIRS

In foreign affairs, too, the brilliant Foreign Secretary Canning pursued a " liberal " policy. After the fall of Napoleon the old rulers had been restored on the Continent. They had quickly set themselves to stifle the principles of free constitutional government, which had everywhere been stimulated by the French Revolution. Canning boldly championed movements for reform in Spain and Portugal and for outright independence in Spain's South American colonies and in Greece; though it must be confessed that he had a shrewd eye to

his own country's interests as well. The Turks had been masters of the Balkans for centuries. When the long-suffering Greeks rose against the brutal tyrants, Canning led Britain to take up arms in their behalf. Here, the British Lion's active intervention was mainly due to the fear that the Russian Bear, if left to itself, would plant its great paws around the eastern Mediterranean and menace our interests there and in the overland routes to India.

The wrongs of the heroic Greeks had aroused the warmest sympathy in British hearts. Their country was endeared to all men of culture by the glories of its classic past. Numbers of ardent volunteers had gone out to strike a blow at the abominated Turk. Amongst the leaders was our noble-hearted poet Lord Byron, who laid down his life for the cause. At last, when the Greek fortunes were desperate, Britain, Russia and France sent out a fleet to intervene. At the battle of Navarino, fought in 1827, they won a complete victory over the Turks and their Egyptian vassals. A few years later plucky little Greece recovered the boon of freedom.

RELIGIOUS TOLERATION

Another forward step, taken at home, though very grudgingly, marked the triumphant advance of religious toleration. The remaining penal laws against Nonconformists and (with a few exceptions) Roman Catholics were abolished in 1828–29. But it was only under the threat of civil war in Catholic Ireland that the Romanists were granted this relief.

The government's attempts at social reform were praiseworthy enough, but they amounted to nothing more than futile tinkerings with an engine that required a thorough overhaul. It was Parliament itself that needed repair. In 1830, when dandy George's worthless life closed, parliamentary reform was the dominant question of the day.

RAILWAYS AND INDUSTRY

A memorable feature of the period was the opening of the Stockton and Darlington railway in 1825, followed by that of the Liverpool

George IV reigned from 1820–30 but had previously acted as Regent during his father's madness.

and Manchester railway in 1830. These ventures marked the beginning of a new era in transport by steam-powered locomotives. As the railway system spread over the country it gave a great impetus to every branch of industry.

Another episode was an expensive little war with Burma in 1824-26 which added Assam and other territory to Britain's Indian empire.

WILLIAM IV
A Period of
Political and Social Reform

WILLIAM IV, the next surviving younger brother of George IV, commenced his seven-year reign in 1830, when the country was stirred by the agitation for parliamentary reform. He was a simple, warm-hearted old sailor, very genial and breezy, as befitted an old tar, but sometimes a little queer in his conduct. He favoured moderate reforms.

The sufferings of the poor, the exclusion of the lower and middle classes from due representation in Parliament, and the consequent neglect of their grievances, had by this time created a somewhat explosive situation. And it was made additionally explosive by events abroad. In 1830 France threw out her despotic King, Charles X, and the Belgians rose against the Dutch House of Orange and demanded their independence. Britain now had a forceful Foreign Secretary in Lord Palmerston. He was in many ways a delightful character, refreshingly brisk and gay, and always ready to lecture poor ignorant foreign diplomats on the British principles of free constitutional government and to uphold British interests abroad. It was with his support that Belgium gained her freedom. But revolutionary ideas are apt to spread and Britain had caught a touch of the infection. The demands put forward by the people amounted to a full-scale assault on the landed aristocracy's monopoly of political power. These demands were two-fold.

THE PEOPLE'S DEMANDS

One was for a fairer rearrangement of the antiquated parliamentary constituencies—the county areas and the boroughs (towns). These constituencies elected two members apiece, quite regardless of how many voters each contained. Indeed, all the evils and injustices described under the reign of George I still remained uncorrected and even intensified. Populous new factory towns such as Birmingham and Manchester returned no separate representatives. But the " pocket boroughs " and " rotten boroughs," some of them with only one or two voters (Old Sarum, near Salisbury, was actually an unpeopled waste).

William IV. 1830–37.

still elected their pair of members. And the old flagrant bribery, the buying and selling of borough seats, and the widespread control of elections exercised by the gentry, went on merrily.

The other demand was for an extension of the franchise, or right to vote. At that time, in the English counties, it was restricted to landowners, small as well as large. Tenant-farmers and farm labourers had no say. In the boroughs, the varied qualifications were as senseless as if they had been invented by a lunatic; but in most places the voters were relatively few. In Scotland and Ireland things were just as bad—if not worse.

THE WHIG AND TORY VIEWS

The Whig and Tory parties in Parliament both agreed that something must be done. But both were also reluctant to surrender the power enjoyed by the governing class to which they belonged. Where they differed was on the question of what concessions should now be made to pacify the people. The Tories were, by temperament, opposed to sweeping changes. The Whigs were more open-minded. They felt that fundamental reforms were essential, partly as a matter of justice, but also to prevent any

A contemporary cartoon of 1832 when the question of the Reform Bill was of tremendous interest. The reformers hack at the Rotten Tree, whilst the diehards shore it up.

further outcry. Only the small group of Radicals (that formed the extreme Whig wing) stood, as a body, wholeheartedly for reform in principle, as a step towards democratic government.

THE REFORM BILL

This was the situation when a Whig government under Earl Grey introduced the great Reform Bill of 1831. The bill proposed to sweep away a host of pocket and rotten boroughs, to reduce the representation of other small towns and to give seats to the unrepresented factory towns. At the same time the franchise (as later amended) was extended to the middle classes—the farmers in the country and the shopkeepers in the towns who owned or rented property of a certain minimum value.

To the old Tories the bill came like a blow between the eyes. It scraped through its second reading by a single vote, but got no farther. Grey resigned. A fresh general election reestablished him with a handsome majority.

The people had set their hearts on the bill with hungry enthusiasm. This time Grey got his measure through the Commons and sent it up to the Lords. The Tory peers threw it out.

The fight was now on outside Parliament. The country was seething. Riots broke out. Public buildings were sacked and burned. The military were called out. Grey piloted a third bill through the Commons. The Lords fell on it and proceeded to cut its heart out. After that the issue was stark and clear beyond all question. Peers or People—which was it to be? The peers had shown themselves resolute. What would the people do? Would they submit? Or would they raise the banner of revolution?

The fateful issue was never tried. It was in the King's power to cancel out the Tory majority in the Lords by creating new peers. To avert the threatening storm he consented to exercise the power. From that moment the Lords were beaten. When the bill next came before them a hundred peers absented themselves and, on 4th June, 1832, the storm-

William Wilberforce who worked unceasingly
for the abolition of slavery.

1832. But it could be only a matter of time
before the workers followed. And there is
another significant point. The House of
Commons had manifested its power. It had
shown that, when resolutely supported by the
people, the Lords could not stand against it.

SOME SOCIAL EVILS ABOLISHED

Next year the Whig government in a reformed Parliament quickly got down to tackling
some crying social evils. There was the scandal
of child-labour. Little children of seven were
kept at work in the textile factories for twelve
or more hours a day. The Factory Act of 1833
(one of a long series to come) prohibited the
employment of children under nine and limited
the hours of those under thirteen to forty-eight
per week. Then, by way of a change, the latter
group were sent to school for two hours daily.
The government also made a money grant for
educational purposes. These modest provisions
were the first effective steps taken by the State
towards the free, compulsory, universal education that children enjoy to-day. In the same
year, mainly as a result of the persistent
endeavours of William Wilberforce and his
fellow-workers, the monstrous institution of
slavery was abolished throughout the British
Dominions.

tossed Reform Bill at last reached port. So
the people breached the ancient stronghold of
aristocratic privilege. True, it was only the
middle classes who entered the fortress in

THE COMING OF THE KING

Yet if His Majesty, our sovereign lord,
Should of his own accord
Friendly himself invite,
And say, " I'll be your guest to-morrow night,"
How should we stir ourselves, call and command
All hands to work! " Let no man idle stand!

" Set me fine Spanish tables in the hall;
See they be fitted all;
Let there be room to eat
And order taken that there want no meat.
See every sconce and candlestick made bright,
That without tapers they may give a light.

" Look to the presence. Are the carpets spread?
The dais o'er the head?
The cushions in the chairs,
And all the candles lighted on the stairs?
Perfume the chambers, and in any case
Let each man give attendance in his place! "

Thus, if a king were coming, would we do;
And 'twere good reason, too.
For 'tis a duteous thing
To show all honour to an earthly king,
And after all our travail and our cost
So he be pleased, to think no labour lost.

But, at the coming of the King of Heaven,
All's set at six and seven;
We wallow in our sin.
Christ cannot find a chamber in the inn.
We entertain Him always like a stranger,
And, as at first, still lodge Him in the manger.

Anon

In a building made mainly of glass (and later known as the Crystal palace) the Great Exhibition of 1851 was opened officially by Queen Victoria, here seen with Prince Albert, who took a very active part in organising the Exhibition, and their family.

VICTORIA
A Prosperous and Progressive Age

IN 1837 Victoria, daughter of Edward, Duke of Kent (William IV's next younger brother), ascended the throne. She was an inexperienced young lady of eighteen, endowed with character, grace and dignity and filled with a deep sense of her royal duties and responsibilities. On her accession the personal connection with Hanover was broken, for the succession to that kingdom was barred to females. In 1840 the Queen was happily wedded to Albert of Saxe-Coburg-Gotha, the future Prince Consort.

Of all the domestic events of Victoria's long reign none is more significant than the rise of the working classes. The Reform Act of 1832, by omitting them from the extended parliamentary franchise, had left them deeply disappointed. They still felt that, so long as they remained voteless, Parliament would continue to neglect their grievances. Accordingly, a number of their leaders drew up a " People's Charter." The principal demands of the

" Chartists," as they were called, were for universal male suffrage (or the right to vote), voting by secret ballot (to avoid bribery and influence) and the payment of members of Parliament (to allow poor men to stand for election). Between 1839 and 1848 three monster petitions were presented to Parliament. But, under the influence of the more violent tub-thumpers, the movement was accompanied with riots and strikes and threats of insurrection. Parliament rejected the petitions and the agitation died out. The workers were left to nurse their grievances till another day. Meantime they concentrated on seeking to improve their condition by means of the growing trade unions and co-operative associations.

SIR ROBERT PEEL AND FREE TRADE

The Tory party had been badly shaken by their defeat on the Reform Bill. They were, however, rallied by Sir Robert Peel, and the

211

new party that gathered round him declared themselves sympathetic towards all necessary popular reform. Peel held office as Prime Minister from 1841 to 1846. He improved the hours and conditions of labour in mines and factories. He took a long step towards Free Trade by removing or reducing a host of duties. He imposed the direct tax on incomes that has remained with us ever since. And then he took a further Free Trade plunge. As a protection to agricultural interests, the existing Corn Laws, by a system of duties, restricted the import of foreign grain. The cry now was that this benefited landlords and farmers but made corn dear. The poorly paid workers were suffering acutely from the high price of bread. Peel carried a measure through Parliament abolishing the unpopular laws. His action was a bold one and it split his land-owning Tory party into two opposing camps—Free Traders and Protectionists. It was not long, however, before Britain went over almost entirely to Free Trade. For a great while after this party politics got rather confused. Indeed the very names of the parties underwent a change: "Conservative" for "Tory," "Liberal" for "Whig."

THE YEAR 1848

The year 1848 was a year of headaches for rulers, at home and abroad. The Chartists were giving the British Government a fright. In Ireland there had long been an agitation for the repeal of the Act of Union and the grant of Home Rule (under the British Crown) by an Irish Parliament. From 1845 onwards the unhappy country had been woefully smitten by famine and disease. Now, there arose an attempt at armed insurrection. In France, Hungary, Italy and Germany revolutions flared up in support of progressive government and national freedom. But all these risings fizzled out like damp squibs.

THE CRIMEAN WAR

In 1852 the leading Free Trade Conservative followers of Peel (who had died two years earlier) joined the Whigs, or Liberals, in a new government. One of the Liberals was Lord

In 1856 Queen Victoria instituted the Victoria Cross, as a naval and military decoration for conspicuous bravery in the face of the enemy. Here she makes awards in Hyde Park.

The Residency at Lucknow was used as a hospital by the garrison during the Indian Mutiny in 1857. It was attacked by native troops and the building badly shattered. This contemporary photograph shows the remains of the Gateway and Banqueting Room.

Palmerston, who had shown himself a live wire as Foreign Secretary in the previous reign. The new cabinet had need of all, and more than all, its abilities. The Turkish empire was breaking up and Russia was hungering after some of the pieces. Britain looked with unfriendly eyes on that aggressive tyrant power as an enemy to freedom. And she had always feared its advance in the Balkans and Near East especially on Constantinople, as a menace to her Indian empire. France, too, was an interested party. All attempts at holding back the hungry Bear miscarried. Palmerston was for firm action. He got his way and the Crimean War of 1854–56 followed. The bitter combats of the Alma, Balaclava, Inkerman and Sebastopol, the heart-stirring, suicidal charge of the Light Brigade " into the jaws of death," and the sublime mission of Florence Nightingale to the neglected sick and wounded, are events in the struggle that will always fire the blood of Englishmen. The peace terms duly chained up the Bear. But it was only a light chain and Palmerston (who had become Prime Minister and would have fought on till the beast was

crippled) rightly prophesied that it could not hold. It was in 1856 that the Queen instituted the Victoria Cross decoration " For Valour."

THE INDIAN MUTINY

Only a year later Palmerston's government was faced with a more perilous trial of strength in India. Since 1839 a series of wars had added Sind, the Punjab and Lower Burma to our eastern empire, while several other States had been peacefully annexed. Then suddenly, in 1857, the Mutiny exploded like a thunder-clap. The causes were numerous: a considerable decline in discipline among native troops; discontent and suspicion over British measures affecting native customs, caste and religion; and many others. The accumulated grievances were touched off by a mere mischance. Cartridges issued to the Sepoy soldiers, the tops of which had to be bitten off before use, were rumoured to be smeared with the fat of animals sacred to Hindus or untouchable by Moslems. Inflamed by this " outrage," the revolt spread with lightning speed over the northern and central provinces. The fighting took on the fury and ferocity of a struggle of wild beasts. The British power in India seemed in danger. Yet within a few months the back of the mutiny—it was purely a military revolt, never a national rising—was broken. By the following year, 1858, British authority was restored. The rule of the East India Company was thereupon taken over wholly by the Crown. In 1877 the Queen assumed the title of Empress of India.

THE ITALIAN STATES UNITE

The years following the Mutiny saw some notable events in Europe. In 1861 most of the disjointed States of Italy, hitherto languishing under foreign rule, won their freedom and became united in a single kingdom. The remainder followed within ten years. Palmerston gave the movement his blessing. The patriot-hero Garibaldi and his famous thousand red-shirts nobly co-operated in it.

THE RISE OF PRUSSIA

Another state that came to the fore was Prussia. Since its theft of Silesia from Maria Theresa of Austria over a century before, and its setback in the Napoleonic wars, it had enormously expanded its bounds. Now, under

William Ewart Gladstone (1809-98), the Liberal leader whose powerful personality and speaking ability made him a great parliamentarian.

the steady guidance of the " Iron Chancellor " Bismarck, it made a further menacing advance. By 1866 it had seized Schleswig-Holstein, lowered the crest of Austria and brought together under its own ambitious leadership an all-too-powerful confederation of North German states.

GLADSTONE AND DISRAELI

In 1861 the Prince Consort died. He was followed four years later by Palmerston, whose death left the stage clear for the contests of two famous political rivals—Gladstone and Disraeli.

Benjamin Disraeli, the Conservative leader, was the baptized son of a Spanish Jew. He was clever, quick-witted and ambitious. His great aims in life were to advance the cause of the workers, to popularise the monarchy, to foster the unity, might and glory of the British Empire and to exert Britain's influence boldly in foreign affairs. Gladstone, who became the Liberal leader, was a man of strong moral and religious principles who took his political responsibilities very seriously. He had a terrifically powerful personality and a torrential gift of speech that made him the greatest parliamentarian of the age. He disliked Disraeli's

Benjamin Disraeli, Earl of Beaconsfield (1804-81), a famous premier of Queen Victoria's reign.

In 1897 Queen Victoria had reigned for sixty years, the longest reign in the history of the king-dom. The Queen drove in an open carriage to a Diamond Jubilee Thanksgiving Service at St. Paul's along a route lined with her loyal subjects, including the cheering Christ's Hospital boys.

"Imperialism"—his inflated and aggressive notions of empire—and he strongly opposed over-much meddling in the affairs of other nations. He was a master of finance and an enlightened social and political reformer.

THE FRANCHISE EXTENDED

The popular demand for a further extension of the franchise had again become a burning question. Liberals and Conservatives alike realised that it was irresistible, and both parties were out to catch the workers' votes once they were granted. In the end it was Disraeli who got his bill through. The Reform Act of 1867 (by reducing the property qualification and bringing in a number of lodgers) gave the vote to almost all the working class except agri-cultural labourers. These had to wait till 1884. The workers were now in a position to com-mand the respectful attention of the two rival parties. Later on, however, they learned to organise their own Labour Party.

FURTHER REFORMS

In 1868 the Liberals under Gladstone came into office. Ireland was still suffering—and giving—trouble. The bomb-throwing "Fenian" agitators had been clamouring for an in-dependent Irish republic. Gladstone tried to right some of their wrongs. He rid the Catholic nation of the dominance of the Protestant State Church. He improved the hard lot of the peasants by reforming the harsh land laws. Turning to England, he carried through, in 1870, an Education Act which set up local School Boards and provided for the building of more schools. It was not, however, till twenty-one years later that children's education became everywhere both compulsory and free. In 1872 the old Chartist demand for the secret ballot in parliamentary elections was at last conceded.

THE FRANCO-PRUSSIAN WAR

Meantime, abroad, the Prussian Eagle had

After the defeat of the French in 1870
Napoleon III surrendered his sword.

dug its talons deep into France during the war of 1870–71. Alsace-Lorraine was torn from her. France once more became a republic. And, in the hour of Bismarck's triumph, the German Empire—a combination of the northern confederation and the southern States—was born.

TROUBLE ABROAD

A few years later Disraeli secured another turn of office. He carried out several useful reforms concerning public health, housing, trade unions and other matters. Then he turned to deal with a tangled situation abroad. In 1877–8 the Russians, free now of their flimsy chain, defeated Turkey and liberated the greater part of the Balkans from the Moslem tyranny. " Imperialist " Disraeli (now Earl of Beaconsfield) thought the peace terms gave Russia far too much control in the Near East and backed up his protests with a persuasive display of troops and warships. Whereupon Russia sullenly climbed down. The terms were drastically modified, and Turkey placed the island of Cyprus in British hands.

Another tangle was Egypt and the recently opened Suez Canal, which provided a new sea-route to India. Britain and France held a considerable financial interest in the Canal and the

country. When, therefore, the spendthrift Khedive, the ruler (nominally under the Sultan of Turkey), suspended payment of the State debts, something had to be done about it. What Disraeli did, in 1879, was to arrange for Britain and France to take over administrative and financial control of the country. Next year the whirligig of home politics brought Gladstone back into power and in 1881 Disraeli died. In this and the following year the Egyptian Army rose against the foreigners. The French withdrew from the scene and the peace-loving Gladstone was compelled to send ships and men to suppress the rising and protect the Canal. The next complication was a fanatical religious outbreak in the Sudan. Gladstone refused to take it in hand, but sent out General Gordon to withdraw the scattered native garrisons serving under British officers. Gordon, unfortunately, got cut off in Khartoum and in 1885 the dilatoriness of Gladstone's Cabinet in sending troops to his relief resulted in his tragic death. The people never forgave Gladstone for that. Britain remained in occupation of Egypt and in 1896–8 Sir Herbert Kitchener brilliantly reconquered the Sudan.

IRISH HOME RULE

At home the irrepressible Irish demand for Home Rule had broken out in violent excesses, not excluding murder. Gladstone became convinced that it would be wise and just to concede it, and he exerted all his great powers of oratory to steer the necessary bill through Parliament. But all he succeeded in doing, before he retired in 1894, was to split the Liberal Party on the issue. Many of his followers went over to the Conservative Party, who were determined enemies of Home Rule. That was in 1885 and for most of the remaining years of the reign the Conservatives, with their new " Liberal Unionist " allies, were in power. The Radical—or extreme Liberal-Unionist Joseph Chamberlain, who became Colonial Secretary in 1895, carried on Disraeli's Imperialist policy with immense ardour, so that it continued to be a distinctive slogan of the Conservative-Unionist Party.

THE BOER WAR

In 1899 the unhappy Boer War broke out in South Africa. (Those of the Liberals and Radicals who denounced it said that it was the outcome of blatant Imperialism.) Sixty years earlier some thousands of Boers (the descendants of the original Dutch settlers) had trekked northwards into the wilderness to escape from British rule. A series of unfriendly contacts ensued as the British, in their native wars and annexations, followed them up. Eventually the Boers were established in the Transvaal and Orange Free State as two independent republics, subject to certain British treaty rights. When gold was discovered in the Transvaal, outsiders—mostly British—poured into the country. Although these " uitlanders " paid enormous taxes, President Kruger wilfully refused to give them citizenship and treated them very oppressively. His ideal had always been " South Africa for the Boers." At last, in 1899, his offensive attitude and military preparations led to the outbreak of war between Britain and the two republics. The Boers proved unexpectedly tough and elusive fighters and the first operations were a long tale of British disasters. In 1900, however, Lord Roberts and Lord Kitchener (the Sir Herbert of the Sudan war) got the upper hand, though the stubborn Boers still kept up an exasperating irregular resistance.

Queen Victoria. 1837–1901.

THE VICTORIAN AGE

The end was still delayed when, in 1901, Queen Victoria died. Her passing plunged the Empire into mourning. Her wise and sympathetic rule had won her people's reverence and affection and made the monarchy the binding link of the empire.

The Victorian age was a period of notable achievements in every phase of national life. The working classes, newly educated and organised, rose to political power. Britain, "the workshop of the world," multiplied its commerce and manufactures and national wealth, though there was a serious set-back in the collapse of her agriculture under the pressure of foreign competition. The reign saw the development of the electric telegraph and telephone. These are only a few of a host of material gains. There were others of another character: the growth of a more humane attitude towards the underdogs of society; and a deep concern with religion. The long literary Roll of Honour of the reign is starred with such household names as the poets Tennyson, Browning and Mathew Arnold; the novelists

Dickens, Thackeray, " George Eliot " and the Brontës, besides those spell-binders Kipling and Robert Louis Stevenson; the historians Macaulay, Carlyle and John Richard Green; and countless writers on various subjects of thought and learning. As for worldly dominion, Britain stood forth as a great world-power and mistress of the seas. Her empire, with its civilising mission, included Gibraltar, Malta and Cyprus in Europe; Canada, Australia and New Zealand; a greatly expanded India; broad domains in Africa; innumerable scattered islands in the East and West Indies and elsewhere in the Atlantic, Pacific and Indian Oceans; mainland settlements in Central and South America; and stations in China.

It was indeed a prosperous and progressive age. Yet, at the end of the century, there were clouds on the horizon.

Foreign competitors were challenging Britain's commercial supremacy.

And Germany was making a sudden and enormous increase in her existing modest navy.

DAVID LIVINGSTONE

The Man who opened up

the Dark Continent

LIFE was not easy in the little Scottish village of Blantyre, Lanarkshire. Hours of work were very long, and the young men in the factory found that, after fourteen hours' work, they had little time for anything else. Perhaps it was that David Livingstone was a little different from the others. Perhaps it was that he wanted to better himself, for he had only received a humble education.

Whatever his motive, he found time, after work, to go to evening classes, and spent most of his pocket money on books. Nothing appealed to him so much as books on travel and nature. On these subjects he could sit and read for hours, and he soon had a good general knowledge.

Then, one day, he decided to leave his homeland and sail to other lands to tell the people of the God in whom he believed. After he had studied medicine, he was accepted by the London Missionary Society, and it was agreed that his knowledge could be of the greatest advantage in Africa. Thus, in 1840, this young man of twenty-seven arrived on the continent where he was to spend most of his life.

His objective was Kuruman, in Bechuanaland, where Dr. Moffat was working, and it was from here that he operated, travelling many hundreds of miles through unexplored territory.

Soon, the natives who were with him came to respect him, for they discovered that he was fearless, and, what was more important, he never expected them to do anything that he would not do himself.

It was when he returned to Kuruman that he married Dr. Moffat's daughter, who left with him for the post he had founded about two hundred miles farther north. They had four children, and it was because of them that Mrs. Livingstone returned to England, leaving her husband to explore for about four years on his own.

David Livingstone, the missionary who combined spreading the Gospel with exploration.

ATTACKED BY A LION

Let it not be imagined that the work was easy. Journeying through uncharted country is never easy. Often his way was barred by thick trees, and many times he had to follow the course of a river for some way before he could cross. There was always the danger of wild animals, too, and, on one occasion, he was attacked by a lion, which broke his arm before his men were able to kill it. His arm never set properly afterwards. Other dangers, though much smaller, were the mosquitoes and flies, which carried disease, and many times he was forced to rest to get over a bout of fever.

The people with whom he came into contact were not always helpful either. Wherever he went, he taught of God, but the Negro was still very much bound by his old superstitions and by the witch-doctor. Sometimes, the tribes

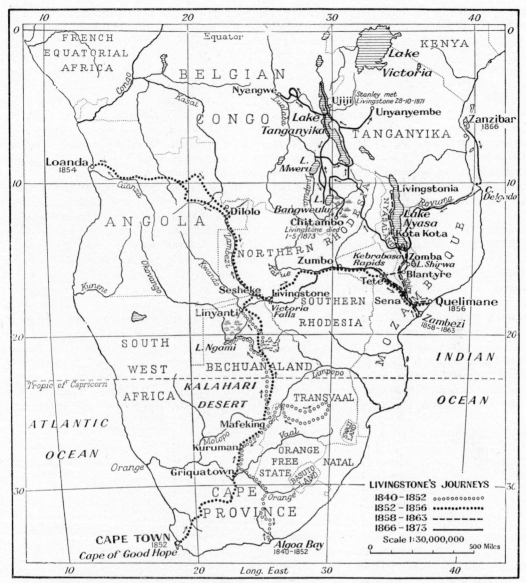

Livingstone's journeys in Africa are clearly shown on this map. Livingstone traced many rivers to their sources, discovered the Victoria Falls and opened up the continent for future travellers.

were openly hostile, and demanded goods from him. Great comfort came in the knowledge that he had some good, faithful Negroes with him.

After sixteen years, he returned to Britain, where he received a hero's welcome. He had accomplished that which no other man had been able to. He had seen the Victoria Falls, he had touched the Kalahari Desert, and he had taken extensive notes of all that he had observed. These were received with great joy by the Royal Geographical Society, to whom they were of the greatest value.

EXPOSING THE SLAVE TRADE

Another aspect of his work was that he exposed the slave trade, with all its associated evils, in such a way that the people of this country were immediately up in arms, and many demanded that it should be stopped.

His next trip to Africa was to last for six years. He set out to explore the river Zambezi, and soon discovered Lake Nyasa, which was to become British territory. One of the hardest blows of his life was dealt here, for his wife, who had travelled out with him, died after four years of the African climate. Two years later he returned home.

Once again he left for Africa, but this journey was not to be as successful as the previous ones. Everything seemed to go wrong, from losing many of his stores to losing many of his men. A rumour was spread that he had been murdered, and an expedition was sent by an American newspaper to see what it could find.

"DR. LIVINGSTONE, I PRESUME?"

The leader was Henry Stanley. He discovered that Livingstone had been seen in the Tanganyika district, and it was at Ujiji that one of the most famous meetings of all times took place. Stanley, walking forward, said simply, " Doctor Livingstone, I presume? " People everywhere rejoiced in the knowledge that Livingstone was alive and well. Stanley tried to persuade him to return home, but there was no stopping Livingstone. The supplies he had received gave him new courage.

No one, however, could spend all that time in the jungle with all its difficulties, and remain in the best of health. His work had told on him, and Livingstone soon began to feel that he could not continue much longer. He even had to be carried on a litter, a kind of stretcher, by his faithful followers.

Then, one day, he was discovered in an attitude of prayer by his bedside. This was by no means uncommon, but, on this occasion, he was so still. David Livingstone, who had opened up the Dark Continent, had started on his last journey.

His heart was buried under the tree where he had died, but these faithful followers decided that his body must rest in his homeland. Embalming it and wrapping it in bark, they carried the body for many hundreds of miles, taking eight or nine months to reach the coast. There, after a rough, difficult and dangerous journey, they handed their treasure over to the authorities in Zanzibar, who had Livingstone's remains shipped back to England.

He was laid to rest in no less a place than Westminster Abbey, where may be seen a stone with letters of brass: " Brought by faithful hands over land and sea, here rests David Livingstone," a fitting memorial to a great man, but also to his faithful friends.

THE SWIMMER

How many a time have I
Cloven with arm still lustier, breast more daring,
The wave all roughen'd; with a swimmer's stroke
Flinging the billows back from my drench'd hair,
And laughing from my lip the audacious brine,
Which kiss'd it like a wine-cup, rising o'er
The waves as they arose, and prouder still
The loftier they uplifted me; and oft,
In wantonness of spirit, plunging down
Into their green and glassy gulfs, and making
My way to shells and sea-weed, all unseen
By those above, till they wax'd fearful; then
Returning with my grasp full of such tokens
As show'd that I had search'd the deep: exulting,
With a far-dashing stroke, and drawing deep
The long-suspended breath, again I spurn'd
The foam which broke around me, and pursued
My track like a sea-bird—I was a boy then.

Lord Byron

FATHER DAMIEN

The Friend of the Leper

JOSEPH DE VUESTER was born in 1840 in Louvain, Belgium, of rather poor parents, and he spent much of his time in his younger days in the fields near his home. His brother, who was older, was training to be a Roman Catholic priest, and when Joseph was nineteen he went to visit this brother. For several years he had taken an interest in the work of the Church, and he had decided that there was a great opportunity of service ahead of him.

It was while he was visiting his brother that he felt a call to join the Church, and to dedicate himself to the service of others. Little did he know that his name was to become one of the great names of the world, or that to him was to come great honour in the eyes of millions of people.

His opportunity came some time later and quite by accident. He had gone to see off his brother, who was going to the Hawaiian Islands as a missionary, when his brother was taken ill and unable to go. Quickly young Joseph, now known as Father Damien, begged to be allowed to take his brother's place, and this wish was granted. Collecting together a few belongings, mainly articles that he would need on the journey, he bade his family farewell and left his homeland for what was to be the last time.

When he arrived in the islands he soon made himself liked by all the people. It was nothing to see this fine upstanding young man climbing the cliffs, or swimming in the seas. He was a fine figure of a man, but what was more important, he had a great personality.

One of the pictures which hurt him most and which left a deep impression on his mind, was of a man of his parish who had been struck with leprosy and was forced to leave his wife and children to go and live, without help, on a nearby island named Molokai.

THE ISLAND OF LEPERS

This may seem rather harsh treatment, but leprosy is a dreadful disease which eats away the flesh and eventually causes death, with

Father Damien, who died to save lepers.

untold sufferings. To ensure that as few people as possible caught the disease, all cases, however slight, were sent to this island, where they were compelled to lead a life of misery with others afflicted like themselves.

One day in 1873, a conference was being held between the bishop and the missionaries about their work, when the subject of the lepers arose. If only there were someone who could help them! Father Damien then volunteered to go.

Probably he guessed what lay in store for him as he left the island, which had been his home for the nine years since he left Belgium. This was to be his last real touch with his fellow-workers, for Molokai was a place to be avoided. Admittedly boatmen took stores to the island, but they made off again as soon as they could. They had no intention of allowing the disease to get anywhere near them. For the first few months, Damien realised what might happen to him, and the thought filled him occasionally with horror, but soon he found that there was little time in which to think.

The lepers, he discovered, were living in a colony at one end of the island, where a flat piece of land jutted out into the sea. Their condition was dreadful. Many were so badly

In olden days people believed in the divine power of kings, thinking they had healing powers which could be transmitted by touch. It was sufficient, in some cases, for the patient to touch something the king had held in his hand. Here Edward I is giving a " touchpiece to a leper."

stricken with the disease that they were unable to do anything for themselves. Those who were not so badly afflicted lived some distance away, but knew that, in course of time, they, too, would be condemned to the same fate. They lived in the open, their only shelter being the branches of trees, which were placed over rough walls to give some protection. The men and women themselves were in despair and many of them were drinking a local alcoholic drink made from roots until they were insensible.

Into this picture of despair and misery walked Father Damien. His work was to be very exacting, for there were to be many demands upon his time. In fact, for many days, he lived under a great tree which grew on the island, for he had no time to build himself a house.

CONDEMNED TO DEATH

At first, the lepers were not very pleased to see him, for they had a grudge against people in general; but, gradually, they came to regard him as a friend who was there to help them. Soon, Damien was busy helping the people in every possible way. There was no doctor and he had to bind up the sores of these unfortunates. There was no water supply, and Damien sent for materials to build one from a spring to the settlement. There were no special burial arrangements, and those who died were just cast into a shallow grave and covered with earth. Damien soon found that he had to carry out the task of undertaker and, because there was no one who could make the coffins, he had to do so himself.

Gradually, by sheer hard work, he was able to improve the lot of these people until they led a more or less civilised existence.

Then, one day, Father Damien was busy washing himself, and, placing his feet in water that was too hot for him, he noticed that the skin was blistering but he could feel nothing. That could mean only one thing. He had leprosy.

After the initial horror of feeling that he was condemned to a slow painful death, he realised that this would help him in his work, for it was no longer " My brethren " when he addressed the people in the little church he had built, but " We lepers."

Without sparing himself, he continued to work, until in 1889, four years after contracting the disease, he died. Working to the very end, he was eventually called to the God whom he had so faithfully served and, amid great sorrow, his body was buried beneath the great tree, the branches of which had given him shelter when he first landed on Molokai.

In Louvain, a statue was erected to him; on Molokai he is remembered with gratitude; but his greatest memorial is in the work that has followed his death. Hearing of his unselfishness, a society was formed and funds were raised, and it is said that, in his death, Father Damien was able to do more for the lepers of Molokai than in his life—a great tribute to a really great man.

DO YOU KNOW?

Where does rubber come from?

Rubber is really the sap obtained from tropical trees.

It was first found out hundreds of years ago by natives who saw a beetle boring its way into the trunk of a tree. A juice oozed out, which killed the beetle and quickly filled up the hole which the insect had made, so that the tree's growth would not be stunted.

The natives cut off the juice and rolled it into a ball which they used for playing games. To-day the sap is gathered and made use of in many different ways.

When the natives found out that white men were willing to pay them for the juice that came from the trees, they set about gathering it in large quantities. To-day the collecting of this sap is a great industry, and we should all be grateful to the little beetle who first found it out.

Why is a pebble sometimes put in a kettle?

Many people keep a small pebble or marble in the kettle. There is a reason for this. Some water is *hard*. Hard water comes from that part of the country where the rocks are limestone. Water flowing from limestone hills has lime chalk in it. If you try to wash with it you will find you cannot get a good lather.

Water of this kind, when boiled, leaves a solid substance behind. This settles on the inside of the kettle. Then mother says the kettle is *furred* inside.

If a small stone or marble is placed in the kettle it dances around as the water warms. Thus it rubs round the inside walls of the kettle and prevents the *fur* or deposit from forming.

In districts where the water is *soft*, and easily gives a good lather, no stone is required in the kettle, as there will be no deposit.

Experts at work in the National Gallery on a wooden panel whose fabric was being eaten away by wood worms, and would shortly have been ruined.

THE PRESERVATION AND RESTORATION OF OLD PAINTINGS

THE galleries of the world are full of pictures covered with an age-darkened varnish, and, although they may be admired, we have very little idea of what they looked like when they were first painted. Quite an outcry was caused when the National Gallery cleaned a number of old masters—amongst them Rubens's " Chapeau de Paille "—so thoroughly that the original colours became visible again, for people found it hard to believe that the glowing colours had been so dimmed by the dirt of centuries.

NEW SCIENTIFIC METHODS

Until the end of last century, restoration was mainly in the hands of private practitioners, some of whom were skilful and conscientious, although to very many others all that seemed necessary was to clean the surface dirt and retouch. Even during the present century, under the controlled conditions of the National Gallery, less than one picture a year was cleaned between 1900 and 1933. The war years, however, provided an unusual opportunity, not only to repair some of the pictures that were removed for safety, but to bring the latest devices of science into play. New methods of restoring pictures have been discovered, and by using X-rays, infra-red and ultra-violet light, it is possible to see the changes and improvements made by the artist —and also, of course, to detect forgeries. It

CLEANING OLD MASTERS

"Portrait of a Man" by Titian (1477-1576)

WITH the passage of years the colours of many Old Masters have become dim and dulled, hiding to a great extent the original beauty of the painting. Due to the advance in scientific methods of treatment it is now possible to remove the accrued dirt of centuries without damaging the painting in any way, and the National Gallery in London, whose collection of Old Masters is second to none, employs a special staff to carry out this work. Here you see two famous paintings from the National Gallery. One, by Titian, photographed whilst still in process of being cleaned, shows how dark the colours had become, before the dirt of centuries was removed. The other, by Giovanni Bellini, with whom Titian worked for a time as a pupil, is shown after cleaning has been completed, and the full splendour of the clear colours glows again, just as it did when the picture was first painted more than four hundred years ago.

"The Madonna of the Meadows" by Giovanni Bellini (1428-1516)

Reproduced by courtesy of the Trustees, the National Gallery, London

is possible, with the help of a tintometer, to detect changes in colour, thus assisting the work of restoration and giving fascinating new information about the studio methods employed by some of the old masters.

THE EFFECTS OF DAMP AND DUST

The chief diseases of old pictures are caused by damp. Many of them have reposed in churches and castles for hundreds of years, and their only protection has been a coat of varnish. Yet if you look at some of the ancient Egyptian paintings preserved in the British Museum, which are thousands of years old, you will be struck by their extraordinary freshness. They kept their bright colours because the atmosphere of Egypt is so dry, but without air conditioning they would quickly deteriorate in London. Until the time of the French Impressionists, who ceased to use varnish because they thought that it spoiled the vibrant effect at which they aimed, varnish was generally used as a protection. When it was not used impurities in the air sank into the paint and dulled the colours, red assuming a purplish hue and yellow turning brown. Unfortunately when dust is worked by moisture into the very texture of a painting, there is no way of cleaning without doing irreparable damage.

REMOVING VARNISH

Dirty varnish, on the other hand, can be removed by various ingenious methods. Some varnishes can be rubbed off by the fingers. The most rapid and simple method is to apply a mixture of essence of turpentine and alcohol. Unfortunately this often proves rather dangerous, and the safest solvent is one that acts more gradually and gently. In the case of an old picture there may be several coats of varnish of different kinds and the restorer must select an appropriate solvent for each type.

No matter what patience and care are exercised, however, varnish is seldom totally removed without some slight injury to the surface. It then becomes necessary to undertake the delicate job of retouching. This has to be done more freely when a tear has been mended, or if some of the paint has worn away in the course of time. The problem is not merely to match the artist's colours at the moment of application, but to foresee how the new colour will look in years to come. The great artists of the past made their own paints and often kept their recipes secret. But even if we knew the exact ingredients, it would still be necessary to allow for changes in the pigments due to the passage of time.

SOME OF THE DIFFICULTIES OF RETOUCHING

The method most commonly used is to grind colours with turpentine, and apply them with varnish. They change much more slowly than if ordinary paint were used, but they still change; sooner or later the retouching can be detected. Better results can be obtained by using colours ground with white of egg. This makes great demands on the restorer's skill, because tempera colours, as these are called, dry soon after they are applied. However, they settle down to a permanent tone in a few days, and it is this state which the restorer has to predict.

In the past repainting was sometimes done even to famous pictures on a reckless scale. Rubens and Raphael have both suffered from the zeal of the restorer. By means of ultraviolet rays it is usually possible to see whether the paint on a given canvas is all of the same chemical composition. Any retouched part is then seen to be of a different colour even though this is undetectable in ordinary daylight.

TRANSFERENCE

The most astonishing restoration operation consists in removing the painting like a shell from a canvas or wooden panel. This is known as " transference " and was invented about the middle of the eighteenth century when two masterpieces of Raphael, " St. George " and " La Petite Sainte Famille," were treated in this way. The first step is to glue paper and tarlatan to the painting itself to protect the surface. Then it is turned over, and by the cautious use of damp and heat, the glue between the actual canvas and the coating on which the picture is painted is softened until the canvas comes away. There are various kinds of coating, but the basis is either size mixed with plaster, or carbonate of lime, or white lead upon size. Without some such coating, the canvas would not be flexible and the paint would very soon crack, and as a

This painting was badly damaged during the war. With care and patience the tears have been mended, the painting retouched and the havoc almost obliterated. The expert here marks each affected area before starting work.

consider it to be more reliable than the alternative method of reinforcing the old canvas or panel.

RELINING

Reinforcing or " relining " has been applied to many famous pictures, including Velasquez's "Venus" in the National Gallery. Relining is a useful technique if a canvas is torn. The back of the damaged canvas is cleaned and covered with glue. Then a gauze is applied, and finally the new canvas. After it has been ironed, the relined canvas is stretched and the gaps made by the tear are filled in with a mixture of carbonate of lime and glue. This is a well-tried way of concealing the tear, but there are, of course, risks of unfortunate after-effects. The mastic used to fill the gap may scale off, or if the work is carelessly done serious trouble might arise from air bubbles between the two canvases.

AIR-CONDITIONING ESSENTIAL

The work carried out in its own laboratory by the National Gallery has proved of great value to all collectors. It has been proved beyond all doubt that the controlling of humidity and temperature is of supreme importance for the preservation of paintings, and therefore air-conditioning should be installed in all public galleries. This, however, is hardly practicable in churches and all private houses, but where a valuable painting has to be hung without such a precaution, it should be protected by glass. Paintings should, in fact, be regarded as " living " things which need to be looked after in order to retain their full beauty.

result, transference would not be possible·

It may be even more difficult to detach the picture from its support if it has been painted on wood. This has to be gradually planed away until only the painting remains. The next stage is to glue a new canvas to the detached painting. Transference is a much more lengthy and complicated operation than this brief description suggests, but experts

SENDING A COLLINS

When you have stayed with friends it is your duty—as it should be your pleasure—to send them a note of thanks for their kindness.

Some people call these notes " bread-and-butter letters," which is not very romantic. Others call them " Collins," and you may wonder why.

The term comes from Jane Austen's famous book, *Pride and Prejudice*. Mr. Collins, in the novel, paid a long and not appreciated visit to the Bennets. When at last he left, he said: " Depend upon it, you will speedily receive from me a letter of thanks for this as well as for every other mark of your regard during my stay in Hertfordshire."

These letters, if they are to mean anything should be sincere and informal. The happiest one that I ever received read: " We had an awful journey home, but, bless you, our visit was worth it."

Mary Slessor, with some of her native friends of Calabar in West Africa. This brave woman won the love and respect of the primitive people to whom she dedicated her life.

MARY SLESSOR
The Friend of the Native

IN 1848 a baby was born in Aberdeen who was to be one of the greatest women who has ever lived. Her name was Mary Slessor; her father was a drunkard; her home life was poor; and there was little to suggest that one brought up in such circumstances would be named with the heroines of the world.

At the age of eleven, she went to work in a factory in Dundee and there, in the evenings, she would make her way to the little mission which stood in one of the worst slum districts in the town. Gradually, as she grew older, she became one of the workers there, trying to help those who were in need.

It is here that we have one of our earliest pictures of Mary Slessor, for there were certain gangs of boys who were not anxious to see the work of the mission spreading. It was one of these which cornered Mary regularly and endeavoured to stop her from getting into the mission.

On one occasion, they had her with her back to the wall, while they threatened her with a piece of metal. She remained there unflinching, though grazed by the metal, and the gang was so impressed by her bravery that they became her helpers. This picture of Mary, with her back to the wall, is very apt, for so much of her life was to be spent courageously with her back, as it were, to the wall.

A GIRL MISSIONARY

In 1875 she resolved to be a missionary and see what she could do to help the people of Africa. The place she felt she ought to go to was the Calabar district on the west coast of Africa. After undertaking a certain amount of necessary training, she sailed for Duke

227

Town, which was to be her home for several years.

The missionary there was amazed to think that a girl should be sent to such a place, but he soon found that Mary, with her winning way, was to be a great asset to the station.

Soon Mary was taking her place with the men, going round the village to call people to church, unflinching at the dreadful filth and squalor she found, and doing all she could to help the people who were in particular need.

But, though Mary was getting on well, and though she was well liked, she was not really happy, for she had heard that there were people living up-country, in small villages, who needed to be taught of Christ. These people were particularly fierce and cruel, and stopped at nothing to get rid of anyone they did not want. The authorities did not feel that it was safe to send anyone, let alone a woman, and they refused to allow her to go. Mary, however, was very insistent and, after twelve years' work on the coast, permission was eventually given for this arduous task.

A DANGEROUS JOURNEY

Mary fully realised the difficulties, as did also the people she was leaving behind. At first it seemed that she must go alone, but, at the last moment, another missionary, by the name of Bishop, agreed to accompany her. Within three months of permission being given, she had started on her journey to Okoyong, accompanied by Bishop and by her family. Her family consisted of a small group of orphans, who had been cast out of home by their families and left in the jungle to die.

The journey, itself, was sufficient to strike fear into the heart of anyone. By day, there were strange sounds coming from the jungle, and by night these were magnified. The sight of many wild animals looking for a meal and the word that she had received of the nature of the people to whom she was going, were sufficient to scare anyone, but Mary Slessor knew her friends back at the coast were praying for her and she felt that all would be well.

It was a strange little band of people that eventually found its way into the village. Bishop, with the stores, had been left four miles away on the river, while Mary, together with a group of very tired, crying children, entered the village.

There began a most difficult task, for the natives had many strange and evil customs to be fought. She found that much of the time was spent in trying to get better conditions for the women and the slaves, who, in many cases, were treated no better than, if as well as, the animals.

A PRIMITIVE SCHOOL

There she began a school. A very primitive one it was, for there was little at her disposal. On the veranda of a house a few logs were placed on which her pupils sat as she taught. There, too, she conducted the worship of God every night in the yard which belonged to the chief. There, the people came to understand the God who had sent this strange white woman to help them, and soon many were joining her in the singing of the hymns. Soon, too, they came to regard her advice as good. In matters of justice, she often won the natives over to her side, though it was often after great persuasiveness on her part.

One of her greatest triumphs was when she stopped a battle between two tribes. Hearing of the squabble, she set out to do what she could to stop trouble. Being rather weak, she had to be carried as she followed behind the army which was marching, but she never seemed to be able to catch up with the warriors.

Eventually, she caught up with them just as they were making ready to attack. Chiding the chief, she tried to persuade him to stop the nonsense. Eventually an old man stepped forward and thanked her for coming. Immediately she let them know that she was not going to stand by and watch them fighting, and told each side to choose two or three men to come and talk with her. The trouble was over.

Wherever she went, she received attention from the natives, who were always ready to listen to her. For thirty-six years, with the exception of short periods, this great Christian woman travelled the country, helping those in distress and ever increasing the sphere in which she worked. In the end, she would take no honour for herself, but gave glory to God for all she had been able to do in His name.

To-day, the results of her work still live, and it may be said that she probably did more than any other woman to bring civilisation to Darkest Africa.

Miss Florence Nightingale who brought hope and healing to wounded soldiers in the Crimean War and revolutionised nursing.

FLORENCE NIGHTINGALE

The Lady of the Lamp

IT WAS in 1820, when a well-to-do Englishman and his wife were holidaying in Italy, that a daughter was born and named Florence, after the city in which they were staying. Little did they realise that this baby was to become one of the most loved and most respected people whose names have graced the pages of a history book.

Florence, it was expected, would take her place in society, for she had received a very good education, was of a very respectable family, and had been presented at court.

This, however, was not the kind of life which appealed to Florence, for she greatly wished to be able to care for those who needed her help. One of the earliest stories which is told of her is that, as a girl, on her father's estate, she cared for a sheep-dog which had been hurt, restoring it to health, although the shepherd had thought that the dog would have to be destroyed.

Her family showed the greatest possible disapproval of her wish to become a nurse, for, in those days, nursing was looked down upon as being anything but a respectable career. Florence was adamant, and, as there were no training hospitals in England, she travelled to Germany to undertake training there at a hospital which she had heard of through Elizabeth Fry.

There she worked hard and qualified as a nurse, returning to this country when her training was completed.

It was about this time that the Crimean War broke out between Turkey and Russia, with Britain and France supporting Turkey. After the battles of Balaclava and Inkerman, there were so many wounded and they were in such

229

a dreadful condition that an appeal was sent for help from Britain.

The response to this appeal was to send a group of nurses, with Florence Nightingale in charge. When they arrived, however, they found opposition from the military leaders, who had certainly not expected, nor did they want, women in the hospital. It was with the greatest difficulty that Florence was able to get permission to do what she thought ought to be done, and, at first, the nurses were employed only on cleaning the place up. It was one frustrated attempt after another, until the military authorities agreed to let the nurses do what they had been sent out to do.

The hospital they found was a large Turkish barracks, and it was filthy. The soldiers lay on the hard wooden floor, and the rats could be seen running around the room and across their feet. However, the place was speedily cleaned up and reorganised, and what had been a very poor state of affairs for the soldiers very quickly improved.

Difficulty was found in getting supplies, because the army regulations would not permit their issue, but Florence overcame this problem by buying her own supplies.

Every day she worked, thinking nothing of herself, and the nurses who were with her worked equally unselfishly, nursing the injured, helping them to write letters home if they were unable to do so themselves, speaking words of comfort to those who had particular problems. Then at night she would go the rounds of the hospital, carrying with her a small lamp to light the way, and, as she passed, the soldiers smiled at the one who became affectionately known as the " Lady of the Lamp."

One day she was delighted to receive a letter from Queen Victoria herself, showing that the Queen was taking a great interest in the work she was doing.

VISITING WOUNDED MEN AT THE FRONT

Having been at Scutari for six months, Florence wished to see what conditions were like at the front, and she travelled to the battlefield so that she could see what could be done for the wounded men at the front.

While she was there, she unfortunately caught a fever and had to be kept in a hospital near the front. It is interesting to see that the commander, who had been so much against

Florence Nightingale is here seen at Scutari, in the Crimea. On arrival she devoted herself to the cleaning up and reorganisation of all the hospitals, and enforced rigid cleanliness and careful nursing. She also bought her own supplies when the Army was slow in sending them.

the arrival of the nurses, thought so much of Florence and her work after only six months that he risked the fever to go and visit her personally.

Attempts were made to send her home, but she refused to go. " They need me," was her main thought, as she considered the soldiers; and it was not until the last of the wounded had left Scutari at the end of the war that she agreed to come home.

A welcome for a heroine awaited her, but she would have none of it. She turned down the offer of a civic reception or of bands on the quay, and came back as quietly and as unobtrusively as she could.

But having returned, she did not consider her work to have finished. One thing that was urgently needed was a training-school for nurses in this country. She had shown that nursing was a profession to be proud of, and she wanted to feel that those who took it up could have the advantages of training such as she herself had received. Accordingly, a special training-school was opened at St. Thomas's Hospital in 1871.

Not only did she help the nurses, but she never forgot the soldiers, and, back in England, she did much to encourage the building of canteens.

In 1907, a great honour was bestowed upon Florence Nightingale when she received the Order of Merit, and was the first woman to do so. It was only three years later, at the age of 90, that she died, having won the hearts of all. Many were the hearts that felt very heavy when the news was announced, and many old men, veterans of the Crimean War, remembered with gratitude the grace of the " Lady of the Lamp," whose shadow on the hospital floor men bent to kiss.

CHRISTMAS BELLS

I heard the bells on Christmas Day
Their old, familiar carols play,
   And wild and sweet
   The words repeat
Of peace on earth, good-will to men!

And thought how, as the day had come,
The belfries of all Christendom
   Had rolled along
   The unbroken song
Of peace on earth, good-will to men!

Till, ringing, singing on its way,
The world revolved from night to day,
   A voice, a chime,
   A chant sublime
Of peace on earth, good-will to men!

Then from each black, accursed mouth
The cannon thundered in the South,
   And with the sound
   The carols drowned
Of peace on earth, good-will to men!

It was as if an earthquake rent
The hearth-stones of a continent,
   And made forlorn
   The households born
Of peace on earth, good-will to men!

And in despair I bowed my head;
" There is no peace on earth," I said,
   " For hate is strong,
   And mocks the song
Of peace on earth, good-will to men! "

Then pealed the bells more loud and deep
" God is not dead, nor doth He sleep!
   The Wrong shall fail,
   The Right prevail,
With peace on earth, good-will to men! "

Henry Wadsworth Longfellow

RUDYARD KIPLING

A Writer For All Ages

MOST of you will have heard of Rudyard Kipling long before you see his name at the top of this page, and many of you will have read the *Just So Stories* and at least one of the *Jungle Books*. What I hope to do now is to give you a glimpse of some of the other wonderful things Kipling wrote, and to make you want to read them yourselves. For if you get a liking for Kipling when you are young, you will never tire of him; all his magnificent stories and verses will be yours for life—for you will quickly find you can read all his things over and over again, and every time you do so you'll discover something new and exciting.

Rudyard Kipling was born in Bombay in 1865. When he was only five, he was sent to England to be educated; and this early part of his life was very unhappy. For six years, in fact, he was in the care of a woman whose ideas of discipline amounted to a kind of tyranny. When he was seventeen he returned to India where he worked very hard for seven years as a newspaper reporter, a job which took him all over India and gave him his unrivalled knowledge of that fascinating country. He achieved fame with his first book, written when he was twenty.

KIPLING'S NOVELS

Most of Kipling's work consisted of short stories and poems, and it is principally those we shall be looking at, but he did also write four full-length novels, two of which have boys for heroes and are thrilling stories for both young and old. The first is *Captains Courageous*, written in 1896. It's about a very spoilt and conceited boy who falls overboard from a liner off Newfoundland, and is picked up by a fishing boat. He has, of course, first to have the conceit knocked out of him, but once that's been done he soon makes friends with the crew and shares their exciting life: trawling, battling with storms, and, best of all, racing

to find fish and bring off the biggest catches, thus beating the other boats back to port. It gives a vivid picture of experts at their own special job—which always appealed to Kipling.

The other full-length book is *Kim* (1900), one of the most fascinating novels ever written, though you'll like it even better when you're older. It's about an orphan boy whose father and mother were British, but who was brought up in India and entirely among Indians—so much so that he can easily pass for one himself. Being quick-witted and fearless, he gets into countless scrapes and adventures. But soon an important Englishman learns his story, and realises what a valuable recruit he would be for the Secret Service—after which his adventures become much more exciting and very much more dangerous. When you read *Kim* you will find that Kipling has brought a whiff of the warm, scented air of India into your own home, so that you, too, smell the woodsmoke and taste the spicy foods, and, like the hero (who never wore shoes if he could help it), feel " the caress of soft mud squishing up between the toes."

THE " JUST SO STORIES "

In 1902 Kipling wrote the *Just So Stories*. Probably you know these already—or you may perhaps think, because the title page says " For Little Children," that you're too old for them. Actually, when you're grown-up and have children of your own, you'll love to read them again, and if you've a young brother or sister who's reading them now do please have another look at them, because you're sure to find plenty you missed before. Take the black and white pictures, for instance. Kipling drew these himself, and wrote those rather delicious bits underneath—as when he describes the sea as " ooshy-skooshy " because of the whale's sucking. They're well worth further study. You'll also get a lot of new fun out of the poems after each story; if you've a small sister who asks endless questions, you'll appreciate " The Elephant's Child " one, and you probably don't know that in the beautiful verses after " How the Alphabet was Made " Kipling is speaking of his own little daughter, who died when she was only six.

THE " JUNGLE BOOKS "

The Jungle Book and *The Second Jungle Book* were written several years earlier. Make sure you read them *both*, as they are really one book and their stories interlock. Eight of them are about an Indian boy named Mowgli, who is lost by his parents in the jungle and brought up by wolves. We meet a whole forestful of animals and birds, and hear not only their talk but the way they look at Life: from the wise old bear who teaches jungle law, to the gluttonous crocodile who is " never quite full." Probably the best Mowgli story is " Kaa's Hunting," where the boy is kidnapped by monkeys, and his friends the bear and panther have given him up for lost, for they would stand no chance against such a mob. Suddenly the old bear remembers the one creature the apes are terrified of, the one who alone can strike all their myriads helpless at once—Kaa, the great rock python. The way he saves Mowgli makes a thrilling story.

An interesting thing about the Mowgli stories is that the first one Kipling wrote is not in the jungle books at all, but was written some years earlier. The story is called " In the Rukh " (Rukh = Forest) and tells of Mowgli as a young man with extraordinary power over animals. It was inventing this story that planted the idea of the others in Kipling's mind.

Of the seven other jungle book stories, the best known is " Rikki-Tikki-Tavi," the exciting one about the mongoose and the cobras—but what you can't help noticing is that through *all* the tales, especially those about the wolf-pack, there runs the spirit of law and discipline that Kipling thought so important in life. Read the poem in the second book called " The Law of the Jungle," and you will find the same sort of rules of conduct for wolves as exist in your own school: rules that put the team first, but insist on your being self-reliant also; rules such as:

" *When ye fight with a Wolf of the Pack ye must*
fight him alone and afar,
Lest others take part in the quarrel, and the
Pack be diminished by war."

OTHER ANIMAL STORIES

Kipling was very fond of animals, and they come into many of his stories. Dogs were his favourites, and if you, too, care for dogs you'll be fascinated by the way he brings them to life—every one a character and every one different. Here is an extract from the story of a jealous little terrier whose master is looking after someone else's dog as well:

She settled her head on the pillow several times, to show her little airs and graces, and struck up her usual whiney sing-song before slumber. The stranger-dog softly edged towards me. I put out my hand and he licked it. Instantly my wrist was between Vixen's teeth, and her warning *aaarh!* said as plainly as speech, that if I took any further notice of the stranger she would bite. . . . The big dog's tail thumped the floor in a humble and peace-making way."*

Can't you *hear* that " aaarh! " and *feel* those strong, sharp teeth on your wrist in the dark, while the big, lonely stranger-dog waits patiently on the floor?

Kipling's best dog-story is called " The Woman in His Life "—about how a little black Scottie saves his master from losing his reason. You will love this story, though the rest of the ones in that book won't appeal to you till later on.

Then there's a splendid tale of polo-ponies in India, called " The Maltese Cat." " Play

*From " Garm—A Hostage " (*Action & Reactions*).

for the Side " is the cry running through it all, and it tells how a dozen cheap, humble ponies, welded into a team and led by the clever little " Cat," fared in a big match against twice their number of highly-bred expensive ones—who are not, unfortunately, in the least used to helping each other. It's impossible to read the story without catching the thrill of galloping after the flying, bounding ball, the thunder and thwack of a high-speed shot at goal, and the roar of the frantic crowds straining along the side-lines.

MACHINES AS STORY-HEROES

You are sure to be keen on machines; so was Kipling, but he was the first to picture them as having human feelings: shyness, pride, discontent and even humility. ".007 " is about a brand-new express railway engine, and when he meets his elders for the first time he's as terrified as you and I were when we walked into the big class-room on our first day at school. His driver has run him into the round-house where the older engines live, and he " would have given a month's oil for leave to crawl through his own driving wheels into the brick ash-pit beneath him." But you can't keep a good engine down, and it's not long before .007 gets his chance. "The Ship that Found Herself " tells of a new 1,200-ton cargo steamer. No shyness about *her*; thinks she's Queen of the Ocean—till the first lift of the swell sets every separate bit of her grumbling and groan-quarrelling with its neighbours, yelling for more room:

> " Ease off! Ease off, there! " roared the garboard-strake. " I want one-eighth of an inch fair play. D'you hear me, you rivets! . . . Ease off, you dirty little forge-filings. Let me breathe! "

It's not till they've driven the ship across the Atlantic through the stormiest of seas that all her parts get used to working together, and realise at last that none of them can function without the rest. As she steams up the distant harbour the ship,

for the first time, speaks with one voice.

GREAT STORIES OF ENGLAND

Kipling loved India, loved animals and loved children, but most of all he loved England. He realised better than any other writer that England stands as she does to-day —beautiful and strong—because of what her people did and endured in the past: the ships they built, the wars they fought (not always against men), and, most of all, the just way in which they governed. Whenever he looked at his beloved Sussex countryside he saw people living their lives on those same slopes hundreds of years ago, and with his genius he was able to conjure those lives back from the past and put them vividly before us. In two books of stories—*Puck of Pook's Hill* and *Rewards and Fairies*—a boy and his sister are constantly meeting, near their own home, folk of the past who helped to make our history: a flint-man who fought wolves with the first iron knife, a Norman knight who had to live here after Hastings among Saxons who hated him, a doctor who discovered the secret of the Great Plague, and many more— and many of the stories these people tell took place in the actual valley, and beside the actual stream, where the children are

One of Kipling's own drawings for his book of *Just So Stories*.

Some *Jungle Book* characters. Can you name them all?

standing. Well does the wise little Puck sing:

" *See you the dimpled track that runs,*
All hollow through the wheat?
O that was where they hauled the guns
That smote King Philip's fleet."

In these books you meet the men who hauled such guns—or perhaps they were really meant for a pirate ship, and the ironmaster who founded them was being paid ten times their value for risking his neck—and his foundry stood down there, where the little mill is innocently clacking away under your very eyes!

KIPLING AS A POET

Rudyard Kipling is quite as famous for his poetry as for his short stories—in fact, the many snatches of him that have become everyday language (phrases like " Triumph and Disaster ") nearly all come from his verse. Probably his best-known poem is " Recessional " (" Lest We Forget "), which is sometimes sung in church to the tune of " Eternal Father, strong to save . . ." but he wrote verses about as many different subjects as he did stories: Indian ones, war ones, poems about the countryside, animal ones, funny ones and sad ones. Many of the poems " go with " a particular story, like the camel's hump one; others were written for a special occasion or purpose, such as to get money for the families of soldiers who were away fighting (" The Absent-Minded Beggar "). These often first appeared in a great newspaper like *The Times*. There are hundreds of poems you will love at your present age (a few suggestions are given at the end of this article), and your best plan is to get hold of a volume of *all* his verse and browse through it.

THE IMMENSE RANGE OF HIS WORK

I have only touched on a fraction of Kipling's stories and poems, trying to pick on those that will appeal to you *now*, as an introduction to the treasure-hoard that will still lie under your hand when you've read them. For instance, there is *Stalky & Co.*, the strangest school story you've ever dreamt of. It's really more about masters than boys, but the older ones among you will enjoy the way Stalky and his friends are constantly turning the tables—as when another house accuses theirs of not washing and calls them stinkers. Deadly was the revenge they took! Then there are funny tales, more wonderful tales of England, tales of the sea, air, doctors, soldiers, even tales of heaven.

WHAT HE STOOD FOR

You will only have to read a very little of his work to realise that the things Kipling believed in were loyalty, devotion to duty, and freedom—and for him the great champion of freedom was England. At the start of the Great War of 1914 he wrote:

> " *What stands if Freedom fall?*
> *Who dies if England live?* "

He believed that without those three things life could not be full and happy; and with them went another thing: compassion—or, if you like, pity and love. Nowhere in his works will you find anything that's really meant to hurt, unless it's hurting something that he detested: arrogance, cruelty, bullying, injustice. Later on you'll find that he wrote much about illness, but always with the idea of curing it, of healing.

Putting it shortly, Kipling believed in 'guts' and kindness.

HIS HABITS AND HOME

He was a very shy man, and spent years hunting for a home where he could escape crowds. He found it at Burwash, a little village deep in Sussex; even to-day it is miles from a station. The house is called Bateman's. Kipling bought it in 1902, and lived there till he died on 18th January, 1936. He wrote much of his best work there, and in 1907 he was awarded the famous Nobel Prize for Literature —won in 1953 by Sir Winston Churchill. Bateman's now belongs to the National Trust, so we are allowed to visit it. The best time to go is just after reading the " Puck " stories, as the brook and old mill near the house are the very ones that come into them so much, while a short way off stands Pook's Hill itself. You will love Kipling's work even more after seeing the home of this great man, who wrote so much for both old and young, and so much that can never die, that in every sense he deserves the title of A Writer for All Ages.

WHERE TO FIND KIPLING'S STORIES AND POEMS

The best way to start reading Kipling is to get some of his books from your school or Public Library. (As long as your father is a ratepayer you can use the latter.) But once you catch the magic of his writings you will want some of the books for your own, so here is a list of those recommended for *now*, together with any special stories you should look out for. They are all published by Messrs. Macmillan.

Book	Stories Recommended
Just So Stories	All.
The Jungle Book	All (includes "Kaa's Hunting" and "Rikki-Tikki ").
The Second Jungle Book	All
Many Inventions	" In the Rukh " (the first Mowgli story).
The Day's Work	" The Maltese Cat." ".007." " The Ship that Found Herself."
Limits and Renewals	" The Woman in His Life " (dog story. *No* others).

Puck of Pook's Hill	{ All, but read " Puck "
Rewards and Fairies	{ before " Rewards."
Stalky and Co.	All.
Captains Courageous	A novel.
Kim	A novel.

Messrs. Macmillan also publish the following collections, with coloured plates:

Animal Stories
All the Mowgli Stories

VERSE

You cannot do better than get the Definitive Edition of Rudyard Kipling's Verse, published by Messrs. Hodder & Stoughton. This is absolutely complete. Here are a few poems that will appeal to you at once:

All the poems that go with the stories you like.
" His Apologies " (a dog poem).
" The Land " (about the men it *really* belongs to).
" The Ballad of East and West."
" The Truce of the Bear " (when he begs

Bateman's, Kipling's home at Burwash in Sussex. The pond is full of goldfish.

for mercy—you must certainly beware!).
" The Bell-Buoy."
" Gunga Din."

If you would like to know more about Kipling, there is a quite excellent little book called *Son of Empire*, by Nella Braddy, published by Collins and available in many libraries. It was written specially to bring Kipling to the notice of young people.

All quotations from Rudyard Kipling's Works which appear in this article and the illustrations from the Just So *Stories are by kind permission of Mrs. George Bambridge and of Messrs. Macmillan & Co.*

DO YOU KNOW?

Where does sand come from?

When you are enjoying yourself at the seaside in summer do you ever wonder where all the sand comes from?

Most of it comes from rock which has broken apart and has been washed away by the action of the water. A great part of the ocean bottom is made up of sandstone, which wears away by the continual washing of the sea and floats up to the surface. The waves wash it to the shore, where it piles up on the beach.

Sand often differs in colour, depending on the rocks from which it comes. Sometimes valuable ores, such as gold, copper and iron, are found mixed with the sand.

The great sandy deserts, which we find many miles inland, mark the places where the sea once swept over the land.

What does " get the sack " mean?

The story goes that in olden times a Sultan of Turkey, ruler of his country, had a curious way of ridding himself of people who troubled him. He had them put in sacks and thrown into the sea!

This story came to our islands, and when people were dismissed from their jobs it was said that they had " been given the sack."

This expression is still used in our country, and when a person is told that his services are no longer needed, he is said to have been sacked.

HOW PLEASANT

TO KNOW

MR. LEAR

JUST over a hundred years ago a young man—rather awkward in appearance and untidily dressed—rang the front door bell at the royal residence of Osborne and asked to see the Queen. The footman was puzzled: Queen Victoria did not make a habit of receiving uninvited guests. However, he was shown into an ante-room where an equally puzzled equerry tried, tactfully, to discover the caller's business. The visitor was amiable but vague, and the equerry was soon convinced he was dealing with a lunatic until the guest at length casually remarked that he was " Lear, you know. The Queen wanted some drawing lessons."

For Edward Lear, remembered now for his nonsense verse, was by profession a landscape painter whose sketches were so much admired in his lifetime that Queen Victoria specially commissioned him to give her a series of twelve lessons. The absent-minded painter had typically forgotten to mention this on his first visit.

Absent-mindedness was indeed one of Lear's characteristics, and he tells the story against himself of how—once wishing to return the salute of a friend—he raised his right hand to his forehead thereby smartly plastering himself with the colours on the palette his hand was holding at the time.

THE QUEEN'S DRAWING MASTER

By the time he had begun his lessons with the Queen—(" Mr. Lear was very much pleased with my drawing and very encouraging about it," wrote his royal pupil in her diary)—young Edward had suffered more than one reversal

of fortune. All his adult life he suffered from periodic " tinlessness," as he called his lack of money, but his early youth had been passed in wealth.

With twenty brothers and sisters he lived in a large house in Highgate, then a quiet village, from which his stockbroker father departed each morning to the City and the not too arduous business of making money But one day Papa did not return—and news came instead that, having been involved in unfortunate speculations, he was now lodged in the debtors' prison. Servants were dismissed, the house and twelve carriages sold, and the sorrowful Lears moved into apartments near their father's prison.   And Edward, not yet thirteen, wrote a poem to mark the occasion:

In dreary silence down the bustling road
The Lears, with all their goods and chattels,
*   rode.*

For the next few years Edward was looked after by his beloved elder sister, Ann. Short-sightedness and ill-health made regular schooling inadvisable, and instead he was instructed by Ann and—in drawing—by another sister, Sarah. His particular interest was to draw flowers and birds, and by the age of fifteen he was already beginning to earn money by his paintings. His reproductions of birds were so accurate that the Zoological Society commissioned him to paint the parrots at the London Zoo—and the young man who hated noise found himself shut up in the Parrot House for a year!

When the drawings appeared, his reputation

was made: he had combined the technical skill of an artist with the knowledge of a naturalist and commissions began to flow in. Among them was the one which by an odd chance was to make his name.

ILLUSTRATING A MENAGERIE

The then Earl of Derby had formed a unique collection of birds and animals at his house, Knowsley Hall, and he now invited Lear to make an illustrated record of the menagerie. Life at Knowsley, where Lear spent most of the next four years, was an introduction to a new world. In the great galleries of the enormous house hung famous paintings by Holbein and Rembrandt. Here too, were entertained " half the fine people of the day," as Edward wrote. Young Lear, who had arrived as a junior employee, soon became friendly with some of the most influential people in the land, for he possessed wit and charm: above all, as a friend afterwards wrote of him, he was " gettonable with."

Sometimes, Lear confessed, the grand society overpowered him dreadfully. " There is nothing I long for half so much as to giggle heartily and to hop on one leg down the Great Gallery."

But there was one section in that large household where he was quite free to giggle and hop as much as he pleased, and in the nurseries, where quantities of Lord Derby's grand-children and great-nephews and nieces were brought up together, he was a welcome visitor. There his funny drawings were received with peals of laughter, and there he began to scribble the nonsense verses for which he is

to-day remembered. People of wealth and importance might give him their friendship and patronage, but it was the children of Knowsley who first inspired the work for which he became famous.

THE ORIGIN OF LIMERICKS

Lear did not invent the limerick form, though it is always associated with his name. Indeed, the origin of the name itself is obscure, though it is thought to have been taken from a chorus " Will you come up to Limerick ? " following extemporised nonsense verses. But it was Lear who popularised the form, and everyone—from the Poet Laureate, Tennyson, downwards—began to compose them.

> *There was a young girl of Majorca,*
> *Whose aunt was a very fast walker,*
> *She walked seventy miles,*
> *And leaped fifteen stiles,*
> *Which astonished that girl of Majorca.*

During his years at Knowsley, Lear finally decided to become a landscape painter. Asthma and bronchitis made English winters a danger, and when the Knowsley commission was ended he determined to travel abroad. For the rest of his life most of his time was spent out of England. He travelled in Italy—which he loved—in Greece, Egypt, Palestine, Corfu, Corsica, India—and wherever he went, he painted. His pictures were hung in the Royal Academy and the drawings of his travels were collected and published.

In Rome, where he lived for several years, the Prince of Wales—later Edward VII—

" . . . She walked seventy miles, and leaped fifteen stiles . . ."

visited his studio. He met and liked Robert and Elizabeth Barrett Browning after their famous elopement; the Tennysons were intimate friends. Lear set many of his songs to music—yet for all his charm and popularity Lear was not a happy man. Frequently ill, lonely and depressed, he felt he had missed in his life the tranquil happiness he so desired. He had no children, for although he had several times thought of marriage, he died a bachelor.

A year before his death he sent from San Remo—where he now lived—for the woman to whom he had for many years thought of proposing marriage. But her visit came to an end and she returned to England with the question unasked. He never saw her again.

THE MAN WHO UNDERSTOOD CHILDREN

Yet wherever he went he collected children. Some of the happiest hours of his life must have been those in which a circle of intent small faces surrounded him while delighted eyes watched the sketches flow from his pen. Children felt "safe" with this tall, bearded man with the twinkling glasses: they felt he "understood."

Lear never sat down specially to compose his nonsense verses: like Topsy in *Uncle Tom's Cabin*, they "just growed"—on the backs of envelopes, on scraps of paper—written to amuse the children of his friends, of his landlord, the guests in the same hotel:

> *The Owl and the Pussy cat went to sea*
> *In a beautiful pea-green boat*
> *They took some honey, and plenty of*
> *   money,*
> *Wrapped up in a five pound note.*

The Jumblies go to sea in a sieve.

He invented words, too, and there is no need to ask their meaning: there are the pelicans who stamp their feet " with a flumpy sound "; there is scenery which is " pomskizillious and gromphibberous," and of course there is " runcible," which might be applied to a hat, a cat or a spoon; there are the enchanting story-poems of " The Dong with the Luminous Nose " and " The Pobble who had no Toes." (At least, he began by having toes, but he unscrewed them.)

LEAR MADE THOUSANDS LAUGH

Lear seldom referred to his verses, yet there is an underlying sadness in some of them which seems to show that in them he was expressing some of his deepest feelings. How haunting are some of the verses:

> *Far and few, far and few*
> *Are the lands where the Jumblies live;*
> *Their heads are green, and their hands are*
> *   blue,*
> *And they went to sea in a sieve . . .*

And there is the portrait of Lear himself— as the Yonghy-Bonghy-Bo—living his last years in Italy alone save for his servant and Foss, his cat, who lived to be seventeen and who has been immortalised in his master's drawings.

Years before, someone had remarked " How pleasant to know Mr. Lear," and Lear had

The Yonghy-Bonghy-Bo, whose head was very large and whose hat was very small.

gleefully seized on the remark and made it into the first line of a poem:

How pleasant to know Mr. Lear!
Who has written such volumes of stuff:
Some think him ill-tempered and queer,
But a few think him pleasant enough.

His words were prophetic but too modest: not merely " a few " have found his writings " pleasant enough ": thousands of people have laughed at them and many thousands more will laugh at them. How pleasant indeed it would have been to have known Mr. Lear.

THE POBBLE WHO HAS NO TOES

. . . *The Pobble swam fast and well,*
    And when boats or ships came near him
He tinkledy-binkledy-winkled his bell
    So that all the world could hear him.
And all the Sailors and Admirals cried,
When they saw him nearing the farther side,
" He has gone to fish for his Aunt Jobiska's
" Runcible Cat with crimson whiskers!"

MARCO POLO

Special Envoy
for the Great Khan

IN THE year 1295, three men, wearing shapeless Tartar dress, were refused entry to their own house in Venice. In vain they insisted that they were the brothers Nicolo and Maffeo Polo and Nicolo's son, Marco. No one believed them. The Polos, they were told, had gone off to the Far East over twenty years ago and had died there. After some difficulty, the returning travellers established their identity; but for the rest of his life, Marco never succeeded in getting people to accept his stories of the marvels he had seen in Kublai Khan's distant realms. Instead, everyone laughed at him and called him Marco Million because he was always talking about Kublai Khan's millions of horses and millions of jewels and millions of soldiers.

Marco Polo, the Venetian traveller whose story of his travels was disbelieved.

AT THE COURT OF KUBLAI KHAN

Marco Polo's story really began in 1260 when his father and uncle went trading to the Crimea. Their business there finished, they explored farther and eventually reached Cambulac—now Peking—where they were received at the Court of Kublai Khan, the Great Khan of China. Kublai Khan listened to and was impressed by all that the two Venetians had to tell him about Europe: so much so that he asked them to undertake a mission on his behalf to the Pope, requesting that a hundred learned men be sent to preach to his Tartars, bringing with them some holy oil from the lamp that burned over the Holy Sepulchre at Jerusalem. The Polos returned home, after a nine-year absence, to discover that the Pope had died and that his successor had not yet been appointed.

A JOURNEY OF THREE AND A HALF YEARS

It was not, in fact, until 1271 that the Polos were able to set off on the return journey to the Court of Kublai Khan. With them went Marco Polo, a sturdy youth of seventeen, and, instead of the hundred learned men requested, only two Dominican friars, who deserted the expedition at Palestine whither the Polos had gone to obtain the holy oil. Undismayed, the Polos went on alone. They travelled past Baghdad and Mosul down to Hormuz, on the Persian Gulf where they at first intended to take ship for India. Here, however, they changed their minds and decided to complete the journey by land. They turned north and crossed the salt desert of Kerman, then struck east through Northern Afghanistan. Marco fell ill and the journey was held up for a year while he recovered. They went on again across Pamir —the roof of the world—with its horned sheep which are still called *Ovis Poli* in honour of the man who first described them. The travellers then descended into Eastern Turkestan and eventually arrived near Lake Lob. Having provisioned themselves, they undertook a frightful journey of thirty days across the Gobi Desert. They arrived safely and in May 1275 they were ushered into the presence of the Great Khan after a journey that had lasted three and a half years.

From the moment that Nicolo ushered Marco forward with the words: " Sire, this is your servant and my son," it was obvious that Kublai Khan recognised in the young Venetian a kindred spirit. Soon Marco Polo had adapted himself to the customs of the Tartars and had learned to read and write four languages. He became a kind of Special Envoy for the Great Khan, travelling in this capacity to Tibet, Burma and Japan. He won great renown, too, by navigating a Tartar fleet to India and as a reward for this, he was appointed governor of the important city of Yangchow. Honours were heaped on him. Ancient Chinese records mention that in 1277, Marco Polo was a member of the Imperial Council.

MARCO POLO SETS OUT ON A DANGEROUS MISSION

Meanwhile the years were passing quickly and Kublai Khan was growing old. The Polos began to think of returning to Venice once more. They had been in China for seventeen years and no doubt they were homesick; but there was an even more urgent reason for their return. Their success and the favour shown to them by Kublai Khan had made them a great many enemies among the nobles, and the Venetians were only too well aware of what might happen to them when the Great Khan died. Kublai Khan, however, turned a deaf ear to all their pleas. He would give them anything for which they cared to ask except the one thing they really wanted—permission to leave his realm. Then suddenly, in 1291, there came an unexpected opportunity. Ambassadors arrived from the Khan of Persia with the news that his favourite wife had died and that on her death-bed she had begged him to take another wife from her own Mongol tribe. They found one at Peking but their overland route on the return journey lay through war-torn country and a voyage by sea seemed, therefore, the only alternative. The ambassadors petitioned Kublai Khan for the

An early artist's impression of Marco Polo's departure from Venice. The Polo family embarked on their journey in 1271, but did not reach Kublai Khan's Court until 1275.

A drawing showing Marco Polo and his father kneeling before Kublai Khan, when they arrived at his court in 1275 after a journey lasting four years.

services of the three Venetians, a request that was not at all well received. In the end, the Great Khan agreed. He made the Polos promise to return after they had spent some time in Christendom and sent them on their way with letters to all the principal European monarchs, including Edward I of England. Early in 1292, the escorting fleet of fourteen vessels set sail and after a two-year voyage of incredible hardship arrived at its destination, only to find that in the meantime the Khan of Persia had died. Marco Polo handed over the Mongol princess to the Khan's successor and the three Venetians set off overland.

THE ADVENTURERS RETURN HOME

The end of 1295 saw, too, the end of their journey which had lasted, in all, twenty-four years. The Polos settled down once more in Venice. They were wealthy and important for they had brought back with them a huge fortune in jewels; and every evening the young men of Venice would foregather at the Ca'Polo to hear the fantastic stories of life among the Tartars. It was then that Marco acquired his famous nickname.

Marco's adventures were not yet over. In 1298, Genoa, the greatest commercial rival of Venice, sent a fleet to attack the Venetians.

Among the ships that sailed to meet the Genoese was a galley under the command of Marco Polo. The battle resulted in a shattering defeat for the Venetian fleet which lost sixty-eight galleys. Seven thousand men were dragged off to Genoese prisons, among them the man who had been the favourite of the great Kublai Khan. Soon, all Genoa was flocking to the prison to hear the marvellous stories of the captive Venetian captain. Tired of the constant demand, Marco decided to put the whole thing in writing. He managed to get a letter through to his father in Venice, asking that all the notes of his travels which he had brought back from Tartary be sent on to him; and at that moment he found, in the prison, the ideal man to help him with the task of writing his book.

THE GREATEST TRAVEL BOOK EVER WRITTEN

The man was a prisoner called Rusticiano, a native of Pisa. He had been in prison for two years but had been, previous to that, a writer of romances, with an excellent knowledge of French. He agreed to act as scribe and together he and Marco Polo whiled away the dreariness of captivity by putting down on paper what has since then been called the greatest travel book ever written. It was this book that inspired the poem " Kubla Khan " which came to the poet Coleridge in a dream. But in his own day, the book was regarded by Marco Polo's friends as an essay in drawing the long bow and a collection of the tallest of tall tales. It was only centuries later that the accuracy of its facts and observations was fully established.

Marco Polo spent just over a year in the Genoese prison and from then, until his death in 1324, he lived quietly and prosperously as an honoured citizen of the Venetian Republic. Frequently he was to be seen on the Rialto, accompanied by his Tartar servant, Peter, whom he released at his death " from all bondage as completely as I pray God to release mine own soul from all sin and guilt." On his death-bed, he was implored by well-meaning friends to admit to such parts of the book as were untrue or exaggerated. Marco Polo answered them in typical fashion. He had not told, he replied indignantly, half of what he had seen. Marco Polo's will can still be seen in the library of St. Mark's.

In the annals of exploration, there is no greater name than that of Marco Polo. It was he who first bridged the gap between East and West and his pioneering led directly to the later Age of Discovery. In fact, the extent of Marco Polo's influence on later history is nothing less than fascinating. He wrote one of the greatest travel books in literature. He introduced to Europe a Chinese delicacy which later evolved into ice-cream. His book inspired one of the finest poems in English literature. And that same book was the constant companion of an unknown Genoese captain who read it incessantly and made notes on more than seventy of its pages. The captain's name, later to become so well known, was Christopher Columbus.

ODD ADVERTISING

Advertising is as old as the hills; indeed a piece of Egyptian pottery, placed by the experts at 1300 B.C., bore a phrase which to-day we would call a slogan. There is no end to the ingenuity of those who have something to sell or something to say. And they did not wait for the introduction of printing.

It has been said, with some truth, that there is a buyer for everything—if he can be found.

It was an optimist in Bolivia who offered a volcano for sale, but the advertiser was probably right in claiming that it would produce enough steam to develop prodigious electrical energy.

A furrier in Quebec drew attention to his shop by placing outside a 15-ft. figure of a beaver in ice.

An Essex firm, some years ago, scattered gifts among all who passed their premises. They drew attention to their business all right, but the crowds that gathered resulted in a police summons for obstruction.

A Paris optician drew attention to his business by training a cat to sit, wearing spectacles, on his porch.

The backs of playing cards are often used for advertisements and the under sides of loaves baked in tins sometimes carry an embossed advertising slogan. Italian postage stamps were once sold with every other " stamp " in the sheet bearing an advertisement. New Zealand stamps once had an advertisement printed on the back.

In 1924 the fortifications of Paris were offered for sale, and the famous Eiffel Tower has been used for advertising purposes. During the Second World War there were suggestions that the world-famous Nelson Column in Trafalgar Square should be used for patriotic advertising.

A periodical was once published, soaked in eucalyptus, which was said to ensure that its readers did not catch a cold.

In one city where a famous Charlie Chaplin film, *The Gold Rush*, was showing, leaflets were handed out which ensured the payment of a thousand dollars if anyone died of laughing while witnessing the film.

Sometimes the efforts of enterprising tradesmen, when venturing into foreign languages, have effects that they do not anticipate. For instance, a Japanese outfitter displayed a notice which read: " Ladies please have fits upstairs."

THE INDUSTRIAL REVOLUTION

A Period of Transition

IN the seventy years between 1760 and 1830 a series of events happened in England which changed the face of the world. England was the first country to pass from an agricultural to an industrial economy, and this period is consequently known as the Industrial Revolution. It is one of the great turning points in the history of civilisation.

It is easier to see where the Industrial Revolution began than where it ended, because once the process of invention started it never ceased. The mainspring of the change was the discovery of a new source of power—steam. At first this was used in mining, then it was taken to textile factories, and finally it was applied to transport when the Railway Age opened in 1832.

If you try to imagine what England looked like in the middle of the eighteenth century, you must picture a landscape without railways and with very few roads or canals. There were no coal-mines in South Wales and Yorkshire, no big factories or mills or blast furnaces. The chief fuel used at this time was still wood and charcoal, for although a certain amount of coal was brought by sea from Newcastle, it was too expensive to employ in such industries as existed. Many tons of wood would have been required to smelt one ton of iron.

A NETWORK OF CANALS

It was a fortunate thing in the long run that our forests were becoming exhausted. The fact of a fuel famine gave the impetus to seek cheap transport for coal. To carry coal by road from Manchester to Liverpool, for example, cost forty shillings a ton. The Duke of Bridgwater was the pioneer in this development, and in 1759, he cut a canal between his Worsley collieries and Manchester, thus causing the price of coal in Manchester to fall by half. A few years later another canal was built linking Manchester to the sea, and before long a network of canals spread across England. Not only coal but wheat, pottery, and iron could be carried to all parts of the country, and although roads were much improved in the years that followed, thanks largely to the engineering skill of Macadam, the waterways remained the principal means of transport for heavy goods until the advent of the railway.

It was now possible to open up new coalfields in South Wales, Scotland, Lancashire and Yorkshire. At the same time improvements in the technique of smelting enabled the iron industry to develop. The production of pig iron increased from 17,350 tons in 1740 to 125,079 tons in 1796. A new Iron Age had begun, and led the way to steel in the following century. The first iron bridge over the Severn was built in 1779; the first iron ship in 1790.

THE INVENTION OF THE STEAM ENGINE

The production of cheap cast iron stimulated the invention of various kinds of machinery. By far the most important was the discovery by James Watt of a steam engine which could be employed for pumping coal-mines. Steam engines were soon in demand for all mining districts in England and orders came from France, Russia, and Germany. In 1781 the first attempts were made to use steam power on ships, and in 1801 Trevithick made a clumsy start with a locomotive. It was some time before the technical difficulties in both cases could be overcome.

THE BEGINNING OF MASS PRODUCTION

Meanwhile the inventors were active in the textile industry. Weaving and spinning were handicrafts largely carried out in the homes of individual workers on a small scale. The invention of the flying shuttle, however, enabled weavers to double their output, and it was followed by the spinning-jenny, Cartwright's power loom and Arkwright's water-frame. These devices marked the beginning of mass production.

Until the middle of the eighteenth century cotton cloth had been imported from India, but when this was prohibited there was a far greater demand for yarn than could be met by the traditional method of hand-spinning. The first factories to be built employed water power, but,

The spinning machine invented by Richard Arkwright in 1769, was one of the devices which marked the beginning of mass production.

by 1785 Watt's steam engine became available to them.

There was a world market for textile goods and the new mills that sprang up obtained ample supplies of cotton from the North American colonies. Capital was invested eagerly in what promised to be an easy way of making a fortune. Machinery displaced for a time many of the skilled workers and there were plenty of routine jobs that could be done by women and children. Another source of labour was the farm workers who had been driven out of employment by drastic enclosures of land.

CHANGES IN AGRICULTURE

English farming was also undergoing a great change in this period. The smaller farms were unable to compete with improved but more costly methods of agriculture which required capital. Villagers, who had made use of common land, lost the rights which they had held by custom from time immemorial but without any legal sanction. Gradually an army of unemployed was created and they naturally turned to the new industries that were in need of unskilled labour.

An old print showing the early machinery which was used for stocking framework knitting.

The spinning-mill of a large cotton factory. This complicated machinery with a very large output can be looked after by a relatively small number of employees.

POVERTY AND PLENTY

It is a strange and bitter irony that a period which vastly increased the wealth of this country should also have intensified the poverty of so many people. Because labour was plentiful it was cheap, and although prices rose steeply wages were virtually at starvation level. The inevitable result was the bread riots, which broke out in 1795 in almost every county. To meet this situation, a system of public relief which started at Speenhamland in Berkshire, spread throughout the country. It was decided that " every poor and industrious man " should have for his support, 3s. for himself and 1s. 6d. for each member of his family, " either procured by his own or by his family's labours or an allowance from the Poor Rates."

EMPLOYMENT OF CHILDREN

The extent of the distress can be judged from the fact that the Poor Rate rose from about £2,000,000 in 1790 to £7,000,000 in the first decade of the nineteenth century. The unhappy

and perhaps unintended result was to bring down wages still further. Another sequel was the creation of workhouses, a large proportion of the inmates of which were children. They were taught a trade and then sent to the mills of Lancashire. They were entirely defenceless and compelled to work long hours in appalling conditions for a pittance.

The allowance for children under the Speenhamland Act induced paupers to raise large families in order to add to their income, and these children also drifted to the mines and factories. The general misery of the poor in the first phase of the Industrial Revolution was made even worse by an uninterrupted series of bad harvests between 1789 and 1802.

England was involved in a costly continental war, which was followed by a severe slump and widespread unemployment. Except for the few who were able to profit by the transformation that was taking place, it must have been impossible to realise that the Industrial Revolution was other than a disaster. The unemployed

Appalling conditions prevailed in the eighteenth and early nineteenth centuries in the coal mines. Coal was manhandled by barrow, often by women and children.

A modern mechanical loader at work in a mine to-day. The loading rate is about four tons per minute and it therefore conserves the miners' energies for coal-cutting.

blamed the introduction of machinery for their plight and once more serious riots broke out.

To the average worker the victory over Napoleon probably meant less than the Corn Laws, which were introduced in 1815 in order to keep the price of wheat at the level it had reached when supplies from Poland and France were prevented from reaching England owing to the war. It was forbidden to import wheat whenever the price fell below 50s. a quarter.

A PERIOD OF UNREST

A fierce agitation was started to repeal the Corn Laws and reform Parliament. The general ferment caused by the industrialisation of the country now found more definite political expression. Those in favour of reform were called Radicals and the government was

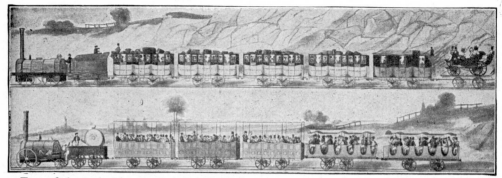

Two of the early Liverpool and Manchester Railway trains. The top one is a mail train with first-class carriages and the bottom one consists of second-class carriages.

alarmed lest there should be risings on the scale of the French Revolution. In order to understand the mood that prevailed we need only compare it with the fear of Communism that followed the Bolshevik Revolution of 1917.

Rioting broke out in London. In Bridport and Bideford there were riots on account of the high price of bread. There were disturbances among the miners in Newcastle, the weavers in Preston, and the unemployed in Birmingham. The Luddites in Nottingham destroyed thirty stocking frames because the machines had made it impossible for hand-knitters to make a living. Machines were also wrecked in the West Riding and elsewhere.

THE PETERLOO MASSACRE

Hunger marches were organised in many parts of the country, and the government took stern measures to suppress the Radicals. The climax came in 1819 when a huge demonstration was held at St. Peter's Fields, Manchester, and addressed by a famous Radical orator. The Yeomanry charged a crowd of 80,000 people, killing eleven and wounding four hundred. The Peterloo massacre, as this was called, shocked public opinion and increased the demand for Parliamentary reform in spite of the repressive legislation that followed which made all legal agitation impossible.

INCREASING PROSPERITY

Yet with all this unrest, prosperity, measured in terms of increased production and trade, soon returned. England became the workshop of the world. It had been first to apply science to industry and other countries were still far behind. Commerce was expanding and the

The first Cunard liner to cross the Atlantic was the *Britannia*. She was powered by steam, paddles and sail, for ship design in mid-nineteenth century was in a state of transition.

The Great Exhibition of 1851, held in the Crystal Palace, Hyde Park, was symbolic of the Industrial Revolution, and new machinery was on display for all the world to see.

factories were gradually squeezing handicrafts and small-scale domestic industry out of existence. It is worth noting that the inventions which had brought all this about owed very little to pure scientific research, but were mostly the work of mechanics and engineers employing trial and error methods. The application of advances in scientific theory came later with the development of electricity and chemistry.

To begin with, the Industrial Revolution was a brutal affair, and looking back at it from this distance it seems almost incomprehensible that people could be so insensitive to suffering. Yet the concern for social welfare and a reasonable standard of living, which we are inclined to take for granted, grew out of this stormy period of transition. No one at the time grasped the full significance of changing from an agricultural to an industrial economy—industrialism had never existed before, and so there was nothing to learn from history.

CHILD LABOUR

When the conditions in the early factories came to be known, there was a revulsion of feeling which resulted in demands for reform. From 1802 onwards legislation began to be introduced to limit working hours. It met with stubborn opposition on the part of factory owners and had to be introduced piecemeal. An Act was passed in 1819 forbidding the employment of children under nine in cotton factories and limiting the daily working hours of those between nine and sixteen to $13\frac{1}{2}$. It was not until 1833, however, that a general prohibition of employing children under nine came into force and even then the silk factories were exempt.

The worst abuses of child labour were to be found in the mines and as these were not covered by Factory Acts, the young children who could no longer work in factories only too often found their way into the mines. The wages of their parents were so low that they virtually had no option but to send their children to work. The demand for coal and the introduction of machinery into mines led to deeper seams being opened up and long working hours. Sir Humphry Davy invented a safety lamp in 1816 which was designed to

In the early days of railways there were many claims that a horse and carriage were faster than a train. One such claim was put to the test and on this occasion, in 1830, the horse and carriage won, though it was not long before the speed of the trains increased.

prevent explosions in gaseous mines, and he fondly believed that it was a gift to humanity, and so he refused to reap any financial reward for it. Unfortunately its use led to more risky workings and the number of accidents increased.

On the whole, the Factory Acts resulted in the installation of better machinery, because this was the only way to compensate for shorter working hours. As many of the smaller firms could not afford to change their methods they were frequently absorbed by bigger concerns. The tendency had already begun for industry to become concentrated in ever fewer hands.

THE POLITICAL PARTIES

It is impossible to disentangle the political consequences of the Industrial Revolution from other causes in such a rapidly changing world. Undoubtedly it helped to create Radicalism—which contained the seeds of Socialism—and created a sense of solidarity among the industrial workers which issued later in the formation of trade unions. The wealthier classes, depending on industry and trade, turned towards the Whig Party, which gave rise to Liberalism; and the Tories represented the interests of the farmers and landed aristocracy. The Liberals took up the cry for free trade, but the Tories had a stake in tariffs, particularly on imported corn.

The political outcome of the Industrial Revolution was the Reform Bill which passed into law on 7th June, 1832, after a long, hard fought struggle. It increased the electorate and by giving more power to the industrialists and the middle classes it made possible the emergence of the Liberal Party, which dominated politics throughout a great part of the nineteenth century.

RAILWAYS

By then the steam engine entered on its final triumph, thanks to the genius of George Stephenson. The Stockton-Darlington railway was opened in 1823, and six years later Stephenson's *Rocket* took the prize on the new line between Manchester and Liverpool. The locomotive had at last arrived and all that remained was to make it faster and more efficient. During the next decade railway lines were laid down with feverish energy and within two years £70,000,000 was invested in construction. The English landscape changed. The Industrial Revolution, as it is generally understood, was over and a new age dawned in which England became the richest and most powerful nation in the world.

HOW WE GOT OUR PARLIAMENT

WE know that to-day we are ruled by men and women sent to Westminster, to sit in the House of Commons, and to make laws for our benefit. To-day the representatives chosen by the ordinary men and women of the country govern us. In other words, we choose for ourselves who shall govern us, look after our country and make good laws. This is known as *Democracy*, which comes from two Greek words: *Demos*, meaning " people " and *Kratos* meaning " power." So, translated more simply, it means " The people rule for the people."

It was not always like this, for a long struggle had to be undergone, which lasted for hundreds of years, before the ordinary people were able to vote as to who should represent them in Parliament. You will learn all about this in school: perhaps you are already studying this very subject. Here, in this book, however, we will try to show you clearly the various stages in this struggle, and we do it by means of charts.

We begin in the days of the Anglo-Saxons, over a thousand years ago, and not long after the Romans had left Britain. Our story fills eleven charts, and each of these has been designed not to tell you everything, but to illustrate what you read and hear at school, and to make you want to read more in your spare time.

Try to understand each chart, and use a history book to help you fill in the story. You will find it great fun searching facts out for yourself. Indeed, this is one of the very best ways of learning anything properly, so that it will never be forgotten. Once you have read the wonderful story of our country's history, you will find that these charts become like picture-galleries, showing you actual happenings of the past. The happenings are stepping-stones in the growth of our land, and thus the charts will be reminders to you and will help you to remember your history.

Our first selection of charts deals with Parliament from the days when the King was not living in a palace, but constantly moving about his country, and ruled the people himself,

to the present day, when our Sovereign no longer makes our laws, but signs and approves the laws made by our own representatives in Parliament. This shows the change from Absolute Monarchy, with all power in the Monarch's hand, to Constitutional Monarchy, when the Monarch does not interfere with law-making, which is left to the people's own selected law-makers—The Members of Parliament.

Take the charts one at a time, read the captions beneath the picture, and then try to understand the whole message of the chart, before turning to the next one. These charts will help you to understand at a glance what the Feudal System of Norman times was, and how it worked. Later you will see how, through Tudor and Stuart times, the King was really the government, until at last the people, little by little, won their way to leadership. It was a long fight, and a hard one, as you will see in chart No. 7—" Rise of Democracy." The men who fought for the People's Charter of 1838—called The Chartists—had no easy task, and suffered for their efforts, but their demands have practically all been granted and we run our country to-day by the resultant laws. Learn especially the six things the Chartists demanded, and note when these at last became law. Then read your history books and learn how keen was the struggle of those brave people, and how, little by little, their demands were one by one acknowledged as fair and just.

Next study carefully charts 10 and 11 which will show you how Parliament opens, works, and finally, after five years, must resign. The Chartists demanded a new Parliament every year, but it has been found that a period of five years is best, so that an elected Parliament may really do what it promised the people it would perform if elected to rule.

The last chart shows how a Bill becomes an Act of Parliament. Your daily newspapers will help you to understand this more clearly, for laws are being dealt with in Parliament almost every day.

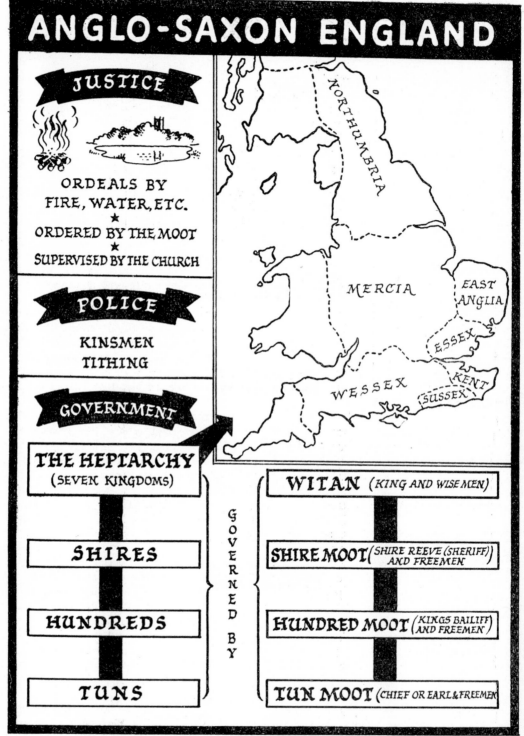

ANGLO-SAXON ENGLAND

JUSTICE

ORDEALS BY FIRE, WATER, ETC.
★
ORDERED BY THE MOOT
★
SUPERVISED BY THE CHURCH

POLICE

KINSMEN
TITHING

GOVERNMENT

THE HEPTARCHY (SEVEN KINGDOMS)

SHIRES

HUNDREDS

TUNS

GOVERNED BY

WITAN (KING AND WISE MEN)

SHIRE MOOT (SHIRE REEVE (SHERIFF) AND FREEMEN)

HUNDRED MOOT (KINGS BAILIFF AND FREEMEN)

TUN MOOT (CHIEF OR EARL & FREEMEN)

NORTHUMBRIA

MERCIA

EAST ANGLIA

ESSEX

KENT

SUSSEX

WESSEX

1. Note how Anglo-Saxon England was divided into Seven Kingdoms, known as the Heptarchy. The chart shows how each Kingdom was split up, and how each part had its own moot, or council, to look after its affairs. The Witan was the council for the country.

THE FEUDAL SYSTEM

THE KING

OWNED ALL
THE LAND

RECORDED HIS
POSSESSIONS IN
DOMESDAY BOOK

GAVE LAND TO
TENANTS-IN-CHIEF
IN EXCHANGE FOR···

TENANTS-IN-CHIEF

1. MILITARY SERVICE
2. ADVICE
   (IN CURIA REGIS)

GAVE PART OF THEIR
LAND TO BARONS IN
EXCHANGE FOR···

BARONS

1. MILITARY SERVICE
2. ADVICE
   (IN BARONIAL CURIA)

GAVE LAND KNOWN AS
A KNIGHT'S FEE IN
EXCHANGE FOR ···

KNIGHTS

1. MILITARY SERVICE
2. SUPPLY OF FOOT
   SOLDIERS

GAVE LAND TO NORMAN
AND SAXON FARMERS
IN EXCHANGE FOR···

FARMERS

1. MILITARY SERVICE
   (AS FOOT SOLDIERS)
2. WORK ON THE LAND

ALL OWED FIRST ALLEGIANCE TO THE
KING AND THEN TO THEIR
RESPECTIVE OVERLORDS

SERFS WITH FEW RIGHTS WORKED THE LAND

2. This chart and the next explain the Feudal System, showing the King in control and then
down, step by step, from Tenants-in-Chief to the ordinary people, who owned land. There
still were serfs, the labourers, who had no land, and had no power or right of any kind.

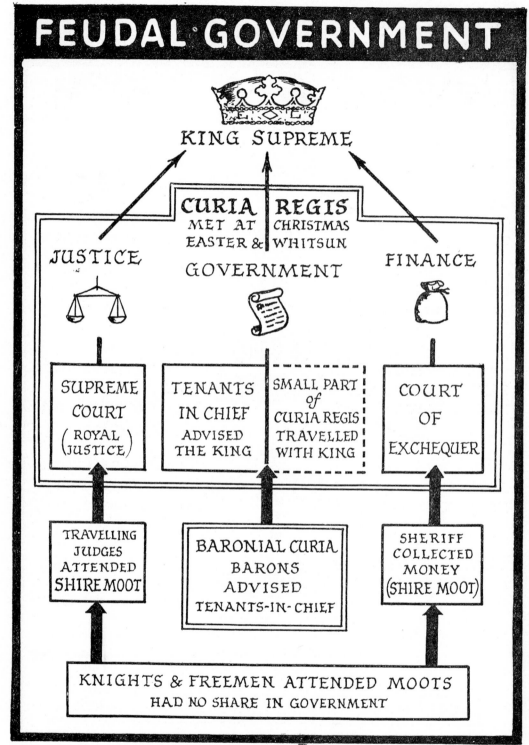

FEUDAL GOVERNMENT

KING SUPREME

CURIA REGIS
MET AT | CHRISTMAS
EASTER & | WHITSUN

GOVERNMENT

JUSTICE   FINANCE

| SUPREME COURT (ROYAL JUSTICE) | TENANTS IN CHIEF ADVISED THE KING | SMALL PART of CURIA REGIS TRAVELLED WITH KING | COURT OF EXCHEQUER |

| TRAVELLING JUDGES ATTENDED SHIRE MOOT | BARONIAL CURIA BARONS ADVISED TENANTS-IN-CHIEF | SHERIFF COLLECTED MONEY (SHIRE MOOT) |

KNIGHTS & FREEMEN ATTENDED MOOTS
HAD NO SHARE IN GOVERNMENT

3. Here we see the way in which the King dispensed justice. It will be best to read this chart from the bottom upwards. Thus you may follow the course of government from the village to the King and the Council—the *Curia Regis*—over which he presided.

RISE OF PARLIAMENT

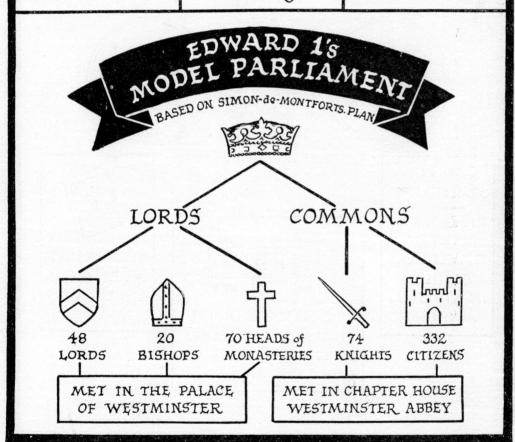

1215	1258	1265
'THE PARLIAMENT' AT RUNNYMEDE	THE MAD PARLIAMENT' *(Curia Regis at Oxford)*	THE BACHELORS VERSUS THE ROYALISTS
◆	◆	◆
KING JOHN *sealed the* MAGNA CARTA	HENRY III BRIDLED *Provisions of Oxford* COUNCIL *of* 15	SIMON *de* MONTFORT *set up* MODEL PARLIAMENT

EDWARD 1's MODEL PARLIAMENT

BASED ON SIMON-de-MONTFORTS. PLAN

LORDS   COMMONS

48 LORDS	20 BISHOPS	70 HEADS of MONASTERIES	74 KNIGHTS	332 CITIZENS

MET IN THE PALACE OF WESTMINSTER   MET IN CHAPTER HOUSE WESTMINSTER ABBEY

4. The early Parliaments are now beginning to form themselves and develop, until we have the Model Parliament of Edward I, which was based on the idea of Simon de Montfort, in 1262. Thirty years passed before Edward carried out Simon's plan successfully.

P.H.

THE TUDOR PERIOD

MONASTERIES DESTROYED

MANY LORDS KILLED IN WARS OF THE ROSES

THE COMMONS HAD BECOME THE MORE IMPORTANT

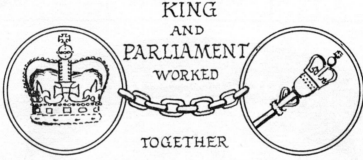

KING AND PARLIAMENT WORKED TOGETHER

COURT OF STAR CHAMBER

DISREGARDED MANY OF THE CITIZENS' RIGHTS IN JUDICIAL MATTERS

ST. STEPHENS CHAPEL (PARLIAMENT HOUSE) GIVEN TO THE COMMONS BY EDWARD VI

BEGINNING of RELIGIOUS INFLUENCES in PARLIAMENT

5. The Tudor period is one of the most important and interesting in all our country's history. Starting in 1485 after the Battle of Bosworth, when Henry Tudor became Henry VII, it stretched to 1603, and ended with the death of Queen Elizabeth.

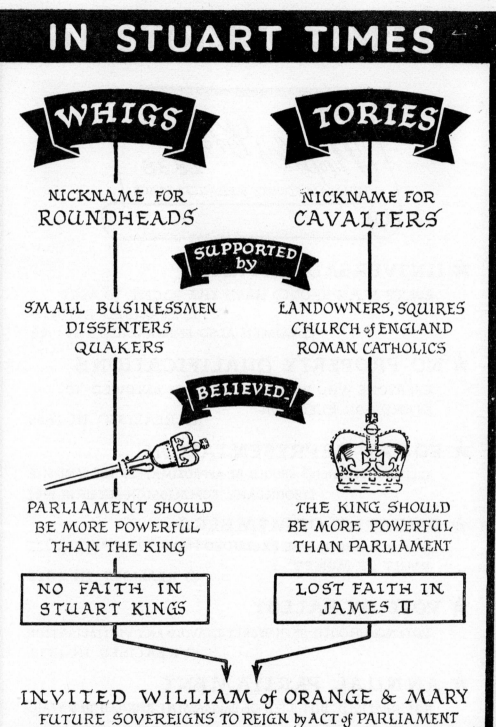

IN STUART TIMES

WHIGS	TORIES
NICKNAME FOR ROUNDHEADS	NICKNAME FOR CAVALIERS

SUPPORTED by

SMALL BUSINESSMEN DISSENTERS QUAKERS	LANDOWNERS, SQUIRES CHURCH of ENGLAND ROMAN CATHOLICS

BELIEVED

PARLIAMENT SHOULD BE MORE POWERFUL THAN THE KING	THE KING SHOULD BE MORE POWERFUL THAN PARLIAMENT
NO FAITH IN STUART KINGS	LOST FAITH IN JAMES II

INVITED WILLIAM of ORANGE & MARY
FUTURE SOVEREIGNS TO REIGN by ACT of PARLIAMENT

6. After the strong rule of the Tudors came that of the Stuart Kings, and the idea held by them that Kings ruled by Divine Right roused the people to demand power to rule themselves through Parliament. Thus the Civil War began, and Charles I was beheaded.

RISE OF DEMOCRACY

★ **UNIVERSAL SUFFRAGE**

EVERY MAN SHOULD HAVE THE RIGHT TO VOTE
☆ REALISED BY 1918
☆ WOMEN ALSO ENFRANCHISED BY 1928

★ **NO PROPERTY QUALIFICATIONS**

EVERYONE WHO WISHED SHOULD BE ALLOWED TO
STAND FOR ELECTION
☆ REALISED IN 1858

★ **EQUAL REPRESENTATION**

ALL CONSTITUENCIES SHOULD BE APPROXIMATELY THE SAME SIZE
☆ BOUNDARY COMMISSION SET UP IN 1944

★ **PAYMENT OF MEMBERS**

NO-ONE SHOULD BE EXCLUDED FROM PARLIAMENT FOR
WANT OF MONEY
☆ REALISED IN 1911

★ **VOTE BY BALLOT**

VOTING SHOULD BE IN SECRET TO AVOID ANY VICTIMISATION
☆ REALISED IN 1872

★ **ANNUAL PARLIAMENT**

NOT REALISED BUT LIFE OF PARLIAMENT REDUCED TO 5 YEARS

7. The Chartists, as they were called, were a body of people who wished in the early nine-teenth century to see the country ruled by a Parliament representing all the people. The chart shows what they demanded and when their demands were finally granted and became law.

8. Who can vote for a Member of Parliament? This chart shows how, from 1832 to the present day, there has been a widening of the *franchise* (that is, the people who may *vote*). Now all men and women over 21, unless insane, in prison, or in the House of Lords, may vote.

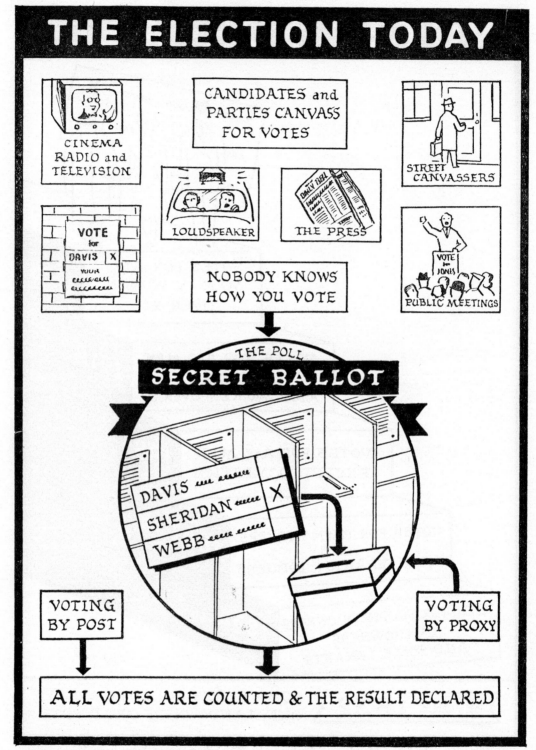

9. This is how an election is carried on to-day. The voting is by ballot. No one knows for whom you vote. It is your own secret and your own personal affair.

PARLIAMENT TODAY

GENERAL ELECTION
THE PEOPLE ELECT THEIR MEMBERS OF PARLIAMENT

THE QUEEN INVITES THE LEADER OF THE
LARGEST PARTY TO FORM A GOVERNMENT

STATE OPENING OF PARLIAMENT
THE QUEEN READS HER SPEECH
FROM THE THRONE OF THE HOUSE OF LORDS
(OUTLINES THE GOVERNMENT'S PROGRAMME FOR THE YEAR)

HOUSE of COMMONS	HOUSE of LORDS
THE SPEAKER THE PRIME MINISTER GOVERNMENT & OPPOSITION --- --- --- INTRODUCES LEGISLATION DISCUSSIONS, DEBATES, QUESTIONS, DIVISIONS	THE LORD CHANCELLOR LEADER of the HOUSE of LORDS GOVERNMENT & OPPOSITION --- --- --- BUSINESS IS SIMILAR TO THAT OF THE HOUSE OF COMMONS
THE GOVERNMENT MUST RESIGN AFTER 5 YEARS OR IF IT IS DEFEATED ON A MAJOR ISSUE	AS THE LORDS IS THE HEREDITARY CHAMBER MEMBERS DO NOT RESIGN

THIS ALLOWS THE PEOPLE TO RE-ELECT THE SAME GOVERNMENT
OR TO MAKE A CHANGE AT THE ENSUING
GENERAL ELECTION

10. This is Parliament as it works to-day. A *general* election is when Parliament is dissolved and members for all constituencies must be elected. When a member resigns or dies there is a *by*-election in his constituency.

AN ACT OF PARLIAMENT

A BILL
CLASSIFIED AS
A PUBLIC BILL
A FINANCE BILL
A PRIVATE BILL
OR A HYBRID BILL

INTRODUCED BY A MINISTER
OR A PRIVATE MEMBER AT THE
FIRST READING
(FORMALITY ONLY)

SECOND READING
DISCUSSION. AMENDMENTS PROPOSED
BY THE OPPOSITION. DIVISIONS

COMMITTEE STAGE
DETAILS ARE DISCUSSED
BILL IS REPHRASED IF NECESSARY

ANY AMENDMENTS ARE REPORTED
TO THE SPEAKER AT THE
REPORT STAGE

THIRD READING
FINAL VOTE IN HOUSE OF COMMONS

ALL BILLS, EXCEPT FINANCE BILLS,
ARE PASSED TO THE
HOUSE OF LORDS
FOR APPROVAL

THE BILL IS SENT TO THE QUEEN
TO RECEIVE THE
ROYAL ASSENT
IT IS SEALED AND SO
BECOMES AN ACT OF PARLIAMENT

**AN ACT OF
PARLIAMENT**
BECOMES THE LAW OF
THE COUNTRY & MUST BE
OBEYED BY EVERYBODY

11. Study this chart carefully, for it shows clearly, beginning at the top left-hand corner, how a bill originates. Then are shown the various steps in the progress of the bill until it receives the Royal Assent and becomes law,

THE BRITISH ARMY

A Pictorial Review

DURING the period of the Commonwealth and Cromwell's rule in the seventeenth century, the Army was all-powerful and it was also extremely unpopular. On the Restoration of Charles II in 1660, the decision was immediately taken to disband the New Model Army, as it was called, but conditions being unsettled this had to be done slowly.

One of the regiments was kept in being, however, since it was called upon to deal with a small rising of malcontents, and this was the Coldstream Guards. In addition Guards for the King's person were created, and these were known as the First (later Grenadier) Guards and there were also two regiments of mounted guards, known as the Life Guards and the Blues.

Many of the soldiers forming the new regiments were, of course, already trained in the New Model Army, and merely joined up again, and so the foundations of the British Army were laid.

1st Tangier Regiment of Foot in 1687. Pikes, muskets and swords were all in use.

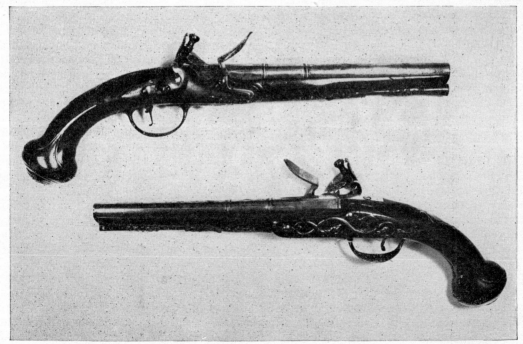

A pair of flintlock holster pistols of the reign of Queen Anne. These were carried in holsters on either side of the saddle by mounted troops.

A panoramic view of the Battle of Malplaquet, fought near Mons on 11th September, 1709, in which the Duke of Marlborough defeated the French. It was, however, an empty victory and the casualties amongst the troops commanded by Marlborough amounted to 20,000 men.

The foot regiments, which were subsequently raised, were chiefly for use abroad in such possessions as Tangier (which had come into Britain's possession as part of the dowry of Charles II's wife, the Portuguese Princess, Catherine of Braganza). Tangier was abandoned in 1684 and the troops returned to Britain. The 1st Tangier Regiment continued to be known by its old name for some time, although it was renamed the Second, or Queen's, Regiment of Foot.

THE EIGHTEENTH CENTURY

At the beginning of the eighteenth century most armies consisted mainly of mercenaries, who hired themselves as soldiers to whomsoever paid best. These men, who were of many different nationalities, would, if captured, often switch their allegiance in exchange for their liberty.

Under Marlborough (described by Wellington as the greatest general who ever appeared at the head of a British Army) the British Army was victorious in Europe during the War of the Spanish Succession. It was due to his efforts that the balance of power in Europe was maintained, at a time when it seemed that Louis XIV of France would carry all before him, including perhaps even Britain itself.

By Marlborough's time the use of gunpowder was more general, pikes being regarded as obsolete. A musket and bayonet were the usual weapon issue to the British Army as early as 1706.

Some units of the Grenadier Guards, whose uniforms you see opposite, served under the Duke of Cumberland at the time of the Jacobite Rebellion in 1745–46, and other units also served under the personal command of George II during the War of the Austrian Succession (1740–48).

The 42nd Highland Regiment was raised in 1725 to assist General Wade when he was sent to Scotland to disarm the Highland clans. The Regiment became known as The Black Watch from the dark colour of their kilts.

The 4th Regiment of Horse (later to become the 3rd Dragoon Guards) was raised in 1685 at the time of the Monmouth Rebellion. They were equipped with both sword and musket, the latter being just visible behind the rider at his right side. The musket was for use dismounted.

The uniforms worn in mid-eighteenth century by the Grenadier Guards. *Left to right:* A private of the Centre Companies, a drummer and a sergeant.

Officer and sergeant of 42nd Highland Regt.

The 4th Regiment of Horse in 1742.

A view of the taking of Quebec on 13th September, 1759. This was the result of an extremely well-planned and successful combined operation organised by General Wolfe. His troops are here seen in control of the Heights of Abraham, the high ground overlooking the town.

A 1770 mortar. This gun fired shot at a high elevation, so that it fell vertically.

The Honourable Association of City and Westminster Horse Volunteers off to exercises by Expedition or Military Fly. The volunteers wore red tunics, white breeches, black gaiters and black hats with a " busby " effect. The artist was Thomas Rowlandson.

The magnificent figure of a sergeant of infantry in the year 1791.

Sergeant and privates of the 87th (Prince of Wales's Own Irish) Regiment in 1813.

The Volunteers were raised to defend the country during the Napoleonic wars. They received pay for completing two days' drill out of seven, but they were in other respects civilians. The City and Westminster Horse Volunteers were obviously a " smart " regiment, no doubt assisted financially by wealthy business men, rather than the Government.

The sergeant of the 87th Regiment, here seen on active service, is taking the eagle emblem from a dead French soldier during the Peninsular War.

Uniforms during the early nineteenth century reached a zenith of elaborate splendour. *Left:* an officer of the 62nd Regiment (infantry) in 1828, whose uniform, although ornate, does not compare for magnificence with the cavalry officers' (*centre*) of the Royal Regiment of Horse and 9th Lancers. The undress uniform of a 3rd Light Dragoons officer is on the right.

The Royal Horse Artillery in action. The guns and gun-and-ammunition carriages are shown here in Holland during the Napoleonic war period.

There was no sign at this period of "battle" uniform, as distinct from "dress" uniform. In fact as late as 1854 at the time of the Crimean War, the 11th Hussars, who took part in the charge of the Light Brigade, wore their magnificent uniforms, including dolman jackets slung across their shoulders, in action.

The charge of the Brigade must have been a truly spectacular one, as, led by Lord Cardigan, whose uniform had lost none of its pristine splendour owing to his having lived in a yacht off-shore and not shared the discomforts of camp life with his men, swept in review formation along the "valley of death."

At the Battle of Balaclava in October 1854 : The Charge of the Light Brigade. The 11th Hussars, on reaching the Russian guns, cut down the gunners.

Alexis Soyer, chef of the Reform Club, London, went at his own expense to the Crimea to improve the cooking of army rations. This he did and also invented new cooking stoves.

In the midst of the Battle of Omdurman (1898), the 21st Lancers charged two or three thousand dervishes, who were on foot. With lances couched and led by their officers with drawn swords, the Lancers attacked in close order at full gallop. In such a situation infantry faced with charging cavalry will usually either keep their heads and shoot the cavalry down,

or they will break into confusion and be speared as they attempt to run. The dervishes, however, were not afraid of cavalry, and, although their fire was not accurate enough to stop the charge, they were able to give the British troops considerable punishment at close quarters, for the fighting was then mostly with sword and lance, in almost medieval style.

The Boer War (1899–1902) in South Africa. The 1st Welch Regiment arrives in camp. The troops relax, the cooks get busy and one soldier sits down to write a letter home.

History keeps repeating itself: in 1899 the young wife, tight-lipped, says good-bye to her husband, and, in 1914, she is saying good-bye again, this time to her son.

In the 1914–18 war, armament grew bigger and more destructive. Eight-inch howitzers fire a barrage during the Battle of the Somme in August 1916, from behind a hillock. The bleak devastation wrought by war in the surrounding countryside can be seen.

The tank, a British invention, was first used in the 1914–18 war in 1916 to end the deadlock of trench warfare. These Mark V tanks, together with infantry (New Zealand and 37th Divisions) move forward at Grevilliers in August 1918.

The First World War was more mechanised than any that had gone before, but there are times in every war when the work of each soldier is important. Shell-carrying pack mules have to be got through the mud somehow with their precious load.

Nature can take a hand with a vengeance in a battle. Rain has turned the ground into a quagmire, and the gun must be hauled out of the mud by hand, for no wheeled or tracked vehicle could grip such an impossible surface. So the soldiers have to strain and heave.

The Royal Scots Greys, with their beautifully groomed mounts, rest on the roadside near Montreuil in May 1918. The cavalry had had no opportunity for a charge on anything but a minor scale during the war, though they had been used successfully to cover the retreat from Mons. They expected, however, to be used for the " gap scheme," which meant charging into a gap created by an artillery bombardment followed by an infantry assault. But no such gap was ever achieved and so no cavalry charge was possible.

Mounted troops are now only used on ceremonial occasions. Mechanisation during and after the First World War became more complete. Sword and lance and the cavalry charge gave way to armoured cars and tanks and guns.

The glamour of war departed with the horse, for, despite all its horrors, war has always had a romantic appeal. Now the ruthlessness of modern weapons far out-does any damage which could be inflicted by a man with a musket, a sword or a lance. The chivalry of knightly contest, which has spurred on many a soldier of the past, seems to have been obliterated.

Looking back across the last two and a half centuries the role of the soldier has changed very radically and is still changing. During the Second World War the advent of the unmanned missile, and subsequently the guided missile and the bombs of phenomenal power, has turned even the possibility of war into a threat to the very existence of the human race.

In this review of the British Army we have tried to show you how a great tradition has been built up, a tradition of loyalty and service and pride, a tradition of which we may all be proud. Over the years and in a great many different parts of the world, our soldiers have fought with courage and determination to right wrongs, to assist the oppressed, to prevent any upset to the balance of power in Europe. It is indeed an honourable record. We hope that there will not be any call upon us to test our Army in the future, as it has been tested so many times in the past, but should it in any way prove necessary to use our Army, it will assuredly live up to its great past and do worthy battle for what is right.

Mrs. Pankhurst and her daughter welcomed by their fellow Suffragettes on their release from prison in December 1908. The courage and determination of these women was astounding.

THE SUFFRAGETTE MOVEMENT

IN 1928, the House of Lords gave its approval to a measure with the colourless name of the Equal Franchise Bill by which women were entitled to vote on the same terms as men. The bill was passed quietly, without speeches, almost apologetically in the manner of someone repairing a rather obvious oversight. Thus ended, undramatically, a struggle which had lasted just over sixty years and which had been waged, at times, with the most relentless bitterness on both sides.

THE BEGINNING OF THE STRUGGLE

The struggle to obtain equal rights for women can be said to have begun in 1792 with the publication of Mary Wollstonecraft's book, *Vindication of the Rights of Women*; but as a political issue and something more than just a vague desire, it can be conveniently dated from 1867 when the philosopher John Stuart Mill brought in a Women's Suffrage amendment to

the Reform Bill. This amendment was rejected. During the next twenty years, agitation was kept up by the various branches of the National Society for Women's Suffrage which sprang up all over the country under the leadership of Mrs. Henry Fawcett. These societies, though very active, were intent on achieving their ambition by constitutional means and enlisted the sympathy of a great many politicians. Certain minor gains were made but the real goal—the vote for women—was as far off as ever due to the fierce hostility of the men in power. The quiet, reasonable approach of Mrs. Fawcett's Suffragists appeared to have failed. Now a new tactic came into being, the method of Mrs. Pankhurst's Suffragettes.

MRS. PANKHURST

Mrs. Pankhurst had been connected with the Manchester Suffragist movement from 1889 and by 1901 she was on the committee.

Impatient at the lack of progress, she decided that shock tactics might be more effective. In this way the Women's Social and Political Union was formed and later became the Militant Suffrage Society. They were to begin with a very small group, hardly bigger than the Pankhurst family. There was Mrs. Pankhurst with her three daughters, Christabel, Sylvia and Adela, a teacher called Theresa Billington; and about twenty other women. Soon there arrived to join them a valuable new recruit, a mill-girl named Annie Kenney whose courage and tenacity and devotion remind one irresistibly of Joan of Arc. The W.S.P.U. began operations in Manchester and right from the start they meant business. They denied themselves all luxuries so that the money could go to the cause. They submitted themselves to a strict discipline and worked ceaselessly to put their viewpoint before the public. Then in 1905, at a huge meeting of the Liberal Party, there came the incident which put the Suffragettes on the offensive. Annie Kenney waving a small white banner emblazoned—" Votes for Women "—asked the speaker, Sir Edward Grey, if the Liberal Party would give women the vote. The question was ignored and she shouted the question again. She was joined by Christabel and a riot ensued, ending when the two women were summarily ejected from the hall by the stewards and the police. The following morning Annie and Christabel were brought up for trial *for assaulting the police.* Fines were imposed on them with the option of going to gaol for seven days. They chose prison. A packed meeting welcomed them when they were released. Annie Kenney was sacked from her job at the mill and became practically a member of the Pankhurst family. From now on, she was a full-time worker for the cause. The attacking phase had begun.

THE MOVEMENT GAINS IMPETUS

During the general election of 1906, the Manchester Suffragettes were perpetually in action and grew steadily in numbers. Yet their leaders were not satisfied with the results. They decided to switch the scene of operations to the

In November 1910 Mrs. Pankhurst (*right*) and Dr. Elizabeth Garrett Anderson went to Westminster, broke through the police cordon and entered the House.

A Suffragette parade through London was held in June 1911 and attracted a great deal of attention. It took place three days before the Coronation of George V.

At the Derby in June 1913 a Suffragette called Emily Davison threw herself in front of the King's horse at Tattenham Corner and died from the injuries she received. Her funeral was made the occasion of a Suffragette parade.

enemy headquarters—London. Annie Kenney was sent on ahead as organiser and so well did she play her part that on the day when the new Parliament assembled, 350 women marched to Caxton Hall where they held a protest meeting. Soon the Suffragette Movement had developed into a tremendous force. Its membership and sympathisers included women—and men— from all classes of society, while its increase in numbers made it no longer possible for its enemies to dismiss it as the cranky notion of a few women. The Suffragettes were helped, too, rather than hindered by the stupidity and brutality of those in authority. Time and again, these brave women were sent to prison where they were treated with less consideration than the commonest and vilest criminal. They were locked up in narrow cells with practically no ventilation. They were denied the customary hour of exercise. When they protested they were put in solitary confinement or strapped up in leather jackets. They were occasionally handcuffed for a whole day, their hands only being freed for meals. When they went on hunger strike, they were forcibly fed. A great many people, who had not cared one way or the other about votes for women, changed their minds when they learned of such indignities.

THE STRUGGLE GROWS SERIOUS

Meanwhile, the struggle increased in ferocity. The Suffragettes invaded the House of Commons and were thrown out. They travelled all over the country, whenever there was a by-election, and made life miserable for the candidate who did not support their cause. At one of these elections, in Devon at the beginning of 1908, Mrs. Pankhurst was severely beaten up by a crowd of roughs, only one of whom was punished with a fine of five shillings. At another meeting, a young woman who resented the candidate's remarks about the Suffragettes, signalised her displeasure by turning up at all his subsequent meetings armed with a large and very loud muffin bell. On 21st June, 1908, the largest gathering ever witnessed in Hyde Park was organised by the women who were anxiously—and unnecessarily as it happened—supervised by a total of no less than six hundred police. The government, however, took no notice and refused to meet a delegation from the various organisations that had assembled. This merely had the effect of

making the women more determined than ever. Twenty-one of them attempted to rush the House of Commons. A Suffragette in a dirigible balloon drifted over the building on what was probably the first leaflet raid. Three members of the Women's Freedom League went into the Ladies' Gallery of the House, chained themselves to the grille with padlocks and kept shouting: " Votes for Women! " A locksmith had to be fetched before they could be removed. On one occasion, a vehicle made up to represent a Black Maria appeared in the streets. Women in prison dress descended from it and began chalking the streets and distributing hand bills to passers-by. In Glasgow, a girl climbed on to the roof of St. Andrew's Hall and lay there in a downpour, interrupting a meeting inside by calling down through a skylight. One Member of Parliament had just begun his speech when he was interrupted by Suffragette slogans which came, apparently, from an organ in the hall. Two women had hidden in it all night. Ladders had to be fetched to get them out and the meeting was abandoned.

THE CONCILIATION COMMITTEE

At last it began to look as though the government was about to yield. In 1909, the new Parliament formed a committee for Women's Suffrage which came to be known as the Conciliation Committee. The Conciliation Bill was drawn up with the object of granting the vote to about a million women householders. The Suffragettes called a truce during which they indulged only in propaganda. Between July and September, no less than four thousand meetings took place. By November, it became obvious that the Bill was being quietly side-tracked. A deputation of the W.S.P.U. went to the House and there was a violent scene during which the Prime Minister was showered with glass and one of his colleagues had his hat kicked to pieces by the infuriated women. The truce was ended on that day which came to be called Black Friday and which ended with the arrest of over a hundred women. From then on, the Suffragettes abandoned any attempt at moderation. A campaign of window-smashing was started. The windows of the big West-End stores were shattered as were the windows of houses and offices belonging to those hostile to the cause. From the beginning of 1913, the policy of

This was the scene outside Buckingham Palace after the police had foiled an attempt to present a petition to the King. One of the Suffragettes involved has been arrested.

violence was stepped up to include fire-raising. Two churches were burnt down and Lloyd George's house set on fire. Attempts were also made to cut pictures from their frames in the National Gallery. There were hundreds of arrests including most of the Suffragette leaders who promptly went on hunger strike. Forcible feeding having been discontinued, the Home Secretary tried to checkmate this move with the Prisoners' Temporary Discharge for Ill Health Bill. Prisoners released on licence under this bill—the famous Cat and Mouse Bill —were sent to a house, nicknamed Mouse Castle by the Suffragettes, and there they were nursed back to health under police supervision. Time and again, many of them, including Annie Kenney, escaped in disguise and turned up at meetings to continue the struggle. In 1913, the cause acquired its first martyr in the person of Emily Davison. Miss Davison had just been released after serving a six months' sentence for firing a letter-box. She went straight from prison to the Derby and stationed herself at Tattenham Corner with a Suffragette petition in her hand. As the King's horse came galloping up, she rushed out and threw herself in front of it. She died four days later from the injuries she received.

WORLD WAR I INTERVENES

Throughout the year 1914, the Suffragettes kept up the pressure and in May of that year, they attempted to reach Buckingham Palace where they hoped to present a petition to the King. The attempt was foiled. In a way, it was the climax of the Suffragette Movement. The storm clouds were gathering over Europe and very soon the question of Votes for Women was swallowed up in the greater question of the deadly battle with Germany. The women who had chained themselves to railings now drove ambulances, made munitions, worked on farms, and took the places everywhere of the men who were fighting at the front. In the war, the women proved themselves. When it ended, there was no longer any hostility to their demands; and the granting of their rights was merely a matter of time.

Edward VII and Queen Alexandra, with the French President, visit an Exhibition in 1908.

EDWARD VII

The Peacemaker

EDWARD VII, who succeeded his mother, Queen Victoria, in 1901, was favoured with great charm, good nature and social tact. These qualities, coupled with his love of the national sports, his devotion to the country's affairs and his concern for the poor, made him a much esteemed and highly popular king.

In 1902 the Boers surrendered. Only five years later they were granted self-government.

A Unionist (Conservative plus Liberal-Unionist) government was still in office in 1901 and one of its most useful measures was the Education Act of 1902. This abolished the School Boards, placed education in the hands of Town and County Councils and provided for additional technical and secondary instruction.

IMPERIAL PREFERENCE

In the same year the ardently Imperialistic Colonial Secretary, Joseph Chamberlain, presided over a sort of empire family gathering or conference of colonies which had been granted self-government—Canada, Australia, New Zealand, Newfoundland, Cape Colony and Natal. Resolutions were passed favouring Imperial Preference—the fostering of trade within the empire by taxing foreign goods more highly than empire goods. A year later Chamberlain boldly launched a crusade for renouncing Free Trade (which Britain had practised for half a century) and adopting Imperial Preference as a step towards closer empire union. The Unionist Party, however, was in two minds on the subject. And the electorate, fearing that the new system would mean dearer food, expressed *their* mind in 1906 by turning out the Unionists and putting in the Liberals with a record majority.

RISE OF THE LABOUR PARTY

The new government was distinguished by advanced Radical ideas of social reform. But the outstanding feature of the Parliament was

283

the first appearance of a strong Labour Party
—fifty-three members in all. The House of
Commons was no longer to be a preserve of the
upper classes. The working class had arrived to
stay. And amongst their luggage were some
disturbing and revolutionary notions. The most
widespread was the doctrine of Socialism:
which means, among other things, a war on
capitalists and private profits, and State ownership and control of land and industry for the
benefit of the community.

Under the increased influence of the Labour
movement the government, between 1906 and
1909, tackled a variety of social evils, and
beginnings were made in providing school
meals for the children of the poor, old age
pensions for their parents, better pay and conditions for " sweated labour " and Labour
Exchanges to help the unemployed to find
work.

THE PEOPLE'S BUDGET

Then came a battle royal. In 1909 the
Chancellor of the Exchequer was David Lloyd
George, a fiery Welsh Radical with a gift of
popular oratory as overwhelming as Niagara
Falls. Lloyd George introduced a " People's
Budget " which was avowedly intended, by
means of new and increased taxation, to take
from the rich in order to help the poor—like
Robin Hood. The House of Lords indignantly
cast out the measure, though they were not
supposed to interfere with " money bills." The
Liberals, even more indignant, thereupon, in
January, 1910, went to the country. And the
country re-elected them, though with a reduced
majority.

After that the budget was duly swallowed by
the chastened Lords. But before this happened
the government had begun to whet their knives
preparatory to hamstringing the Upper House;
for they had determined to abolish once and
for all the power of that body of hereditary
peers (the majority of them Conservatives) to
override the House of Commons. The Prime
Minister, Asquith, introduced a Parliament Bill
providing that any measure passed by the
Commons in three successive sessions over a
period of two years should become law whether
the Lords rejected it or not. That was, however as far as the hamstringing operation of
the Upper House progressed during the course
of Edward VII's reign.

Edward VII. 1901-10.

THE " ENTENTE CORDIALE "

Meantime, abroad, the aggressive attitude of
Germany and the mutual distrust of the great
powers were shaping towards a world catastrophe. The nations were lining up and in
1904 Britain concluded the *Entente Cordiale*
with France and extended it to Russia in 1907.
(See *The First World War*.)

It was in this uneasy situation, at home and
abroad, that, in May, 1910, suddenly King
Edward died.

The reign had been marked by some notable
mechanical developments. The petrol-powered
motor car began to come into general use. In
1901 the first transatlantic wireless message
was transmitted from Cornwall to Newfoundland. In 1909 the Frenchman Blériot achieved
the first epoch-making aeroplane flight across
the English Channel.

NOBEL
OF THE
NOBEL PRIZES

THE 10th December is prize-giving day for the world! The winners are grown-ups—does that surprise you?—men and women, born in any country, who have "contributed most materially to the benefit of mankind during the year immediately preceding." The prizes, known as the Nobel prizes, after their founder, Alfred Bernhard Nobel, are awarded to those who have done most to enrich the fields of science, literature and peace.

Too often we do nothing to thank or honour those scientists, doctors and inventors, who by their selfless devotion, arduous researches, and ultimate discoveries, add immeasurably to the comfort and well-being of our lives. Gladly we accept their gifts of discovery, without as much as a word of appreciation.

Perhaps we are therefore a little astonished to find that it was left to the vision of Alfred Nobel—himself a scientist and inventor—to think up and provide the means of encouragement, recognition and reward of all such, who are for ever rendering the greatest services to humanity, and consequently, to us.

How did this come about?

To answer that question, we must really know more about Nobel, who gave his name to the languages of the world in creating the Nobel prizes.

His family hailed from Skane, or Scania, in southern Sweden, and were descended from peasant stock. When, in the seventeenth century, his great-great-grandfather, Petrus Olofsson, sought entrance to the University of Uppsala he took, as was the custom then, a Latinised surname, calling himself Nobelius after the village of Nöbbelöf, his birthplace. This name was handed down from one generation to the next, but through the years its spelling altered slightly, until it took the form we know it to-day—Nobel.

Alfred Nobel was born in Stockholm on 21st October, 1833. In later years he wrote that "his miserable existence should have been terminated at birth by a humane doctor."

Alfred Nobel, the explosives manufacturer, who founded the Nobel Prizes.

Perhaps he was prompted to such a statement thinking of his health, which troubled him all his life, so that from childhood he was continually forced to fight against illness. But he never indulged in self-pity, and there was more than a little truth in his words, when he jokingly referred to his principal virtues as "Keeping his nails clean and never being a burden to anyone."

Alfred was born at a time when his parents were almost penniless. His father, Emanuel Nobel, was an inventor; a born genius, who, without proper opportunities of study or instruction in engineering and building, had so succeeded in these spheres as to add hitherto undiscovered knowledge to them. When Alfred was four, his father went to Finland in search of work, and in 1842 to Russia. There he was able to interest the Russian Government in sea and land mines for defensive purposes. With the outbreak of the Crimean War, orders poured in for these and for ships' engines for the Navy, and in meeting their demand he built factories and prospered.

Meanwhile the entire Nobel family, Alfred, his two elder brothers, Robert and Ludvig, and his younger brother Emil, moved with their mother to St. Petersburg to join their father. There they received their schooling, first from a Swedish tutor, and later from a Russian.

POET OR ENGINEER?

Soon the three eldest sons were helping their father in his engineering works; though Alfred appears to have spent two years travelling abroad to finish his education, and to have visited the United States. It is just at the outset of this journey, when he is about eighteen years of age, that he pauses; poet or engineer, which is it to be? In him is the urge to write poetry, like our own Percy Bysshe Shelley, whom he admires tremendously, and whose pacifist and humanitarian principles were to influence his life in later years. He picks up his pen and, writing in the English language, decides that life is

"... *a precious gift*
A gem that Nature gave to each of us
That we might polish it until its sheen
Should finally reward us for our pains."

How well Alfred Nobel was to polish the gem of life!

On his return to St. Petersburg, he entered his father's engineering firm. But with the conclusion of the war, the family's fortunes changed and Emanuel Nobel was compelled to hand over his plant and machinery, and return to Sweden with his wife and youngest son.

Alfred remained in Russia and worked on chemical research, particularly studying the uses of nitro-glycerine, which he first caused to explode, under water, in the summer of 1862. Elated by his discovery, he joined forces with his father in Sweden, where he carried his great invention a step further, producing a compound of powder and nitro-glycerine, which considerably increased the blasting capacity of gunpowder. Obtaining a patent for his invention, a small factory was set up for the manufacture of the new explosive and to facilitate further experiments.

In 1864 a serious explosion wrecked the

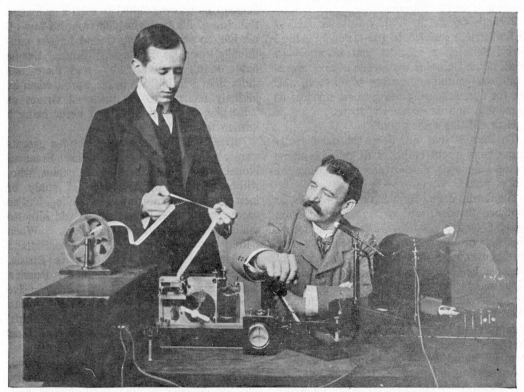

As a crown to the success of his discovery of radio telegraphy, Guglielmo Marconi, an Italian engineer (seen here with his assistant, and some of the apparatus he used in 1898), was presented with the Nobel Prize for Physics in 1909.

workshop, killing Emil. This proved too great a shock for Alfred's father, who took no further part in the work of explosives. But Alfred, undaunted, forged ahead. Forbidden to manufacture explosives within the precincts of the city, he promptly and literally started a "floating concern," mooring a lighter, on the shores of Lake Mälaren, on which work progressed. For, after all, wasn't there already a demand for the new explosive? Weren't the mines and the State Railways using it for the blasting of tunnels?

Help was forthcoming. The importance of the discovery being recognised, a company was founded for the manufacture of nitro-glycerine, The Nitro-Glycerine Company, and permission granted to erect a factory just outside Stockholm.

This was the first of many factories engaged in the making of explosives. Yet, though busy with the intricacies of acquiring foreign patents for his invention, and in founding and setting up factories in Norway, Germany, England (with an important off-shoot in the Ardeer factory in Scotland), France and the United States, Alfred Nobel did not forsake his experiments. There was still much to do.

The new explosive was dangerous to handle, and anything which would make it safer to use would naturally increase demand for it.

THE DISCOVERY OF DYNAMITE

It was the practice to transport and ship nitro-glycerine in zinc containers, packed in crates with a filling of sawdust for protection. Notwithstanding, accidents occurred. If, however, nitro-glycerine could be solidified, much of the danger would be eliminated. All kinds of absorbents were tried; powdered charcoal, sawdust, brick-dust, even cement, but none of these was suitable. Then one day, when Nobel was in the Krümmel works, a faulty crate was returned from the docks at Hamburg. Apparently the nitro-glycerine, eating its way through the zinc container, had leaked—but what was this? Instead of the usual sawdust padding, the crate had been lined with *kieselguhr*, a sort of clay, and to Nobel's astonished delight the oily liquid had been entirely absorbed by it, while leaving the clay still in a granulated form. Might this be the solution? Subsequent tests showed that it was so. Dynamite had been invented!

It is for this invention, perhaps, that Alfred Nobel is best known, but he went on to make many other far-reaching discoveries in explosives, inventing blasting gelatine, special detonators, and ballistite, a smokeless powder, which greatly interested military circles for its use with rifles and guns, and its influence on tactics.

But behind his life's work on explosives lay a man's keen desire for the world's peace, and a belief that the progress of science could in time prevent wars altogether. "The day when two army corps will be able to destroy each other in one second, all civilised nations will recoil from war in horror and disband their armies," he said.

War or peace; the choice remains the world's to this day, though paradoxically Alfred Nobel has provided for both. He was a man of supreme imagination who had his eyes on horizons afar off. "There are plenty of screws loose in my head, and I am a super-idealist. . . . I can digest philosophy better than food . . . I am not one to ask the impossible, if I like a person I let my demands collapse like a house of cards."

It is only in snatches like these from his letters (he wrote about thirty a day) that we catch a glimpse of the real man, for he shunned all forms of outward show. "I am not aware that I have deserved fame, and I take no pleasure in its clatter," he states.

He hated public functions, refused to have his portrait painted, or supply his would-be biographers with personal details. "No one reads essays except those about actors and murderers, preferably the latter . . ." he hits back. But though in public he was reticent, in private, as "one of my few favourite people," you could expect to enjoy the company of a most excellent and charming conversationalist, interested in a host of subjects beyond the immediate scope of explosives. It is quite likely the conversation would turn from the latest developments in the construction of rocket projectiles, the possible manufacture of artificial silk, experimental research on blood transfusions, the good news from the oil-wells at Baku in which he shared a common interest with his brothers, to talk of literature and the preservation of world peace. For all these subjects commanded his attention.

A popular winner of the Nobel Prize for Literature in 1953 was Sir Winston Churchill. Lady Churchill is seen receiving the Prize on his behalf from King Gustav of Sweden.

At the presentation ceremony many famous Professors of Physics, Chemistry, Medicine, Physiology and Literature from all over the world gather to receive their Prizes. Bertrand Russell, the philosopher, is seen at the end of the row on the right.

He was a ceaseless worker, untiring in all he set himself to do. Ill-health continually dogged his footsteps, but despite this he travelled widely in the course of his business, yet always finding time for research.

HELPING THE DREAMERS

During his life, he amassed an immense fortune which he gave generously for the benefit of humanity. In a will, written in his own hand, he set forth the visionary objectives and shining aim of the future Nobel prizes to be awarded internationally, in the following categories: Physics, Chemistry, Physiology or Medicine, Literature, and Peace. " I would like to help dreamers . . . Dreamers such as possess the gift of poetry, but are unknown to the many, or are misunderstood by them, meditative young research workers who are on the very threshold of a great discovery in physics, chemistry or medicine, but lack the means to achieve it." Such were the generous motives which prompted him to invent his Nobel prizes; and who knows, it may yet turn out to be his greatest invention of all!

The story of the prize-winners is history; their names being synonymous with the finest achievements of the world. Looking down the list of awards, we recognise Pierre and Marie Curie, whose joint researches won for them the Physics prize in 1902, and led Marie Curie to the discovery of radium and polonium in 1911, for which she was awarded the Chemistry prize, becoming thus the only person to gain two awards in different subjects. Her discovery not only introduced a new science but provided a means of treating that most deadly of diseases, cancer. Her daughter, still developing the science her mother began, was similarly honoured by the Nobel Foundation in 1935.

Think of a world without radio or wireless telegraphy. Yet, before Guglielmo Marconi, an Italian engineer, discovered it, there was no such thing. How glad we are to know that there was a Physics Nobel prize to crown his success in 1909. His discovery has affected our everyday life, universally, and to an extent he could never have imagined possible.

Likewise, the miracles that have been

Dr. Albert Schweitzer, winner of the Nobel Peace Prize in 1954, is also a gifted musician. He is pictured here with the celebrated violinist, Telmanyi, who uses a special Bach bow.

Earl Russell (Bertrand Russell) receives the Nobel Prize for Literature from the King of Sweden at a ceremony in 1950.

discovered in medical science are beyond all praise. Investigations concerning malaria, digestion, tuberculosis, diabetes, and the discovery of the blood groups which made possible the practical use of blood transfusions, have been responsible for saving countless lives; but what of the men who made this knowledge available? Were it not for the Nobel prize-list the names of Sir Ronald Ross (1902), Ivan Petrovic Pavlov (1904), Robert Koch (1905), John James Richard Macleod (1923) and Karl Landsteiner (1930) respectively would go unrecorded in public memory.

Nobel himself, we are told, would have liked to devote some of his time to biological research, for he was of the belief that a layman, unhampered by existing medical theories, might more readily strip a problem to its solution. It is therefore not surprising that he established this prize for physiology and medicine. As also, remembering his inborn desire to be a poet, he honours those who each year in the field of literature produce "the most distinguished work of an idealistic tendency."

SIR WINSTON CHURCHILL'S PRIZE

Many of these prize-winners will be known to you. There's our own Rudyard Kipling (1907), W. B. Yeats (1923), George Bernard Shaw (1925), John Galsworthy (1932), Bertrand Russell (1950), and Sir Winston Churchill (1953). At the presentation ceremony, these words were addressed to Sir Winston:

" Generally the Nobel Prize gives lustre to the prize-winner. In this case the prize-winner gives lustre to the prize." A magnificent tribute to one of the greatest men this age has seen.

When we consider the monetary value of the prizes, approximately £12,000 each, we cannot help wondering what it would have meant to Chaucer, Charles Lamb or Robert Burns to have been similarly honoured?

The final prize is the coveted one for Peace, awarded to the person who has done most to promote the fraternity of nations. In the first year of its conception, 1901, it was awarded to Henri Dunant, for his humanitarian qualities, for his part in founding the Red Cross and originating the Geneva Convention, which provides for the humane treatment of all prisoners-of-war; and more recently, to General George Marshall of the United States of America, for his work in the rehabilitation of the nations after the Second World War.

The presentation of the prizes for Physics, Chemistry, Medicine and Literature takes place at a solemn and impressive ceremony at Stockholm in the presence of the Royal Family, the winners receiving their prizes, diplomas and gold Nobel medallions, from the hands of H.M the King of Sweden. The Peace Prize is presented in Oslo on the same day at a meeting of the Norwegian Storting (parliament), specially convened for that purpose.

The medallions bear Nobel's likeness, with birth and death dates (1833-1896); the reverse side of the Swedish medals bears a paraphrase of a line from Virgil's Æneid, " Inventas vitam juvat excoluisse per artes " (He enriches life who makes discoveries), and the Norwegian medal for Peace, the motto, " Pro pace et fraternitate gentium " (For peace and the brotherhood of man).

Prize-giving day is also the anniversary of Alfred Nobel's death, and on the evening of the 10th December at a banquet a silent toast is drunk to the memory of this distinguished and beloved son of Sweden, who gave his high ideals and his hope to the world.

ANDREW CARNEGIE

The Millionaire Philanthropist

IN 1919 there died a man who had declared and tried to live up to the belief that: he who dies possessed of wealth that he was free to distribute, dies disgraced. He was one of the richest men in the world and his name was Andrew Carnegie.

Carnegie was born in Dunfermline, Scotland, in 1835, the son of a struggling weaver. Life was hard in these days when factories were arising to put the handloom weavers out of business, but young Carnegie enjoyed his schooldays; and when, in 1848, his family set out for America in the hope of better things, the boy wept as he watched his beloved town vanish from sight. After a horrible voyage that lasted some three months, the Carnegies arrived at the dismal town of Allegheny in Pennsylvania and soon discovered that their move from Scotland had been a move from the frying-pan into the fire. At the age of thirteen, Andrew found himself working in a factory as a bobbin boy. His hours were from seven in the morning until six at night. His wages were five shillings a week.

Andrew Carnegie, the poor boy who made good in the United States. His wealth he devoted to charitable purposes.

CARNEGIE'S SENSE OF OPPORTUNITY

After a year spent in a cellar smelling of oil, Andrew found a new job as a telegraph clerk. This was much more congenial work and the boy felt that at last he had a future. Soon he was in charge of the office and when, in 1853, the Pennsylvania Railway Company set up its telegraph system, Andrew Carnegie, aged eighteen, was offered the job of secretary to Robert A. Scott, the superintendent. He accepted, and was soon singled out as a coming man. Once, when an accident blocked the whole line, Carnegie acted promptly, sending out telegrams in Scott's name, sorting out the tangle and getting the lines back into commission. It was natural, therefore, that when Scott moved on to a more important job, his place as superintendent should be taken by Carnegie. This promotion gave freedom of action to the young man's driving ambition and uncanny sense of opportunity; and it is hardly surprising that it was Carnegie who first saw the possibilities of sleeping cars and

put them into operation on the Pennsylvania Railway.

SKILFUL INVESTMENTS

When the Civil War broke out in 1861, railways suddenly became vital factors in the struggle between North and South. Robert A. Scott was put in command of all Northern railways and telegraphs and asked that Carnegie be made his assistant. By the time that the war ended in 1865, the young Scotsman found himself an established and wealthy man. He had a salary of £600 a year but he had invested his money with such skill that his income was in the region of an annual £10,000, a fantastic achievement for someone who had only just reached his thirtieth birthday. Carnegie, however, was not content to rest on his laurels. So he resigned from the railway service and struck out on his own. The railways were expanding rapidly and this, plus the aftermath of the fighting, meant that there would be a demand for iron. With a few partners, Carnegie set up a company which built the first iron bridge across the Ohio River.

A NEW WAY OF MAKING STEEL

Carnegie became wealthier than ever but he did not become either cautious or complacent. When he heard of the Bessemer process, then newly developed, he began to think in terms of steel. There, he saw, was the thing of the future. Steel was malleable and durable: it bent under pressure but did not break, whereas iron railway lines were constantly having to be replaced because they cracked easily. Until now, the manufacture of steel had been a costly process but Bessemer's method of producing it from iron ore reduced the cost tremendously. While Carnegie was weighing up the pros and cons, the news arrived of the discovery of a great field of iron ore in the vicinity of Lake Superior. It was like an omen. His partners, however, failed to share his enthusiasm and Carnegie promptly sold out all his investments and formed a new company with its head-quarters and works at Pittsburgh. Almost from the start its success was sensational and by 1888, Carnegie owned a colossal steel plant, a line of steamships, over four hundred miles of railways and vast coal and iron fields. By the end of the century all records for steel production were shattered and Andrew Car-negie was one of the most powerful figures in America; and when, in 1901, the United States Steel Corporation took over the vast Carnegie industrial empire, the handloom weaver's son from Dunfermline received one hundred million pounds for his holdings and was now, almost certainly, the richest man in the world.

GIVING AWAY A FORTUNE

Having made this fantastic fortune, Carnegie now occupied himself with equal determination in the rather more unusual business of giving it away. A fanatical believer in the power of education, he set about endowing libraries and colleges where knowledge would be available to all. Over a million pounds went to set up branch libraries in New York. Dunfermline and Pittsburgh were showered with gifts. The four Scottish universities received a grant of more than two million pounds to help to pay the fees of needy students. A Hero Fund was set up to reward acts of outstanding courage.

Skibo Castle on the Dornoch Firth, which Carnegie built and where he lived during the last years of his life. At the flagpole you can see the composite flag which Carnegie insisted should fly over the castle, composed of the Union Jack and Stars and Stripes sewn together.

Carnegie is here seen sitting in the centre with members of the Carnegie Trust, which he created, believing that a man who dies possessed of wealth that he was free to distribute, dies disgraced. He set up many philanthropic projects before his death.

When, in his old age, he asked his secretary how much he had given away, the secretary could reply, " 324,657,399 dollars, sir." In 1902, St. Andrews, Scotland's oldest university, returned the compliment by appointing him Lord Rector.

RETURN TO SCOTLAND

The last years of his life were spent in the native land he had wept to leave as a boy of twelve. He built a castle at Skibo on the Dornoch Firth and lived there quietly. In the mornings, he would awaken to the skirl of the pipes; and often he was to be seen proudly wearing the kilt. On the castle flagstaff, a queer composite flag, made up of the Union Jack and the Stars and Stripes sewn together, fluttered in the breeze. The feverish days in the American business world seemed very remote.

A LONG AND FRUITFUL LIFE

A new world was, in fact, coming into being as Europe drifted towards World War I. Carnegie saw the signs and tried vainly to persuade the German Emperor of his folly. When he failed, he threw his energies into the British war effort, handing over huge sums to the Red Cross and the Y.M.C.A. At the same time he bombarded the American president, Woodrow Wilson, with letters, urging him to bring his country into the struggle on the side of the Allies. In 1917, a German submarine sank the *Lusitania* and brought about the thing that the old man at Skibo Castle so earnestly desired. Now, at last, the flag that fluttered from the flagstaff meant something more than a pious wish. In a year, the struggle was over and the might of Germany was crushed; and in another year, having lived long enough to see the final victory, Andrew Carnegie died at the age of eighty-four. He left behind him 2,505 libraries. He had given away something like seventy million pounds. He had lived up to his maxim: he who dies possessed of wealth that he was free to distribute, dies disgraced.

Militarism in Germany was carefully fostered by the Kaiser, Wilhelm II, who, throughout his long reign, arranged and enjoyed frequent military parades. This one is typical.

THE FIRST WORLD WAR
" The War to end War "

THE underlying causes of the war of 1914–18 were many and mixed and muddled. For many years beforehand the great powers were suspicious and fearful of each other's designs. Among them Germany was becoming the bully of Europe. The Prussian military caste and the blustering Emperor, or Kaiser, William II, were arrogantly bent on punching their way to the fore. Germany's mailed fist and, in their own sphere, the punier paws of her weaker partner Austria-Hungary were a standing provocation. Austria and Russia were rivals for control in the Balkans. Germany and Russia were rivals in the Near East, where the former had gained a dominant influence over Turkey. France was still smarting from her crushing defeat in 1870–1, as well as from later humiliations. As for Britain, while Germany's designs in the Near East challenged her interests there, Germany's ambitious naval plans threatened her very existence.

THE OPPOSING GROUPS

By 1907 the uneasy powers had formed themselves into two opposing groups. Germany, Austria-Hungary and Italy made up the Triple Alliance. Britain, France and Russia had come together in the Triple Entente to balance it. This had developed from the historic *Entente Cordiale*, or cordial understanding, established between Britain and France, and cemented by Edward VII's personal tact and charm, in 1904.

In 1914 Europe was heading like a high-powered car out of control straight for the abyss of war, and all Britain's desperate efforts to apply the brakes were powerless. What precisely Germany's ambitions were, and whether or not she was spoiling for a fight, are even now

By chance a photographer happened to be there when Princep (here marked with a cross), the man who assassinated the Austrian Archduke and his wife at Serayevo in June 1914, was arrested.

disputed questions. She was the strongest military power in Europe. Her neighbours feared that she aimed at dominating them. Germany feared that the Triple Entente, having encircled her, sought her destruction.

THE OUTBREAK OF WAR

The spark that actually lit the fuse that fired the powder that shattered Europe was a relatively trivial affair—as sparks are. The heir to the Austrian throne was assassinated. Austria, with some show of reason, blamed Serbia for the crime and deliberately rushed to war against her. Russia, Serbia's patron, prepared to come to her aid. Germany, supporting Austria, declared war on Russia and France. Britain entered the lists on 4th August, after Germany had invaded Belgium: for that brutal act was an infringement of the little kingdom's guaranteed neutrality and a direct threat to Britain's maritime security. So Europe drifted into the war. And it was to be a war on a new

and mighty scale, with the combatant nations throwing all their resources into a struggle to the death: men by the million; the new aeroplanes and airships; improved submarines; heavier artillery and more machine-guns; poison gas; and Britain's surprise invention—the tank.

THE MIRACLE OF THE WAR

Germany had to cope with a war on two fronts. She counted on a swift victory and acted on a preconceived plan. This was to strike through Belgium, sweep round towards Paris, squeeze the French armies together and destroy them and so bring France to her knees before the slow-moving Russian legions were ready to engage. The plan might have succeeded had it been followed out closely. The Belgian frontier fortresses tumbled down. The French in the north, and the British Expeditionary Force under Sir John French on their left flank, were in grave danger of being enveloped. The

A famous recruiting poster of Lord Kitchener. Wherever you stand, to the left, right, centre, above or below, his eyes will still be on you.

dogged British stands at Mons and Le Cateau enabled them to extricate themselves; but by the end of August the enemy stood within striking distance of Paris. Then the exultant Germans, overrating their successes, made a false move and Joffre, the French commander, saw that they paid for it. On 5th September he turned and counter-attacked and drove the startled enemy back from the River Marne and across the Aisne. This was the famous "miracle of the Marne" that saved Paris and perhaps France.

YPRES

In Belgium, the fall of Antwerp on 9th October was followed by a German drive for the Channel ports, the possession of which would have cut Britain's communications. But the British blocked the way at Ypres and, in a series of battles that raged with unsurpassable fury from 19th October to 22nd November, they fought the enemy to a standstill. The German hopes of a swift victory were shattered. Thenceforth the struggle became static along

Before the Battle of Albert in July 1916, the 1st Lancashire Fusiliers fix bayonets. This trench is typical of many where the men lived and fought whilst they were in the firing line.

The Kaiser studies the war map with Field Marshal von Hindenburg (*left*) and General Ludendorff. Hindenburg became President of the German Republic in 1925.

a 350-mile line of trenches stretching from the North Sea to Switzerland. The Allies had suffered over a million casualties.

In the East the Russians were tasting a mixed diet of defeat and victory. In East Prussia they were knocked spinning in the battle of Tannenberg. In the south they routed the Austrians in Galicia.

GALLIPOLI

In 1915 the deadlock on the Western Front led the Allies to look eastwards. Turkey had joined the enemy powers in the previous October; whereupon Britain had annexed the island of Cyprus and declared Egypt a British protectorate. Russia was being hard pressed. Accordingly, a plan was formed for forcing the Dardanelles and taking Constantinople. This would give a knock-out blow to Turkey in Europe and enable aid to be sent to Russia. When a naval bombardment failed to silence the forts, troops were landed on the Gallipoli

peninsula. It was an operation of immense difficulty and only the dare-all spirit and superb dash of the attackers, especially the " Anzacs " from Australia and New Zealand, made it possible. Even so their valour was of no avail. There was bad staff work and bad luck and around the end of the year the hopeless project was abandoned.

Meantime Turkey in Asia was receiving attention. Indian divisions advanced up the River Tigris in Mesopotamia (Iraq) and in September captured Kut. There, however, General Townshend was later besieged by a superior Turkish force. All attempts to relieve him were repulsed and in April, 1916, after a fighting siege of nearly five months, the garrison was forced to surrender.

ITALY CHANGES SIDES

The combats on the Western Front during 1915 produced little change. Sir John French was then superseded by Sir Douglas Haig as

Gallipoli: North Beach, Anzac, after the August offensive in 1915. Hospital tents are in the foreground, ordnance and supply stores, centre, and a terrace of dug-outs, right centre.

General von Falkenhayn (*left*,) Commander of the German Army on the Rumanian front.

commander of the British forces. At home, Asquith's unsatisfactory ministry was replaced by a coalition government of all parties. Italy, renouncing the Triple Alliance, joined the Allies and kept the Austrian armies occupied. On the eastern front the Russians were driven back and badly shaken. Serbia was crushed and Bulgaria joined the Austro-Germans in the crushing.

VERDUN

In 1916 Britain realised that she must throw her full weight into the scale to help make good the Allies' appalling casualties: she adopted conscription. This year Falkenhayn, the German commander, worked on the idea of bleeding France to death by continuous attack on a vital point. From February to September he battered away at the great fortress system of Verdun. France bled indeed, but not to death. Haig, at the cost of 750,000 casualties, relieved the pressure on the fortress by a sustained offensive in the Somme valley, and Verdun remained untaken. Russian successes led Rumania to join hands with the Allies in the wild war dance; three months later she lay

In the First World War women began to play an active part in hostilities. A contingent of National Motor Volunteers, Women's Reserve, being addressed by their inspecting officer.

The scene outside Victoria Station, London, shortly before the departure of the trains taking soldiers back to the Front after an all-too-short period of leave.

At Advanced General Headquarters, Beauquesne, in August 1916. *Left to right:* General Joffre, President Poincaré, H.M. King George V, General Foch and Sir Douglas Haig.

prostrate beneath the enemy's jack-boot. In Britain, the end of a year of exhaustion and failure brought a new vigour to the conduct of the war when the human dynamo, Lloyd George, became Prime Minister.

SUBMARINE WARFARE

The British Navy was bearing the brunt of the operations at sea and strangling Germany with its ever-tightening blockade. Only once —in the Battle of Jutland on 31st May, 1916— did the main fleets engage. The immediate result was disappointing and inconclusive. But the German Navy, having prudently retired to harbour, never afterwards ventured far out again except to surrender at the end of the war. Instead, contrary to international law, the enemy, from January, 1917, concentrated on unrestricted submarine warfare. Shipping of every kind or nationality, armed or unarmed, proceeding to or from British ports, was attacked without warning. Germany was feeling the pinch of Britain's hunger-blockade.

The war in France was in a condition of stalemate. An all-out submarine campaign, it was confidently expected, would reduce Germany's arch-enemy to starvation and submission in six months. The expectation came perilously near to being realised, and only the Allies' tireless exertions and clever devices enabled them to swat the mosquito-like swarms of U-Boats that assailed them. Innocent-looking " Q "-ships that lured the enemy to destruction, camouflaged hulls to reduce visibility, depth charges and mines, guarded convoys and new shipbuilding—all these are among the measures that slowly gained the mastery over the deadly pests. What the piratical submarine campaign did do, however, was to bring the United States into the war in April, 1917. And *that* was counted a decisive happening—provided Uncle Sam could don his armour in time.

GAIN AND LOSS

Unfortunately the heartening event was accompanied by another *dis*heartening event,

Wounded British prisoners being brought into St. Quentin (which was in German hands during most of the war) under the charge of a very young German guard.

In March revolution broke out in Russia. The royal government was overthrown; the army fell to pieces; and in December the country's new masters signed an armistice with Germany. Russia was " out."

There was no lack of fighting in the West during 1917. The Allies had mustered nearly four million men, a third of them British, with more coming. The Aisne, Vimy Ridge, Messines, Paschendaele and Cambrai (where the British tanks first definitely showed their possibilities) are names associated with local or incomplete successes and failures, with dauntless valour and limitless endurance, but also, alas! with hideous and colossal slaughter. To add to the tale of disappointment, the Italians suffered a heavy defeat at Caporetto.

THE NEAR EAST

The most cheerful campaigning news came from two minor fronts. In Palestine a British force under the brilliant cavalry commander Sir Edmund Allenby thoroughly trounced the Turks at Beersheba and went on to capture Jerusalem. Next year the army gave the enemy another good licking and reached Aleppo, right up in northern Syria. In these masterly campaigns Allenby received valuable aid from that romantic and almost legendary hero " Lawrence of Arabia" and the wild Arab tribesmen who fought under his magnetic leadership. In Mesopotamia the shame of Kut was wiped out in 1917 by the recapture of the town and the taking of Baghdad, nicely clinched in 1918 by the conquest of the whole country.

THE SOMME AND VICTORY

The year 1918 brought the long and bitter contest to a crisis. Ludendorff, who had taken over the German command in the West, massed all his forces for a determined snatch at victory before the American armies were ready. The submarine campaign had failed. The British blockade was succeeding. From March to July Ludendorff delivered a series of terrific attacks that were savagely driven home. The Allied armies reeled before the staggering blows. The British front was pierced. The onrushing Germans once more reached the Marne. But it was their final effort and the Allies recovered in time. Foch, now Supreme Commander in France, was able to strike back. And American aid was coming in fast to make ultimate victory sure. Then, on 8th August, in the Somme area, Haig, with 450 tanks rumbling ahead of his troops, launched an offensive that broke the German front and scored a spectacular triumph. The victory was followed up by repeated attacks that stabbed all up and down the enemy line. The Germans were forced back in a general retreat. Haig's mighty blows smashed through their final defences. Germany's military power cracked. All her partners were throwing up the sponge. Mutiny broke out in the fleet. Revolution flared up at home. The Kaiser left Germany for Holland. On 11th November Germany surrendered and signed armistice terms dictated by the victors. The Allies, with the British Commonwealth and Empire forming the hard core of their exertions, had won

what was perhaps the most titanic war in history.

THE SETTLEMENT AND LEAGUE OF NATIONS

Germany was disarmed and forbidden to re-arm. She was presented with a colossal, and quite impossible, war bill. Alsace-Lorraine was restored to France. The enemy colonies, which had already been captured, were divided among the Allies. Britain and the Dominions received German South-West and part of German East Africa (the latter now Tanganyika), together with other colonies in Africa and in the Pacific. They were to be governed by the new possessors as trustees or guardians under the newly-created League of Nations. Britain also received Palestine and Mesopotamia on the same terms, but later these areas were formed into independent States.

The peace treaties (that of Versailles, 1919,

A scene during the Third Battle of Ypres, August 1917. A 12-inch Mark I Howitzer is being manœuvred along a partially wrecked railway mounting at "Salvation Corner."

A scene of utter desolation near Arras in " No Man's Land." Destruction such as this was widespread both in France and Belgium, where fighting ebbed and flowed for four years.

Field-Marshal von Hindenburg arrives with his staff for an inspection of troops near Noyon in June 1918. Five months later the war was over and Germany defeated.

Refugees returning to their homes in Courtrai the day after the liberation of that town in October 1918. The old lady, who has all her worldly possessions in the cart drawn by a strange pair of draught-animals, questions a British officer.

The signing of the Peace Treaty in the Hall of Mirrors, Versailles, on 28th June, 1919. The German representative signs.

and others) redrew the map of Central Europe with the aim of securing the liberation of the smaller peoples from their former masters and regrouping them in new democratic States. The ramshackle Austro-Hungarian Empire had already broken up. From its parts were formed the republics of Austria itself, Czechoslovakia and Hungary. Republics were also set up in Germany, Poland, Yugoslavia (the former Serbia much enlarged) and the Baltic countries. Remembering the suffering and havoc of the war years (the British Empire alone mourned nearly a million dead), the victors laboured to prevent further armed conflicts by means of a great League of Nations. A solemn Covenant, signed eventually by member states all over the world, was made to submit future disputes to arbitration and to combine against any aggressor. Unhappily the noble aim failed. From the beginning it lacked the support of the people of the United States, who feared to entangle themselves in more European quarrels. In any case it was too high to reach—yet.

NURSE EDITH CAVELL
A Very Brave Woman

A DAUGHTER was born to the Vicar of Swardeston, near Norwich, in 1866, and she was christened Edith. Little did her parents realise that one day the name of Edith Cavell would rank with the greatest.

It was not until she was twenty-nine years of age that she decided to take up nursing as a career and entered the London Hospital. There she settled down to her studies and proved herself to be so capable a nurse that, when a bad attack of typhoid fever broke out at Maidstone, in 1897, Edith Cavell was chosen as one of the best nurses of the hospital.

No task seemed to be too great for her, and she was held in high esteem by all at the hospital; but after five years she left the London Hospital to take up a post as superintendent night nurse to the St. Pancras Guardians, where she stayed for a further three years.

Here again, no one could speak too highly of her work as a nurse, as a lecturer and as a friend. A beautiful little story is told of how she sent a poor child for a holiday at Hastings, though she knew that it had not long to live. She rejoiced in the fact that she had at least been able to give it some enjoyment.

Her next post was at the Hoxton Infirmary, where, after seeing her at work as a nurse and as an organiser, the director said: " She is a heroine, in my eyes, of the type of Joan of Arc." Even so, it soon became obvious that she could not stand up to the strain for much longer, and she was compelled to take a holiday abroad for six months.

Shortly after she returned she was offered a post in Belgium. Nursing in Brussels, at this time, was all in the hands of the Roman Catholic Church, but, though Edith was a Protestant, she did so well that everyone admired her work. Though not of the same Church or even the same country, she was appointed as the head of the Berkendael Institute, which was patronised by the King and the Queen of the Belgians.

When the Great War broke out, in 1914, Edith Cavell was on holiday with her friends in Norfolk, but as soon as she heard the news she realised that she must return to Brussels. By this time she had endeared herself to the people of that city.

When she arrived she found there was some confusion. The German nurses, who had been at the Institute, had been recalled, and her first task was to see them safely away and into the waiting train. Then followed a period which proved to be most difficult, and which eventually ended in her death.

FRIEND OR FOE?

Soon, under her influence, the hospital was prepared for the wounded soldiers who, it was realised, would soon be coming. One town fell after another, and soon the Germans were in Brussels itself. Edith knew her job was to nurse, and whatever nation the injured belonged to, she always had a kind word for them. Later she discovered that Brussels was

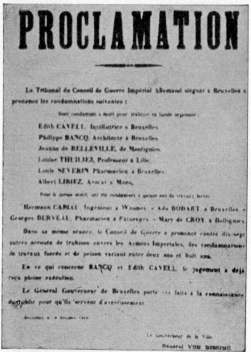

The Proclamation announcing the sentence of death, which was posted throughout Belgium in 1915, by order of General Von Bissing, who ordered Nurse Cavell's execution.

Edith Cavell faced her German accusers with dignity and courage.

not a very healthy place in which to live, for no one knew who was a friend and who a foe. People did not speak to one another any more than was necessary, lest a word out of place might mean suspicion of spying—and there was only one penalty for a spy—death.

Still, she set about her work, helping the children who had been stranded, and caring for the wounded. Her hospital included men of many nationalities, on either side, and she took the same thought and showed the same consideration for all.

In the meantime Edith had taken the opportunity to help some of her fellow-countrymen to find a way out of Brussels. It was most dangerous, but in any war there is always an underground movement to help the man on the run. Few knew of this, not even many of her friends. The task became even more dangerous after the new German governor of the city had proclaimed that anyone harbouring or helping an enemy alien would be subject to the greatest penalties.

HELPING HER ENEMIES

Edith continued to show great consideration to the German soldiers and was able to help them quite considerably, but this aroused the suspicions of the governor and some of his friends. Spies were set to watch her every movement. The Germans could not understand why an Englishwoman, who was so admired by the Belgians, should be giving help to her enemies in this way.

Soon, small charges were brought against her. Most of them were petty and insignificant, but, if all were added together, they made quite a formidable list against her.

Then, by accident she was betrayed. One of the Germans had pretended to be an English soldier who wanted to get home, and a young English servant girl, with whom he had made friends, said that she would endeavour to arrange something, as Nurse Cavell had helped many people in a similar way before. With great rejoicing the news was received. The Germans had at last discovered how the English were getting out of Belgium.

On 5th August some soldiers entered the hospital ward as she was bandaging a patient, and told her to follow them. She asked to be given permission to continue dressing the wound, but this was not granted. For the last

time, she left her hospital and was taken to St. Gilles Prison, where she waited in a cell for two months.

FACING A FIRING-SQUAD

Her arrest was a close and guarded secret, but, when the news leaked out, entreaties were made for her release. However, they were of no avail, for Edith Cavell had broken one of the laws of war, by helping the enemy.

Her trial was held in the October, and she was sentenced to death for treason. The verdict was faced with courage and calmness. In the death cell she spoke with the English chaplain before being taken out to face the firing party at 2 a.m. There, she remained calm to the end, professing her faith and saying that she was proud to die for her country.

Her memorial service in St. Paul's Cathedral was impressive; her memorial was erected near Trafalgar Square, where it may be seen to-day; but her greatest memorial is in the hearts of a people who cherish such courage and fortitude as were shown by this heroine of the war.

Edith Cavell, the brave woman who faced a firing-squad, seen in more peaceful days.

GEORGE V

The First King
of the House of Windsor

George V. 1910–36.

GEORGE V, another sailor-king, succeeded his father, Edward VII, in 1910. His solid virtues were quickly appreciated. Throughout his reign his sober sense of duty, his unfailing sympathy and understanding, were devoted to the welfare of " his very dear people."

The reign began in a lively political atmosphere. Asquith's Liberal Government had just introduced the Parliament Bill for curtailing the powers of the House of Lords. The Lords side-tracked it. Asquith appealed to the country. The electors returned him to power again. None the less, the Lords tried to mangle the bill. But their resistance ended, in 1911, under Asquith's threat to swamp the Conservative majority in the Upper House by creating a host of new peers. So the Lords lost their absolute power of veto over legislation. They could only hold up bills for a period of two years. And they could not even do that with " money bills."

It was at this time that members of Parliament first received payment for their services. The grant was designed to help the workers' representatives to enter Parliament.

In the same year a measure of the highest social value was carried through by the Chancellor of the Exchequer, Lloyd George. The National Health Insurance Act gave manual workers and many other employees pay and free medical attention during sickness. For these benefits the employee paid a weekly sum by way of insurance and the employers and the State supplemented it. The Act also granted unemployment pay to workers in certain selected trades. (In 1920 the benefit was extended to most of the other industries.)

These were troubled times, filled with industrial disputes and strikes that well nigh paralysed the country's trade. And Ireland was getting fighting mad again over Home Rule. In 1912 the Liberals introduced a new bill to grant it. On this occasion the excitement centred round the attitude of Ulster, the north-eastern province. The greater part of Ulster was predominantly British and also intensely Protestant. It wished for nothing more than to remain under the United Kingdom Parliament. And it declared that, rather than submit to an Irish Parliament dominated by Catholics, it would fight. Civil war would certainly have blazed out had not the coming of a greater clash of arms in 1914 caused the whole matter to be shelved. (See *The First World War*.)

Inevitably after the war trade crashed, causing mass unemployment, grave labour unrest and bitter want throughout Europe. In Britain (to the horror of old-fashioned politicians) the first—very shaky—Labour, or Socialist, government came into office in 1924. A National Government, formed from all parties and elected in 1931, definitely abandoned Free Trade and adopted the policy of Protection and Imperial Preference for which Joseph Chamberlain had fought so strenuously at the beginning of the century. Gradually

A group of royal mourners at Buckingham Palace to attend the funeral of Edward VII in 1910.
Left to right, back row: Haakon VII of Norway, Ferdinand I of Bulgaria, Manoel II of Portugal,
Wilhelm II of Germany, Gustav V of Sweden, Albert I of Belguim. *Front row*: Alfonso XIII of
Spain, George V and Frederick VIII of Denmark.

trade conditions improved and somewhat better times followed.

Women had been demanding the right to vote for years past. Their splendid services during the war, in filling the gaps left by the soldiers gone overseas, now made their claims irresistible. Accordingly, in 1918, women of thirty or over possessing a property qualification were given the vote. Adult suffrage for all males (irrespective of the previous property and lodgers' qualifications) was also granted. Ten years later women were put on the same footing. Thus the ideal of equal adult suffrage was at length attained.

In the early 1920s the voice of radio, or wireless broadcasting, began to bring public affairs, education and entertainment into almost every household.

In 1922 Britain withdrew her protectorate over Egypt and declared the country to be an independent State. British troops, however, remained in occupation for defence purposes.

In Ireland, during the war, a new " Sinn Fein " party, encouraged by German agents, had started another insurrection and proclaimed an independent republic. Eventually, in 1920-22, an agreement was come to under which the country was divided into two regions: six counties of Ulster (thenceforth called " Northern Ireland "), and the rest of the island (to be known as " the Irish Free State "). Each was given its own Parliament; but, while Northern Ireland still remained a part of the United Kingdom, the Free State became a self-governing Dominion, like Canada. The republican party, however, bitterly opposed the agreement and in 1932 they came into power in the Free State Parliament. From then onwards down to the end of the reign their leader, Mr. de Valera, proceeded to break one

The Kaiser drives in an open landau with his cousin King George when on a visit to London before the first World War.

A keen yachtsman, the King frequently raced his yacht *Britannia* at Cowes Regatta, The scene on board before the start of a race.

In 1935, when George V had reigned for twenty-five years, his Silver Jubilee was celebrated amidst great popular enthusiasm. With Queen Mary he drove in state through London.

The Royal Procession during one of the King's ceremonial drives at the time of his Silver Jubilee. The entire route was lined with affectionately cheering people.

link after another in the slender chain that bound the Free State to Britain.

During the war the self-governing Dominions had eagerly rushed to the aid of the mother country. Side by side with their magnificent efforts the already growing feeling of their own separate nationhood had strongly developed. To this sentiment effect was willingly given at an Imperial Conference held in 1926 and confirmed by the Statute of Westminster in 1931. Great Britain and the Dominions were declared to be equal, self-governing communities, united by a common allegiance to the Crown and freely associated as members of the British Commonwealth of Nations. The Dominions concerned at this date were Canada, Australia, New Zealand, Newfoundland, the Irish Free State and South Africa—the last-named being a Union, effected in 1909, of Cape Colony, Natal, the Transvaal and the Orange Free State. India had not yet attained " Dominion " rank; but it was training hard to achieve self-government, and a few years later, in 1935, an All-India Federation was foreshadowed.

While these more or less peaceful changes were occurring, other countries were seeking their ideals of government by violent means. Russia became a completely Communist country, in which the State controlled everything, including labour, and threatened war on all capitalist nations. In Italy Mussolini, with his " Fascist " followers, set up a dictatorship after seizing power in 1922. In 1935, cynically disregarding the Covenant of the League of Nations (see *The First World War*), he made a pretext for invading and annexing Abyssinia. The League proved incapable of bridling him, and its feeble attempts only embittered Italy against France and Britain, and threw her into the arms of Germany.

And what of fallen Germany? In 1918 she was fallen indeed. But by January, 1936, when our own good and well-beloved King George passed away, the dictatorship of Adolf Hitler, established in 1933, was setting her on her feet again. (See *The Second World War*).

EDWARD VIII
The King Who Abdicated

EDWARD VIII ascended the throne on the death of his father, George V, in January, 1936. But he was never crowned. He wished to contract a marriage which the Cabinet knew would arouse the strongest disapproval as being contrary to British traditions and principles. The Cabinet's views were supported by the overseas Dominions, to whom the Crown was the honoured symbol of their union with Britain. The King's intentions, however, remained fixed. Accordingly, if a constitutional crisis was to be avoided, he was compelled to choose between his affections and his throne. He chose the former. In December he abdicated and his brother, the Duke of York, assumed the Crown as George VI. The ex-King was created Duke of Windsor and he and his duchess have since lived mostly in America.

Abroad, Nazi Germany provided a sensation of another kind when Hitler suddenly marched his troops into the Rhineland. (See *The Second World War*).

Edward VIII. January–December 1936.

German mounted troops in Cologne in 1936 when they re-occupied the Rhineland.

312

GEORGE VI

A much-loved King

George VI.   1936–52.

GEORGE VI's sudden call to the throne, on the abdication of his brother Edward VIII in December, 1936, set the new King and his Queen Elizabeth an all-unexpected task. How nobly they performed it, every year of the reign testified. There was never a king and queen who so completely won their people's hearts. They delighted in public service. They shared the dangers and hardships of the coming war with gay and steadfast courage. Their happy family life endeared them to millions of other happy British families. And the unconquerable spirit with which the King endured and triumphed over an impediment in his speech won the respect and admiration of all.

The subject that dominated Europe at this time was the growing menace of Nazi Germany. Hitler swallowed up Austria in 1938 and Czechoslovakia in that and the following year. His threat to Poland was the final outrage that led to the Second World War.

When the six-year conflict was over it remained for the victors to clear up the mess. Europe was bankrupt and ravaged. Industry and commerce were in chaos. Millions of people were hungry and homeless. Political discontent was rife. Had it not been for the generous economic aid of the United States it is hard to see how the stricken countries could ever have struggled to their feet again.

Even before victory was in sight the Allies had begun to plan for the future, and in 1945 fifty countries signed the Charter of the United Nations Organisation that was to supplant the old League of Nations. It was a further brave endeavour to prevent future wars, besides undertaking various social and economic services on an international scale.

The Allies remained in military occupation of Germany and Austria: Russia controlling the eastern parts, the United States, Britain and France the western. The central and southeastern States of Europe which had been overrun by Germany were restored, with some boundary alterations. But, unhappily, none except Greece enjoyed real independence. They lay under the huge shadow of Communist Russia. And that shadow threatened to spread over all Europe. To Russia, Communism was almost a religion and, notwithstanding her obligations under the Charter, it was her avowed purpose to force it on her neighbours by stirring up discontent and revolution and, if need be, by war. The German Eagle had been well and truly strangled, but now the mammoth Russian Bear towered up in its place as a new menace to Europe. The production of the atom bomb added to the tension. At first the United States held the lead, but their monopoly was broken when Russia herself succeeded in manufacturing the bomb.

The western Allies, including the United States, were anxious to set up a repentant Germany, under due safeguards, as a useful member of European society and a counterpoise to Russia. This, of course, did not suit Russian designs. Accordingly, in 1949, Western Germany alone was formed into a Federal Republic and closely associated with the western powers.

A year later the United Nations Organisation was winning its spurs in Korea. Communist forces in the north, backed by China and Russia, were threatening to sweep over the entire peninsula. But they were resolutely checked by United States forces, in company with troops from Britain, the Dominions and other nation-members of U.N.O.

Meantime Britain was struggling with the same post-war difficulties as the rest of Europe. In the general election of July, 1945, the Socialists swept the country. The war had done much to level class distinctions and promote ideas of equality. It was strongly felt by many that society must be created anew on truly democratic lines. The State must ensure a higher standard of living for the masses, with full employment, shorter working hours and freedom from economic anxieties. All the political parties were pledged to social reform, but there were fundamental differences in their general principles of government. Labour stood for State ownership and control in industry and the public services. The Conservatives believed in private ownership, free competition and individual enterprise. The Liberal Party hardly counted. It had been declining since the end of the First World War and was now practically eclipsed.

The Socialist government made the most of its sensational triumph in the election. Now was its chance to build up the brave new world, the " Welfare State," of its dreams! In its five years of office it nationalised the Bank of England, the coal mines, railway and road transport, cables and wireless, gas and electric light. (It brought in the great iron and steel industries too, but the Conservatives denationalised them, as well as road transport, after they were returned to power under Mr.— later Sir—Winston Churchill in 1951.) But its finest social achievement was the passing, in 1946 and 1948, of the National Insurance, Assistance and Health Service Acts. Under these measures the State provides a generous scale of sickness, unemployment, old age and other benefits (in return for weekly contributions from certain groups) and a free health service for all. Since the weekly contributions do not cover the cost, however, general taxation is

The Trooping the Colour Ceremony in 1937. King George, followed by his brothers the Dukes of Gloucester and Kent, inspects the Guards prior to the march past.

In 1940, when London was badly bombed, the King refused to leave the capital for the safety of the country. He visited the districts which had suffered most to cheer the people and he inspired them with his own courage. Here he inspects the Pioneer Corps.

heavily drawn upon to pay for these benefits. The Socialists also further clipped the wings of their old enemy, the House of Lords: the the period during which it could hold up legislation was reduced from two years to one.

One effect of the war was to strengthen the growth of nationalism among the peoples of the near and farther East. The British Labour Government was all in favour of such growing-up movements. Under legislation passed in 1947, Burma became a free and independent State, while " India " and " Pakistan " (the States into which the Indian Empire split) and Ceylon were made independent, self-governing Dominions of the British Commonwealth of Nations. In 1949 Eire became a republic and seceded from the Commonwealth.

On 6th February, 1952, the whole empire was stunned by the news that George VI, the best of kings, had passed away.

After the end of the war a Victory Parade was held in London. The naval contingent marches past the King and Queen and the country's war leaders, who flank the royal platform.

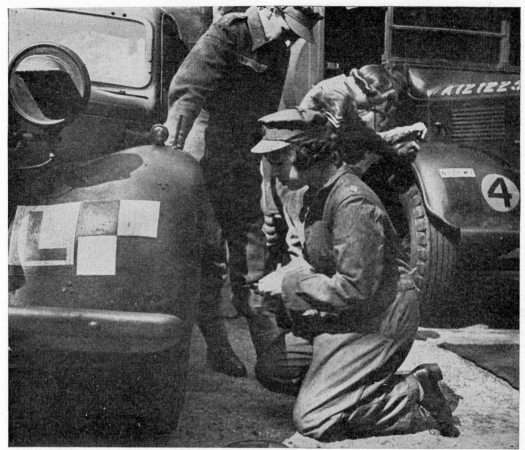

During the 1939–45 war, as Princess Elizabeth, the Queen joined the A.T.S. (now known as the W.R.A.C.) and she is here seen at a Training Centre learning to change a wheel.

ELIZABETH II

Our Gracious Young Queen

THE Princess Elizabeth, in company with her husband, the Duke of Edinburgh, was in Kenya when she received the tragic news of the sudden death of her father, George VI, on 6th February, 1952. Immediately the travellers embarked on the 4,400-mile flight home. At her first Privy Council the new Queen earnestly declared her resolve to follow her father's shining example of service and devotion to his people. She was crowned in Westminster Abbey on 2nd June of the following year. On the same day she had the pleasure of sending congratulations to the British expedition which had scaled the hitherto unconquered summit of

Mount Everest, the world's highest mountain.

Her Majesty was nearly twenty-six at the date of her accession, having been born on 21st April, 1926. Few children, royal or otherwise, can have enjoyed a happier home life and up-bringing. After she became heiress-presumptive to the throne the Princess was trained for her high station by careful teaching and an increasing practical experience of public life. During the Second World War she went into uniform, like millions of her father's other subjects. At eighteen she was granted a commission in the Auxiliary Territorial Service and passed all her driving tests. Through all these

She learns to tricycle, whilst her sister Margaret is still in her pram.

At a Charity Concert, shortly after her father had come to the throne.

A happy family group taken in 1946 at Windsor Castle, showing King George and Queen Elizabeth with their daughters and, of course, a favourite Corgi.

Princess Elizabeth with Prince Philip just after their engagement was announced.

The formal but very happy picture taken after the wedding in 1947.

In 1951 Princess Elizabeth and her husband pose with their children in the gardens of their home, Clarence House. Princess Anne, tired of photographers, crawls towards the flowers.

The State Coach waits as the Queen leaves Westminster Abbey annexe after her Coronation.

years her character was growing in strength and individuality, and her ideals of good faith and public service were developing. In 1947 she shared with her parents the novelties and excitements of a tour in South Africa, including 8,000 miles of journeying by special train. At Cape Town her twenty-first birthday was celebrated. The next great event of the year was the Princess's marriage, on 20th November, with Lieutenant Philip Mountbatten, a great-great-grandchild of Queen Victoria, formerly Prince of Greece and now Duke of Edinburgh. It was an ideal royal romance. On 14th November, 1948, Prince Charles was born, to be followed by Princess Anne on 15th August, 1950. Further lengthy travels followed these happy events. In 1951 the Princess and her husband flew the Atlantic for a tour of Canada.

The Queen steps ashore at Sydney, Australia, to begin her Royal Tour. The very extensive tours which the Queen and her husband have undertaken since her accession, have bound the countries of the British Commonwealth ever more closely together.

Then, in the succeeding year, while they were in Kenya, on their way to visit Australia and New Zealand, came the news of King George's death.

The Queen's unwearied devotion to her royal duties has made her gracious presence and happy smile familiar to her subjects on countless public occasions. And the popular Duke of Edinburgh, with his keen interest in industry and science and national activities in general, has been similarly prominent. In 1953 the royal pair made a six-month, 50,000-mile tour of the West Indies, Australasia and Ceylon, returning by Aden, Uganda, Malta and Gibraltar. A trip to Norway in 1955 gave them a sight of the famous and fascinating Kon-Tiki raft. Not the least successful of their overseas expeditions to date was a visit to Nigeria in January-February, 1956. This honour immensely gratified the Queen's white and coloured subjects and, indeed, completely turned the heads of the enraptured natives.

In 1954 Britain agreed to the progressive withdrawal of her remaining troops from Egypt. In 1956 Egypt seized the Suez Canal from the Canal Company and the whole question of ownership and use has since been the subject of considerable upheaval.

In Europe generally the coming of the longed-for era of settled peace and international concord was, and still is, delayed by the attitude of Russia. In 1955 the German Federal Republic, by arrangement with the western powers, became an independent sovereign State and joined the defence system which the West was building up to meet possible Russian aggression. Meantime the world's scientists were still blissfully engrossed in peering into the secrets of atomic power. In 1952 Britain made her first test explosion of an atomic bomb. Since then the United States, Russia and Britain have manufactured the even more shattering hydrogen bomb. Repeated endeavours to come to an agreement with Russia for banning atomic warfare and generally reducing armaments have so far been frustrated by mutual distrust. This is the prime problem which mankind has to solve. The choice lies, as Sir Winston Churchill once said, between supreme catastrophe and measureless reward. We have been warned!

The Royal Family photographed at Buckingham Palace after the Coronation of Queen Elizabeth II. *Left to right:* H.R.H. Princess Alexandra of Kent, H.R.H. Prince Michael of Kent, H.R.H. the Duchess of Kent, H.R.H. Princess Margaret, H.R.H. the Duke of Gloucester, H.M. The Queen, H.R.H. the Duke of Edinburgh, H.M. Queen Elizabeth, the Queen Mother, H.R.H. the Duke of Kent, H.R.H. the Princess Royal, H.R.H. the Duchess of Gloucester. H.R.H. Prince William of Gloucester. H.R.H. Prince Richard of Gloucester.

ALBERT SCHWEITZER

A Life spent in the Service of Others

IT IS strange that a doctor who treats negroes in Equatorial Africa should spend his holidays rescuing old organs from the scrap-heap; but Dr. Albert Schweitzer has a regard not only for all living things but for beautiful things as well. The old organs of Europe, with their somewhat old-fashioned look, gilded pipes, richly decorated cases with carvings of angels and cherubs, seemed to be out-of-date and rather silly in the modern age of electric trains, radio and high-speed aeroplanes.

" Can't we have a new organ? " said many church councils, " one with bright new shining pipes—a high-powered electric motor to blow the wind—a bright new console with all the latest gadgets for our fine organist, who can play faster than most, or we shall lose him to a church with a more modern outlook than our own! " Thus, several old organs were torn down from their galleries, and fine, bright, efficient factory organs, with three or four times their power, were put in their place.

When such stories came to the ears of Dr. Schweitzer, he was moved to serious action. It takes a lot of courage to tell a committee that they are wrong and you are right, and it is surprising how obstinate a committee can be in such matters. But, Albert Schweitzer is an obstinate man, too. In fact, he is about the most obstinate man there is.

Son of a parson, he studied theology and music, and wrote, when still a young man, one of the most outstanding books in theology, *The Quest of the Historical Jesus*. He also wrote a book about Bach, which was to become the standard work on this composer. He was therefore regarded as one of the most promising men of his generation, and he travelled far and wide giving organ recitals, and at the same time his reputation as a theologian was recognised as very considerable. His future therefore was assured, for he had

A man of outstanding character, Dr. Schweitzer combines the professions of theologian, missionary, surgeon, writer and musician.

gifts far above the average both intellectual and artistic; he had, moreover, a strong constitution.

SCHWEITZER'S GREAT DECISION

In the year 1905 Schweitzer carried out the resolve that had been in his mind for some time. It was, that as he had by now reached the age of thirty, he would henceforth devote his energies and talents to the service of his fellow-men. The chief difficulty that confronted him was the means of doing this effectively. Just preaching the Gospel did not seem to him enough; even music seemed to him to be inadequate as a means of benefiting his fellows. He felt the need for doing something more practical.

Now, when a great and sincere mind is in doubt as to what to do next, and is in no great hurry to try and do silly and inadequate things, just to still his conscience, there comes very often a direct answer to the appeal for guidance. It came to Schweitzer.

One day, while idly turning over the pages of a magazine of the Paris Missionary Society, he read that the Mission had not enough workers in the Northern Province of the

Congo Colony. From that moment he knew where his own work was to be done. He decided to be a medical missionary in Equatorial Africa.

To some people things come easily—certain skills and gifts are bestowed upon the few that are denied to others. Schweitzer always seemed to have to work the hard way—and it must be admitted that the hard way takes the longest time. He had now, therefore, to take up another study besides Theology, Philosophy and Music. He had to study medicine, and this meant that at the University where he was already a member of the staff as a lecturer he had to re-enlist himself as a student!

Here then was his first hurdle: hours and hours of wearisome study in subjects in which often he found little to interest him; but Schweitzer cultivated the art of making difficult and uninteresting subjects a personal challenge.

During the next eight years he spent his time preparing himself for his great work. He had not only to learn the theory of medicine, but he had to learn and practise his skill at surgery, and master that special field of medicine to heal diseases to be found in the tropics. The hard way was always for Schweitzer.

There are many places on the surface of the globe where missionaries are required, in cities as well as in country districts, by white people as well as black, and in temperate climates as well as in tropical areas. But Schweitzer chose the most helpless and backward people in the remotest and most uncomfortable spot on the face of the earth, because he believed that only by doing the work that a Christian was expected to do could he be truly fulfilling the task he felt he had been called upon to perform.

A LONE PILGRIMAGE

When Christian in *The Pilgrim's Progress* set out on his lone pilgrimage, he encountered difficulties and opposition on all sides. The opposition was sometimes open, sometimes secret, and came from both friends and enemies. And so it was with Schweitzer when he embarked upon his chosen path. The first piece of opposition came from the Paris Missionary Society itself. They could not accept Schweitzer because of his heretical views, and only on the promise that he would not teach religion would he be allowed to

practise as a doctor! Then, too, opposition came from his own personal friends who tried to persuade him, either that he was running away from life, or maybe that he was trying to hide his grief over an unfortunate love affair, or that perhaps he was unhappy because he was not making sufficient reputation for himself in music.

When these persuasions failed, they tried to tell him that he was too good a man for Europe to lose—he ought to remember his debt to civilisation in Europe, instead of hiding himself in the African jungle—looking after a lot of sick negroes who would not appreciate him anyway.

But Schweitzer had made up his mind and he had considered one thing further, which shows us one of the finest traits in his character; he considered that, should he fail (a fact he could not overlook), he would still have sufficient courage left to face the fact and his friends on his return.

But he was not to fail. The oppositions he faced—he faced calmly and serenely, for in his own words, " anyone who proposes to do good must not expect people to roll stones out of his way, but must accept his lot calmly even if they roll a few more upon it."

PREPARING FOR HIS NEW LIFE

The study and development of his own knowledge and skill as a doctor did not complete his preparations for Africa—he had to gather together all the equipment, stores and medicines. Nor was this easy to a man who had for many years been a student of Theology, Philosophy and Music.

The tedious job of making lists, inspecting stores, packing equipment, and at the same time studying this, to him, new science, was a further trial; and let it not be thought for a moment he was the " happy warrior " who is so frequently the hero of fiction. He summed up his difficulties " that the study would mean a tremendous effort, I had no manner of doubt—I did, in fact, look forward to the next few years with dread." And then he went on to say " but the reasons . . . weighed so heavily that other considerations were as dust in the balance."

There was the ever-present further difficulty of obtaining the necessary money to furnish his hospital and maintain it once it was

Doctor Schweitzer directs work in the plantation at Lambaréné. There they grow many thousands of fruit trees as well as palm oil trees, bananas, manioc, rice and vegetables which keep the hospital supplied with food.

After supper the Doctor's time is divided between writing and music. Behind him on the wall are the finished pages of his latest book where they are hung to protect them from ants.

In the hospital grounds two gentle young gazelles come to Dr. Schweitzer to be petted. The one on the right is nuzzling his pocket hopefully for titbits.

before the doctor had unpacked his instruments and opened his medicines, there were natives from many hundreds of miles away, awaiting his treatment. The difficulty of housing the patients was made worse, as many of them had come with a companion, and these, too, had to be fed and housed. Food for these companions had to be found, and the natives schooled in the elementary facts of behaviour and cleanliness. Gratitude for the help given was best shown by them giving to the doctor gifts of money and food in exchange for medicines.

With the ever-growing number of patients, it was necessary to build huts and houses to accommodate those who were bedridden, and to house their companions, and in some cases their entire families. This was accomplished by arduous labour, the doctor himself helping in all the heavy toil involved in sawing and planing the timber and digging the foundations

HEALING, PREACHING AND MUSIC-MAKING

To the doctor's great joy he was permitted by the authorities, after a short time, to preach as well as heal. A specially-made pianoforte with organ pedals attached, that the Paris Bach Society had given him, enabled him to practise for half an hour each day. So, very slowly, but surely, the hospital in Lambaréné, founded in a hen-house, began to grow in size and stature.

In August, 1914, war in Europe broke out, and Schweitzer was forced to abandon his medical work in Africa to benefit the negroes, because white people in Europe were at war with one another. The irony of the situation! A white man forced to end his work in benefiting primitive negroes who were not even Christian, because so-called Christian nations, with all the benefits and advantages of civilisation, were at war.

Many men would have railed and fumed and wasted their energies in such a predicament. We must not think that Schweitzer was not disheartened—he would have been a lesser man than he is had he not felt the awful injustice of the situation—but the fact is, he was not quite so sure that " civilisation " was the ideal way of life, in any case.

He was not sure that progress, in the accepted sense of the word, was inevitably to the good.

established. The royalties on sales of his book on Bach helped to finance his undertaking, and his recitals, and the generosity of his friends who, when they could see he was really bent on his undertaking, and that nothing would dissuade him, made handsome gifts. On the afternoon of Good Friday, 1913, Schweitzer —now thirty-eight—and his wife left Günsbach for Equatorial Africa.

A HEN-HOUSE FOR A HOSPITAL

When we see a modern hospital to-day with its imposing brick front, its polished plate-glass doors, its shining corridors, its spotless linen and its brisk and business-like nurses, sweet-smelling disinfectants and airy rooms, we feel we are in an establishment that works with the precision of a machine, and the efficiency of a factory. It was doubtless in such hospitals that Schweitzer was trained and there, too, his wife, a nurse, also learned her craft. It is such an establishment as this that we think of when we hear or see the word hospital. But that is not what awaited Schweitzer in Lambaréné. Labourers were hard to obtain and most of the buildings were of corrugated iron, and so Schweitzer's first hospital was housed in a fowl-house.

In tropical Africa news travels fast, and

A leper arrives at the hospital after travelling for more than five days by dug-out canoe. He
used his paddle to help him hobble from the river and it lies beside him as he wearily unwraps
the filthy rags with which he has bound his feet, swollen with leprosy.

He was not sure that because we in our time have advantages of civilisation not granted to our forbears, we are from that fact better men and women, and automatically more worthy than our ancestors. He felt it nothing less than a duty, therefore, to express these doubts in some form that could challenge and if possible arrest a doctrine which suggests that progress, without a sense of direction, is even sensible.

" REVERENCE FOR LIFE "

Within two days of his internment he set to work to write a Philosophy of Civilisation. To accomplish this task he had to examine the philosophies of many civilisations and aspects of thought. In contemplation of these problems he discovered what can be called the kernel of his own philosophy in the phrase " reverence for life." This is a very difficult philosophy to understand, with all that it implies, but it does imply that if thought be given to any action with this end in view, considerable amendment to our ways and behaviour will result.

In 1917, three years after the outbreak of war, Schweitzer, who had only recently been allowed to resume his work, was hustled out of Lambaréné by the authorities to be taken back to Europe to be placed in a camp for prisoners-of-war.

In the prison camp he had to be content to practise the organ by playing on the table and imagining the pedals on the floor; and try as best he could to write a few chapters of his book on civilisation. In time, with the exchange of prisoners being effected, Schweitzer and his wife found themselves once again in

The only way of getting supplies to and from the hospital by river is in these dug-out canoes. The wine-keg which the Doctor is holding is used for carrying the precious filtered water.

Alsace. Weary, ill and destitute, they returned to the valley, now in the throes of bombardment, whence they had gone forth in the name of civilisation to help the savages of Equatorial Africa.

In 1919 he was sufficiently recovered from a serious operation to accept a lecture tour in Sweden. The following year he wrote his most popular account of his experiences in a book, *On the Edge of the Primeval Forest*, which has gone into countless editions and been translated into many languages. Now followed extensive work throughout Europe as a lecturer and recitalist, and as a preparation for another expedition to Lambaréné he took a further course in the study of tropical diseases, obstetrics and dentistry. In 1924 he again embarked for Lambaréné.

A SAD RETURN

When he arrived the scene which greeted him was one of heart-breaking desolation and decay. His hospital was a shell, the roof rotted away, the native-built structures had collapsed, paths were so overgrown that the tracks were almost impossible to trace. So now, eleven years after his first assault on the jungle, Schweitzer had to begin all over again.

One can hardly believe a man would have enough courage to begin again a work that

Seen here with her pet monkey, Trudi Bochsler, a Swiss nurse, has come to Lambaréné to devote her nursing skill to the African lepers.

had almost been obliterated, not only by the folly of man, but by Nature herself.

One of the most poignant diaries in existence is the diary of Captain Scott of the Antarctic, when he describes the misery, desolation and despair of his condition and that of his comrades. Not less poignant is the description that the doctor writes of his assistants and himself in this first year of his second period in Lambaréné.

Out of this period of desolation was born a new and even greater resolution. The whole of the hospital must be moved two miles upstream to a site more suitable for expansion. Of course, by now there were helpers who had given their services to the hospital; nurses and doctors from Europe, and natives had again been enlisted for much of the manual labour; but as Dr. Seaver has written, " there was only one man who could plan and design, only one who could superintend the building, for his was the only authority the natives would recognise without question." This labour alone would take a year, but as Schweitzer was planning a long-term policy, one year was not considered too much time to give to the project.

BUILDING UP A NEW LIFE

By 1927 things were once more sufficiently established to allow the doctor to return to

A nurse taking a sick child to hospital. The mother had given her a witch-doctor's "cure" which only aggravated the illness. Ignorance and superstition are difficult to eradicate.

Europe to give recitals and lectures, and thus to obtain money for his hospital. By the end of 1929 the doctor was back in Lambaréné and was not in Europe again until 1931.

Such was the pattern of his life, incessant arduous labour in Equatorial Africa which exhausted him in mind, body and spirit; a return to Europe to refresh his exhausted body and soul, collecting money by giving lectures and organ recitals and publishing books, until he had built a hospital to accommodate 400 patients and attended by several doctors and nurses from Europe, who had been inspired by the personal devotion of the great doctor, to join him in his selfless task of caring for the less fortunate in the tropical jungle.

He does not work a mere eight-hour day. He begins work at 6.45 a.m. and does not finish until after midnight, fighting not only disease, but his own fatigue. His whole life is a life of devotion—in active service for his fellow-men.

A GREAT MAN PLAYS GREAT MUSIC

Fortunately for us, Schweitzer has made a large number of gramophone records of his organ-playing, and we can, if we wish, listen to him playing the works of the great Bach on the organ at All Hallows, Barking, St. Aurélie, Strasbourg, and the organ at Günsbach, which

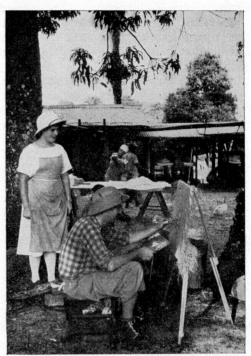

Fritz Hug is shown here with his sister, Vrene, who is the hospital dietician.

Working on a canvas woven from palm fronds, Fritz Hug paints Dr. Schweitzer's portrait.

has been reconstructed to his specification.

Some of these records may be a disappointment to the hearer who expects dazzlingly brilliant performances. The slow tempo of the music as played by Schweitzer, the long passages without changing the stops or manuals, and the somewhat inflexible rhythm have all been criticised, but the overwhelming sublimity of the content of the music is so clearly brought out and the clarity of each part so well moulded, that one gradually becomes conscious of hearing familiar music, as it were, for the first time.

Herein lies the charm of Schweitzer's interpretation. We are drawn towards the inner heart of the music itself—and only a great artist can give us this experience. It is small wonder that a great man plays great music in a great way. For Schweitzer is one of the greatest men of our generation and, like Chaucer's poor parson,

He waited after no pomp and reverence
Nor made him a light conscience
But Christ's love, and His apostles twelve,
He taught, but first he followed it himself.

SIR WINSTON CHURCHILL

THE hour, it is said, brings the man; and when the story of the twentieth century is written, the name of one man will blaze through it gloriously, the name of Winston Leonard Spencer Churchill, who rallied the shattered forces of freedom at a time when the dark shadow of tyranny lay triumphantly across half the world.

A FAMOUS NAME

The name of Churchill, of course, was by no means unknown in other eras. It had resounded throughout Europe at the beginning of the eighteenth century when John Churchill, first Duke of Marlborough and commander of the armies of the Grand Alliance, smashed the power of France in a series of magnificent victories that proved him one of the greatest soldiers of all time. Parliament acknowledged its debt to him by gifting him the fifteen hundred acres of the manor of Woodstock, near Oxford. In addition, Blenheim Palace was built for him and named after his greatest triumph. It was in this palace that Winston Churchill was born on 30th November, 1874. His father was Lord Randolph Churchill, a younger son of the seventh Duke of Marlborough and a well-known politician. His mother was Jeanette Jerome, a beautiful American heiress.

SCHOOLDAYS

The future Prime Minister's schooldays were neither happy nor encouraging. He was sent first of all to a small private school run by a cruel and senseless brute. Young Winston's defiance of this man became legendary in the school but the experience, which lasted two years, undermined his health and twice he was dangerously ill with pneumonia. This explains why he later went to Harrow instead of to Eton, where the Churchills usually went. Harrow was on a hill and therefore, in the view of Winston's mother, more suitable for a boy with a weak chest. The staff at Harrow, however, may have suspected, when young Churchill arrived there, that it was rather his brain that was weak. He made a deplorable showing at the entrance examination. Soon he was firmly established in the lowest position in the lowest class. During his whole stay at Harrow, he never advanced beyond the Lower School. Latin, Greek and mathematics he refused steadfastly to learn; yet he won a prize for reciting, faultlessly, twelve hundred lines from Macaulay's *Lays of Ancient Rome*. He despised cricket and football too, but he won the Public Schools' Fencing Championship.

SANDHURST AND THE ARMY

Lord Randolph Churchill was disappointed by his son's apparent shortcomings and decided that the only career that held out any hopes for him was in the army. Winston passed the examination for Sandhurst at his third attempt, finishing so far down the list that he was only accepted for the cavalry, a branch of the army that was willing to do without cleverness as long as a young officer could afford the considerable expense that was involved in the upkeep of his horses. Yet it was against this unpromising background that young Churchill began to find himself and to show the earliest signs of the phenomenal energy and drive that were to propel him to greatness. He was commissioned in 1895 and posted to the 4th Hussars, stationed at Aldershot. Two months previously, his father had died and the brand new 2nd Lieutenant was forced to consider some method of supplementing his income. There was a minor revolution going on in Cuba against the Spaniards at that time and Winston Churchill saw here an opportunity of turning to advantage the five months leave to which cavalry officers were entitled annually as a kind of compensation for being paid a mere fourteen shillings a day. He approached a newspaper and offered to cover the Cuban campaign. The newspaper agreed and Winston Churchill's career as a writer was launched. He returned from Cuba, having enjoyed himself immensely, to discover that his regiment was under orders for India.

SERVICE IN INDIA AND EGYPT

In India, he studied fiercely to make up for the years wasted at school. He was supremely happy in the army, but he was conscious, too, that it was not enough. When fighting broke out on the North-West Frontier, he pulled various strings and travelled two thousand miles across India to take part in the campaign as correspondent for an Indian newspaper. When it was all over, he wrote a book called *The Malakand Field Force* which gave an account of the fighting and was a great success. In 1898, he was in the thick of battle again, this time in Egypt where a campaign was being waged against the Dervish Army. The critical battle was at Omdurman where the British Army won a great victory against overwhelming odds. Winston Churchill, by now with the 21st Lancers, took part in what was to prove the last cavalry charge in British military history and sent back an account of it to the *Morning Post* for which he was acting as correspondent. Later he wrote *The River War*, which was hailed by the critics but made him a great many enemies, because of his forthright criticism of certain aspects of the campaign. Churchill was unperturbed. He had already decided that the great future that he had planned for himself lay elsewhere. He had become preoccupied with politics. In March, 1899, he resigned from the army. In June of the same year, he stood for Parliament at Oldham but was defeated. The setback was temporary; for by the end of the year Winston Churchill was a national hero.

THE BOER WAR

It was the Boer War that catapulted him to fame. Shortly after its outbreak in 1899, the

In 4th Queen's Own Hussars uniform in 1895.

Morning Post commissioned him to act as their special correspondent at the huge salary—for those days—of £250 per month. Churchill sailed for South Africa and, having reached there, began to make his way towards Ladysmith where the fiercest fighting seemed likely to be. At the town of Estcourt, he learned that Ladysmith had been cut off and that no one apparently knew what was likely to happen to Estcourt itself. An armoured train was sent out to reconnoitre and one of its passengers was the *Morning Post*'s special correspondent. The train was ambushed and Winston Churchill distinguished himself in the fierce fight that ensued. Victory went to the Boers, however, and Churchill found himself a prisoner in Pretoria. He had not the slightest intention of remaining there; so one night he climbed over the wall and walked off into the darkness. He found a railway line and hid himself in a goods train. He jumped off this at dawn and spent the daylight hours hidden in a clump of trees. That night he made contact with an Englishman who kept him hidden for three days down a coalmine. At the end of that time, he smuggled himself aboard a train bound for Lourenço Marques in Portuguese East Africa where he arrived safely, concealed among bales of wool.

Lord Randolph Churchill, father of Sir Winston, and a well-known politician.

On 7th January, 1911, a group of anarchists barricaded themselves into a house in Sidney Street in the East End of London and fired from the windows at the police and the fire brigade who tried to deal with them. A detachment of the Scots Guards was ordered to the scene. Churchill, as Home Secretary, witnessed the " battle " and later gave evidence in court.

A steamer took him to Durban and a triumphal welcome. He discovered that the Boers had put a price—£25—on his head and that the newspapers in Europe had been headlining his exploits. For the next few months, he served with the South African Light Horse. Then another election became imminent and he obtained permission to return home. Once again, he stood as Conservative candidate for Oldham; but this time the result was different. He won the seat and at the age of twenty-six began his parliamentary career.

THE POLITICIAN

It was to be a career of ups and downs; and there were to be times when, as a career, it would seem to have come to an end. Winston Churchill was too dynamic a personality ever to fit easily into the pattern of a party. He very quickly proved this in 1904 when he found himself unable to agree with the Conservative Party, of which he was a member, on the issue of Free Trade. Accordingly, he left their ranks and threw in his lot with the Liberals. Promotion soon followed and at the age of thirty-one, he was Under-Secretary of State for the Colonies. In this capacity, he was responsible for putting through the measures which gave complete self-government to the Transvaal and the Orange Free State. By a strange coincidence, one of the Boer leaders with whom he came in contact at this time was Louis Botha, the very man who had taken him prisoner during the attack on the armoured train.

FIRST LORD OF THE ADMIRALTY

It seemed at this time as though nothing could stop the young and ambitious politician. Soon he was a Privy Councillor. At the age of thirty-four, he was a Cabinet Minister. Soon he was Home Secretary and in 1911 there came his most important and fateful appointment to date when he was appointed First Lord of the Admiralty. For several years now, Churchill had been increasingly aware of the growing power and menace of Germany and her challenge to Britain. The two nations had hovered on the brink of war following the Agadir incident of 1911 and the actual outbreak seemed only to be delayed. Churchill threw himself almost passionately into the task of making use of the time that remained. He reorganised the Admiralty, putting it on an immediate war footing. He recalled the fiery

Lord Fisher, the greatest sailor since Nelson according to knowledgeable opinion, from his retirement in Italy and together these two thrustful men reorganised the British Fleet; so that when war did finally break out in 1914, the Navy was thoroughly prepared for immediate action. As the war grew in intensity, however, a clash between the two powerful personalities became almost inevitable. It came to a head over the question of the Dardenelles campaign, a campaign which, although brilliant and audacious in conception, turned out, for various reasons, to be completely disastrous in practice. Winston Churchill was made the scapegoat for the debacle and in May, 1915, he was removed from his post. It seemed that his political career, that had so recently seemed so promising, was now in ruins. Meanwhile the war raged on and Winston Churchill, returned to the army and commanded the 6th Royal Scots Fusiliers in France. He arrived there in November and for the next seven months, he was involved in the war at close quarters. It was not until June, 1916, that he returned to his parliamentary duties and another year elapsed before Lloyd George, the new Prime Minister and a lifelong friend of Winston Churchill, brought him back into the government as Minister of Munitions.

IN AND OUT OF OFFICE

The end of the war brought its own problems and following the election just after the Armistice, Churchill was made Minister of War. In 1921, he was shifted to the Colonial Office where he dealt very efficiently with the Middle East problem and brought about a settlement of the grievous Irish question. But already he was beginning to be less and less in sympathy with the Liberal Party. Ideally, he would have liked the Liberals and Conservatives to settle their differences and had even gone so far as to put forward the idea of a Centre Party which would be made up of the moderates of both sides. When this idea failed, Churchill was forced to consider his own position which more and more inclined to the Conservatives. In 1922, he was defeated in an election at Dundee and was out of politics for two years. He used the time to write *The World Crisis*, an excellent book on the war that had only recently ended. This, apparently, was not able to absorb all his astonishing energy; for he began to turn out paintings which were highly praised by experts

In 1911 H.M.S. *Centurion* was launched as part of the programme for the reorganisation of the Fleet. Churchill (*second right*) arrives for the launching ceremony with Lord Fisher (*second left*), whose expert assistance Churchill had sought to improve the Navy.

Churchill with Lloyd George in 1915.

like the great Augustus John. Writing and painting, nevertheless, were merely incidental. He was unhappy outside the stirring world of politics; and he had made up his mind to rejoin the Conservatives. In 1924, the Labour Government fell and the country returned a Conservative Government to power. Stanley Baldwin was the new Prime Minister and one of his first actions was to appoint Winston Churchill Chancellor of the Exchequer. The next five years were the least successful of his career. By 1929, he was out of office and out of favour everywhere. For the next ten years, he was, politically speaking, condemned to wander in the wilderness.

A PERIOD " IN THE WILDERNESS "

Perhaps at no other time in his long life was Winston Churchill called upon to display, to such an extent, all his reserves of courage, patience and endurance. He was without power to influence events, yet he alone, of all the men in Parliament, really saw clearly the trend of these events. He watched the emergence of a

Churchill is seen with ambassadors of this country's allies during the 1939-45 war. Represented here are the U.S.A., Poland, China, U.S.S.R., Greece, Yugoslavia, and Norway.

As the Royal Family wave to the cheering crowds from the balcony of Buckingham Palace on the day Germany surrendered, there beside them stood Churchill, the architect of that victory.

new and aggressive Germany and time and again warned the Government precisely what the intentions of this new Germany were. He brought forward evidence that the Germans were secretly and illegally re-arming and on this subject he was better and more accurately informed than the Foreign Office. Yet all his warnings were jeered at and went unheeded. Even when he was proved right, nothing was done about it. Looking back at the history of the thirties, it is almost incredible that such a state of affairs could have existed. It is saddening, too, to reflect that had Churchill been heeded, the Second World War might never have happened.

CHURCHILL TAKES COMMAND

However, he was not heeded. Hitler came to power in 1933 and worked hand in glove with the Italian dictator Mussolini to undermine the democracies of Europe. Year by year, the situation became more and more beyond control. The Italians seized Abyssinia. The Germans tried out their new aircraft in Spain. The British Government stood weakly by, content to try a policy of appeasement; but in the end, appeasement was not enough and on 3rd September, 1939, Neville Chamberlain broadcast to the nation that Britain was now at war with Germany. On the 10th May, 1940, with the German troops attacking Holland, Chamberlain resigned and the new Prime Minister, Winston Churchill, took over. For the next five years, he was Britain. Never before

in history has a leader commanded such a completely united nation. When things were going badly, he came before them and told them the truth and they responded with courage. Even when the country stood alone, surrounded by gloating and triumphant enemies, there was no thought of surrender. The German *Luftwaffe* was shattered in the Battle of Britain. The night bombing of the cities began and the country endured, spurred on by its dauntless Premier. Gradually, the tide began to turn. America was brought into the war and Britain began to take the offensive. That she was able to do so, after all the punishment she had taken, was largely due to one man; and the victory was the outcome of his leadership.

A GREAT MAN

When the war ended, he lost office when the Labour Government came to power. He regained the Prime Ministership, then retired, handing the reins over to Sir Anthony Eden. He remained, however, in Parliament for the simple reason that politics had been and always would be his life. The only reward he accepted was a knighthood. He asked for nothing more. For services such as his there can be no adequate reward. General Eisenhower, Supreme Commander of the Allied Expeditionary Force and later President of the United States, summed it all up when he said of Britain's wartime leader:

" *Only history can measure even remotely the service he rendered to us all.*"

In September 1938 the Rt. Hon. Neville Chamberlain, M.P., the Prime Minister, flew to
Germany to establish personal contact with Hitler and, he hoped, avoid war.

THE SECOND WORLD WAR

THE war of 1939–45 was a natural consequence of the First World War and the
Treaty of Versailles that concluded it; which
is rather pitiful when you recall that the first
conflict was fought as " the war to end wars."

The ruinous economic depression that
blighted Europe after World War I hit Germany
all the harder because of the staggering burden
of reparations, or compensation for war
damage, heaped on her shoulders by the
victors. She was let off eventually; but, in the
universal trade slump then prevailing, the
miseries of want and mass-unemployment remained to afflict her people. Added to these
hardships were the bitter humiliation of defeat,
the widespread illusion that her armies had not
really been broken in the war and the feeling
that the Allies had tricked her into submitting
to the harsh terms of the peace treaty. The
resulting sense of national grievance prepared
the way for the uprising of the ex-corporal
Adolf Hitler and his National Socialist (Nazi)

party. Hitler was unquestionably a genius of
sorts, but he was an evil genius for Germany.
His daring aims and fanatical personality in-
toxicated his followers with bright visions of a
fatherland restored to power and prosperity in a
glorious triumph over its oppressors.

HITLER'S RISE TO POWER

In 1933 Hitler made himself dictator. Then,
shrewdly judging that the war-weary Western
Powers would not use force to restrain him, he
proceeded to flout the Versailles treaty by
building up his country's armed forces anew.
In March, 1936, he defied the treaty again by
marching his troops into the Rhineland—the
German province bordering Belgium and
Luxembourg which Germany had agreed to
leave demilitarised as a security measure. The
Western Powers might there and then have
taken him by the scruff of the neck and hurled
him back again. But, though seriously alarmed,
they lacked the unity and resolution to act.

APPEASEMENT

In 1937 Neville (son of the noted Imperialist Joseph) Chamberlain was head of the National —practically Conservative—Government in Britain. Above all things, Chamberlain dreaded another world war. He thought he could " appease " Hitler by a sympathetic discussion of Germany's grievances. He was to get a painful shock. In 1938 the dictator seized Austria. Next, he cast a hungry eye on the strongly-fortified Bohemian frontier districts of the republic of Czechoslovakia, which were largely German in population. But Czechoslovakia was allied with France and Russia, and Britain, too, might be aroused if he attacked it. Unfortunately, the republic's backers were not prepared for war. In September, Chamberlain, pursuing his policy of appeasement, practically handed the coveted districts to Hitler on a plate. The gratified tyrant thereupon declared that his territorial appetite was satisfied. Henceforth all was to be peace and concord. . . . Six months later he swallowed the remainder of the republic— which was *not* largely German in population. Chamberlain woke up. Hitler's design to dominate Europe had become plain to all.

THE OUTBREAK OF WAR

Poland's turn came next. Hitler demanded the cession of Danzig, which had been made a free city by the Treaty of Versailles. Poland refused and France and Britain promised to back up her resistance. War was drawing very near now and both sides angled hopefully for the friendship of Russia. It was Germany that hooked the monster fish, by a treaty securing Russia's neutrality in the event of war. On 1st September, 1939, Hitler invaded Poland. Two days later Britain and France declared war. So began the Second World War.

The destructive powers of military weapons had expanded enormously since the earlier conflict, and the sufferings and horrors they were now to inflict on Europe were proportionately intensified. The new or improved weapons and equipment revolutionised warfare. Armies were mechanised. Tanks, used in hundreds, gave them their " punch." Aeroplanes dominated land, sea and sky. Radio transformed communications and radar contributed its uncanny aid in tracking aircraft and shipping.

As in 1914, the British overseas Dominions rallied to the mother country. But the Irish Free State (which in 1937 had proclaimed " Eire "—in English " Ireland "— a sovereign, independent State, though retaining some ill-defined connection with the British Commonwealth), remained neutral.

THE PAUSE AND ATTACK

Unhappy Poland was throttled in a month and then carved up between Germany and Russia. In the West things were singularly quiet till April, 1940. Then suddenly the Germans pounced, by land, sea and air, on Denmark and Norway, largely to gain a base for attacks on British shipping. Gallant British and French attempts to oust the invaders failed. On 10th May the Germans burst into Holland and Belgium. In Britain, acute dissatisfaction over the failure in Norway and the critical situation in Belgium and northern France overthrew Chamberlain's government. The hour brought forth the man and Mr. Winston Churchill was called upon to form a more efficient and truly national government. Thenceforth his powerful and many-sided genius was to be the supreme directing force of all his country's energies.

DUNKIRK

The Germans now launched a masterly non-stop surprise attack in the Ardennes with their *Panzer* ("mail ") divisions of armoured troops. Employing a new technique of massed tanks and low-flying dive-bombers against an enemy woefully inferior in mechanisation and aircraft, their columns smashed clean through the Allied line. By 20th May they had driven right across northern France to Abbeville and reached the English Channel. The Anglo-French-Belgian forces cut off in the north were hemmed in. The Belgians, exhausted, gave up the fight. Their Allies were relentlessly squeezed into a narrow bridgehead around the French seaport of Dunkirk. Annihilation threatened them and only a miracle could avert it. The amazing thing is that the miracle happened. Ships of the British Navy and merchant fleet, seconded by a host of yachts, tugs, barges and other odd craft, many of them manned by their volunteer owners, performed the impossible. Between the end of May and early June no less than 338,000 of the hemmed-in British and French troops were snatched from the German jaws

The beach at Dunkirk at the height of the evacuation at the end of May 1940. It was painted by an eye-witness, the war artist Charles Cundall, who admirably conveys the scene.

Some of those evacuated from Dunkirk come thankfully ashore at Dover. French and British servicemen mingle, some with equipment, some without, but all determined to fight again.

A " Fieseler Storche " landing in the Place de
la Concorde, Paris—France was defeated.

that were closing on them and brought safely
across to England.

THE DEFEAT OF FRANCE

But France was beaten. Her more southern
armies were still in the field; but the country
was infected with political unrest and the troops
had little heart for continuing the struggle. On
22nd June the aged Marshal Pétain's government signed an armistice which surrendered all
northern and western France to Hitler's control.
Meantime the " valiant " dictator of Italy,
Mussolini (who had previously allied his
country with Germany after falling out with
the League of Nations over the seizure of
Abyssinia), decided that the time was ripe for
declaring war on France and Britain.

BRITAIN STANDS ALONE

Britain, sadly battered but defiant, stood
alone amid the wreckage of the Allied cause,
and the triumphant Hitler now bent all his
efforts to the task of smiting her down. Invasion preparations began; but first German
mastery of the air must be assured. In early
July a contest of deadly intensity was waged
between the R.A.F. and the German *Luftwaffe*
of four times its strength. On London the
bombs rained down death and devastation
regularly night and day for three weeks and
more. But her tight-lipped citizens showed an
awestruck world that " she could take it." The
ruinous raids were extended to the big industrial areas and ports and continued through-

out the winter and spring of 1940–41. But by
October, 1940, Hitler had been forced to admit
defeat in the air and to postpone his unsolicited
visit to England indefinitely. For the rest of the
war, with intervals, air raids (including the
later flying bombs and rockets) became an
accepted feature of everyday existence.

The land war that had been lost in the West
could only be re-won, if at all, by a stupendous
effort. That effort was not staged till 6th June,
1944 (known to the Allies as " D-Day "). We
can, therefore, turn to the other theatres of war
and follow the operations there up to that date.

WAR IN AFRICA

One of the liveliest of these theatres was
North Africa. There, the fortunes of the desert
war ebbed and flowed like the tide. The enemy's
purpose was to destroy Britain's power in the
Mediterranean, Egypt and the Red Sea and
thereby sever her communications with the
East. Already their submarines and aircraft
had made the Mediterranean a perilous place
for Allied shipping. Now, the completion of
the work was left to the braggart Mussolini.
Italy's land, sea and air power, being free
from other commitments, was overwhelmingly
superior to that which Britain could muster on
the spot. The Italian General Graziani, therefore, was in high hopes when, in September,
1940, he invaded Egypt from the neighbouring
Italian colony of Libya. In December General

British infantry charge an enemy position
during the campaign in North Africa, through
the dust and smoke of the battle.

Wavell's Army of the Nile went out to meet him. By February, 1941, his tanks and infantry had done some remarkable work. They had driven the Italians out of Egypt, reached Benghazi (500 miles from the starting point), annihilated a great enemy army and taken 130,000 prisoners, 400 tanks and 1,290 guns. The British losses were under 2,000 men. So much for Graziani's hopes.

GREECE, SOMALILAND AND ABYSSINIA

Unfortunately these dazzling successes were now to be interrupted. Greece was being attacked by Germany, and General Wavell's force was heavily drawn upon to aid her. The aid, especially in aircraft, proved insufficient. Greece fell and the British troops were transferred to Crete. But there too, when the Germans followed with airborne troops in May, their complete mastery in the air won the day. So Germany established her footing in the eastern Mediterranean.

Incidentally, in 1941, some slight consolation

In the Western Desert shortly before the Battle of El Alamein, Lord Trenchard with Lt.-Gen. Montgomery, G.O.C., Eighth Army.

for these failures was forthcoming from East Africa. British Somaliland, which had been taken by the Italians in the previous year, was regained. Italian Somaliland and Eritrea were captured. And stolen Abyssinia was recovered for its rightful ruler.

ROMMEL AND EL ALAMEIN

Back in Libya, in March-April, the first ebb tide in the fortunes of war had set in. The Germans, under the daring Rommel, had taken over and the British, drained in numbers and weakened in tanks, lost almost all their recent gains. The valuable seaport of Tobruk, now besieged, still remained to them, but General Wavell's main force was hustled back into Egypt. In the ensuing period (during which General Auchinleck replaced Wavell) the tide ebbed and flowed in the most bewildering manner. At length, in May-June, 1942, Rommel's superior tanks and guns had their way. Tobruk fell. The British were forced back, in a dour fighting retreat, deep into Egypt. At El Alamein they stood only sixty miles from Alexandria, the key to communications with the East. But there they turned at bay.

General Alexander now assumed control in Egypt. Under him General Montgomery, a careful organiser and gifted strategist, was given command of the reinforced army soon to become famous as " the Eighth Army." On

Gen. Rommel, German G.O.C. in North Africa.

During the great British offensive against the Germans and Italians in North Africa in the autumn of 1942, columns of British tanks and armoured cars moved up towards the front.

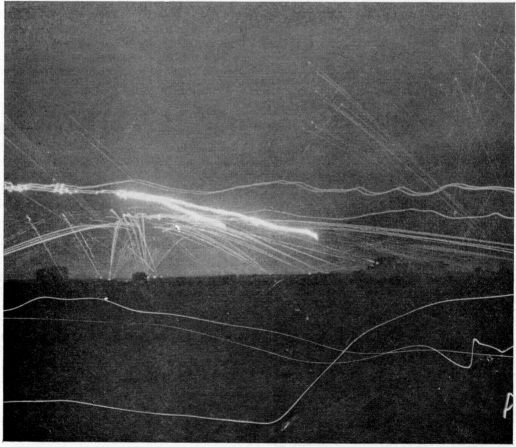

This night picture was taken during enemy air attacks on the new forward British position on 27th October, 1942, in the midst of the eleven-day Battle of El Alamein.

A knocked-out German tank's crew surrenders.

23rd October the decisive eleven-day battle of El Alamein began. It ended in the complete rout of the German and Italian Army. The tide had turned again in Britain's favour and this time finally. Montgomery now trundled the beaten foe before him westwards for a matter of 1,400 miles till he reached Tripoli in January, 1943. So much for the daring Rommel.

MOROCCO, ALGERIA AND TUNISIA

In December, 1941, the United States had entered the war in circumstances to be related presently. In November, 1942, Anglo-American armies, under the American General Eisenhower, had effected landings in the French colonies of Morocco and Algeria, which were still under the control of Pétain's defeatist government. Later they were joined by an army of French and colonial troops, ready to strike a blow for fallen France. The Allies' purpose was to co-operate with the Eighth Army in expelling the enemy from North Africa. This would open up the Mediterranean for Allied shipping and for further promising ventures. In April, 1943, the armies of Generals Eisenhower and Montgomery joined hands. The Germans were feverishly pouring fresh

Appropriate war-time reading matter.

troops into neighbouring Tunisia; but in May General Alexander, acting as Deputy Commander of the Allied forces, gave them the knock-out blow. A quarter of a million prisoners went into the bag and North Africa was cleared.

THE ITALIAN CAMPAIGN

The first of the further promising ventures was General Alexander's conquest of Sicily in July-August. The next comprised landings on and around the " toe " of Italy in September. Already, however, Mussolini had been thrown out by his own people and a new Italian government secretly agreed to unconditional

As the British advanced so the prisoners trekked in thousands to the rear.

General Alexander, Deputy Commander of the Allied Forces, defeated the Germans in Tunisia and was later victorious in Italy.

The capture of Cassino, Italy, in May 1944, was only effected after heavy fighting. Scots Guards Bren gunners amidst the ruins.

surrender. But the Germans took over the defence of the country, and the Anglo-American and other troops (the Eighth Army among them) had to fight their way up the leg of Italy bit by bit. On 4th June, 1944, two days before D-Day, they got about as far as the knee. The Americans jubilantly entered Rome and the enemy was in full retreat to new positions farther north.

THE INVASION OF RUSSIA

The next theatre of war to be visited is an unexpected one. Hitler's treaty of friendship with Russia in August, 1939, had been a mere stop-gap. He had never felt sure of his new and powerful friend's sincerity and a time came when, apart from other considerations, he needed to secure command of Russia's vast resources in food, oil and other supplies. So in

Winter warfare north-west of Stalingrad. White-clad Russian shock troops run to the attack. The conditions in which this campaign was fought were appalling and casualties were heavy.

Britain sent large consignments of war material, which she could ill spare, to Archangel to assist her ally, Russia. A near miss when a convoy was attacked.

June, 1941, he suddenly turned about and launched his armies against her. Britain no longer stood alone. She had gained an ally. True, her new partnership was an uneasy one. Russia was a revolutionary, Communist and aggressive state and there could never be any real trust or cordiality between the two countries. But all differences were for the moment submerged in the immediate need to smash the common enemy. Britain regularly sent large consignments of war material to Archangel, though she could ill spare them and the convoys suffered heavy losses from German submarines.

Hitler's legions, operating over a front that reached from the Baltic to the Black Sea, drove rapidly and confidently forward. By December, 1941, they stood within forty miles of Moscow. In the south they reached the River Volga in August, 1942. But there, at Stalingrad, a titanic three-month contest ended in complete disaster. It was war on a gigantic scale, with millions of troops and thousands of tanks and guns engaged on fronts hundreds of miles long. The weight of the inexhaustible Russian masses —" the Russian steam-roller "—told in the end. The invading hosts were ground down, or pushed back, with staggering losses When D-Day dawned the Russians had almost entirely liberated their homeland and were still pressing westwards on the heels of the exhausted foe.

PEARL HARBOUR

The Far East front opened even more sensationally than the Russian. Japan, like Italy, had sided with Germany because of the opposition of the League of Nations to a war of aggression, in this case against China. Possessing the third largest fleet in the world, her ambition was to be top dog in the East. On 7th December, 1941, when the United States were still at peace, she made a diabolically

Pearl Harbour, where the American Pacific Fleet lay at anchor, after the Japanese attack in December 1941, with ships on fire or sunk and dockside petrol installations ablaze.

Men of the Buffs during the Burma campaign had to hound out the Japanese individually.

treacherous raid by carrier-borne aircraft on Pearl Harbour, in the Hawaiian Islands, and put the unsuspecting American Pacific Fleet out of action. It was a major catastrophe; but it brought the United States into the war. For several months afterwards the faithless Japanese were indeed top dog in the Pacific. Britain could do little against them. Her resources were already stretched to breaking point in other quarters and she was lamentably weak in the Far East.

WAR IN THE FAR EAST

The top dog was quick to take advantage of the situation and bite and bite again. The greater portion of the East Indies, the Philippines and New Guinea, was snapped up. On 15th February, 1942, British arms suffered a humiliating disaster: the key naval base of Singapore, attacked from landward, was

Photographed at Yalta in the Crimea with their advisers, Churchill, Roosevelt and Stalin,
who met to discuss the future conduct of the war.

stormed. In March, Rangoon, the capital of Burma, fell and the whole country was yielded up when the British and native army withdrew behind the Chindwin River into Assam. India itself stood in danger.

By May, however, Uncle Sam was recovering his breath after the foul blow below the belt at Pearl Harbour. During the ensuing two years a series of combats (in many of which Australian units distinguished themselves) raged with sustained and devastating fury. The naval air-battles of the Coral Sea and Midway Island, and the sea-land-air contests for the Solomon Islands (notably Guadalcanal), New Guinea, the Gilberts and the Marshalls, are among the star American victories in that vast ocean war. By D-Day the United States were edging towards Japanese home waters.

The world position of the Allies had tremendously improved since 1941–42. Everywhere their cause was on the up-grade. Thus it was that, in 1944, a reinforced and re-equipped army, trained in jungle fighting and covered, transported and supplied by a powerful air force, was able to stage a come-back in

Burma. (American and American-trained Chinese forces co-operated in the ensuing campaigns.) A notable victory in the battle of Arakan, on the south of the fighting line, put the army in good heart. But then the ferocious and fanatical little brown men launched a heavy attack in the centre and actually won a foothold in India. The critical battle was still undecided on D-Day.

THE WAR AT SEA

The last front to be surveyed is the sea front. The whole Allied position depended on command of the ocean routes for the transport of troops, food, munitions and other supplies. The responsibility, for this and for all the other multifarious operations at sea, was almost entirely Britain's till the United States came in. Apart from the Pacific area, no really considerable actions were fought, though there were many notable smaller engagements. Aircraft, carrier-borne or shore-based, became a dominating factor in all naval operations. The most dramatic episode was the chase of the *Bismarck*, Germany's powerful new 45,000-ton

The surrender of the German forces on the British Front on 4th May, 1945. Field-Marshal Montgomery reads the terms to General Admiral von Friedeburg and Kontur Admiral Wagner.

late July the break-out began and grew and grew into a grim pursuit across northern France and Belgium of a desperate and failing foe. General Eisenhower had taken over operational control on 1st September. Enemy resistance now stiffened, and the autumn and winter were periods of hard and steady slogging. But the end of March, 1945, saw the Germans driven over the Rhine with the Allies forcing the crossing after them. Then followed the drive into the heart of Germany. Before April was out the enemy lines buckled and broke beneath the Allies' relentless hammer-blows. Prisoners surrendered by the hundred thousand. Connection was made with the Russians advancing from the east. Hitler committed suicide. In Italy, General Alexander had reached the top of the " leg " and Mussolini had been shot by Italian patriots; while on the 2nd May nearly a million German troops laid down their arms.

Five days later Germany herself surrendered unconditionally.

VICTORY IN THE FAR EAST

Only Japan was left to be reckoned with and the reckoning—which was aided by a new British Pacific fleet—was short and sharp. Already the Americans were back in the Philippines and other strategical islands and Burma had been recovered. By the end of July Japan's remaining naval power was utterly destroyed. In August military history was made with the dropping on her towns of the first atomic bombs. On 14th August she gave up the struggle. The Second World War was over.

Britain, supported by the Commonwealth and Empire, could review her part in the conflict with justifiable satisfaction. She had given her all and bled herself white. And she had added another name to the roll of the world's great men. Winston Churchill had proved himself the grandest war leader of all times. His rock-firm faith and unflinching courage, his rousing ardour and limitless energy, had inspired Britain to defy the German tyrant when his power seemed unassailable. So Britain had once more saved Europe by holding, alone and unaided, the last bastion of freedom till the time arrived when Russia and the United States marched forward with their saving power.

INDEX